C000113407

BANNING 'CONVERSION THERAPY'

This book looks at why and how states should legally ban LGBTQ+ 'conversion therapy'. Few states have legislated against the practice, with many currently considering its legal ban.

Banning 'Conversion Therapy' brings together leading academics, legal and medical practitioners, policymakers and activists to illuminate the legislative and non-legislative steps that are required to protect individuals from the harms of 'conversion therapy' in different contexts.

The book considers how best to address this complex and interdisciplinary legal problem which cuts across human rights law, criminal law, family law and sociolegal studies, and which represents one of the key contemporary problems of LGBTQ+ equality and national and international human rights activism.

Banning 'Conversion Therapy'

Legal and Policy Perspectives

Edited by
Ilias Trispiotis
and
Craig Purshouse

•HART•

OXFORD • LONDON • NEW YORK • NEW DELHI • SYDNEY

HART PUBLISHING

Bloomsbury Publishing Plc

Kemp House, Chawley Park, Cumnor Hill, Oxford, OX2 9PH, UK

1385 Broadway, New York, NY 10018, USA

29 Earlsfort Terrace, Dublin 2, Ireland

HART PUBLISHING, the Hart/Stag logo, BLOOMSBURY and the Diana logo are
trademarks of Bloomsbury Publishing Plc

First published in Great Britain 2023

A catalogue record for this book is available from the British Library.

A catalogue record for this book is available from the Library of Congress.

Library of Congress Control Number: 2023943023

ISBN: HB: 978-1-50996-115-3
        ePDF: 978-1-50996-117-7
        ePub: 978-1-50996-116-0

Typeset by Compuscript Ltd, Shannon

FOREWORD

Banning 'Conversion Therapy' is a timely and important book. Although so-called 'conversion therapy' is banned in a small number of countries around the world, there is increased awareness of these practices, and a recent global impetus toward confronting them. Several countries are considering outlawing 'conversion therapy', especially after victims and survivors have become more visible and motivated through recent interventions by the United Nations, the Council of Europe, and many other international, regional and domestic organisations.

Addressing the damage created by 'conversion therapy' has been one of my priorities as the UN Independent Expert on Sexual Orientation and Gender Identity (IE SOGI) since 2018. In 2020, I published a Report on these practices, which was based on extensive research and engagement across the globe, which showed, beyond any doubt, that so-called 'conversion therapy' practices are deeply discriminatory and profoundly damaging on the physical and psychological integrity of lesbian, gay, bisexual, and trans and other gender diverse persons (LGBT). That is why my recommendations to states were to ban the provision and advertisement of practices of 'conversion therapy', raise awareness about the invalidity and ineffectiveness of these practices, and support their victims and survivors. Ending practices of conversion is one of the three global calls for action that I have made during my tenure as Independent Expert, a call that has been incorporated in the strategic plans of the Equal Rights Coalition and the LGBT Core Group at the United Nations, a call that is increasingly answered by Member States.

'Conversion therapy' comes in many guises, depending on different political, social, and religious contexts. Understanding these contexts and their historical origins is key to the design of legislation and public policy to end it. In addition to the importance of designing and implementing appropriately tailored legal measures, we have to pay attention to institutional designs for achieving effective protections of LGBT equality. Institutional frameworks that condition how rights operate can be as important to securing LGBT equality as addressing the abstract rights themselves.

Outlawing so-called 'conversion therapy' raises pressing and complex questions that cut across human rights law, criminal law, family law, and socio-legal studies. Even though my mandate – and other high-profile multilateral actors – has called on states to take action, remarkably little legal research has been published on the justifications for a ban on 'conversion therapy'; on what the scope and shape of a legal ban should be; and on what non-legal measures ought to be considered, alongside a legal ban, in order to end those practices.

This edited collection answers those pressing questions sensitively and comprehensively. Trispiotis and Purshouse bring together an eclectic and diverse group of law academics, medical and legal practitioners, activists and survivors from different geographic and disciplinary places. The chapters of this book are based on a substantive body of research and a great deal of critical reflection. They explore a wide range of evidence and arguments on the harmfulness of so-called 'conversion therapy', on the scope of a potential ban, and on the actors and organisations that have to be leveraged to bring this practice to an end.

The chapter authors are to be congratulated for delivering on two fronts. The book illuminates why targeted legal intervention against 'conversion therapy' is essential, and it offers a host of practical suggestions on the legal and non-legal steps that ought to be taken to protect LGBT individuals from the harms of this practice in different contexts.

The analysis and arguments offered are premised on excellent insights into a complex and misunderstood area of international human rights law, which the chapter authors address with sophistication and rigour. Through these insights, the book as a whole not only tackles the phenomenon of 'conversion therapy' but also provides important clarifications of the principles shaping LGBT equality, the prohibition of torture, inhuman or degrading treatment, and the ties of human dignity to equal respect.

The chapter authors are well aware of the obstacles to ending 'conversion therapy'. While we can celebrate the positive momentum towards denouncing those practices, research about how national legislatures can ban those practices, and how this ban can be applied effectively to bolster LGBT equality, is essential. Through the book, we learn that analysis is necessary to expose the strengths and weaknesses of international and regional human rights decisions, especially from the perspectives of LGBT people, to strengthen our awareness and thinking on equality.

This book answers the call made by many victims, during conversations held in dozens of countries around the world, for comprehensive legal language and doctrine that describes the pain and suffering to which they have been subjected and the legal response that is owed to them, not only to recognise their pain, but also to ensure non-repetition against others. *Banning 'Conversion Therapy'* is essential reading for anyone wishing to understand what can be done, through the law and beyond, to put an end to these forms of cruel, inhuman and degrading treatment or punishment.

Victor Madrigal-Borloz
United Nations Independent Expert on Protection against
Violence and Discrimination Based on Sexual
Orientation and Gender Identity

ACKNOWLEDGEMENTS

We have been very lucky to work with numerous colleagues – at Liverpool and Leeds, and elsewhere in the academic community – who have been supportive of this project.

We would like to thank everyone at Hart for their help with the publication of this book, particularly Kate Whetter and Verity Stuart.

We are very grateful for the diligent research assistance of Lewis Lockwood, which was generously funded by the Centre for Law & Social Justice at the University of Leeds.

Guido Noto La Diega and Tania Phipps-Rufus enabled the first-named editor to host a panel at the Open Section of the Society of Legal Scholars Annual Conference at KCL in September 2022. Some of the papers in this collection were presented at this event and the audience provided very useful feedback.

Finally, we would like to thank our contributors for their excellent work and Victor Madrigal-Borloz for writing the foreword.

Ilias Trispiotis and Craig Purshouse
April 2023

CONTENTS

LIST OF CONTRIBUTORS

Lui Asquith is a solicitor of the Senior Courts of England and Wales.

Lee Davies is a postgraduate researcher at Birmingham Law School, University of Birmingham, UK.

Jack Drescher is Clinical Professor of Psychiatry in the Department of Psychiatry at Columbia University, New York, USA.

Javier García Oliva is Professor of Law, School of Law, University of Manchester, UK.

Helen Hall is an Associate Professor at Nottingham Law School, Nottingham Trent University, UK.

Jonathan Herring is Professor of Law at the University of Oxford and DW Wolf-Clarendon Fellow in Law at Exeter College, Oxford, UK.

Hannah Hirst is a Lecturer in Law at School of Law, University of Sheffield, UK.

Victor Madrigal-Borloz is the United Nations Independent Expert on Sexual Orientation and Gender Identity and the Eleanor Roosevelt Senior Visiting Researcher in Human Rights at Harvard Law School, USA.

Natasa Mavronicola is Professor of Human Rights Law at Birmingham Law School, University of Birmingham, UK.

Jayne Ozanne is Director of the Ozanne Foundation and Director and Founder of the UK's Ban Conversion Therapy Coalition.

Noam Peleg is a Senior Lecturer at Faculty of Law, University of New South Wales, Australia.

Craig Purshouse is a Senior Lecturer at Liverpool Law School, University of Liverpool, UK.

Senthorun Raj is a Reader in Human Rights Law at Manchester Law School, Manchester Metropolitan University, UK.

Nick Schiavo is Founder of No Conversion Canada, a national, non-profit, grass-roots coalition dedicated to ending 'conversion therapy' in Canada.

Jordan Sullivan is SOGIECE/CP Prevention & Survivor Support Coordinator at the Community-Based Research Centre, Toronto, Canada.

Ilias Trispiotis is Professor of Human Rights Law at School of Law, University of Leeds, UK.

ABBREVIATIONS AND ACRONYMS

AACAP	American Academy of Child and Adolescent Psychiatry
ACTSI	Alliance for Therapeutic Choice and Scientific Integrity
APA	American Psychiatric Association
APsA	American Psychoanalytic Association
CAT	UN Convention against Torture
CBRC	Community-Based Research Centre
CEDAW	UN Convention on the Elimination of Discrimination Against Women
CIDT	Cruel, Inhuman or Degrading Treatment
DSM	Diagnostic and Statistical Manual
ECHR	European Convention on Human Rights
ECtHR	European Court of Human Rights
EqA 2010	Equality Act 2010
GIDS	Gender Identity Development Service
IFTCC	International Federation for Therapeutic and Counselling Choice
IICSA	Independent Inquiry into Child Sex Abuse
ILGA	International Lesbian, Gay, Bisexual, Trans and Intersex Association
MOU	Memorandum of Understanding on 'Conversion Therapy'
NARTH	National Association for Research and Therapy of Homosexuality
PTSD	Post-Traumatic Stress Disorder
SOGIE CE	Sexual Orientation, Gender Identity or Gender Expression Change Efforts
UKGEO	UK Government Equalities Office

UN	United Nations
UNCRC	United Nations Convention on the Rights of the Child
UN SOGI	UN Independent Expert on Sexual Orientation and Gender Identity
VAW	Violence against Women

Introduction

ILIAS TRISPIOTIS AND CRAIG PURSHOUSE

This book examines legal responses to LGBTQ+ 'conversion therapy'. The seeds of this collection began with a discussion about the 2019 Oscar Best Picture race. As colleagues at the University of Leeds at the time, we would sometimes discuss cinema when passing each other in the corridor. Although we disagreed about the merits of Alfonso Cuarón's *Roma* over Yorgos Lanthimos's *The Favourite*, we thought that the film adaptation of *Boy Erased* should have got a bit more love during awards season.[1] The film, starring Lucas Hedges, Nicole Kidman and Russell Crowe, is based on Gerard Conly's account of his time in a Love in Action 'conversion therapy' centre and sees the 'students' subject to a parade of abusive behaviour including mock funerals where they are hit with Bibles and dunked in a bathtub, being barricaded into a room and forced to make humiliating confessions. A few months earlier, another 'conversion therapy' film, *The Miseducation of Cameron Post*, had been released starring Chloë Grace Moretz.[2] Based on the novel by Emily M Danforth, it detailed the emotional abuse suffered by 'disciples' at the God's Promise 'conversion therapy' programme.

Surely, we thought, this would be unlawful? How could people get away with running such centres without being immediately sued and/or arrested? The first-named editor, a specialist in human rights and equality law, thought that 'conversion therapy' involves a distinctive combination of discrimination and abuse, which could constitute degrading treatment. As a torts lawyer, the second-named editor thought that the torts of battery, false imprisonment and negligence might capture much of the wrongdoing in these films. We decided to look further at the issue and maybe write an article on the topic, if there was nothing else out there. Our initial research showed that, while some US academics had discussed the matter and Theresa May's LGBT Action Plan had discussed a ban on 'conversion therapy' in the UK, it had been underexplored in English legal scholarship.[3]

---

[1] J Edgerton et al (Producers), *Boy Erased* (Focus Films, 2018) based on the memoir by G Conly (London, William Collins, 2018).

[2] MB Clark et al (Producers), *The Miseducation of Cameron Post* (Beachside Films and Parkville Pictures, 2018) based on the novel by EM Danforth (London, Penguin, 2017).

[3] See C Purshouse and I Trispiotis, 'Is "Conversion Therapy" Tortious?' (2022) 42(1) *Legal Studies* 23, fn 12 for some of the US sources. For details of the LGBT Action Plan see UK Government Equalities Office, *LGBT Action Plan: Improving the Lives of Lesbian, Gay, Bisexual and Transgender People* (GEO, 2018).

Our naïve plan for a single article covering all of the legal issues raised by 'conversion therapy' became a bigger job than we anticipated. One article soon became two: one on the human rights issues, published in the *Oxford Journal of Legal Studies*, and one on the torts issues in *Legal Studies*. The *OJLS* article argued that 'conversion therapy' is disrespectful to the equal moral value of LGBTQ+ people and violates specific protected areas of liberty and equality that are inherent in human dignity. As such, all forms of 'conversion therapy' amount at a minimum to degrading treatment in violation of human rights law, particularly Article 3 of the European Convention on Human Rights (ECHR).[4] The *Legal Studies* work argued that, while many tort claims against 'conversion therapists' had the potential to succeed, particularly in egregious cases, some types of claim would fail.[5] For example, a negligence claim might fail if the claimant does not suffer a medically recognised psychiatric injury, and a claim under the rule in *Wilkinson v Downton* would fail if the 'conversion therapist' had a benign motive. Reform of the law would be needed if the practice was to be stamped out.

Realising not only that our two articles were barely scratching the surface on the law surrounding this practice, but also the limitations of our own experience and expertise, we decided to assemble a range of voices to look at whether and how 'conversion therapy' should be banned in law. All the chapters in this collection support using the law to ban 'conversion therapy', but do not necessarily agree about the best way of doing so. We wanted to select authors who think differently from each other and from us, and who have had various kinds of experiences in advancing LGBTQ+ equality, whether through scholarship, legal advocacy, activism, or a combination thereof. We chose authors with different disciplinary and geographic perspectives and at various stages of their careers because we had learned so much from being involved in diverse intellectual spaces throughout our research project on 'conversion therapy'. We chose contributors whose scholarship we had read and taught, and/or whose work we admired. We also chose contributors who have survived 'conversion therapy' and/or have worked with survivors: their insights into the practice, and the non-legal steps that ought to be taken to end it, are invaluable and penetrate all parts of the book. Countless other scholars and activists have advanced our understanding of 'conversion therapy' and LGBTQ+ equality, many of whom are referenced in this collection.

This chapter introduces the collection by highlighting points that struck us as particularly significant in understanding the practice and effects of 'conversion therapy'. The book is intended to be read in many ways. Egalitarian, emotional and dignitarian ideas that are introduced in the first part continue throughout the book, where different aspects of the scope and limitations of a legal ban on 'conversion therapy' are discussed. For example, the dignitarian harms of 'conversion

---

[4] I Trispiotis and C Purshouse, '"Conversion Therapy" as Degrading Treatment' (2022) 42(1) *Oxford Journal of Legal Studies* 104.
[5] Trispiotis and Purshouse (n 4).

therapy' are explored in different ways in several chapters, while legal protection for gender identity and expression is pursued in others. Cross-cutting themes pervade many chapters – such as coercion and consent, and the type and formulation of laws in this area – as do themes addressing activism and transitional justice. But before moving on, it is important to address two key points. First of all, what is 'conversion therapy'? Second, what is the right term to refer to it?

According to the UN, 'conversion therapy' is a widely discredited set of practices which aim to 'cure' LGBTQ+ people by changing or repressing non-heteronormative sexualities and gender identities.[6] As the Memorandum of Understanding on 'Conversion Therapy' in the UK, which was signed in 2022 by leading UK health bodies, including NHS England and NHS Scotland, puts it

> 'conversion therapy' is an umbrella term for a therapeutic approach, or any model or individual viewpoint that demonstrates an assumption that any sexual orientation or gender identity is inherently preferable to any other, and which attempts to bring about a change of sexual orientation or gender identity, or seeks to suppress an individual's expression of sexual orientation or gender identity on that basis.[7]

So, 'conversion therapy' describes 'a multitude of practices and methods' to change or suppress an individual's sexuality or gender identity.[8] All involve 'attempts to pathologize and erase the identity of individuals'.[9]

A wide range of 'conversion therapies' have been reported, including 'corrective' rape and sexual assault,[10] imprisonment and kidnapping,[11] physical abuse,[12] electroconvulsive shock treatments,[13] hormone treatments,[14] and 'aversion therapy'.[15] However, not all forms of 'conversion therapy' involve overt violence. Some take the form of 'talking therapies', which involve psychotherapy, peer support, or pastoral counselling.[16] Techniques utilised there include trying to make recipients behave in conformity with gender stereotypes;[17] encouraging them to sever ties with their families; and promoting celibacy.[18]

---

[6] UN Human Rights Council, *Practices of So-Called 'Conversion Therapy': Report of the Independent Expert on Protection Against Violence and Discrimination Based on Sexual Orientation and Gender Identity*, 1 May 2020, A/HRC/44/53, para 2. Also, Independent Forensic Expert Group, 'Statement on Conversion Therapy' (2020) 72 *Journal of Forensic and Legal Medicine* 101930, 1.

[7] BACP et al, *Memorandum of Understanding on Conversion Therapy in the UK*, November 2022, version 2 https://www.bacp.co.uk/events-and-resources/ethics-and-standards/mou/.

[8] *Practices of So-Called 'Conversion Therapy'* (n 6) para 17.

[9] ibid para 19.

[10] ibid paras 18 and 39.

[11] ibid para 39.

[12] ibid paras 39, 50 and 52.

[13] *Report of the Special Rapporteur on the Question of Torture and Other Cruel, Inhuman or Degrading Treatment or Punishment*, UN General Assembly, A/56/156, 3 July 2001, para 24.

[14] *Practices of So-Called 'Conversion Therapy'* (n 6) para 46.

[15] ibid para 43.

[16] KA Hicks, '"Reparative" Therapy: Whether Parental Attempts to Change a Child's Sexual Orientation Can Constitute Child Abuse' (1999) 49 *American University Law Review* 506.

[17] *Practices of So-Called 'Conversion Therapy'* (n 6) para 45.

[18] ibid para 37.

There is significant evidence that the use of psychotherapy or pastoral counselling as a practice of 'conversion therapy' can cause grave, life-long harm.[19] So, the distinction between physical and 'talking' forms of 'conversion therapy' does not downplay the harmfulness of the latter. People who have undergone such 'therapies' have reported 'loss of self-esteem, anxiety, depression, social isolation, intimacy difficulty, self-hatred, shame, sexual dysfunction, suicidal ideation, and post-traumatic stress disorder'.[20] And arguably, many forms of 'conversion therapy' might be difficult to classify as they constitute both physical and emotional abuse.

To recap, 'conversion therapy' refers to any sustained effort to change or suppress a person's sexual orientation or gender identity *because* their sexuality or gender identity are considered inferior or problematic. Moreover, there is incontrovertible evidence from across the world that 'conversion therapy' is consistently aimed at effecting a change from non-heterosexual to heterosexual and from trans or gender diverse to cisgender.[21] The assumption that LGBTQ+ sexualities and gender identities are inherently inferior, and ought to be changed or suppressed for that reason, lies at the core of 'conversion therapy'.

We noted earlier that curbing 'conversion therapy' relies on understanding what such practices constitute, as well as their harmfulness. Language is central to drawing attention and action towards 'conversion therapy'. But is 'conversion therapy' the right term to describe the litany of harmful practices described above?

There are at least four problems with the term 'conversion therapy'. First of all, the term 'therapy' suggests that a person's sexuality or gender identity, or their expression, amount to some sort of illness or condition that can be 'cured'. Second, 'therapy' also conveys the misleading idea that there is sound medical or scientific evidence backing conversion practices, just as there is with most legitimate therapies. Both those connotations are patently false. LGBTQ+ identities are not illnesses or pathologies,[22] nor is there any evidence that they can be changed through 'treatment'.[23] Apart from its falsity, the message conveyed by the term 'therapy' reproduces, and promotes, the social image of LGBTQ+ people

---

[19] J Turban et al, 'Association between Recalled Exposure to Gender Identity Conversion Efforts and Psychological Distress and Suicide Attempts Among Transgender Adults' (2020) 77(1) *JAMA Psychiatry* 68; J Devlin et al, 'Sexual Orientation Change Efforts Among Current or Former LDS Church Members' (2015) 62(2) *Journal of Counseling Psychology* 95; D Halderman, 'Therapeutic Antidotes: Helping Gay and Bisexual Men Recover from Conversion Therapies' (2002) 5(3–4) *Journal of Gay & Lesbian Psychotherapy* 117.

[20] *Practices of So-Called 'Conversion Therapy'* (n 6) para 56. See also J Fjelstrom, 'Sexual Orientation Change Efforts and the Search for Authenticity' (2013) 60(6) *Journal of Homosexuality* 801.

[21] *Practices of So-Called 'Conversion Therapy'* (n 6) para 17.

[22] Homosexuality was removed from the DSM in 1974 and the ICD in 1990. See *American Psychiatric Association Diagnostic and Statistical Manual of Mental Disorders II* (6th printing, APA Publishing, 1974) and *World Health Organisation International Statistical Classification of Diseases and Related Health Problems* (WHO, 1990).

[23] See eg 'Editorial' (2016) 387 *The Lancet* 95; Independent Forensic Expert Group (n 6) 5.

as abnormal and disgusting – a social image which grounds their pre-existing stigma. 'Therapy' therefore relays a demeaning message that affects not only survivors of 'conversion therapy', but LGBTQ+ people in general, and the attitudes of other people towards them. A third problem with 'therapy' is that it fails to capture the abusive nature of many forms of 'conversion therapy'. Many conversion practices are nothing other than violence, rape, humiliation, intimidation – practices that cannot possibly be included in any legitimate definition of therapy. But the term 'conversion' is also problematic. 'Conversion' implies that sexual orientation or gender identity can be changed, despite the complete lack of credible evidence that any such interventions work.

For all those reasons, some advocates and organisations have started to favour the term Sexual Orientation, Gender Identity or Gender Expression Change Efforts (SOGIE CE) instead of 'conversion therapy'. Although the term 'change' may not accurately reflect how such attempts operate, SOGIE CE avoids the problems of the term 'therapy'. However, at the time of writing, SOGIE CE is not widely used or understood, perhaps with the exception of certain advocacy spaces.[24] Even though it is arguable that a common, agreed-upon terminology does not exist yet, 'conversion therapy' remains the most widely used and understood term across the world. 'Conversion therapy' is used in the relevant UN reports,[25] in national and local bans, in advocacy and in common parlance in most countries we are aware of. By contrast, in our experience, SOGIE CE is not widely understood among activists and policy-makers, or by the general public, even in the Global North.

We have decided to use 'conversion therapy' in many parts of this collection, including its title. In other parts of the book, the term *conversion practices* is used. None of those terms is unproblematic. However, research, advocacy and mobilisation within global or multilateral spaces benefit from tapping into the common terminology we have at the time of writing, at least until we build a unified understanding of the practice of 'conversion therapy' and determine which terms can be used to describe it and draw attention to it. We want to make one thing clear though: 'conversion therapy' is a misnomer. That is why both 'conversion' and 'therapy' are between inverted commas throughout the book – to remind the reader that they convey a delusive perception of the abuse they are used to describe.

While researching this topic we have been involved in advising policymakers about a ban in the UK (though the second-named author has since stepped back from this work). One of the reasons why a ban on 'conversion therapy' has proved contentious in the UK is due to the fierce debates about transgender rights. It is worth briefly discussing this important issue here. To an extent, a ban aimed at

---

[24] Advocates often use completely different terms to 'conversion therapy' or SOGIE CE. For instance, certain advocacy organisations in South Africa use a local term, *Inxeba Lam*, which means 'My Wound' in Xhosa, to describe 'conversion therapy'.

[25] See n 6 above and n 29 below.

gay, lesbian and bisexual 'conversion therapy' would be more straightforward to implement, as it is easier to define sexual attraction than gender identity. With trans or gender-diverse people, any likely ban is more complicated, particularly with children. This is because healthcare professionals prescribing puberty blockers and, eventually, cross-sex hormones to children with gender dysphoria could be seen as offering a form of 'conversion therapy', potentially transforming a gay cis-gendered person into a straight trans person. We would not want a position where therapy to assist someone to become more comfortable with their biological sex, or their sexuality, was outlawed or discouraged. Questioning and reflecting before undergoing significant medical interventions cannot be anything other than good practice.[26] As Lemma and Savulescu argue, it is important that transgender patients have the opportunity to have a reflective space and, as such, we have ethical grounds to advocate a 'respectful, collaborative, and inquisitive approach so as to ensure that the desire to medically transition can be said to be autonomous'.[27]

Any ban on 'conversion therapy' therefore needs to strike a fine balance between ensuring that the rights of trans people are respected, while also ensuring that legitimate forms of talking therapy, with the aim of making sure that those undergoing gender reassignment are actually transgender, are not captured by a ban. These barriers are not unbreachable and some jurisdictions seem to have handled them delicately by carving out important exemptions covering therapeutic interventions that do not pathologise any sexualities or gender identities but aim to provide acceptance and support for a person's exploration of their identity.[28] Those exemptions are justified because such types of therapeutic intervention do not constitute 'conversion therapy'. They are not based on the assumption that some sexualities or gender identities are inferior to others, and do not aim to change or suppress them for that reason.

Despite the fact that the United Nations has repeatedly called on states to take action against 'conversion therapy',[29] and so have many other international and regional organisations including the European Parliament,[30] the Council

---

[26] A Lemma and J Savulescu, 'To Be or Not To Be? The Role of the Unconscious in Transgender Transitioning: Identity, Autonomy and Well-being' (2023) 49 *Journal of Medical Ethics* 67.

[27] ibid 71.

[28] See eg the legislation adopted in Queensland (Public Health Act 2005, s 213F as amended by Health Legislation Amendment Act 2020, s 28) and Victoria (Change or Suppression (Conversion) Practices Prohibition Act 2021, s 5).

[29] See eg *Practices of So-Called 'Conversion Therapy'* (n 6). Also, UN Joint Statement, *United Nations Entities Call on States to Act Urgently to End Violence and Discrimination Against Lesbian, Gay, Bisexual, Transgender and Intersex Adults, Adolescents and Children* (September 2015); Annual Report of United Nations High Commissioner for Human Rights, *Discriminatory Laws and Practices and Acts of Violence against Individuals Based on Their Sexual Orientation and Gender Identity*, 17 November 2011, A/HRC/19/41, para 56; *Report of the Special Rapporteur on the Question of Torture and Other Cruel, Inhuman or Degrading Treatment or Punishment*, UN General Assembly, 3 July 2001, A/56/156, para 24.

[30] European Parliament, Committee on Civil Liberties, Justice and Home Affairs, *Amendment 8 to the Report on the Situation of Fundamental Rights in the EU in 2016*, 21 February 2018, A8-0025/8.

of Europe,[31] and the UN Committee Against Torture,[32] 'conversion therapy' is banned in only a small number of countries around the world. At the time of writing, out of the 46 members of the Council of Europe only Malta, France, Germany and Greece have introduced nationwide bans on 'conversion therapy', either fully[33] or partly.[34] In Spain, there are regional-level bans in non-discrimination legislation.[35] The practice is not banned in the United Kingdom.[36] Beyond Europe, Canada and New Zealand have introduced general national bans on 'conversion therapy', whereas medical professionals are banned from providing 'conversion therapy' in Brazil, Ecuador and Taiwan. In the United States, so far twenty States have introduced bans on the practice,[37] although many exempt religious counsellors and organisations from the scope of the prohibition. A similar exemption is part of the ban on 'conversion therapy' in Queensland, one of the three Australian jurisdictions banning the practice at the moment.[38]

At the time of writing, many countries across the world are considering legal bans on 'conversion therapy'. Even so, widespread uncertainty and disagreement prevail with regard to whether states are under a legal duty under international human rights law to ban 'conversion therapy'; what practices and exemptions should be included in a ban; what legal mechanisms ought to be used; and what other steps, beyond a legal ban, ought to be taken to prevent this practice and support its survivors. Those are only some of the pressing questions that these chapter authors are looking to answer.

This collection is divided into three parts. Part I sets out the reasons that justify a legal ban on 'conversion therapy'. Part II explores the scope of a ban on

---

[31] D Mijatović, 'Nothing to Cure: Putting an End to So-Called "Conversion Therapies" for LGBTI People' (Strasbourg, 16 February 2023), https://www.coe.int/en/web/commissioner/-/nothing-to-cure-putting-an-end-to-so-called-conversion-therapies-for-lgbti-people.

[32] See eg UN Committee Against Torture, 'Concluding Observations on the Seventh Periodic Report of Ecuador' (CAT/C/ECU/CO/7, 11 January 2017) para 49. Also UN Committee against Torture, 'Concluding Observations on the Fifth Periodic Report of China' (CAT/ C/CHN/CO/5, 3 February 2016) para 55.

[33] There is a full national ban on 'conversion therapy' in Malta. See Affirmation of Sexual Orientation, Gender Identity and Gender Expression Act, s 3.

[34] In 2020, Germany criminalised the provision of 'conversion therapy' to minors. The provision of 'conversion therapy' to adults is outlawed provided that there was coercion, deceit or misapprehension. This is also the case with the 2022 Greek ban.

[35] At the time of writing, 'conversion therapy' is banned in the Spanish regions of Madrid, Valencia, Andalucía, Aragon, Cantabria, Navarra, Murcia, Canary Islands and Rioja.

[36] A private member's bill outlawing 'conversion therapy' was lost when the UK Parliament was prorogued in 2019. In October 2021, the UK Government opened its proposals to ban 'conversion therapy' for consultation (as part of this consultation, the first-named author gave evidence in the UK Parliament in November 2021) but those proposals were pulled in April 2022 and nothing concrete has been re-introduced since. As noted earlier, a Memorandum of Understanding signed by the NHS and leading counselling, psychotherapy and mental health bodies seeks to ensure that no registered medical practitioners offer the practice in the UK (n 7 above).

[37] At the time of writing, these are: New Jersey, California, Oregon, Illinois, Vermont, New Mexico, Connecticut, Rhode Island, Nevada, Washington, Hawaii, Delaware, Maryland, New Hampshire, New York, Massachusetts, Colorado, Maine, Utah and Virginia.

[38] The others are Victoria and the Australian Capital Territory.

'conversion therapy' and how a ban might interact with specific rights. Part III looks beyond a legal ban on 'conversion therapy'. This part includes the voices of activists and survivors who broach the non-legal steps that are required to end 'conversion therapy' and support LGBTQ+ survivors. However, many chapters touch upon all three areas, and the themes of the normative justification of a ban and its scope and implementation pervade most chapters.

Opening Part I on the reasons in support of a ban, Ilias Trispiotis's chapter considers the extent to which there is a legal duty on states to ban 'conversion therapy' under international human rights law. Trispiotis claims that all forms of 'conversion therapy' involve a distinctive combination of two serious moral wrongs. First, all forms of 'conversion therapy' put LGBTQ+ people at a proved, real risk of grave harm. Second, all such 'therapies' directly discriminate on the grounds of sexual orientation and gender identity. This combination of wrongs means that all forms of the practice fall qualitatively within the scope of the prohibition of degrading treatment. As a result, states are under a positive legal duty to ban all forms of 'conversion therapy'.

Jonathan Herring focuses on the criminalisation of 'conversion therapy'. His chapter argues that the wrongs inflicted by 'conversion therapy' are of sufficient severity to justify criminal intervention against all forms of the practice. Herring shows that, in many ways, 'conversion therapy' is analogous to the criminal offence of coercive control. Drawing analogies to the offences of domestic abuse and domestic violence in the UK, the chapter highlights the relational nature of the wrong in 'conversion therapy', as well as the fact that autonomy and consent should not be a defence to it. In fact, according to Herring, focusing on the value of personal autonomy greatly strengthens the case in favour of criminalisation of 'conversion therapy'.

Jack Drescher was an early critic of what were once known as 'reparative practices' and was author of the landmark article 'I'm Your Handyman', one of the first pieces that detailed the harms of, and ethical concerns with, the practice from a psychiatric perspective. The article is reprinted here, together with a coda detailing what has changed in the almost-25 years that have passed since its publication.

Finishing off Part I, Senthorun Raj considers the emotional grammar of banning 'conversion therapy'. Considering the personal testimonies of victims, together with the language of parliamentary debates on a ban in the UK, Raj shows how emotions such as pain and shame have featured in the discourse surrounding a ban – and the role that such emotions can play in justifying and structuring legal intervention in this area.

Opening Part II on the scope of a ban are two chapters considering the relationship of 'conversion therapy' with children's rights, albeit from different perspectives. Noam Peleg argues that 'conversion therapy', when directed at children, violates a host of rights under the UN Convention on the Rights of the Child (UNCRC) and breaches some of its key guiding principles, such as the principle of non-discrimination, children's best interests, and their right to participation in decision-making. Peleg's chapter takes children and their rights as its focal point of analysis, against a reality where discussions about banning 'conversion therapy' tend to focus on the role of parents in relation to children's sexual rights and gender identity, and rarely consider the rights of children in those areas.

Hannah Hirst's chapter specifically focuses on gender-diverse children. Hirst analyses the scope of a ban on 'conversion therapy' through the lens of the child's right to develop under the UNCRC and UK law. Hirst argues that a ban on all forms of 'conversion therapy' that seek to change children's gender identities is necessary to protect the right of gender-diverse children to develop into adulthood – not just physically, but also mentally and socially – and guarantee them a 'maximally open future'.

Staying on the theme of gender identity, Lui Asquith's chapter looks at how a ban on 'conversion therapy' should be formulated to protect trans people whilst ensuring individual access to responsible healthcare in relation to gender identity. Asquith makes two key points: the first is that a ban on 'conversion therapy' has to be informed by an adequate definition of gender identity and gender expression, and has to protect both. The second is that a ban has to explicitly exempt legitimate gender-related healthcare services. The chapter analyses those points through examples coming from UK and comparative law.

In the last chapter of Part II on the scope of a ban on 'conversion therapy', Javier García Oliva and Helen Hall address the important question of the compatibility of a ban with the right to freedom of religion or belief. García Oliva and Hall argue that, as a matter of principle, banning religious forms of 'conversion therapy' does not amount to a disproportionate interference with the right to freedom of conscience under Article 9 ECHR. Drawing on specific examples of spiritual 'conversion therapies', such as exorcism, García Oliva and Hall conclude that a ban that exempts such spiritual practices would breach central principles of human rights law – and would also lack efficacy.

Part III of the book looks beyond a legal ban on 'conversion therapy'. This part of the book opens with Jayne Ozanne's chapter, which describes religious forms of 'conversion therapy' as a form of spiritual abuse. Drawing on her experience as a survivor of 'conversion therapy' and a leading campaigner to ban it, Ozanne unfolds the different stages of the abuse involved in the practice. The chapter highlights specific steps that ought to be taken to counteract the conditions and structures that make 'conversion therapy' possible. Central among them is engagement with religious communities on the basis of specific, agreed-upon principles that aim to protect LGBTQ+ people. Ultimately, according to Ozanne, ending 'conversion therapy' depends on forging a shared commitment amongst governments and religious leaders to take specific legal and non-legal steps against the practice.

Jordan Sullivan and Nick Schiavo's chapter draws on their research experience working with survivors of 'conversion therapy' in Canada. Their chapter highlights the ways that the lived realities of survivors can be used to build a body of knowledge on the practice and effects of 'conversion therapy'. The chapter argues that any legal ban must engage with that body of knowledge in order to devise sufficient support for survivors. According to Sullivan and Schiavo, unless it incorporates specific support structures, a legal ban on 'conversion therapy' cannot address the barriers faced by LGBTQ+ people to accessing financial, psychological, and culturally and religiously appropriate care – barriers that often propel them into seeking 'conversion therapies'.

Completing the collection is Natasa Mavronicola's and Lee Davies's chapter on using transformative reparations in addition to a legal ban on 'conversion therapy'. Transformative reparations call on the state to transform the unjust circumstances in which serious wrongs have been committed. As Mavronicola and Davies show, this approach has emerged in contexts involving serious human rights violations, not unlike the ones involved in 'conversion therapy'. The chapter shows the specific ways that transformative reparations could be realised in the UK – for instance, through establishing a truth commission on the scope and scale of 'conversion therapies' – and emphasises the importance of prevention of 'conversion therapy' through historical reckoning and through reshaping the social norms and institutions that make 'conversion therapy' possible.

Your journey through this book can take various paths, and you will have different ideas about how the practice of 'conversion therapy' should be brought to an end. Our hope is that you will learn as much from each of these chapter authors as we have in editing this book and that it will inspire further debate on a complicated and topical area of law and policy.

PART I

Reasons for a Ban

1

The Legal Duty to Ban 'Conversion Therapy'

ILIAS TRISPIOTIS

This chapter argues that there is a legal duty under international human rights law to ban all forms of 'conversion therapy'. States are under a positive duty to do so because all forms of 'conversion therapy' fall within the protective scope of the absolute prohibition of torture, inhuman or degrading treatment under international human rights law. Specifically, this chapter claims that all forms of 'conversion therapy' amount at least to degrading treatment because they disrespect the equal moral value of LGBTQ+ people. They do so through a distinctive combination of two serious moral wrongs. First, all forms of 'conversion therapy' put LGBTQ+ people at a proved, real risk of grave physical and mental harm. Second, all such 'therapies' directly discriminate on the grounds of sexual orientation and gender identity: they typically single out LGBTQ+ people to deny them key freedoms related to sexuality and gender identity.

Most parts of the following discussion focus on Article 3 of the European Convention on Human Rights (ECHR). However, the chapter's overarching argument, namely that all forms of 'conversion therapy' amount at a minimum to degrading treatment, is not contingent on the ECHR. The chapter's arguments on the wrongness of 'conversion therapy'; the meaning of degrading treatment in human rights law; and the positive state obligations arising from the relationship between those two, apply more broadly to international human rights law.

The discussion unfolds in four substantive sections. The first section briefly discusses the legal relevance of drawing a distinction between different forms of 'conversion therapy'. The second section analyses the relationship of 'conversion therapy' with human dignity. The third section offers an interpretation of degrading treatment under Article 3 ECHR, which brings to the fore the tight normative links between discrimination, dignity and degradation. The final section analyses the consequences of the claim that all forms of 'conversion therapy' amount at a minimum to degrading treatment under international human rights law for the positive state obligations that arise in this context.[1]

---

[1] Parts of this chapter, especially its first and fourth substantive sections, draw on I Trispiotis and C Purshouse, '"Conversion Therapy" as Degrading Treatment' (2022) 42(1) *Oxford Journal of Legal Studies* 104.

I. Physical, 'Talking', Forcible, Consensual:
The Compatibility of Different Forms of 'Conversion Therapy' with Human Rights Law

Do all forms of 'conversion therapy' amount to a violation of the absolute prohibition of torture, inhuman or degrading treatment under UK and international human rights law? If they do, then states are under a positive legal obligation to ban all forms of this practice. But if they do not, then the relevant positive state obligations would have to be adjusted accordingly. So, before turning to the content of positive state obligations in this area, it is important to clarify whether all different forms of 'conversion therapy' fall within the scope of the prohibition of torture, inhuman or degrading treatment. This and the next section will focus on the ECHR and UK law. However, for reasons that this chapter will mention later, the proposed interpretation of degrading treatment applies to international human rights law more broadly.

Let me start with two specific forms of 'conversion therapy' that clearly violate Article 3 ECHR. First are extreme 'physical' forms of 'conversion therapy', such as those involving rape, electroshocks, forced examinations of genitals, injections of drugs etc.[2] Such extreme violence can cause severe physical and mental suffering, and therefore those forms of 'conversion therapy' violate Article 3 ECHR.[3] Arguably, depending on their severity, such 'physical' forms of 'conversion therapy' may constitute torture rather than degrading treatment.[4] That said, not only the severity of ill-treatment, but also its aim determines its position within the architecture of Article 3. As the European Court of Human Rights (ECtHR) held in *Romanov*[5] and *Cestaro*,[6] the use of gratuitous violence that aims to debase others deserves the stigma attached to torture. Accordingly, because of their intensity and gratuitousness, violent 'physical' forms of 'conversion therapy' would likely amount to torture rather than degrading treatment.

Forcible 'conversion therapy' is a second form that clearly violates Article 3 ECHR.[7] This conclusion flows from case law on forcible medical treatments.

---

[2] *Report of the Special Rapporteur on the Question of Torture and Other Cruel, Inhuman or Degrading Treatment or Punishment*, UN General Assembly, A/56/156, 3 July 2001, para 24.

[3] *Maslova and Nalbandov v Russia*, Application No 839/02, 24 January 2008. Also *Aydin v Turkey*, Application No 23178/94, 25 September 1997, para 86. Threats of violence can constitute torture: see *Selmouni v France*, Application No 25803/94, 28 July 1999, para 101. Torture covers both physical pain and mental suffering: see *Gäfgen v Germany*, Application No 22978/05, 1 June 2010 (Grand Chamber), para 108.

[4] *Jalloh v Germany*, Application No 54810/00, 11 July 2006 (Grand Chamber), para 67.

[5] *Vladimir Romanov v Russia*, Application No 41461/02, 24 July 2008, paras 67–70.

[6] *Cestaro v Italy*, Application No 6884/11, 7 April 2015, paras 182 and 189. Also *Dedovski and Others v Russia*, Application No 7178/03, 15 May 2008, paras 82–83.

[7] 'Forcible' is used to mark cases where a person undergoing 'conversion therapy' is not free to leave or stop the 'therapy'. So, the term 'forcible' does cover those who consented to 'conversion therapy' they knew they would not be able to leave if they changed their mind.

As the ECtHR held in *Herczegfalvy*, unless the forcible treatment inflicted upon a patient were a medical necessity, it amounts to degrading treatment.[8] The UK Court of Appeal reiterated this principle in *Wilkinson*.[9] More specifically, according to *Herczegfalvy* and *Wilkinson*, the forcible imposition of treatment on someone can be justified only when *substantial* benefits can arise from it.[10] Such benefits must be evidenced by 'established principles of medicine',[11] and would often require the cross-examination of medical practitioners.[12] Arguably 'conversion therapy' falls woefully short of this standard. There is evidence of its lasting harmful effects on the physical and mental health of LGBTQ+ people.[13] No health benefits arise from 'conversion therapy', let alone the 'substantial' benefits that the law requires to justify its forcible imposition. Thus, its forcible imposition on children, adolescents or adults violates Article 3. This holds *regardless of* what form forcible 'conversion therapy' takes – eg a violent or a mild, non-physical form – and *regardless of* the age of its victims and their capacity to consent.[14]

That leaves us with mild, non-forcible forms of 'conversion therapy', such as non-physical, 'talking' sessions which pathologise certain sexualities or gender identities and attempt to eliminate them or repress their expression.[15] If non-physical and non-forcible forms of 'conversion therapy' also amount to degrading

---

[8] *Herczegfalvy v Austria*, Application No 10533/83, 24 September 1992, para 82.

[9] *R (on the application of Wilkinson) v The Responsible Medical Officer Broadmoor Hospital* [2001] EWCA Civ 1545, [2001] 1 WLR 419, per Hale LJ, paras 77–80. This applies to both capacitated and incapacitated patients.

[10] ibid para 79; *Herczegfalvy* (n 8) para 82. There is a duty to give reasons whenever a patient should undergo medical treatment without their consent. See *R (Wooder) v Feggetter* [2002] EWCA Civ 554, [2002] 3 WLR 591; *R (B) v SS (Responsible Medical Officer)* [2006] EWCA Civ 28, [2006] 1 WLR 810, para 50.

[11] *Herczegfalvy* (n 8) para 82.

[12] *Wilkinson* (n 9) para 55.

[13] See eg UN Human Rights Council, *Practices of So-Called 'Conversion Therapy': Report of the Independent Expert on Protection Against Violence and Discrimination Based on Sexual Orientation and Gender Identity*, 1 May 2020, A/HRC/44/53. Also, UN Human Rights Council, *Report of the Special Rapporteur on the Right of Everyone to the Enjoyment of the Highest Attainable Standard of Physical and Mental Health*, Anand Grover, 27 April 2010, A/HRC/14/20, para 23. In addition, the harms of 'conversion therapy' are well-documented in medical literature. See eg BACP et al, *Memorandum of Understanding on Conversion Therapy in the UK*, October 2017, version 2, https://www.bacp.co.uk/media/6526/memorandum-of-understanding-v2-reva-jul19.pdf; A Bartlett et al, 'The Response of Mental Health Professionals to Clients Seeking Help to Change or Redirect Same-sex Sexual Orientation' (2009) 9(11) *BioMed Central Psychiatry* 7. See also Chapter 3 of this edited collection, by Jack Drescher.

[14] The compulsion of the medical treatment overshadows whether the patient had the capacity to consent to the treatment. See *Wilkinson* (n 9) para 79; *R (B) v SS (Responsible Medical Officer)* [2006] EWCA Civ 28, [2006] 1 WLR 810, para 50.

[15] This does not include counselling which seeks to provide acceptance, support, facilitation and understanding of a person's sexual and gender identity. Such therapeutic interventions that do not pathologise any sexualities or gender identities but aim to provide acceptance and support to a person, do not amount to 'conversion therapy'. This is because they lack the element of pathologisation of certain sexualities or gender identities that all forms of 'conversion therapy' share, and therefore fall outside its scope. That is why some bans expressly exempt such practices from the scope of 'conversion therapy'. See eg the legislation adopted in Queensland (Public Health Act 2005, s 213F as amended by Health Legislation Amendment Act 2020, s 28) and Victoria (Change or Suppression (Conversion) Practices Prohibition Act 2021, s 5). See also Chapter 7 of this edited collection, by Lui Asquith.

treatment, then every form of 'conversion therapy' – from its ultra-violent to its mildest 'talking' varieties, and in both forcible and non-forcible forms – would fall within the scope of the absolute prohibition of torture or cruel, inhuman or degrading treatment (CIDT) in human rights law.

The argument in the rest of this chapter is based on the following premise. A consistent line of case law in international human rights law suggests that one of the main aims of the prohibition of degrading treatment is to protect individuals from serious violations of human dignity. So, whether 'talking', non-forcible forms of 'conversion therapy' amount to degrading treatment depends on whether they amount to a serious violation of human dignity.

II. 'Conversion Therapy' as a Serious Violation of Human Dignity

'Conversion therapy' involves a distinctive combination of: (1) a proved, real risk of grave harm for the physical and mental health of its victims;[16] and (2) direct discrimination on the grounds of sexual orientation or gender identity. This distinctive combination means that 'conversion therapy' is unlike other harmful practices or pseudo-therapies that are not inherently discriminatory. It also means that 'conversion therapy' is unlike instances of direct discrimination that do not involve a proved real risk of grave harm. That last point is important. 'Conversion therapy' is not homophobia or transphobia, despite typically being motivated by those prejudices. 'Conversion therapy' is a *practice* that aims to change or suppress a person's sexuality or gender identity. It is that practice that ought to be legally banned, for the reasons outlined in this chapter and elsewhere in this collection.

As I mentioned earlier, the prohibition of degrading treatment in human rights law aims to protect individuals from serious violations of human dignity. Does 'conversion therapy' violate human dignity? At first glance, 'conversion therapy' is morally wrong because it endangers the lives and health of LGBTQ+ people. Later parts of this book include qualitative survey results, reports from international organisations, healthcare data and testimonies of survivors, all of which demonstrate the grave injuries that 'conversion therapy' can inflict on LGBTQ+ people. This is wrong in and of itself, regardless of any comparison between people on the grounds of sexuality and gender identity.

At the same time, 'conversion therapy' is morally wrong for reasons that stretch beyond the grave risks it poses for the physical and mental health of its victims.[17]

---

[16] See n 13 above. Numerous studies are included in UN Human Rights Council, *Practices of So-Called 'Conversion Therapy'* (n 13).

[17] This analysis of the wrongness of 'conversion therapy' distinguishes objections based on the proved potential of 'conversion therapy' to cause grave physical and psychological harm from objections to the practice from its inegalitarian nature. However, the two objections are linked. Pain and injury can be

Unlike other harmful or medically negligent therapies, 'conversion therapy' singles out a protected socially salient group of people, ie LGBTQ+ people, for disadvantageous treatment. So, 'conversion therapy' is also, fundamentally, a problem of direct discrimination on the grounds of sexual orientation and gender identity. It is also an intrinsically wrongful form of discrimination, ie it is wrongful regardless of its effects. That is because alongside its proved potential for causing grave physical and psychological harm, 'conversion therapy' is *basically* disrespectful of the equal moral personhood of LGBTQ+ people.[18] All forms of 'conversion therapy' are *basically* disrespectful because, aside from their actual effects on the victims and aside from social conventions about what counts as disrespect, they fail to recognise that all persons are of equal moral value regardless of their sexuality and gender identity. Put differently, they fail to show what Stephen Darwall calls 'recognition respect'.[19] 'Conversion therapies' fail to show recognition respect because they fail to recognise that the status of LGBTQ+ persons as persons has to be appropriately integrated in one's deliberations about how to act. Apart from discounting the interests of LGBTQ+ people to physical and mental health, 'conversion therapy' manifests that *deliberative* failure in two other ways: it attacks core aspects of the identity of LGBTQ+ people by denying them crucial freedoms related to sexuality and gender identity; and it unfairly subordinates them on the grounds of sexuality. Let us look at those in more detail.

First of all, the practice of 'conversion therapy' is disrespectful for the equal moral personhood of LGBTQ+ people because it places less weight on some of their key autonomy interests without any good reason for discounting them.[20] 'Conversion therapy' explicitly marks out LGBTQ+ identities as inferior to heterosexual cisgender identities. As a result of that judgement, it affords less consideration to the interests of LGBTQ+ people.[21] Thus, even though the basis of less consideration is the sexuality or gender identity of the person, the responses constitutive of less consideration are focused on the person and their interests. All forms of 'conversion therapy' share one *autonomy-diminishing* goal: to restrict a host of profoundly important interests in relation to sexuality and gender identity.[22] Out of many possible examples, I will mention two here. The first is the individual interest to develop one's sexual attraction into sexual

---

objected to independently of their consequences to the affected people's options. But pain and injury are harmful also because they obstruct the pursuit of a person's options and relationships.

[18] On basic disrespect see B Eidelson, *Discrimination and Disrespect* (Oxford University Press, 2015) 84–90. Also J Wolff, 'Fairness, Respect, and the Egalitarian Ethos' (1998) 27(2) *Philosophy & Public Affairs* 97, 107–10.

[19] S Darwall, 'Two Kinds of Respect' (1977) 88(1) *Ethics* 36, 38. For the purposes of this chapter it is not necessary to offer a more detailed account of an egalitarian notion of respect. Rather, it suffices to show that 'conversion therapy' undermines respect (including self-respect) in specific ways.

[20] H Frankfurt, *Necessity, Volition, and Love* (Cambridge University Press, 1999) 146–55.

[21] N Kolodny, 'Rule Over None II: Social Equality and the Justification of Democracy' (2014) 42(4) *Philosophy & Public Affairs* 287.

[22] Since 'conversion therapy' breaches autonomy-based duties, state intervention is legitimate. See J Raz, *The Morality of Freedom* (Oxford University Press, 1986) 416–17.

activity. Some forms of 'conversion therapy' are designed to suppress same-sex attraction; others to suppress the option to develop same-sex sexual attraction to same-sex sexual activity.[23] Both forms aim to suppress fundamental choices that are central to personal autonomy.[24] That is, choices that are central to the ideal of an autonomous life shaped by people's successive choices among valuable options of sexuality and gender identity. The second is the interest to take pride in one's sexuality and gender identity and make it part of one's public personality instead of staying 'in the closet'. This is another fundamental choice, central to personal autonomy, because self-repression of one's identity inhibits full participation in valuable aspects of public culture – from music to art to politics – that are influenced and permeated by diverse sexualities and gender identities.[25] As a result of attacking those fundamental choices, 'conversion therapy' also diminishes self-worth because persons measure their own sense of worth according to their ability to realise their capabilities, goals and dreams.[26] So, 'conversion therapy' disrespects the equal value of LGBTQ+ people by discounting, without any good reason, profoundly important interests that are central to personal autonomy. This is one of the reasons why it is wrong.

At the same time, 'conversion therapy' is disrespectful for the equal moral personhood of LGBTQ+ people also for reasons that extend beyond the harms it inflicts on the specific individuals who are subjected to it. 'Conversion therapy' depends on, and reflects, the systematic disempowerment of LGBTQ+ people that occurs in many societies. The message of 'conversion therapy' – a message of contempt or disdain for LGBTQ+ identities, which *can* and *ought to* be eliminated – is demeaning for all LGBTQ+ people, even for those that never get to experience 'conversion therapy' themselves.[27] This is because it reproduces, and promotes, the social images of LGBTQ+ people as abnormal and disgusting, images which ground their long-existing stigma.[28] In these ways 'conversion therapy' affects not only the people who are subjected to it, but also LGBTQ+ people in general and the attitudes of other people towards them. In fact, it is hard to divorce

---

[23] The definitions of 'conversion therapy' in some of the existing laws against it cover practices that aim to convert, cancel or suppress sexual orientation or gender identity. For more details, see the Introduction to this edited collection.

[24] J Gardner, 'On the Ground of Her Sex(uality)' (1998) 18(2) *Oxford Journal of Legal Studies* 167, 172–73. The question of whether sexuality constitutes an immutable characteristic, or a fundamental choice, has no bearing on whether people are entitled to protection from 'conversion therapy'. In either case, sexuality and gender identity are so central to self-determination that the harms of 'conversion therapy' amount to an attack on the autonomy of LGBTQ+ people.

[25] ibid 176–78.

[26] D Réaume, 'Discrimination and Dignity' (2003) 63(3) *Louisiana Law Review* 645, 673; Wolff (n 18) 107; T Khaitan, 'Dignity as an Expressive Norm: Neither Vacuous Nor a Panacea' (2012) 32(1) *Oxford Journal of Legal Studies* 1.

[27] On the demeaning message of discrimination see D Nejaime and RB Siegel, 'Conscience Wars: Complicity-Based Conscience Claims in Religion and Politics' (2015) 124 *Yale Law Journal* 2516, 2574–78.

[28] M Nussbaum, *From Disgust to Humanity: Sexual Orientation and Constitutional Law* (Oxford University Press, 2010) 2–26.

the absence of a legal ban on 'conversion therapy' in most European countries from a social context of historical stigmatisation on the basis of homosexuality.[29] Consider the hypothetical example of a similar practice with the inverse aim, namely a 'therapy' whose express aim is to convert heterosexual people to homosexuals. It is unlikely that such a practice would not be illegal.[30] But people cannot function as equals in their societies if the state does not protect everyone from abusive practices, like 'conversion therapy', targeting sexuality and gender identity. Consider another example, real this time. States do take action against illegitimate forms of coercive interference with important aspects of individual identity, such as religion. The ECtHR, for instance, has repeatedly found that exploiting a power imbalance under specific circumstances, eg in a military environment,[31] in order to coerce someone to change their religion amounts to 'improper proselytism' which enjoys no protection under the ECHR.[32] Comparisons like these illustrate that 'conversion therapy' relies on, and reflects, a social order in which LGBTQ+ people have less power and are shown less respect than heterosexual cisgender people, and in which their needs are marginalised.[33] Those wider, subordinating effects of 'conversion therapy' furnish another decisive objection against it.

It might be objected that the arguments above apply only where LGBTQ+ persons are forcibly subjected to 'conversion therapy' and not in cases where individuals choose to undergo it. If a 'therapy' provider has done enough to warn others about the potential risks from 'conversion therapy', then anyone who nevertheless chooses to undergo it is responsible for any harm they suffer. The next section will rebut this objection: 'conversion therapy' is among those forms of ill-treatment that human rights law prohibits in an absolute sense.[34] Whether an individual consented to their 'conversion' is therefore irrelevant. What matters is whether, in light of the harmfulness of 'conversion therapy', the state did enough to protect people from it.

---

[29] The force of this objection depends on an analysis of socio-historical particularities which determine the meaning of an act. See D Hellman, *When is Discrimination Wrong?* (Harvard University Press, 2008) 34–59.

[30] A historical example can be seen in the debates surrounding the Local Government Act 1988, s 28. See J Moran, 'Childhood Sexuality and Education: The Case of Section 28' (2001) 4 *Sexualities* 73.

[31] *Larissis v Greece*, Application No 23372/94, 24 February 1998, para 51.

[32] This argument does not suggest that there is a positive state obligation to ban all forms of proselytism. It only aims to show that the legitimacy of proselytism depends, to a significant extent, on an evaluation of the background conditions in which it takes place. See *Nasirov and Others v Azerbaijan*, Application No 58717/10, 20 February 2020, para 65; *Jehovah's Witnesses of Moscow and Others v Russia*, Application No 302/02, 10 June 2010, para 122. More broadly, egalitarian considerations can justify restrictions on freedom of religion or belief: see I Trispiotis, 'Religious Freedom and Religious Antidiscrimination' (2019) 82(5) *Modern Law Review* 864.

[33] S Moreau, *Faces of Inequality* (Oxford University Press, 2020) 39–66; N Bamforth, 'Sexuality and Citizenship in Contemporary Constitutional Argument' (2012) 10(2) *I•CON* 477; C Stychin, *Governing Sexuality: The Changing Politics of Citizenship and Law Reform* (Hart Publishing, 2003) 12–13.

[34] Art 3 makes no provision for exceptions and no derogation is permissible under Art 15(2) ECHR. See eg *Soering v United Kingdom*, Application No 14038/88, 7 July 1989, para 88.

There is an additional point though. This consent-based objection is based on an overly narrow interpretation of the moral significance of choice: what matters is the fact of a person's choice, rather than the circumstances under which a person made that choice.[35] However, such an interpretation is misleading because a choice has elevated moral force only when the conditions under which it is made are right.[36] As we saw above, 'conversion therapy' depends on a social context of historical stigmatisation on the basis of homosexuality. The relationship of that context with the pressure on many LGBTQ+ persons to resist their sexuality or gender identity – a pressure that heterosexual, cisgender persons do not experience – has independent moral significance. It is this inherent coerciveness of 'conversion therapy' – which stems from a context of well-known, historical, widespread disapproval of LGBTQ+ identities – that led the 2020 UN Report on 'conversion therapy', submitted by the UN Independent Expert on Sexual Orientation and Gender Identity (UN SOGI) to the UN Human Rights Council, to call for a full ban on 'conversion therapy' regardless of individual consent.[37] As the UN SOGI, Victor Madrigal-Borloz, put it 'the most comprehensive approach is to prohibit all practices of "conversion therapy", including faith-based organization-based counselling, by any person for any reason'.[38]

Several countries have brought in bans on 'conversion therapy'. Those bans differ in their scope, including as to whether they include an exception for individual consent. For instance, Malta was the first country in the Council of Europe to introduce a comprehensive ban on 'conversion therapy' through the Affirmation of Sexual Orientation, Gender Identity and Gender Expression Act 2016. This Act makes it a criminal offence to force 'conversion therapy' on a person; to perform it, regardless of consent, on a vulnerable person; and to advertise its provision. So, although Malta excludes adults who freely consent from the ban, its ban's definition of 'vulnerable adult' opens the door for consent to be invalidated on grounds that are broader than the usual coercion-based grounds required to annul consent.

Closer to the UN recommendations are countries that have introduced comprehensive bans on 'conversion therapy' without exceptions for individual consent. This can be seen in the legislation recently passed by the Parliament of Victoria in Australia. The Change or Suppression (Conversion) Practices Prohibition Act 2021 does not include any exception for adults to provide their informed consent to 'conversion therapy'. In Article 5(1), it is stated that 'a change or suppression practice means a practice or conduct directed towards a person, whether with or without the person's consent'. Another example is Canada, which

---

[35] This distinction draws on Scanlon's distinction between narrow ('forfeiture') and broad ('value of choice') interpretations of the moral significance of choice. See TM Scanlon, *What We Owe to Each Other* (Harvard University Press, 2000) 256–67.

[36] ibid 260. Under a narrow account of the moral significance of choice, the 'background' conditions are important only if they affect the voluntariness of choice.

[37] *Practices of So-Called 'Conversion Therapy'* (n 13) at 21–22.

[38] ibid 18.

in 2022 enacted changes to its Criminal Code in order to effect a comprehensive ban on 'conversion therapy'. Prior to this, partial bans existed in the provinces of Ontario (since 2015) and Nova Scotia (since 2018), which criminalised 'conversion therapy'. The Canadian Government had previously attempted to pass Bill C-6 banning 'conversion therapy', however this was impeded by the dissolution of the Canadian Parliament in September 2021. This previous version of the Bill included a consent exception for adults to undergo 'conversion therapy', which was strongly opposed by campaigning groups such as No Conversion Canada, as Jordan Sullivan and Nick Schiavo discuss in Part III of this edited collection. Importantly, the new Bill C-4 removes the consent exception for adults and creates four new offences related to performing 'conversion therapy'. Other examples of countries which have recently legislated against 'conversion therapy', without setting out any exceptions for adults who consent to the practice, include France and New Zealand.

To be clear, the argument here is not that consent is irrelevant in determining whether a certain conduct amounts to prohibited ill-treatment under human rights law. Indeed, to return to the ECHR, certain treatments may violate Article 3 ECHR precisely because they were forced on someone.[39] However, the argument here is that an overly narrow interpretation of the moral significance of choice, which focuses *only* on consent and overlooks the background conditions under which a decision is made, is under-inclusive. As the next section shows, a narrow account of freedom of choice would be unable to explain key parts of the case law under Article 3 ECHR, where significant emphasis is placed on the circumstances under which someone was ill-treated, such as the existence of widespread and well-known prejudice against a protected group or the vulnerability of the victim, rather than on whether an individual had a choice to avoid ill-treatment. The role of such factors can be captured only by a broader account of the moral significance of choice, according to which in order for a decision to be legitimate the conditions have to be right before passing onto whether the person's choice or consent is sufficient. This broader account is morally preferable, but its full defence cannot be pursued further here.

A final point to emphasise. So far, I have argued that 'conversion therapy' is wrong because it disrespects the standing of LGBTQ+ people as equals. That does not mean that 'conversion therapy' is wrong *because* it is based on incorrect beliefs about the moral worth of LGBTQ+ persons. Of course, the view that LGBTQ+ persons are of lesser value is fundamental to many instances of 'conversion therapy'. But not all instances of 'conversion therapy' necessarily rest on such a judgement of inferior status. Consider a religious group that offers 'conversion therapy' to save gay men from eternal damnation. Their intervention does not necessarily rely on the assumption that LGBTQ+ people are intrinsically less

---

[39] Force-feeding (eg *Nevmerzhitsky v Ukraine*, Application No 54825/00, 5 April 2005) and force-sterilisation (eg *VC v Slovakia*, Application No 18968/07, 8 November 2011) are examples of that.

valuable than others. In fact, their intervention might be taken to suggest the exact opposite, namely that *because* LGBTQ+ people are of equal value, they deserve to be saved through their 'treatment'. Nevertheless, even benevolent forms of 'conversion therapy' that do not rely on a direct judgement about the equal value of LGBTQ+ people as persons fail to accord them the equality of respect that their status as persons demands. This is because their interests – in relation to health and personal autonomy – are unwarrantedly taken to matter less than the interests of others; and, more specifically, less than the interests of heterosexual people in those very matters. Therefore, the wrongness of 'conversion therapy' does not depend on the beliefs of the 'therapist' but on a theory about the normative significance of being a person, which entails that certain considerations should not be taken as a reason for certain actions.

In summary, 'conversion therapy' is wrong because it disrespects LGBTQ+ persons. It disrespects them not only because it places them at real risk of grave physical and mental harm; or only because it denies them key freedoms related to sexuality and gender identity; or only because it depends on, and reflects, their social subordination. 'Conversion therapy' disrespects LGBTQ+ persons for *all* those reasons, at the same time. Both by design and in effect 'conversion therapy' flouts protected areas of liberty and equality which are, as the next section will further discuss, inherent in the idea of human dignity. This partial sketch of the wrongfulness of 'conversion therapy' is meant to offer a set of reasons that, though incomplete, is sufficient for the overall purpose of this chapter, namely, to support the view that all forms of 'conversion therapy' fall within the scope of the absolute prohibition of torture and CIDT in international human rights law.

III. Discrimination, Dignity, Degradation

The previous section set out the reasons why all forms of 'conversion therapy', even 'talking', non-forcible forms, amount to a serious violation of human dignity. This section will link the discussion with the meaning of degrading treatment in international human rights law. It is argued that one of the main aims of the prohibition of degrading treatment is to protect individuals from serious violations of human dignity, which are specified in detail. Although the focus of this section is on Article 3 ECHR, it is submitted that the proposed interpretation applies more widely in international human rights law. That point is confirmed by the interventions in favour of a ban on 'conversion therapy' by the UN SOGI, which was discussed above, as well as by the UN Committee Against Torture, whose position is discussed in the next section.

Recall that my focus here is on so-called 'talking' forms of 'conversion therapy'. For the reasons discussed above, physical and forcible forms of 'conversion therapy' fall clearly within the protective scope of the absolute prohibition of torture, inhuman or degrading treatment. But do 'talking' forms of 'conversion therapy' reach the level of severity that is required to trigger the protection of the prohibition of degrading treatment in law?

Let us examine some examples of the type of degradation prohibited by Article 3 ECHR. Consider the case of *Bouyid*, where the ECtHR held that one slap by a police officer to the face of someone in custody constituted degrading treatment, even though the victim did not experience serious physical or mental suffering.[40] The ECtHR stressed that whenever persons are deprived of their liberty they are in 'a situation of vulnerability'.[41] Vulnerability here is a 'context-sensitive' judgement that reflects the dependency and relative powerlessness of individuals in custody.[42] In that context, the authorities are under a duty to protect them[43] and any recourse to violence which has not been strictly necessary 'diminishes human dignity and is, in principle, an infringement of [...] Article 3.'[44] Under those circumstances, even one slap to the face of a person constitutes a 'serious attack on the individual's dignity'.[45] The ECtHR added two more specific reasons for that finding. First, a slap to the face 'affects the part of the person's body which expresses his individuality, manifests his social identity and constitutes the centre of his senses – sight, speech and hearing – which are used for communication with others'.[46] A slap to the face is therefore a particularly acute form of disrespect for the equal moral personhood of the other. Second, the officers were in a superior position and had power over the applicants when they slapped them. When such a power imbalance exists, even a single slap degrades the person – it puts him down. It expresses that the victim counts for less; that he is powerless under the control of law-enforcement officers and is morally inferior to them.[47]

Thus, looking closely at *Bouyid*, an act is degrading when it satisfies two conditions. First, to degrade is to treat others in ways that express disrespect for their equal moral worth. Treating others as if they are objects rather than human persons or denying others the minimum requirements of personal autonomy and self-respect is incompatible with the inherent dignity of persons.[48] Second, to degrade also requires that the person or entity acting has sufficient power or status to put

---

[40] *Bouyid v Belgium*, Application No 23380/09, 28 September 2015 (Grand Chamber), para 112.

[41] ibid para 107. The vulnerability of an applicant is an aggravating factor when assessing whether ill-treatment is severe enough to fall under Art 3. See L Peroni and A Timmer, 'Vulnerable Groups: The Promise of an Emerging Concept in European Human Rights Convention Law' (2013) 11 *I•CON* 1056.

[42] C Heri, 'Shaping Coercive Obligations through Vulnerability: The Example of the ECtHR' in L Lavrysen and N Mavronicola (eds), *Coercive Human Rights: Positive Duties to Mobilise the Criminal Law under the ECHR* (Hart Publishing, 2020) 93–116; A Timmer, 'A Quiet Revolution: Vulnerability in the European Court of Human Rights' in MA Fineman and A Grear (eds), *Vulnerability: Reflections on a New Ethical Foundation for Law and Politics* (Ashgate, 2013) 162–64.

[43] *Bouyid* (n 40) para 107.

[44] ibid paras 88 and 100.

[45] ibid para 103.

[46] ibid para 104.

[47] ibid para 106.

[48] In *Bouyid*, the ECtHR emphasises the 'strong link' between human dignity and degrading treatment, and that even in the absence of 'actual bodily injury or intense physical or mental suffering' treatment showing 'a lack of respect for or diminishing human dignity' may be classed as degrading.

others down.[49] Those two conditions track the close links between degrading treatment and dignity in our moral vocabulary. It is important to investigate further though whether, when those two conditions are satisfied, an act can be classed as degrading under Article 3 ECHR even in the absence of material effects on the victims.[50] Let us consider some more examples.

The links between degrading treatment and human dignity also emerge in *Identoba*.[51] In *Identoba*, the ECtHR found a violation of Article 3 taken in conjunction with the prohibition of discrimination under Article 14 because the state authorities failed to provide adequate protection to LGBT citizens during their peaceful march on the International Day Against Homophobia.[52] Because of inadequate police intervention, the LGBT demonstrators were subject to homophobic aggression and verbal abuse by counter-demonstrators. LGBT flags and posters were ripped apart; a big mob surrounded the demonstrators, called them 'faggots' and 'perverts', and threatened to 'crush' them and 'burn them to death'.[53]

Similarly to *Bouyid*, *Identoba* shows that the classification of a treatment as 'degrading' under Article 3 is not contingent on its effects on the victims. Even absent any physical injury or serious mental suffering, ill-treatment can still be classed as 'degrading' if it amounts to an 'affront to human dignity'.[54] *Identoba* is a good example of that. What proved significant in this case was that the recipients of the aggression were in a precarious position because of widespread homophobic prejudice against them.[55] It was in this context that the homophobic and transphobic abuse that they experienced had the effect of arousing feelings of fear, anguish and insecurity that were incompatible with their dignity.[56] In such circumstances

> the question of whether or not some of the applicants sustained physical injuries of certain gravity becomes less relevant. All of the thirteen individual applicants became the target of hate speech and aggressive behaviour [...] Given that they were surrounded by an angry mob that outnumbered them and was uttering death threats and randomly resorting to physical assaults, demonstrating the reality of the threats, and that *a clearly distinguishable homophobic bias played the role of an aggravating factor* [...], the situation

---

See *Bouyid* (n 40) paras 87 and 90. See also N Mavronicola, 'Bouyid and Dignity's Role in Article 3 ECHR' (*Strasbourg Observers*, 8 October 2015), https://strasbourgobservers.com/2015/10/08/bouyid-and-dignitys-role-in-article-3-echr/.

[49] Hellman (n 29) 34–58; J Hampton, 'Forgiveness, Resentment and Hatred' in JG Murphy and J Hampton (eds), *Forgiveness and Mercy* (Cambridge University Press, 1988) 52.

[50] The ECtHR suggests so in *Bouyid* (n 40) para 87.

[51] *Identoba and Others v Georgia*, Application No 73235/12, 12 May 2015, para 71.

[52] The police authorities had been informed 'well in advance' of the LGBT community's intention to hold a march in the centre of Tbilisi on 17 March 2012. See ibid para 72.

[53] ibid paras 69 and 70.

[54] ibid para 65. Also, *Eremia v the Republic of Moldova*, Application No 3564/11, 28 May 2013, para 54; and *Gäfgen v Germany*, Application No 22978/05, 1 June 2010 (Grand Chamber), para 103.

[55] *Identoba* (n 51) paras 68 and 70.

[56] ibid.

was already one of intense fear and anxiety. The aim of that verbal – and sporadically physical – abuse was evidently to frighten the applicants so that they would desist from their public expression of support for the LGBT community.[57] (emphasis added)

So, wrongful discrimination is an aggravating factor when considering whether ill-treatment reaches the threshold set by Article 3.[58] The ECtHR has reiterated this principle in *MC and AC*,[59] and in *Aghdgomelashvili*,[60] both of which, similarly to *Identoba*, involved ill-treatment that was motivated by homophobic and/ or transphobic hatred. In *Oganezova*, the ECtHR found a violation of Article 3 in conjunction with Article 14 ECHR in a case involving a sustained and aggressive homophobic campaign against an LGBT activist, including an arson attack against the community club she ran.[61] The applicant did not suffer actual physical injury.[62] However, that was not decisive.[63] Against the background of sustained homophobic harassment against the applicant, which took place in a context of widespread 'negative attitudes' towards the LGBT community in Armenia, the ECtHR found that her ill-treatment must have aroused in her 'feelings of fear, anguish and insecurity which were not compatible with respect for her human dignity and, therefore, reached the threshold of severity within the meaning of Article 3 of the Convention taken in conjunction with Article 14'.[64]

What those cases clearly show is that wrongful direct discrimination plays a key role in the determination of whether an instance of ill-treatment falls within the scope of Article 3 ECHR. Even instances of ill-treatment that do not cause intense physical or psychological suffering can find themselves into the scope of Article 3 ECHR whenever the aim behind them was to discriminate.[65] Notably, those links between discrimination and degrading treatment mirror the interpretation of the prohibition of torture or CIDT by the UN Convention Against Torture (CAT), which has emphasised that the discriminatory use of violence is a determining factor in the classification of an act as torture or CIDT.[66]

Sometimes wrongful discrimination may be in itself so severe as to constitute an 'affront' to human dignity in violation of Article 3.[67] An early example comes from the decision of the European Commission of Human Rights in

---

[57] *Identoba* (n 51) para 70.

[58] ibid para 67. Also *Begheluri and Others*, Application No 28490/02, 7 October 2014, para 173.

[59] *MC and AC v Romania*, Application No 12060/12, 12 June 2016, paras 116–18.

[60] *Aghdgomelashvili and Japaridze v Georgia*, Application No 7224/11, 8 October 2020, paras 44 and 48–49.

[61] *Oganezova v Armenia*, Application No 71367/12, 17 May 2022.

[62] ibid at para 88.

[63] ibid at para 95.

[64] ibid.

[65] *Identoba* (n 51) para 65. The ECtHR has repeatedly held that racial discrimination is a 'special affront to human dignity' and can as such amount to degrading treatment under Art 3. See *Moldovan v Romania*, Application No 41138/98, 12 July 2005, para 110; *Nachova and Others v Bulgaria*, Application Nos 43577/98 and 43579/98, 6 July 2005 (Grand Chamber), para 145.

[66] UN Committee Against Torture, *General Comment No 2*, 24 January 2008, CAT/C/GC/2, paras 20–21. Discrimination also features in the definition of torture in Art 1 CAT.

[67] See eg *Oganezova* (n 61) at para 80.

East African Asians.[68] The case involved the re-imposition of immigration control on the citizens of the UK and Colonies coming from East Africa, who were henceforth not able to enter 'the only State of which they were citizens – the United Kingdom'.[69] A combination of two factors led the Commission to conclude that the discrimination they suffered amounted to degrading treatment. First, differential treatment on the basis of race constitutes 'a special form of affront to human dignity'.[70] Second, the applicants were 'publicly' disadvantaged by discriminatory legislation. The public nature of the measures against them was an additional 'aggravating' factor when assessing whether discrimination constitutes degrading treatment under Article 3.[71] Similarly, in *Cyprus v Turkey* the ECtHR held that Greek Cypriots living in northern Cyprus suffered severe discriminatory restrictions on the grounds of ethnic origin, race and religion.[72] Once again, because of the grounds on which they were discriminated against *and* because their suffered discrimination was 'public' (ie induced by the state[73]), the ECtHR held that it amounted to degrading treatment. A closer look at those two factors, i.e. the ground of discrimination and its 'public nature', is crucial to understand when discrimination can be severe enough to constitute an 'affront' to human dignity and therefore violate Article 3.

First, for the purposes of 'conversion therapy', is sexual orientation discrimination a 'special' affront to human dignity like racial discrimination? After years of evolution, the jurisprudence of the ECtHR suggests that the answer is now yes. Sexual orientation concerns 'a most intimate'[74] and 'vulnerable'[75] aspect of life. Any differential treatment based on sexual orientation requires 'very weighty reasons' to be justified.[76] In *Smith and Grady* the ECtHR held that treatment grounded on 'a predisposed bias on the part of a heterosexual majority against a homosexual minority' may, in principle, fall within the scope of Article 3.[77] An example of sexual orientation discrimination that amounted to degrading treatment under Article 3 comes from *X v Turkey*.[78] In *X*, the prison authorities placed an inmate in solitary confinement because they assumed that his sexual orientation put him at risk of harm from other inmates. No risk assessment was carried out and no explanation was given as to why the applicant was deprived of even limited access to outdoor activities.[79] The ECtHR held that placing the

---

[68] *East African Asians v United Kingdom* (1981) 3 EHRR 76.

[69] ibid para 196.

[70] ibid para 207.

[71] ibid para 208.

[72] *Cyprus v Turkey*, Application No 25781/94, 10 May 2001, paras 306–309.

[73] ibid paras 245 and 292–93.

[74] *Dudgeon v United Kingdom*, Application No 7525/76, 22 October 1981 (Grand Chamber), para 52.

[75] *X v Turkey*, Application No 24626/09, 27 May 2013.

[76] *Vallianatos and Others v Greece*, Application Nos 29381/09 and 32684/09, 7 November 2013 (Grand Chamber), para 77.

[77] *Smith and Grady v United Kingdom*, Application Nos 33985/96 and 33986/96, 27 September 1999, para 121.

[78] *X v Turkey* (n 75).

[79] ibid para 56.

applicant in solitary confinement – a measure reserved for inmates, unlike the applicant, charged with violent offences[80] – without adequate justification was a degrading form of sexual orientation discrimination.[81]

Cases like *X*, *Identoba*, and *Oganezova* bring discrimination on the grounds of sexual orientation or gender identity in line with the earlier discussed cases on racial discrimination: they confirm that, under certain circumstances, wrongful direct discrimination is a special affront to human dignity in violation of Article 3.[82] When state authorities abuse LGBTQ+ people, or when they refuse or systematically fail to protect them from abuse that they knew or ought to have known about, that is a degrading form of direct discrimination. As such, even absent any serious material effects on the victims,[83] it violates the substantive limb of Article 3 read together with Article 14 ECHR. This principle rightly reflects the well-established links between discrimination and degrading treatment in international human rights law. For instance, as the UN High Commissioner for Human Rights has argued, sexual orientation discrimination can dehumanise its victims, which is often a necessary condition for torture and ill-treatment to occur.[84]

Second, we saw that the 'public nature' of discrimination is an aggravating factor when assessing whether discrimination is severe enough to fall under Article 3.[85] This factor reflects the interrelation of control and powerlessness, which is salient in the ECtHR's interpretation of degrading treatment.[86] Cases like *East African Asians* and *Cyprus v Turkey*, where the government institutionalises discrimination, are paradigms of some persons being openly treated as 'objects' in the power of the authorities.[87] In other cases, like *Identoba*, *MC*, *Aghdgomelashvili* and *Oganezova*, questions of abuse of power emerge again, albeit in a different fashion. When the state authorities systematically fail to prevent or investigate hatred-induced violence towards LGBTQ+ people that they knew or ought to have known about, they undermine public confidence in

---

[80] ibid para 53.

[81] ibid para 57.

[82] P Johnson and S Falcetta, 'Sexual Orientation Discrimination and Article 3 of the European Convention on Human Rights: Developing the Protection of Sexual Minorities' (2018) 43(2) *ELR* 167, 175–76.

[83] *Identoba* (n 51) para 70; *MC* (n 59) paras 117–19.

[84] UN Human Rights Council, *Annual Report of the United Nations High Commissioner for Human Rights: Discriminatory Laws and Practices and Acts of Violence Against Individuals Based on their Sexual Orientation and Gender Identity*, 19th Session, 17 November 2011, A/HRC/19/41, para 34.

[85] Of course, being an aggravating factor, the 'public nature' factor is neither necessary nor sufficient to find a case of discrimination in violation of Art 3. See eg *Lyalyakin v Russia*, Application No 31305/09, 12 March 2015, para 69; *Svinarenko and Slyadnev v Russia*, Application Nos 32541/08 and 43441/08, 17 July 2014 (Grand Chamber), para 115.

[86] The approach of the ECtHR is similar to the approach of the UN Committee Against Torture in this regard. See UN General Assembly, *Extra-Custodial Use of Force and the Prohibition of Torture and Other Cruel, Inhuman or Degrading Treatment*, 20 July 2017, A/72/178.

[87] *Tyrer v United Kingdom*, Application No 5856/72, 25 April 1978, para 33.

the state duty to keep everyone physically and morally secure.[88] Moral security depends on having one's moral standing recognised as a limitation to what may legitimately be done to them, and their welfare being treated as morally important by the state.[89] When a protected group is already the target of prejudice, the failure of the authorities to offer them reasonable protection is a paradigmatic affront to their moral standing – it stamps them with a badge of inferiority.

Some of the most egregious forms of direct discrimination degrade their victims precisely because of the open way that they deny them profoundly important autonomy interests[90] and self-respect.[91] This reason might not hold in cases involving non-intentional or indirect forms of discrimination, where the psychological suffering and stigma might be somewhat less.[92] As a result, those would be captured only by Article 14 and not by Article 3 ECHR. Thus, this analysis does not suggest that wrongful discrimination always amounts to degrading treatment under Article 3. An interpretive judgement, similar to that offered by these pages, is required to determine if an instance of discrimination spawns the type of serious degradation prohibited by the provision. Apart from the ground of discrimination, another factor affecting this interpretive judgement is its 'public nature'; although, as we saw, 'public' discrimination does not require that discrimination be widely publicised.[93] The 'public nature' factor is just another way of expressing a paradigm feature of degradation, namely that it rests on a significant disparity in power between two parties. It is because of that power disparity that an action degrades rather than merely insults others.

One final caveat before moving on. The power or status disparity in degrading treatment does not require that ill-treatment is forced on an individual. Although this is often the case, eg when ill-treatment occurs in custody, the requirement for a power/status disparity does not extinguish the possibility for individual voluntary action. In cases like *Identoba*, *Oganezova*, *MC* and *Aghdgomelashvili*, the emphasis of the Court's interpretation was not on whether the ill-treatment in question was forced on the applicants. The emphasis was on the circumstances of widespread prejudice under which individuals were ill-treated and on the fact that, under *those* circumstances, state authorities either outright abused, or refused to provide reasonable protection to, the individuals in question.[94] So, as discussed earlier,

---

[88] In cases involving the rights of transgender people, the ECtHR has held that respect for dignity requires the protection of moral security. See *Van Kück v Germany*, Application No 35869/97, 12 June 2003, para 69; *I v United Kingdom*, Application No 25680/94, 11 July 2002, para 70; *Christine Goodwin v United Kingdom*, Application No 28957/95, 11 June 2002, para 90.

[89] J Wolfendale, 'Moral Security' (2017) 25 *Journal of Political Philosophy* 238, 244. Also C Nikolaidis, 'Unravelling the Knot of Equality and Privacy in the European Court of Human Rights and the US Supreme Court: From *Isonomia* to *Isotimia*' (2018) 18(4) *Human Rights Law Review* 719, 736.

[90] GC Lury, *The Anatomy of Racial Inequality* (Harvard University Press, 2002) 58.

[91] T Khaitan, *A Theory of Discrimination Law* (Oxford University Press, 2015) 126–28; S Bagenstos, '"Rational Discrimination", Accommodation, and the Politics of (Disability) Civil Rights' (2003) 89 *Virginia Law Review* 825.

[92] S Moreau, 'What is Discrimination' (2010) 38(2) *Philosophy & Public Affairs* 143, 177–78.

[93] On the contrary, degrading discrimination can take place in a prison, see eg *X v Turkey* (n 75).

[94] ibid paras 72–73.

although consent is not irrelevant in determining whether conduct amounts to degrading treatment, focusing *only* on individual consent detracts from an evaluation of the background conditions in which ill-treatment was inflicted. Those background conditions have independent moral significance, which stems from the aim of the prohibition of degrading treatment to protect individuals from serious violations of human dignity.

To recap, an act is degrading if it expresses the unequal moral worth of the other *and* if the person acting occupies a position of power over the victim such that their actions can put the other down. This explains why direct discrimination on the grounds of sexual orientation and gender identity can sometimes amount to degrading treatment under Article 3. Before examining whether 'conversion therapy' fulfils those conditions of degradation, two final issues need to be addressed: first, whether the wrongness of a degrading act depends on the intentions of the wrongdoer; and, second, whether it depends on its subjective perception by the victim or others.

In response to the first question, the wrongness of degrading treatment depends on the objective meaning carried by it rather than the mental state of the wrongdoer. A slap to the face of a person has a different, ie degrading, social significance when it happens in a police station rather than outside a pub. Failing to offer reasonable protection to vulnerable people from predictable hatred-induced violence has degrading meaning when we talk about the state authorities rather than one's next-door neighbours. The condition that degrading treatment must express – ie that the other is not of equal moral worth – is satisfied depending on the social or conventional meaning of the conduct. Thus, the intentions of the wrongdoer are not decisive for whether an act is degrading. This objective-meaning interpretation of degrading treatment emerges clearly in the case law of the ECtHR. The ECtHR has repeatedly held that the intention to debase or humiliate is not a necessary condition of degrading treatment.[95] A finding of degrading treatment is possible even when the intention to degrade is absent. In *Gäfgen*, the officers who threatened to torture the applicant claimed that they were trying to save a child's life.[96] Yet their motives made no difference to the Court's assessment, which was that torture or degrading treatment cannot be justified 'even in circumstances where the life of an individual is at risk'.[97]

As for the second question, since what determines whether an act is degrading is its meaning in a particular social context, the emphasis is not on how the victim experienced their ill-treatment. This might appear counter-intuitive because the word 'degrading' focuses on the impact of an act on its victim. Starting from *Ireland v UK*,[98] the ECtHR often reiterates that a treatment is

---

[95] *Svinarenko* (n 85) para 114; *V v United Kingdom*, Application No 24888/94, 16 December 1999 (Grand Chamber), para 71.

[96] *Gäfgen* (n 54) para 107.

[97] ibid.

[98] *Ireland v United Kingdom*, 18 January 1978, 2 EHRR 25, para 167.

degrading if it arouses in its victim 'feelings of fear, anguish and inferiority capable of humiliating and debasing them'.[99] In other cases, the ECtHR stresses that degrading treatment goes beyond the inevitable element of humiliation arising from 'legitimate punishment'[100] or 'mandatory military service'.[101] These terms denote that the subjective experience of ill-treatment is central to its wrongness.

That is not the only available interpretation though. The focus of degrading treatment on its impact on the victims does not mean that the term refers to their subjective experience.[102] It refers to what happens to the person in relation to an objective standard of dignity, ie that each person is entitled to be treated as a moral equal. In the hypothetical scenario that the applicants in *Bouyid* thought that they deserved being slapped whilst in custody, their treatment would still be degrading. That is why the ECtHR has held that although treatment can be degrading when it humiliates, humiliation per se is not a necessary condition of degrading treatment.[103] Nor is it necessary to be humiliated in the eyes of others.[104] A homophobic crowd might not think that it is humiliating for LGBTQ+ people to be publicly abused while police are standing by – as happened in *Identoba*. But insofar as the police inaction expresses the unequal moral worth of the LGBTQ+ people in question, their inaction is degrading.

So far, it has been argued that the ECtHR uses the word 'degrading' as an evaluative term. This section sketched answers to two key components of the complex interpretive judgements that are necessary to flesh out degrading treatment. First, it was argued that an action is degrading if it expresses the unequal moral worth of the victim and if the person acting has power over the victim such that their actions can put the other down. It is for this reason that certain instances of direct discrimination amount to degrading treatment. Second, it was argued that neither the intentions of the wrongdoer nor the subjective perception of the victim determines whether an act is degrading.

IV. Positive State Obligations

So far it has been argued that an act is degrading if it expresses the unequal moral worth of the other and if the wrongdoer has sufficient power over the victim. Wrongful discrimination is a key aggravating factor in this context. It is arguable

---

[99] *Tysiąc v Poland*, Application No 5410/03, 20 March 2007, para 67.

[100] *Lyalyakin* (n 85) para 69.

[101] *Chember v Russia*, Application No 7188/03, 3 July 2008, para 49.

[102] In the jurisprudence of the ECtHR, degradation is closer to being demeaned, in the sense that the person wronged does not have to feel that their moral status has been lowered. See Hampton (n 49) 44–45.

[103] *Poltoratskiy v Ukraine*, Application No 38812/97, 29 April 2003, para 131.

[104] As the ECtHR held in *MSS* it 'may well suffice that the victim is humiliated in his own eyes, even if not in the eyes of others': *MSS v Belgium and Greece*, Application No 30696/09, 21 January 2011 (Grand Chamber), para 220.

that all forms of 'conversion therapy' – not just its 'physical' or forcible forms – fulfil those two conditions of degradation. Treating LGBTQ+ people as though they are of less value is an intrinsic feature of 'conversion therapy'. Every form of the practice manifests contempt for LGBTQ+ identities. That contempt is acted upon through a pseudo-'therapeutic' practice that seriously violates the dignity of LGBTQ+ people by brazenly disrespecting the equal value of their autonomy, health and wellbeing – and by putting them at real risk of grave harm because of their sexuality or gender identity.

It is worth reiterating that 'conversion therapy' is an affront to human dignity regardless of whether any LGBTQ+ persons that go through it are *actually* physically or mentally harmed by it. Physical or mental harm aside, 'conversion therapy' is inherently degrading for its victims and survivors – and for LGBTQ+ people more broadly – because it contemptuously disregards the interests and welfare of LGBTQ+ people.[105] Even when not stated explicitly, the degrading message of 'conversion therapy' is intelligible to its recipients because it reflects and repeats a widely understood message, which is that heterosexual and cisgender identities are 'normal' and desirable, whereas other gender identities or expressions of sexuality are not. This message is intelligible to its recipients because *they* are part of the same community of shared meanings as those who try to 'convert' them. That is why 'conversion therapy' is degrading even when that was not the intention of the 'therapy' provider or how it was conceived by the individual victims.[106]

The expressive harms of 'conversion therapy' encapsulate some of the practice's most profound yet predictable consequences for the interests of its victims. However, it is important to remember that the message conveyed by 'conversion therapy' is not the source of why the practice is wrong. As we saw, 'conversion therapy' is inherently incompatible with the sense of self-worth that we associate with dignity. Self-worth requires that a person is secure in their identity as an individual, including as a member of those communities with which they identify. 'Conversion therapy' eradicates this sense of self-worth. Its aim is to limit the options of LGBTQ+ persons in some of the most valuable and intimate spheres of life. The freedoms 'conversion therapy' brazenly denies would not be denied to a heterosexual cisgender person. Therefore, 'conversion therapy' treats LGBTQ+ people as if they are not of equal moral worth to heterosexual cisgender persons, as if they are second-class. Put otherwise, 'conversion therapy' is degrading *because* it discounts the interests of LGBTQ+ people absent any good reason for

---

[105] Expressive harms can directly injure, and function differently from ideological or purely subjective injuries. 'Expressive Harms and Standing' (1999) 112(6) *Harvard Law Review* 1313; RH Pildes and RG Niemi, 'Expressive Harms, "Bizarre Districts", and Voting Rights: Evaluating Election-District Appearances after *Shaw v Reno*' (1993) 92 *Michigan Law Review* 483.

[106] Subordinated groups do not choose the social meanings imposed on them by society's institutions, such as religious groups or medical experts: L Melling, 'Religious Refusals to Public Accommodations Laws: Four Reasons to Say No' (2015) 38 *Harvard Journal of Law & Gender* 177; M Lim and L Melling, 'Inconvenience or Indignity? Religious Exemptions to Public Accommodations Laws' (2014) 22(2) *Journal of Law and Policy* 705.

doing so. Its degrading character results from the way it wrongs individuals – and this chapter's respect-based account offers a plausible explanation of that wrong.

Recall though that a degrading act also requires that its perpetrator has sufficient power or status over the recipient of ill-treatment. 'Conversion therapy' fulfils that condition too. A significant power imbalance is inherent in the practice. 'Conversion therapy' is typically offered by members of established social institutions, such as faith groups or medical experts, who hold greater power or status in relation to individual victims. The last part of this edited collection includes chapters written by survivors of 'conversion therapy'. All of them point to the significant disparity of status between the religious actors, doctors, psychotherapists etc who act as the 'enlightened' 'therapy'-providers over the benighted 'converts'.[107] It is through this disparity of power or status that the disrespect expressed by 'conversion therapy' does not just insult its victims but degrades them.

So, to sum up, all forms of 'conversion therapy' amount at a minimum to degrading treatment, and therefore violate the ECHR and UK human rights law, because all combine disrespect for the equal moral worth of LGBTQ+ persons with a significant imbalance of power or status between the parties involved. As such, all forms of 'conversion therapy' should be absolutely prohibited, and no consequentialist reasoning provided by the state or others can justify them. Where particular forms of 'conversion therapy' sit on the scale of Article 3 ECHR, ie whether particular 'therapies' constitute torture rather than degrading treatment, would depend on their deliberateness, the involvement of state agents, their specific purpose and the status of the victim in the context of the case.[108]

This chapter grounds the wrongfulness of 'conversion therapy' on its basic disrespect for the equal moral value of LGBTQ+ people. However, my account should not be taken to suggest that the deleterious consequences of 'conversion therapy' for the health and wellbeing of LGBTQ+ persons do not matter. On the contrary, the reasons why all forms of 'conversion therapy' amount at a minimum to degrading treatment are at least partly determined by its predictable consequences for the interests of its victims.[109] That is clearly reflected in international human rights law. According to the Yogyakarta Principles, states are under an obligation to prohibit all forms of 'conversion therapy'.[110] This obligation flows from the absolute

---

[107] *Practices of So-Called 'Conversion Therapy'* (n 13) at 16.

[108] See eg N Mavronicola, *Torture, Inhumanity and Degradation under Article 3 of the ECHR: Absolute Rights and Absolute Wrongs* (Hart Publishing, 2021) Ch 3; M Nowak and E McArthur, 'The Distinction Between Torture and Cruel, Inhuman or Degrading Treatment' (2006) 16(3) *Torture* 147.

[109] So, legal intervention against 'conversion therapy' is justified, at least in part, by appeal to the states of affairs it promotes. This (broadly) consequentialist view differs to rule utilitarianism because it is unconcerned with benefit maximisation. See TM Scanlon, 'Rights, Goals and Fairness' in TM Scanlon (ed), *The Difficulty of Tolerance* (Cambridge University Press, 2003) 33–39.

[110] The Yogyakarta Principles Plus 10, Principle 10 E. Although the Yogyakarta Principles are not legally binding, they are highly influential as they remain the most comprehensive identification of state human rights obligations in relation to sexual orientation and gender identity. See M O'Flaherty and

prohibition of torture or CIDT in international human rights law. The concluding observations of the UN Committee Against Torture on two recent state periodic reports confirm this. Commenting on the seventh periodic report of Ecuador, the Committee called on the state to close all private centres where such 'therapies' are practised and hold to account anyone involved.[111] Similarly, in its concluding observations on the fifth periodic report of China, the UN Committee Against Torture expressed concern about reports that private and state clinics offered 'conversion therapy', including 'involuntary confinement in psychiatric facilities'.[112] Although in 2014 a Beijing court ordered one such clinic to pay compensation to a victim, the UN Committee Against Torture criticised China's 'failure to clarify whether such practices are prohibited by law, have been investigated and ended, and whether the victims have received redress'.[113] The Committee stressed that China should ban 'conversion therapies', as well as all other 'forced, involuntary or otherwise coercive or abusive treatments' against LGBTQ+ people.[114] This last point is crucial because it shows that the UN Committee Against Torture attaches little significance to individual consent to such 'therapies': states are under a duty to outlaw all 'abusive treatments' targeting LGBTQ+ people rather than just forcible 'conversion therapy'.[115]

Moving back to the ECHR, it is clear that public authorities must not engage in the provision of 'conversion therapy' because that would violate Article 3 ECHR. This is not the end of the matter though. Article 3 generates a range of positive state duties, out of which two are particularly important here.[116] The first is the general, or framework, state duty to set up an effective system deterring and punishing acts of ill-treatment, backed up by enforcement mechanisms for the prevention, suppression and punishment of breaches.[117] This framework duty extends to ill-treatment administered by private actors.[118] The second is the more specific positive state duty to take operational measures when the authorities knew or ought to have known at the time of the existence of a real and immediate

---

J Fisher, 'Sexual Orientation, Gender Identity and International Human Rights Law: Contextualising the Yogyakarta Principles' (2008) 8(2) *Human Rights Law Review* 207, 237–47.

[111] UN Committee Against Torture, *Concluding Observations on the Seventh Periodic Report of Ecuador*, CAT/C/ECU/CO/7, 11 January 2017, para 49.

[112] UN Committee Against Torture, *Concluding Observations on the Fifth Periodic Report of China*, CAT/C/CHN/CO/5, 3 February 2016, para 55.

[113] ibid.

[114] ibid para 56.

[115] ibid. Also UN Human Rights Council, *Annual Report* (n 84) para 56.

[116] Apart from 'framework' and operational positive duties, Art 3 ECHR also gives rise to investigative duties. Those fall outside the scope of this chapter.

[117] See eg *Đorđević v Croatia*, Application No 41526/10, 24 July 2012, para 138; *Beganović v Croatia*, Application No 46423/06, 25 June 2009, para 71; *Nachova* (n 65) para 96; *A v United Kingdom* (1998) 27 EHRR 611, para 22.

[118] *Šečić v Croatia*, Application No 40116/02, 31 May 2007, para 53; *Moldovan and Others v Romania*, Application Nos 41138/98 and 64320/01, 12 July 2005, para 98; *MC v Bulgaria*, Application No 39272/98, 4 December 2003, para 151. See also *Gezer v Secretary of State for the Home Department* [2004] EWCA Civ 1730, [2005] HRLR 7. See also, *mutatis mutandis, Commissioner of Police of the Metropolis v DSD* [2018] UKSC 11, [2019] AC 196 per Lord Neuberger at [88].

risk of ill-treatment against identified individuals from the acts of a third party.[119] While the negative duty not to engage in torture or CIDT is absolute, the positive obligations arising from the prohibition are capable of modification on grounds of proportionality. That is, they must be interpreted in ways that do not impose a disproportionate burden on the authorities,[120] and there is also latitude as to how they can be fulfilled.

One important point on the operational duties arising from Article 3 ECHR. As the UN Committee on the Elimination of Discrimination against Women (CEDAW) has noted, the requirement for an immediate risk of ill-treatment, which can be traced back to *Osman*,[121] is problematic in cases of gender-based violence or abuse.[122] This is because that requirement prevents capturing cases where successive episodes of gender-based violence against specific individuals or groups do show that the risk of ill-treatment is real, but where the wrongdoer is not in the direct vicinity of the victim. Drawing on CEDAW's work, in *Volodina* the ECtHR tacitly accepted that in cases of gender-based violence, the standard against which operational state duties are assessed spans a wider window of time, starting from when the risk of ill-treatment is real, even if not imminent.[123] For that reason, states must carefully consider the particular context of the case including any past history of violence.[124] As Judge Pinto de Albuquerque argued, that standard is satisfied if the authorities know or ought to know that a specific group of people is subject to repeated abuse.[125] It is posited that for exactly those reasons, that amended standard of assessment of operational state duties under Article 3 is fully applicable to recurring violent or abusive practices based on sexual orientation or gender identity, such as 'conversion therapy'.[126]

With this amendment to operational state duties in mind, let us go back to the framework state duty under Article 3 ECHR. Recall that the framework duty refers to the primary state obligation to take legal measures designed to ensure that individuals are not subjected to proscribed ill-treatment – including ill-treatment administered by private individuals. Let us focus on how this framework

---

[119] *Osman v United Kingdom*, Application No 23452/94, 28 October 1998 (Grand Chamber), para 116. On the application of the *Osman* test in the context of Art 3 see *Đorđević* (n 117); also *Z and Others v United Kingdom*, Application No 29392/95, 10 May 2001 (Grand Chamber), para 255. The UK courts apply the *Osman* test in cases involving complaints under Art 3. See *DSD* (n 118) per Lord Neuberger paras 92–98; *R (Munjaz) v Ashworth Hospital Authority* [2005] UKHL 58, [2006] 2 AC 148, paras 78–80.

[120] *Đorđević* (n 117) para 139.

[121] *Osman* (n 119) para 116.

[122] UN Committee on the Elimination of Discrimination Against Women, *VK v Bulgaria*, Communication No 20/2008, 15 October 2008, para 9.8.

[123] *Volodina v Russia*, Application No 41261/17, 9 July 2019, para 86.

[124] ibid.

[125] Separate opinion of Judge Pinto de Albuquerque, in *Volodina* (n 123) para 12.

[126] This is congenial to the presumption set in *Re E*, namely that the authorities knew or ought to have known about the existence of a real risk of ill-treatment whenever a breach has occurred, and then recurred, over a period of time. See *Re E v Chief Constable of the Royal Ulster Constabulary and Another* [2008] UKHL 66, [2009] 1 AC 536.

duty applies to 'conversion therapy'. The framework duty under Article 3 often translates to a state duty to mobilise the criminal law against proscribed forms of ill-treatment. We must be careful here, though, because – although criminal law is typically presumed to be an effective tool of deterrence and retribution[127] – widening the web of criminalisation in the name of human rights protection carries significant risks.[128] Criminalisation as part of the framework duty under Article 3 has emerged in a wide range of cases including rape;[129] sexual abuse of minors;[130] disproportionate police violence;[131] ill-treatment in custody;[132] and domestic violence.[133] The reasons behind the state duty to criminalise certain forms of ill-treatment are not always entirely clear.[134] For instance, although the examples above involve physical abuse, the ECtHR has also justified the need for criminal law protection based on the argument that degrading treatment seriously affects human dignity and psychological wellbeing,[135] regardless of whether injuries of a certain degree of severity have been inflicted.[136]

So, does the framework duty under Article 3 require criminal law protection against 'conversion therapy'? For the reasons discussed above, all forms of 'conversion therapy' attain the minimum level of severity to trigger the applicability of Article 3 because all amount to a serious violation of human dignity: they directly discriminate against LGBTQ+ people by placing their physical and mental health at real risk of grave harm; and they can arouse in their victims feelings of fear, anguish and inferiority capable of debasing them.[137] On that account, and applying *Volodina* and *Myumyun* by analogy,[138] the positive framework state duty under Article 3 can justify the criminalisation of the provision of all forms of 'conversion therapy'.[139] Simply put, states must legally ban 'conversion therapy', and they can

---

[127] For a critical appraisal of this presumption see L Lazarus, 'Positive Obligations and Criminal Justice: Duties to Protect or Coerce' in L Zadner and J Roberts (eds), *Principles and Values in Criminal Law and Criminal Justice* (Oxford University Press, 2012) 135–57; F Tulkens, 'The Paradoxical Relationship between Criminal Law and Human Rights' (2011) 9 *Journal of International Criminal Justice* 577.

[128] N Mavronicola, 'Coercive Overrech, Dilution and Diversion: Potential Dangers of Aligning Human Rights Protection with Criminal Law (Enforcement)' in Lavrysen and Mavronicola (n 42) 183–202.

[129] *MC v Bulgaria* (n 118) para 166; *X and Y v The Netherlands*, Application No 8978/80, 26 March 1985.

[130] *M and C v Romania*, Application No 29032/04, 27 September 2011.

[131] *Cestaro* (n 6) para 225.

[132] *Myumyun v Bulgaria*, Application No 67258/13, 3 November 2015, para 77.

[133] *Volodina* (n 123) para 81.

[134] L Lavrysen, 'Positive Obligations and the Criminal Law: A Bird's-Eye View on the Case Law of the European Court of Human Rights' in Lavrysen and Mavronicola (n 42) 29–55, 43.

[135] *Myumyun* (n 132) para 74.

[136] *Volodina* (n 123) para 81.

[137] That is enough for a treatment to qualify as 'degrading' under Art 3 ECHR. See *Identoba* (n 51) para 65.

[138] See n 123 and n 132.

[139] Malta, for instance, has criminalised the provision of 'conversion therapy'. Specifically in the UK, the authorities cannot claim that they were unaware of the risks of 'conversion therapy'. The 2018 National LGBT Survey showed that significant numbers of LGBTQ+ people have been offered 'conversion therapy'. See UK Government Equalities Office, *National LGBT Survey: Research Report*

choose to do so through criminal law. What the framework duty under Article 3 requires is legal provisions that are sufficiently tailored to the human rights offence concerned. So, other options of legal action against 'conversion therapy', such as civil means of redress, could also be used. In fact, as later chapters of this edited collection argue, it might well be that civil means of redress are preferable against certain forms of 'conversion therapy'.[140]

V. Conclusion

This chapter argued that 'conversion therapy' is wrong because it disrespects the equal moral value of LGBTQ+ persons. All forms of 'conversion therapy' combine: (1) well-documented, real risks of grave harm for the physical and mental health of LGBT+ persons; and (2) direct discrimination on the grounds of sexual orientation or gender identity. Through this distinctive combination of wrongs, all forms of 'conversion therapy' amount to a serious violation of human dignity. Therefore, they fall qualitatively within the scope of the absolute prohibition of torture or CIDT under international human rights law. More specifically, this chapter illustrated why all forms of 'conversion therapy' – physical and non-physical, forcible and non-forcible – amount at a minimum to degrading treatment. As a result, states are under a positive obligation to take effective measures to protect LGBTQ+ persons from the harms of 'conversion therapy'. The first important step in that direction is introducing a legal ban on all forms of this practice.

More detail than could be included in this chapter is required on the precise mix of civil and criminal law protections that would be sufficient against 'conversion therapy' in different jurisdictions and legal contexts. The chapters in Parts II and III of this edited collection focus on the specific topics of children's rights, trans rights, religious rights, and transitional justice in the context of 'conversion therapy', as well as on the fundamental importance of engaging with survivors. Legislators and policymakers ought to take those perspectives into account in order to progressively end the abusive practice of 'conversion therapy' through the law but also beyond it.

From the perspective of the prohibition of torture, inhuman or degrading treatment, which was the focus of this chapter, it is unlikely that the Member States of the Council of Europe can fulfil their positive framework duties under Article 3 ECHR without adopting specific legal provisions against 'conversion therapy'

(July 2018) 33 and 83–92. In addition, in 2017, the leading medical professional bodies in the UK, including NHS England and NHS Scotland, signed a Memorandum of Understanding on ending 'conversion therapy': see BACP (n 13) para 3.

[140] *Mitkus v Latvia*, Application No 7259/03, 2 October 2010, para 76. See K Kamber, *Prosecuting Human Rights Offences: Rethinking the Sword Function of Human Rights Law* (Brill, 2017) Ch 1.

that define the scope of the practice and clarify which public authorities have a duty to act against 'therapy' providers. Such provisions must also set out remedies, support, reporting mechanisms for victims, and also the types of interim measures that could be taken in this context. The framework state duties under Article 3 ECHR require this basic legal apparatus firmly in place.

2

Conversion Practices and
Coercive Control

JONATHAN HERRING

Traditional models of criminal law struggle to accommodate claims that conversion practices (often known as 'conversion therapy'[1]) should be a criminal offence. This chapter sets out why that is. It then explores the wrongs of conversion practices by drawing on the literature on coercive control to help overcome these objections to criminalisation. It will proceed as follows. First, it explains the wrong of conversion practices, which can be overlooked by traditional approaches to understanding harm in the criminal law. It argues that conversion practices should be understood as degrading treatment and a breach of trust. Second, it argues that the wrong of conversion practices must be understood in relational terms, rather than the traditional 'incident model' of criminal wrongs. Third, it argues that the consent of the victim to the 'therapy' should not amount to a defence. I provide several reasons for this, particularly that conversion practices draw on and reinforce patriarchal (by which I include cisnormative and heteronormative) forces. So understood, the case for criminalising conversion practices becomes overwhelming, even where there is consent from the victim.

This chapter demonstrates how conversion practices should be seen as squarely within the remit of a modern criminal law. Indeed, if the claims in this chapter are correct then there is a right to be protected from conversion practices. At the same time, it challenges some of the assumptions that underpin the traditional understanding of substantive criminal law.

This chapter will not attempt to discuss alternative definitions of conversion practices, but will adopt that of the Memorandum of Understanding on Conversion Therapy in the UK:

> a therapeutic approach, or any model or individual viewpoint that demonstrates any assumption that any sexual orientation or gender identity is inherently preferable to

---

[1] I use the term conversion practices rather than the more common 'conversion therapy' because as Jayne Ozanne states: 'It cannot rightly be called "therapy" given the harm such interventions are known to cause, which are far from therapeutic': J Ozanne, '"Conversion Therapy", Spiritual Abuse and Human Rights' (2021) 3 *European Human Rights Law Review* 241, 242.

any other, and which attempts to bring about a change of sexual orientation or gender identity or seeks to suppress an individual's expression of sexual orientation or gender identity on that basis.[2]

The history of conversion practices is long and disturbing. Reports from the nineteenth century reveal methods including the use of bicycles for long periods; electric shocks, lobotomies and castration.[3] While in modern forms the practices tend to rely on prayer, psychological techniques and pressure, the aim is the same: to change or suppress a person's sexuality or sexual identity.

While there is widespread support for criminalising conversion practices,[4] putting this intuition within the traditional framework of the criminal law is challenging. This chapter will seek to explore why this is and draw on the recent offence of coercive control as a model that can be used to respond to some of these challenges. Coercive control is the current way of understanding what long ago was called 'wife beating' and more recently domestic violence and domestic abuse. It is an attempt to identify the particular wrong at the heart of domestic abuse. It does so by understanding domestic abuse to be a particular kind of relationship, rather than being a particular kind of act. Evan Stark, a leading commentator on coercive control, defines it as:

> a course of calculated, malevolent conduct deployed almost exclusively by men to dominate individual women by interweaving repeated physical abuse with three equally important tactics: intimidation, isolation and control.[5]

The offence of 'coercive and controlling behaviour' is found in section 76 of the Serious Crime Act 2015:

(1) A person (A) commits an offence if—

(a)   A repeatedly or continuously engages in behaviour towards another person (B) that is controlling or coercive,

(b)   at the time of the behaviour, A and B are personally connected,

(c)   the behaviour has a serious effect on B, and

(d)   A knows or ought to know that the behaviour will have a serious effect on B.[6]

The Family Courts have provided some further guidance in Practice Direction 12J for use in family courts. It states:

> 'coercive behaviour' means an act or a pattern of acts of assault, threats, humiliation and intimidation or other abuse that is used to harm, punish, or frighten the victim;

---

[2] British Association of Counselling and Psycotherapy et al, *Memorandum of Understanding on Conversion Therapy in the UK* (BACP, 4 March 2022) www.bacp.co.uk/events-and-resources/ethics-and-standards/mou/.

[3] G Andrade and M Campo Redondo, 'Is Conversion Therapy Ethical? A Renewed Discussion in the Context of Legal Efforts to Ban it' (2022) 20 *Ethics Medicine and Public Health* 100732.

[4] H Kennedy et al, *The Cooper Report* (Ozanne Foundation, 2021).

[5] E Stark, *Coercive Control* (Oxford, Oxford University Press, 2007) 5.

[6] Serious Crime Act 2015, s 76.

'controlling behaviour' means an act or pattern of acts designed to make a person subordinate and/or dependent by isolating them from sources of support, exploiting their resources and capacities for personal gain, depriving them of the means needed for independence, resistance and escape and regulating their everyday behaviour.[7]

It will be argued that this recent offence opens up criminal law doctrine to being receptive to the criminalising of conversion practices. This chapter will set out three particular problems that traditional criminal law would face in recognising conversion practices as criminal and draw on the offence of coercive control to develop a response to them.

I. Harms

The harm of conversion practices does not fit into traditional understandings of that concept in criminal law. This is problematic because harm plays an important role in the criminal law. First, it is used to justify criminalisation in the first place. The much cited 'harm principle', developed by John Stuart Mill, explains that only acts which cause harm should be suitable candidates for criminalisation:

> The only purpose for which power can be rightfully exercised over any member of a civilized community against his will is to prevent harm to others. His own good, either physical or moral, is not sufficient warrant. He cannot rightfully be compelled to do or forbear ... because in the opinion of others to do so would be wise or even right.[8]

Second, harm is relevant because it is used to rank criminal offences. The worse the harm, the more serious the offence and, usually, the more severe the sentence. For example, offences against the person are often presented as a 'ladder of harms' with battery (a mere touching of person) being at the bottom, leading up through offences involving actual bodily harm and grievous bodily harm until we reach homicide at the top of the ladder.[9]

What is often left unarticulated is how we rank harms. Traditionally, harm was seen in terms of the extent to which the injury impacted on the ability of the victim to fight as a soldier.[10] While clearly we have moved from that, there is still in the criminal law a primary focus on the impact of the injury on the body. Hence in the influential account of Andrew von Hirsch and Nils Jareborg the primary claim protected by the criminal law is to 'physical integrity: health, safety and the

---

[7] Ministry of Justice, 'Practice Direction 12J – Child Arrangements and Contact Orders: Domestic Abuse and Harm' (GOV.UK, 2022) para 3.

[8] JS Mill, *On Liberty* (Indianapolis, Bobbs-Merrill Co, 1956) 13.

[9] J Herring, *Law and The Relational Self* (Cambridge, Cambridge University Press, 2020) Ch 7.

[10] *Wright's Case* (1604) 1 CoLit 127a, 127b; *Bravery v Bravery* [1954] 1 WLR 1169, 1180 (Denning LJ, dissenting). In 1994, Lord Mustill in *R v Brown* [1994] 1 AC 212, 262 declared the common law crime of maim to be 'obsolete'.

avoidance of physical pain'.[11] Indeed, they specifically state that emotional harms are excluded from their analysis because they 'flow from victimisation' but should not be categorised as wrongs themselves.

The wrongs of conversion practices do not easily fit into this model. The injury is not to the body per se. The criminal law has been gradually expanding the concepts of 'actual bodily harm' and 'grievous bodily harm', but only to include psychological conditions, as recognised by professional medical models.[12] The problem is that conversion practices do not necessarily cause psychological conditions.[13]

Drawing on the literature on coercive control we can see conversion practices as involving the kind of harm that the criminal law should cover. That is by recognising conversion practices as causing two forms of harm: degrading treatment and a breach of trust.

A. Coercive Control as Degrading Treatment

The aim of the coercive control is to dominate the victim and diminish their self-worth, through tactics designed to isolate, degrade and exploit the victim.[14] Samantha Jeffries explains that:

> The tactics or behaviours exhibited by perpetrators of coercive control may include: emotional abuse (e.g., victim blaming; undermining the victim's self-esteem and self-worth); verbal abuse (e.g., swearing, humiliation and degradation); social abuse (e.g., systematic social isolation); economic abuse (e.g., controlling all money); psychological abuse (e.g., threats and intimidation); spiritual abuse (e.g., misusing religious or spiritual traditions to justify abuse); physical abuse (e.g., direct assaults on the body, food and sleep deprivation); sexual abuse (e.g., pressured/unwanted sex or sexual degradation).[15]

The regulation of these activities is typically done by the abuser setting down rules which must be followed.[16] A core element of coercive control is rendering the victim dependent upon the abuser by limiting access to external sources of help or independence. Part of generating dependence is to cause the victim to devalue herself. If the abuser can persuade the victim that they are useless and

---

[11] A Von Hirsch and N Jareborg, 'Gauging Criminal Harm: A Living-Standard Analysis' (1991) 11 *Oxford Journal of Legal Studies* 1.

[12] *R v Ireland* [1997] UKHL 34.

[13] Even though there are far too many cases where it has: Ozanne (n 1).

[14] E Stark, 'Looking Beyond Domestic Violence: Policing Coercive Control' (2012) 12 *Journal of Police Crisis Negotiations* 199.

[15] S Jeffries, 'In the Best Interests of the Abuser: Coercive Control, Child Custody Proceedings and the "Expert" Assessments That Guide Judicial Determinations' (2016) 5 *Laws* 14.

[16] C Bishop, *The Limitations Of the Legal Response to Domestic Violence in England and Wales: A Critical Analysis* (Exeter, University of Exeter, 2020).

that the abuser is the only person who would like or support them, this will discourage any attempts to find affection or help outside the relationship.

The harm of coercive control is, therefore, not so much to the physical body per se but to the self. It causes the individual to lose trust in themselves, to hate who they are and blame themselves for bad things that happen to them. The victim of coercive control becomes a tool for the affirmation of the defendant, needed often as a result of their own insecurities about their masculine identity.

B. Conversion Practices as Degrading Treatment

The discussion of coercive control highlighted how, although there may not be physical or medically recognised injuries, the impact on the victim is one of degradation.[17] A victim becomes the tool of the abuser for their own ends. This is true too in relation to conversion practices. As Ilias Trispiotis and Craig Purshouse have argued:

> all forms of 'conversion therapy' are disrespectful of the equal moral value of LGBTIQ+ people and violate specific protected areas of liberty and equality that are inherent in the idea of human dignity.[18]

Just as in coercive control, matters which should be the choice of the victim – what they wear, where they go, what they eat – become taken over by the abuser so that they get to choose nearly every aspect of the victim's life. So too, in conversion practices the defendant is seeking to control the victim's sexual identity and/or sexuality: a core aspect of their identity. This fails to respect what Trispiotis and Purshouse have called the victim's 'moral personhood'.[19] This is done by isolating the victim from other sources of affirmation so that the views of the abuser (eg a religious group or a therapist) become the primary source of the victim's self-validation. When this is done in a way which means the dominant party seeks to mould the victim to confirm to a particular ideal, that is abusive.

By capturing this as degrading treatment there is no need to show that it was intended to be degrading. A person is degraded or treated an inhuman way, regardless of the intent of the actor. It is the objective social message sent by the act, rather than the intent of the person, which matters. The display of a Nazi flag may convey a degrading racist message, even if displayed by a person who was unaware of its significance. Indeed, a person who is aware of the flag but displays it as an attempt at a joke may well be conveying a negative social message by

---

[17] M Higbee et al, 'Conversion Therapy in the Southern United States: Prevalence and Experiences of the Survivors' (2020) 8 *Journal of Homosexuality* 1.

[18] I Trispiotis and C Purshouse, "Conversion Therapy' As Degrading Treatment' (2022) 42 *Oxford Journal of Legal Studies* 104, 113.

[19] ibid 110.

the display, regardless of the joke.[20] Similarly even if the person receiving the conversion practice does not find it degrading that does not mean the practice is not degrading to others. Just the fact that B laughs at the racist joke uttered by A does not mean C cannot be offended and degraded by the joke.

Indeed, it is not even necessary for the person receiving the degradation to be able to recognise it as such. Taking the example of coercive control, the very worst cases are those where the victim comes to accept their treatment as normal and even blame themselves for any violence or abuse, because they have failed to comply with the rules. They will never be able to be good enough for the abuser because they cannot keep in line with all the requirements. This is well captured by the comments of one victim of conversion practices:

> [Growing up], the single message that I kept tucked away in my soul, I guess, was that I was broken and needed to be made complete and whole. So, then of course, as long as I am having gay thoughts, I'm still broken. ['Conversion therapy'] doesn't do a lot for one's self-image, one's recognition, it doesn't do much even for a person's understanding of being a Christian (60- to 64-year-old man who identifies as gay).[21]

It is not surprising, therefore, that domestic violence causes a wide range of mental health problems for victims, ranging from anxiety, depression, post-traumatic stress, substance abuse and suicidal tendencies.[22]

C. Coercive Control as Breach of Trust

The harm done by an abusive intimate relationship goes particularly deep. It is through our intimate relationships that we form our identity and sense of self.[23] This is why domestic abuse is particularly harmful and creates a harm which is not found in other crimes of violence. Intimate relationships typically involve not only trust but also commitment. The individuals invest more in the relationship and commit resources, making the losses that would arise from ending the relationship higher. That can make it harder to leave. All of these factors combine to explain why it is the existence of the intimate relationship which is a key factor in domestic abuse.

Intimate relationship abuse involves a serious breach of 'thick interpersonal trust'.[24] Trust is essential for intimacy and love. An intimate relationship involves

---

[20] ibid 123–24; J Herring and M Madden Dempsey, 'Why Sexual Penetration Requires Justification' (2007) 27 *Oxford Journal of Legal Studies* 467, 481ff.

[21] T Goodyear et al, '"They Want You to Kill Your Inner Queer but Somehow Leave the Human Alive": Delineating the Impacts of Sexual Orientation and Gender Identity and Expression Change Efforts' (2022) 56 *The Journal of Sex Research* 599, 604.

[22] J Singh Chandan et al, 'Female Survivors of Intimate Partner Violence and Risk of Depression, Anxiety and Serious Mental Illness' (2020) 217 *The British Journal of Psychiatry* 562.

[23] Trispiotis and Purshouse (n 18).

[24] D Khodyakov, 'Trust as a Process: A Three Dimensional Approach' (2007) 41 *Sociology* 116.

the disclosing of parts of ourselves (both physical and emotional) that we wish to keep free from another. It is in being able to be completely honest and vulnerable with a partner that relationships can deepen, an understanding of self can grow and sense can be made of life. But all of that depends on trust. In a case of domestic abuse the abuser has misused the intimate sphere, and the knowledge and power they have gained in it, as a tool against the victim.[25]

D. Conversion Practices and Breach of Trust

Conversion practices involve this same breach of trust. First, there is the power relationship between the two parties. The practitioner of conversion practices is typically in a dominant position. This may be by virtue of position of power in a religious group or by virtue of taking on the role of counsellor. Second, the person receiving the 'therapy' is a member of the LGBTQ+ community and so likely to be socially marginalised. In particular, in being willing to seek conversion practices they are impacted by the patriarchal forces in society. As Harish Raju and Ian Bushfield put it, conversion practices:

> medicalizes and pathologizes non-heterosexual and [non-]cisgendered people, treating these people as though they have something wrong with them, and that they as individuals are a problem to be solved through medical intervention, when it is in fact our society that is sick with bigotry.[26]

In relation to the religious context, the person providing the practices is normally taking advantage of their position to represent the dictates of God for the religious group. Religion, which at its best should be a source of affirmation, spiritual assurance and an intense experience of being loved, is used as a weapon against the person. It is used so the person comes to hate their very nature. Far from feeling valued by God, they are told that God hates their essence. They are falsely told that if they have enough faith or pray hard enough they can change who they are. These attempts inevitably fail and then the person's hatred of themselves deepens.

Even outside the religious context a therapist is in a particular position of power and trust in the relationship. As Nick Totten explains:

> Whatever rank they bring with them, psychotherapists and, to a somewhat lesser extent, counsellors are perceived as skilled professionals, with a similar authority to doctors or lawyers; often they are credited with an uncanny and frightening ability to 'see right through' people. Therapy is a middle-class occupation, whatever the self-perception of individual practitioners; and therapists are very often white and from middle-class

---

[25] O Rachmilovitz, 'Bringing down the Bedroom Walls: Emphasizing Substance over Form in Personalized Abuse' (2007) 14 *William and Mary Journal of Women and the Law* 495.

[26] H Raju and I Bushfield, 'A Brief on Bill C-6: An Act To Amend The Criminal Code (Conversion Therapy)' (BC Humanist Association, 2021) 4.

backgrounds. The steadily increasing length and cost of therapy trainings is likely to intensify the difference in rank between practitioners and clients.[27]

This is all the more so as the person engaging with the practices will be in a vulnerable position given their desire to get rid of their sexual identity or orientation. The therapist is using this power to achieve the outcome they desire, rather than seeking to explore the root of the discomfort felt by the person seeking to change their identity. We will explore this issue further when discussing autonomy, later in this chapter.

II. The 'Photograph Approach'

Traditionally, criminal law focuses on a particular moment in time and particular place: the defendant punched the victim outside the pub on Thursday 1 April at a quarter past ten. This has been called the incident model[28] or the photograph approach.[29] This means the criminal law in both its offences and defences has struggled to capture wrongs which take place over time and involve the cumulation, and interaction, of different events. We can see this, for example, in the failures of the defence of provocation (now loss of control) to capture cumulative provocation or to capture the wrong of campaigns of abuse.[30]

The difficulty is that conversion practices can rarely be reduced to a single incident. In some cases it might be possible to identify a particular time of 'exorcisim' or 'prayer', but in many cases there is not a particular moment of the conversion practices. Even where there is, its true nature can only be understood in the context of what has happened in the time leading up to it. It is a process which takes place across time and with intersecting causes. Again, coercive control can give us some insights here.

A. Coercive Control as a Relational Wrong

Traditional understandings of domestic abuse relied on 'the incident model' whereby prosecutions tend to focus on a particular incident of violence. The new offence of coercive control recognises that we should see it as a relationship which is designed to control.[31] Psychologist Mary Ann Dutton explains:

> Abusive behaviour does not occur as a series of discrete events. Although a set of discrete abusive incidents can typically be identified within an abusive relationship, an understanding

[27] N Totton, 'Power in the Therapy Room' (2009) *Therapy Today* 16.
[28] S Zaccour, 'Public Policy and Laws Addressing Men's Violence against Female Intimate Partners' in T Shackelford (ed) *The SAGE Handbook of Domestic Violence* (Los Angeles, SAGE, 2020) 21.
[29] J Herring, *Domestic Abuse and Human Rights* (Amsterdam, Intersentia, 2021).
[30] ibid.
[31] R Pain, *Everyday Terrorism: How Fear Works in Domestic Abuse* (Durham University, 2012).

of the dynamic of power and control within an intimate relationship goes beyond these discrete incidents. To negate the impact of the time period between discrete episodes of serious violence – a time period during which the woman may never know when the next incident will occur, and may continue to live with on-going psychological abuse – is to fail to recognize what some battered woman experience as a continuing 'state of siege'.[32]

The areas of life that are covered by coercive control are extensive. Mary Ann Dutton and Lisa Goodman list nine areas of life which can be subject to control: personal activities/appearance; support/social life/family; household; work/economic/resources; health; intimate relationship; legal; immigration; and children.[33] Evan Stark explains:

> most abused women have being subjected to a pattern of sexual mastery that includes tactics to isolate, degrade, exploit, and control them as well as to frighten them or hurt them physically. ....These tactics include forms of constraint and the monitoring and/or regulation of commonplace activities of daily living, particularly those associated with women's default roles as mothers, homemakers, and sexual partners, and run the gamut from their access to money, food, and transport to how they dress, clean, cook, or perform sexually.[34]

As these examples illustrate, it is often not possible to capture the true impact of the abuse by looking at a single remark or act. It is the combined impact of them which is key. Indeed, an incident in isolation can appear trivial, but as part of a controlling relationship it can take on a new meaning.

The Statutory Guidance has given some indication of what kind of conduct can amount to coercive and controlling behaviour, which include the following:

- controlling or monitoring the victim's daily activities and behaviour, including making them account for their time, dictating what they can wear, what and when they can eat, when and where they may sleep;
- controlling a victim's access to finances, including monitoring their accounts or coercing them into sharing their passwords to bank accounts in order to facilitate economic abuse;
- isolating the victim from family, friends and professionals who may be trying to support them, intercepting messages or phone calls:
- threats to expose sensitive information (eg sexual activity or sexual orientation) or make false allegations to family members, religious or local community including via photos or the internet;
- Intimidation and threats of disclosure of sexual orientation and/or gender identity to family, friends, work colleagues, community and others;[35]

---

[32] M Dutton, 'Understanding Women's Response to Domestic Violence' (2003) 21 *Hofstra Law Review* 1191, 1204.

[33] M Dutton and L Goodman, *Development and Validation of a Coercive Control Measure for Intimate Partner Violence* (US Department of Justice, 2006).

[34] Stark (n 14) 200.

[35] Home Office, 'Domestic Abuse Act 2021 Statutory Guidance' (GOV.UK, 2022) Ch 3, para 50.

The guidance makes it clear that these are just examples of the kind of behaviour which is indicative of coercive control. Just because one of the listed kinds of behaviour is not proved does not mean there is no coercive control.[36]

Proving coercive control can be very difficult. In *F v M*[37] there were many serious alleged incidents of domestic abuse but these were fiercely denied. A key piece of evidence proved to be texts sent by the victim asking for permission to go to the toilet. While far from being the most serious allegations, they shone a powerful light on the nature of the relationship between the couple. This highlights the challenges facing prosecutions for conversion practices and the need to be alert to the nature of techniques applied.

B. Conversion Practices as a Relational Wrong

The coercive control model opens up the possibility of seeing conversion practices as a wrong which is not committed in a moment but is rather typically an abuse of a relationship built up over time. It also shows how apparently minor incidents combine to produce a powerful exercise of control. Understanding conversion practices as a form of relational abuse is important for several reasons.

First, the true impact of an act of conversion practices can only be understood in the relational context. What might appear to be 'just a prayer' or 'a word of advice' can take a completely different complexion when seen as just one part of a larger programme of control. It is the composite impact of the controlling relationships which needs to be captured by the wrong. In cases of religious conversion practices it can be important to understand that words can have particular significance within a group, which might not be appreciated outside the group. To call an activity sinful may not sound a particularly serious matter to some, but within some religious communities that word will carry a particular message, for example one that implies exclusion from God's presence. Further, repeated messages that a person has fallen short of God's ideal can cause them to doubt themselves and their own assessment, but the impact of this can only be appreciated through time.

Second, the emphasis is a description of the defendant's action: they are coercive and controlling, rather than the impact of that behaviour. This is helpful because it ensures that the focus is on the act of the defendant, rather than the impact on the victim. As those who work with victims of coercive control attest, the victim may not present in a way which has obvious harms. Indeed, the ultimate success in coercive control is that the victim comes to accept and agree to the abuse. By focusing on the wrong of seeking to change a person's sexuality or sexual identity through coercive control, we can more effectively capture the wrong.

---

[36] A Nikupeteri et al, 'Coercive Control and Technology-facilitated Parental Stalking in Children's and Young People's Lives' (2021) 5 *Journal of Gender-Based Violence* 395.
[37] *F v M* [2021] EWFC 41.

Third, the concept of coercive control can illustrate the power dynamic which is often at play in conversion practices, where it typically sees a person in a senior position in a religious organisation or person taking on a professional or quasi-professional role in relation to the victim. In any event, the societal structure places LGBTQ+ people in an inevitable position of weakness when their sexuality is portrayed. It is striking that, when a survey was conducted of LGBTQ+ survivors of sexual abuse, a quarter reported that their sexual abuse was initiated in an attempt to convert or punish them for their LGBTQ+ identity.[38] This use of conversion practices as a form of punishment demonstrates the power dynamic often in play and echoes with cases of spiritual abuse where beatings are used to rid a person of their sin. In Andrew Graystone's book *Bleeding for Jesus*[39] he describes the use of physical beatings by leaders in Christian camps of much younger men, which were justified in the name of promoting 'sexual purity'. Conversion practices need to be seen as part of the wider picture of power used to seek to control younger members of faith groups.[40]

III. Autonomy

The third issue is that criminal law is reluctant to punish a defendant for an act to which the victim has consented. There are well established limits to this. A victim cannot consent to acts which cause an injury except in specified circumstances. But generally, it is hard to imagine a prosecution taking place where the victim is perfectly happy with the way the defendant has behaved. So, it is suggested, conversion practices, if they are to be criminalised, should be limited to cases where the victim has not consented to them. After all, if the victim is content with the outcomes why should the criminal law be involved?

One possible response to this argument would be to claim that the harm of conversion practices can be equated to an injury of the kind for which consent is not a defence in criminal law because it involves actual bodily harm or more.[41] I will not pursue that claim. No doubt it is true in some cases, but in others it is unlikely to be straightforwardly the case. So, I will use other arguments on which to base my case.

The starting point is to understand the moral work of consent in the context of a criminal offence. I will adopt that propounded by Michelle Madden Dempsey.[42] In outline, the approach is as follows: consent is only needed when D's act would

---

[38] Galop, 'The Use of Sexual Violence as an Attempt to Convert or Punish LGBT+ people in the UK' (Galop, 2022).

[39] A Graystone, *Bleeding for Jesus* (London, Daron, Longman and Todd, 2021).

[40] Goodyear et al (n 21) 604.

[41] *R v Brown* [1993] UKHL 19.

[42] M Madden Dempsey, 'Victimless Conduct and the *Volenti* Maxim: How Consent Works' (2013) 7 *Criminal Law and Philosophy* 11.

otherwise be wrongfully harming another person's wellbeing. You do not need consent if an act causes no harm. So, looking at a person's car does not require their consent. Consent, therefore, changes an act from a prima facie wrong to one that can be justified.

Consent provides that justifying reason. It does this by allowing D (if they wish) to assume that if V consents, then the act is not – all things considered – contrary to V's wellbeing. That is because D is permitted to rely on V's assessment of their own best interests. We would not think much of D if they said 'I think you will greatly benefit from doing X and I know better than you about that'. Where consent is effective, Madden Dempsey claims that D is entitled to say:

> This is [V]'s decision. He's an adult and can decide for himself whether he thinks the risk is worth it. In considering what to do, I will assume that his decision is the right one for him. After all, he is in a better position than I to judge his own well-being. And so, I will not take it upon myself to reconsider those reasons. Instead, I will base my decision of whether to [harm] him on the other relevant reasons.[43]

This model provides a helpful explanation of what we are looking for with consent: that it gives D sufficient reason to rely on V's assessment of V's wellbeing. Where D knows that V's apparent consent is flawed – for example, it is based on a mistake, or is a result of significant pressure – then D cannot rely on it because they cannot take it as an assessment by V of their own wellbeing. Indeed, given that D is due to perform a prima facie wrongful act on V, D has a responsibility to ensure that V is in a position to make a proper assessment of their own wellbeing.

Applying this to conversion practices and applying the points made earlier in this chapter, we can say that the practices are a prima facie wrong. V's consent, to be effective, needs to give D a sufficiently strong reason to set aside those reasons resting in V's wellbeing that make the act prima facie wrongful. However, I suggest in the context of conversion practices consent will never be able to do this. I offer three reasons: first, consent to conversion practices is too weak to do the work required of it in the model just described; second, the argument just made only gives D permission to set aside reasons resting in V's wellbeing and in this context D should not exercise that permission; third, while the consent of the victim, where sufficiently rich, can justify the wrong against the victim, it does not operate to justify a wrong against others. And conversion practices wrong others.

A. The Lack of Genuine Autonomy

Consent to conversion practices will never be sufficiently strong to perform the moral and legal work just described. I will focus on four aspects of this claim:

---

[43] ibid.

i. Lack of Sufficient Information

There are serious issues around the extent to which consent to conversion practices can be sufficiently informed to amount to strong consent. The Government itself admits 'there is no robust evidence that conversion therapy can achieve its stated therapeutic aim of changing sexual orientation or gender identity' and 'conversion therapies were associated with self-reported harms among research participants who had experienced conversion practices for sexual orientation and for gender identity – for example, negative mental health effects like depression and feeling suicidal'.[44] Following the decision of the Supreme Court in *Montgomery v Lanarkshire Health Board*,[45] patients should be informed of the material risks of any medical treatment in order to protect their rights of autonomy. It is highly unlikely that practitioners of conversion practices do inform their 'clients' of these risks.[46] They therefore lack the necessary information to provide effective consent to the practices.

ii. Authenticity

A key aspect of autonomy is the idea of authenticity: that a person is relying on their own values to determine how they wish to live their life. As McKenzie and Rogers put it:

> [A] person's decisions, values, beliefs and commitments must be her 'own' in some relevant sense; that is, she must identify herself with them and they must cohere with her 'practical identity', her sense of who she is and what matters to her. Actions or decisions that a person feels were foisted on her, which do not cohere with her sense of herself, or from which she feels alienated, are not autonomous.[47]

This is an issue in this context because the desire to change one's sexual identity or sexual orientation is highly likely in our society to result from 'internalized homopbohia' or transphobia.[48] We can see this from the simple fact that all reported attempts and offers of services of conversion practices seek to convert a person away from, rather than towards, being LGBTQ+.[49] As Claudia Man-Yiu Tam puts it:

> it appears difficult if not impossible to separate a history of enforced compulsory heterosexuality from an individual's internalised homophobia. The fears of exclusion and rhetoric of immorality that LGBTQIA+ individuals confront is very different but equally as persuasive as explicit threats or inducements by the state.[50]

---

[44] Government Equalities Office, 'An Assessment of the Evidence on Conversion Therapy for Sexual Orientation and Gender Identity' (GOV.UK, 2021).

[45] *Montgomery v Lanarkshire Health Board* [2015] UKSC 11.

[46] Although there examples of some who do advertise downsides: C Purshouse and I Trispiotis, 'Is "Conversion Therapy" Tortious?' (2022) 42 *Legal Studies* 23, 35.

[47] C Mackenzie and W Rogers, 'Autonomy, Vulnerability and Capacity: A Philosophical Appraisal of the Mental Capacity Act' (2013) 3 *International Journal of the Law in Context* 37, 40.

[48] Andrade and Campo Redondo (n 3).

[49] S Aas and C Delmas, 'The Ethics of Sexual Reorientation: What Should Clinicians and Researchers Do?' (2016) 42 *Journal of Medical Ethics* 340.

[50] C Man-Yiu, 'Conversion Therapy Bans and Legal Paternalism: Justifying State Intervention to Restrict a LGBTQIA+ Individual's Autonomy to Undergo Conversion Therapy' (2021) *LSE Law Review* 1.

iii. Autonomy and Options

Joseph Raz has powerfully argued that a person is only autonomous if they have an adequate range of options to choose from. He discusses two scenarios:

> The Man in the Pit: A person falls down a pit and remains there for the rest of his life, unable to climb out or to summon help. There is just enough ready food to keep him alive without (after he gets used to it) any suffering. He can do nothing much, not even move much. His choices are confined to whether to eat now or a little later, whether to sleep now or a little later, whether to scratch his left ear or not.

> The Hounded Woman: A person finds herself on a small desert island. She shares the island with a fierce carnivorous animal which perpetually hunts for her. Her mental stamina, her intellectual ingenuity, her will power and her physical resources are taxed to their limits by her struggle to remain alive. She never has a chance to do or even to think of anything other than how to escape from the beast.[51]

Raz goes on to explain that neither of these people can be regarded as genuinely autonomous:

> Neither the Man in the Pit nor the Hounded Woman enjoys an autonomous life. The reason is that though they both have choices neither has an adequate range of options to choose from. They present two extremes of failure of adequacy of choice. The one has only trivial options to choose from. His options are all short-term and negligible in their significance and effects. The other person's predicament is the opposite one. All her choices are potentially horrendous in their consequences. If she ever puts one foot wrong she will be devoured by the beast.

This seems particularly relevant in our context. A person seeking conversion practices will be in a similar position to the people in Raz's example. The position of the religious person facing eternal damnation or ineffective conversion practices is like the man in the pit. The person seeking to escape from a homophobic and transphobic society or ineffective conversion practices is like the hounded women. For both, their range of options is so limited that they cannot be said to have genuine autonomy.

iv. Acting on Consent

Going back to the model of consent proposed earlier, it should be recalled that consent operates to give the practitioner permission to provide conversion practices only when they can be satisfied the consent reflects a genuine assessment by the 'patient' of their own best interests. Writing in context of medical treatment Natalie Stoljar writes

> In addition to securing informed consent, health care providers have an important role to play in promoting patient autonomy. Providers must be alert to the social conditions that affect patients' capacities for autonomous reasoning. For example, internalized

---

[51] J Raz, *The Morality of Freedom* (Oxford, Clarendon Press, 1988) 104.

norms may undermine an agent's sensitivity to the options that are available to her; and cultural or family expectations may erode a patient's 'self-referring attitudes' and lead to diminished self-confidence and self-esteem. The provider must therefore take positive steps to counteract these effects, for instance, encourage imaginative reflection on different options and create the conditions in which patients truly feel authorized to speak for themselves.[52]

Exactly the same point applies to therapists and religious leaders before embarking on conversion practices. Very few conversion practitioners will do this. Indeed, their commitment to the conversion inhibits them from undertaking this kind of approach. I conclude that consent to conversion practices is rarely, if ever, sufficiently autonomous to amount to sufficient consent to justify the treatment. Even if it did, it is not used by the practitioner in the way it needs to be if consent is to be used.

B. Undermining Rather than Enhancing Autonomy

A person has no right to demand a medication which is ineffective. Even if one is willing to pay for it, a doctor cannot prescribe lithium to a patient who has no need for it or remove the leg of a person simply because that is what they want. There is no right to demand harmful or ineffective treatment. And conversion practice simply does not work.[53] As Wells writes, 'conversion therapy is not a "therapy" at all, but a fraudulent, deceptive and unscientific practice known to cause significant harm to vulnerable people'.[54]

Indeed, it may be worse than that, because conversion practices will inhibit a person's autonomy by focusing on repression of their identity, rather than seeking to rejoice in it. It can diminish a person's valuing of themselves, which is an important aspect of their autonomy. Indeed, conversion practices seem to double the risk that a person will be subject to suicide[55] and significantly increase the risk of a wide range of mental health difficulties.[56]

C. Harm to Others

Conversion practices harm others. We can again learn from the literature on coercive control. When a partner engages in domestic abuse, their power comes from

---

[52] N Stoljar, 'Informed Consent and Relational Conceptions of Autonomy' (2011) 36 *The Journal of Medicine and Philosophy: A Forum for Bioethics and Philosophy of Medicine* 375.

[53] Man-Yiu (n 50).

[54] K Wells, *Conversion Therapy in Canada: A Guide for Legislative Action* (MacEwan University, 2020).

[55] Ozanne (n 1).

[56] T Jones et al, 'Supporting LGBTQA+ Peoples' Recovery From Sexual Orientation and Gender Identity and Expression Change Efforts' (2022) 57 *Australian Psychologist* 359.

within the relationship but also is supported by broader social forces. As Arendt has observed:

> Power is never the property of an individual; it belongs to a group ... When we say of somebody that he is 'in power' we actually refer to his being empowered by a certain number of people ... *potestas in populo*, without a people or group there is no power ...[57]

Patriarchy is key to understanding domestic abuse, as Madden Dempsey explains:

> the patriarchal character of individual relationships cannot subsist without those relationships being situated within a broader patriarchal social structure. Patriarchy is, by its nature, a social structure – and thus any particular instance of patriarchy takes its substance and meaning from that social context. If patriarchy were entirely eliminated from society, then patriarchy would not exist in domestic arrangements and thus domestic violence in its strong sense would not exist ... Moreover, if patriarchy were lessened in society generally then ceteris paribus patriarchy would be lessened in domestic relationship as well, thereby directly contributing to the project of ending domestic violence in its strong sense.[58]

Domestic abuse in this way reinforces other social structures that inhibit women's access to places of power. Further, it replicates the disadvantages in the outside world within the domestic. For example, the attempts by the male perpetrators of abuse to prevent their female partners entering the workplace or public arena are but imitations of broader attempts to restrict women's access to the workplace.

The social inequalities enable and assist domestic abuse; and the domestic abuse supports and enables the social inequalities to exist. There is a two-way mutual support going on. As the Parliamentary Assembly of the Council of Europe's Committee on Equal Opportunities for Women and Men puts it:

> Violence against women is a question of power, of the need to dominate and control. This in turn is rooted in the organization of society, itself based on inequality between the sexes. The meaning of this violence is clear: it is an attempt to maintain the unequal relationship between men and women and to perpetuate the subordination of women.[59]

This means that domestic abuse needs to be seen as one aspect of the broader phenomenon of abuse of women. Domestic abuse will be experienced with and through a range of other forms of violence against women. The emotional abuse will echo the calls of street harassment; the objectification in sexual relations will reflect the presentation of women in the violence of pornography; and the controlling rules match the messages sent through patriarchy about the expected roles of women.

---

[57] H Arendt, *Crisis of the Republic* (New York, Harcourt Brace, 1972) 143.

[58] M Madden Dempsey, 'What Counts as Domestic Violence?' (2006) 13 *William and Mary Journal of Women and the Law* 301; M Madden Dempsey, 'Towards a Feminist State' (2007) 70 *Modern Law Review* 908, 938.

[59] O Keltošová, *Report on Domestic Violence* (Doc 9525, Council of Europe, 17 July 2002) s 2.2.

As with coercive control in the context of domestic abuse, we can understand conversion practices to reinforce and be reinforced by patriarchal inequality, especially in its cisnormative and heteronormative manifestations.[60] Conversion practices are, in reality, directed towards LGBTQ+ people. While in the literature sometimes references are made to the hypothetical of a person being converted to being gay, the very fact this has to be presented as a hypothetical reveals it does not reflect the true social context within which conversion practices operate.[61] As a social performance, it is directed at those whose sexual orientation and gender identity is perceived to be in need of change. It operates, therefore, with a discriminatory impact against LGBTQ+ people.

As with coercive control, the expressive power of conversion practices reflects and reinforces a patriarchal assumption that a person's sexual orientation or sexual identity is wrong and something to be ashamed of. In sending this message it is replicating the anti-LGBTQ+ messages that abound in society. It draws on them and reinforces them by seeking to shame LGBTQ+ people. It also sends a message that a person's identity is an appropriate subject for therapeutic intervention, placing it alongside illness or problems for which a person might seek help.[62] For those facing transphobia and homophobia, being unsure of whether to live their identity publicly, the message sent is that rather than doing so, they should seek help.[63]

The negative message of conversion practices is demonstrated by the fact that a survey of LGBTQ+ people in 2017 found 5 per cent reporting they had been offered a 'cure' of being LGBTQ+.[64] Notably, nearly half of those offered it had undergone the 'therapy'. The fact that such a high percentage had attempted it is an insight into the high levels of stigma still attached to LGBTQ+ existence. It is hard to believe that, given a genuinely free choice, half of LGBTQ+ people offered a 'cure' would choose to try to change their gender or sexuality. It demonstrates that the patriarchal context impacts on the choices made.

Those who do not do so are impliedly required to justify why they have not undertaken treatment. The permissibility of conversion practices puts considerable pressure on members of the LGBTQ+ community, given our patriarchal society. Gerald Dworkin puts the point this way, in another context: 'once I am aware that I have a choice, my failure to choose now counts against me. I now can be responsible, and be held responsible, for events that prior to the possibility of choosing were not attributable to me'.[65] Parents and friends with more

---

[60] Trispiotis and Purshouse (n 18) 113.

[61] UNHRC, 'Practices of So-Called "Conversion Therapy": Report of the Independent Expert on Protection Against Violence and Discrimination Based on Sexual Orientation and Gender Identity' (1 May 2020) A/HRC/44/53.

[62] C Delmas 'Three Harms of "Conversion" Therapy' (2014) 5 *AJOB Neuroscience* 22.

[63] ibid.

[64] Government Equalities Office, 'The Prevalence of Conversion Therapy in the UK' (GOV.UK, 2021).

[65] G Dworkin, 'Markets and Morals' in G Dworkin (ed), *Morality, Harm and the Law* (Oxford, Westview, 1994) 155.

traditional views may find it harder to come to terms with their relative's sex or sexuality identity.[66] Notably, the Australian Capital Territory's Sexuality and Gender Identity Conversion Practices Act 2020, which bans some conversion practices, expressly states that one of its objectives is to affirm that all people 'have characteristics of sexuality and gender identity' and 'no combination of those characteristics constitutes a disorder, disease'.[67]

Sean Aas and Candice Delmas write 'that it is better for sexual minorities not to have the option to alter their sexual orientation at all, because having the option to alter one's sexual orientation, in a context of heteronormative domination, harms sexual minorities'.[68] They explain that societal pressures on sexual minorities will put pressure on them to undergo conversion they would not seek if it were not an option. It would also require those who do not seek to convert to justify their decision. Imagine, for example, a person 'coming out' to conservative religious parents. Perhaps their best argument may be that there is nothing they can do about their sexual orientation. The option of being able to change it makes that a much more complex conversation as they need to justify to their parents why they do not change it.

As with coercive control, conversion practices typically work to force people into traditional performances of cisnormative and heteronormative behaviour, often reinforcing traditional stereotypes based on sex. For example, religious groups which promote conversion practices often rely on patriarchal assumptions about the role of men and women.[69] This demonstrates the importance of understanding conversion practices within the broader forces of social inequality within which they operate.

IV. The Government's 2021 Proposals

In 2021 the Government produced proposals to ban 'conversion therapy'. At the heart of the proposals is a new offence:

> a talking therapy delivered to either a person under 18 or a person who is 18 or over and who has not given informed consent, with the intention of changing their sexual orientation or changing them to or from being transgender, should constitute a criminal offence.[70]

---

[66] Aas and Delmas (n 49).

[67] Government Equalities Office, 'Closed Consultation: Banning Conversion Therapy' (*GOV.UK*, 9 December 2021) www.gov.uk/government/consultations/banning-conversion-therapy/banning-conversion-therapy, section 5.2.

[68] Aas and Delmas (n 49).

[69] See eg J Dobson, *Bringing up Girls* (London, Tyndale House, 2018), which from an evangelical Christian perspective emphasises the importance of ensuring that girls are protected on their 'journey to womanhood'.

[70] Government Equalities Office, 'Closed Consultation' (n 67).

As this quotation indicates, the proposal is that consent will operate as a defence. The Government explains:

> We recognise that some believe that an adult cannot consent to non-coercive and non-forced talking conversion therapies even when fully aware of the potential for being harmed. However, it is the view of the government that the freedom for an adult to enter such an arrangement should be protected.[71]

The Government indicates that coercive control can be a useful theme in drafting the offence. It suggests:

> Our proposal is to develop a new talking conversion therapy criminal offence that operates on 2 tests: coercion or control and motivation of conversion therapy.
>
> The first test will build on the existing coercive controlling behaviour offence, which will be expanded to be regardless of repetition or the nature of the relationship between the perpetrator and victim. It is not the government's intention to amend the existing definition set out in Section 76 of the Serious Crime Act 2015, rather to apply its principles specifically to the conversion therapy offence. The second test will require a court to be satisfied that the talking therapy act was motivated by conversion therapy.[72]

While drawing the links between coercive control and conversion practices is welcomed, being in line with the arguments made in this chapter, the precise proposal by the Government has some troubling aspects centring on its attempt to separate out coercive control in the context of conversion practices and in domestic abuse.

First, coercive control in the context of domestic abuse is an offence under section 76 of the Serious Crime Act 2015, even where there is consent to the coercive control. This is because there are widespread accounts of how psychological abuse, such as gaslighting,[73] leads to victims coming to blame themselves for any abuse, and understanding the abuse to be beneficial to them.[74] To permit consent as a defence to conversion practices fails to appreciate the arguments made in the previous section, that autonomy cannot be exercised in this context.

Second, as argued in the second section of this chapter, it is crucial that coercive control is understood within its relational context. To recognise that 'conversion therapy' can occur even if it is the only time the parties have met, is to be welcomed, but that incident must be understood in the broader relational context the victims finds themselves in. For example, if a person attends a 'revival meeting' and they go forward to receive prayer for sexuality or sexual identity conversion from a visiting preacher, it is correct that this cannot be seen as falling under any offence. However, if consent is to be recognised as a defence, it is important this incident be seen in the wider context of that person's religious community so that any apparent consent can be recognised as not representing an autonomous decision.

---

[71] ibid.

[72] ibid.

[73] P Sweet, 'The Sociology of Gaslighting' (2019) 84 *American Sociological Review* 851.

[74] See further Herring, *Domestic Abuse* (n 29) Ch 2.

Third, there are serious concerns over the requirement that 'the talking therapy act was motivated by conversion therapy'. This seems to ignore the evidence given earlier in this chapter that coercive control can often appear benign to the outside observer, because remarks can ake on meanings well understood by the parties, but hard to detect to the outside observer. Within the context of 'conversion therapy', remarks stressing the importance of 'living a Godly life' or 'fleeing sin' may seem to an observer to be general advice on living a religious life, but understood within a particular religious community to be referring to sexual desires. In the context of coercive control, abusers commonly present their behaviour as 'loving too much', as way of justifying possessiveness.[75] The requirement of proving a desire to 'convert' offers too ready a loophole for abusive behaviour.

V. Conclusion

This chapter has explored the challenges traditional criminal law faces when responding to conversion practices. It has suggested that drawing on the literature around coercive control can be a helpful way of addressing these. In particular, it has been argued that conversion practices can be understood as involving degrading treatment and a breach of trust. These wrongs, properly understood, are of sufficient severity to justify criminal intervention. Second, it has been suggested that understanding conversion practices as a relational wrong, analogous to coercive control, means that the difficulty of identifying a moment when the crime occurs can be overcome. Finally, it has been argued that autonomy and consent should not be seen as providing a defence to a criminal offence of 'conversion therapy'. Indeed, the autonomy arguments greatly strengthen the case in favour of criminalisation.

With these points in mind, there is much to be concerned about in the 2021 proposals for the creation of an offence prohibiting conversion practices. While the proposed offence seeks to make use of coercive control, it does so without sufficiently appreciating its impact and nature. In particular, by offering consent as a defence to the proposed crime and requiring proof of intent to 'convert', the offence fails to appreciate the invidious impact of coercive control and the hetero/cisnormative environment on those subject to conversion practices. One should no more be able to give legally effective consent to conversion practices than one can to domestic abuse.

---

[75] This is discussed in detail in J Herring, 'Family Law: What's Love Got to do with it?' in J Scherpe and S Gilmore (eds), *Family Matters: Essays in Honour of John Eekelaar* (Amsterdam, Intersentia, 2022).

3

Historical, Clinical and Ethical Perspectives

An Update on *I'm Your Handyman*

JACK DRESCHER

I first began writing about what used to be called 'reparative therapy'[1] in the 1990s. It is now one of several approaches classed under 'conversion practices'. While the last decade has seen advocacy groups address gender identity conversion efforts, most of my work has focused on sexual orientation conversion efforts. I was prompted to write about psychotherapeutic efforts to change homosexuality because of what I was seeing in my own clinical work in New York City: gay men, usually at least ten years older than me, who had previously been in some form of therapy relationship – mostly with psychoanalytic practitioners but sometimes with religious ex-gay groups – in which their goal was to change their homosexual attractions to heterosexual ones.[2]

To put this in context, at the time I started writing about conversion practices, a common belief in the mental health professions was 'there's no harm in trying'. Although my colleague Douglas Haldeman had first sounded the alarm regarding the harms these practices caused,[3] what he had to say back then would not be generally accepted for many years.

It was the late John De Cecco, then editor of the *Journal of Homosexuality*, who approached me in the mid-1990s to write about conversion practices for his journal. At the time I was working on my psychotherapy book which would include a chapter criticising reparative therapies from a psychoanalytic perspective.[4]

---

[1] J Nicolosi, *Reparative Therapy of Male Homosexuality: A New Clinical Approach* (Northvale, Aronson, 1991).

[2] J Drescher, *Psychoanalytic Therapy and the Gay Man* (New York, Routledge, 1998).

[3] DC Haldeman, 'Sexual Orientation Conversion Therapy for Gay Men and Lesbians: A Scientific Examination' in JC Gonsiorek and JD Weinrich (eds), *Homosexuality: Research Implications for Public Policy* (Newbury Park, Sage, 1991); DC Haldeman, 'The Practice and Ethics of Sexual Orientation Conversion Therapy' (1994) 62(2) *Journal of Consulting and Clinical Psychology* 221.

[4] Drescher, *Psychoanalytic Therapy and the Gay Man* (n 2).

I agreed to do the *Journal of Homosexuality* article,[5] reprinted after this coda, which I entitled 'I'm Your Handyman' after a James Taylor song.

In 1997, I also published a preview of some of the points made in 'Handyman' in the newsletter of the New York State Psychiatric Association[6] which, unsurprisingly, provoked an angry letter in response from the late Charles Socarides, a promoter of conversion practices. Consequently, I knew I was headed down the right path.

Which brings us to this volume you are reading and my effort to describe what happened and what has changed in the quarter of a century since I began writing about conversion practices. This includes the changes in the National Association for Research and Therapy of Homosexuality (NARTH) and the ex-gay movement, the position statements of professional health and mental health organisations, and the changing legal landscape around the world.

I. NARTH No More

As recounted in 'Handyman', following the threat of a lawsuit, the American Psychoanalytic Association issued non-discriminatory statements regarding the acceptance of lesbian and gay candidates and the promotion of training and supervising analysts in their affiliated institutes.[7] This decision did not go over well with psychoanalysts who pathologised homosexuality and led to their forming a new organisation, NARTH. Its first president was the late Charles Socarides[8] who was a fierce opponent of the 1973 decision by the American Psychiatric Association (APA) to remove homosexuality from its Diagnostic and Statistical Manual (DSM).[9]

Another important leader, now also deceased, within NARTH was Joseph Nicolosi[10] who coined the term 'reparative therapy'[11] and who, like Socarides, was a frequent media spokesperson, although from a religious Catholic psychologist's perspective, against the mental health mainstream's gradual rejection of pathologising theories of homosexuality.

As I previously noted 'many social issues groups create and then promote self-appointed "experts" and "think tanks" to speak to the media to make a case *to the public* for marginal and discredited scientific theories'.[12] One of NARTH's main

---

[5] ibid.

[6] J Drescher, 'What Needs Changing? Some Questions Raised by Reparative Therapy Practices' (1997) 40(1) *New York State Psychiatric Society Bulletin* 8.

[7] RA Isay, *Becoming Gay: The Journey to Self-Acceptance* (New York, Pantheon, 1996).

[8] M Fox, 'Charles W Socarides, Psychiatrist and Psychoanalyst, is Dead at 83' (*The New York Times*, 28 December 2005).

[9] R Bayer, *Homosexuality and American Psychiatry: The Politics of Diagnosis* (New York, Basic Books, 1981); J Drescher and JP Merlino (eds), *American Psychiatry and Homosexuality: An Oral History* (New York, Routledge, 2007).

[10] R Sandomir, 'Joseph Nicolosi, Advocate for Conversion Therapy for Gays, Dies at 70' (*The New York Times*, 20 March 2017).

[11] Nicolosi (n 1).

[12] J Drescher, 'When Politics Distort Science: What Mental Health Professionals Can Do' (2009) 13(3) *Journal of Gay & Lesbian Mental Health* 213, 220.

purposes was to create credentials for media spokespersons to deny and repudiate the growing cultural normalisation of homosexuality, from what they claimed was a truly scientific perspective. However, in the US and other countries, their efforts failed and the social struggle for marriage equality or same-sex marriage prevailed.

In 2014, NARTH rebranded itself as 'The Alliance for Choice and Therapeutic Integrity' but following the death of its most prominent media spokespersons, the organisation appears to have faded into media obscurity in the US. Today, most of their present leadership appear to be individuals with strong religious backgrounds and ties. And, as stated on their website, the group no longer pretends to be a scientific one but claims that:

> The Alliance exists to encourage human flourishing by promoting a more complete truth, informed by Judeo-Christian values and natural law, about the science of sexual orientation and biological sex through education, advocacy, clinical training, and therapy.[13]

Nevertheless, their rebranded website shows they may still be capable of doing harm to individuals who are unhappy about what conversion therapists call 'unwanted same-sex attractions'.

II. The US Ex-Gay Movement

The US ex-gay movement began in the late 1970s and reached its public relations zenith during the US culture wars over marriage equality in the early 2000s. Its origins, beliefs, history and setbacks have been described and documented by others.[14]

The ex-gay movement found much financial support from religious, social conservative organisations who were opposed to marriage equality and other gay civil rights. As it became increasingly clear that the battle to prevent marriage equality was being lost in the US, financial support began to dry up and the most prominent ex-gay organisation, Exodus International, closed in 2013. Its president at the time, Alan Chambers, admitted that he continued to have same-sex attractions (although he was in a monogamous heterosexual marriage) and apologised for the 'pain and hurt' the organisation had caused.[15]

American ex-gay leaders and NARTH founders never limited their efforts to combating the normalising acceptance of homosexuality to the US alone. Ever in search of an audience, despite growing American rejection of his views, in

---

[13] Therapeutic Choice, 'Homepage' (Therapeutic Choice) www.therapeuticchoice.com.

[14] WR Besen, *Anything But Straight: Unmasking the Scandals and Lies Behind the Ex-Gay Myth* (New York, Routledge, 2003); T Erzen, *Straight to Jesus: Sexual and Christian Conversion in the Ex-Gay Movement* (Berkeley, University of California Press, 2006); M Wolkomir, *Be Not Deceived: The Sacred and Sexual Struggles of Gay and Ex-Gay Christian Men* (New Brunswick, Rutgers University Press, 2006).

[15] J Merritt, 'The Downfall of the Ex-Gay Movement' (*The Atlantic*, 6 November 2022).

1995 Socarides was invited to give the annual lecture at the UK's Association for Psychoanalytic Psychotherapy in the National Health. British psychoanalysts at the time were still of the opinion that homosexuality always represented a form of potentially curable psychopathology.[16] Paradoxically, the invitation 'galvanised a group of psychotherapists, both gay and heterosexual, who were unwilling to accept theories that pathologised all expressions of homosexuality'.[17] Nicolosi was invited to speak about his theories of 'curing' homosexuality in Italy in both 2005 and 2010.[18]

After rebranding itself, NARTH also created an international version of its 'conversion therapy' brand: The International Federation for Therapeutic and Counselling Choice (IFTCC). According to Wayne Besen of Truth Wins Out, a watchdog group documenting activity of the ex-gay movement, IFTCC organised a conference in Slovakia in 2020, offering 'conversion therapy' seminars in three languages: Slovakian, Polish and Hungarian. According to Besen, IFTCC and the ex-gay organisations are 'planting their toxic flag in undemocratic regimes where LGBTQ people can't mount a proper defense. Their most recent targets for expansion are authoritarian countries in Eastern Europe'.[19]

As in the case of NARTH, as ex-gay messaging declined in influence and media representations in the US, ex-gay messengers tried to extend their message that 'change is possible' to other countries. This was not altogether surprising, as many members of the late Exodus International come from evangelical, proselytising religious traditions. For example, Don Schmierer, a board member of Exodus International, between 2008–2009 was reported to have brought his 'ex-gay' message to Korea, Ukraine and most notably to Uganda prior to the introduction of legislation that carried a death penalty for engagement in homosexual acts.[20]

Sadly, while their influence had been greatly diminished in Western countries, the conversion therapy and ex-gay movement is still active around the world.

III. The Two APAs

At the time of the publication of 'I'm Your Handyman', two US mainstream mental health organisations, the American Psychiatric Association and the American

---

[16] ML Ellis, 'Challenging Socarides' (1997) 7(2) *Feminism and Psychology* 287; D Twomey, 'British Psychoanalytic Attitudes Towards Homosexuality' (2003) 7(1–2) *Journal of Gay and Lesbian Psychotherapy* 7.

[17] Twomey, ibid 13.

[18] C Atzori, 'A Tribute to Dr Nicolosi from a Physician in Italy' (Joseph Nicolosi's website, March 2017) www.josephnicolosi.com/collection/a-tribute-to-dr-nicolosi-from-a-physician-in-italy.

[19] Letter from Wayne Besen to author.

[20] J Burroway, 'Exodus Board Member Joins Nazi Revisionist at Uganda Conference' (*Box Turtle Bulletin*, 24 February 2009) www.boxturtlebulletin.com/2009/02/24/9098; J Burroway, 'Slouching Toward Kampala: Uganda's Deathly Embrace of Hate' (*Box Turtle Bulletin*, 24 February 2009) www.boxturtlebulletin.com/slouching-toward-kampala.

Psychological Association, weighed in on the issue of conversion therapy. The psychiatric APA's position, in a statement that recognised the potential harm of such procedures, was that the

> APA opposes any psychiatric treatment, such as 'reparative' or 'conversion' therapy, that is based on the assumption that homosexuality per se is a mental disorder or is based on the a priori assumption that the patient should change his or her homosexual orientation.[21]

The psychology APA, on the other hand, was unwilling to take as hard a line about possible harm, noting that 'the ethics, efficacy, benefits, and potential for harm of therapies that seek to reduce or eliminate same-gender sexual orientation are under extensive debate in the professional literature and the popular media'.[22] Nevertheless, the statement concluded with the resolution

> that the American Psychological Association opposes portrayals of lesbian, gay, and bisexual youth and adults as mentally ill due to their sexual orientation and supports the dissemination of accurate information about sexual orientation, and mental health, and appropriate interventions in order to counteract bias that is based in ignorance or unfounded beliefs about sexual orientation.[23]

By 2000, the psychiatric APA, increasingly concerned about the potential harm of conversion practices, went a step further and recommended that 'ethical practitioners refrain from attempts to change individuals' sexual orientation, keeping in mind the medical dictum to First, do no harm'.[24] The psychology APA returned to this issue once again in 2007 by appointing a Task Force (of which, although I am a psychiatrist, I was appointed as a member) on the Appropriate Therapeutic Response to Sexual Orientation, which issued its report in 2009.[25] After an extensive dive into all the peer-reviewed literature on 'conversion therapy', the Task Force, among other things:

- concluded that there is insufficient evidence to support the use of psychological interventions to change sexual orientation;
- encouraged mental health professionals to avoid misrepresenting the efficacy of sexual orientation change efforts by promoting or promising change in sexual orientation;

---

[21] American Psychiatric Association, 'Position Statement on Psychiatric Treatment and Sexual Orientation' (1999) 156 *American Journal of Psychiatry* 1131.

[22] American Psychological Association, 'Resolution on Appropriate Therapeutic Responses to Sexual Orientation' (1998) 43 *American Psychologist* 934.

[23] ibid.

[24] American Psychiatric Association, 'Commission on Psychotherapy by Psychiatrists (COPP): Position Statement on Therapies Focused on Attempts to Change Sexual Orientation' (2000) 157 *American Journal of Psychiatry* 1719, 1721.

[25] American Psychological Association, Task Force on the Appropriate Therapeutic Response to Sexual Orientation, *Report of the Task Force on the Appropriate Therapeutic Response to Sexual Orientation* (2009).

- concluded that the benefits reported by participants in sexual orientation change efforts can be gained through approaches that do not attempt to change sexual orientation.

In subsequent years, the psychiatric APA continued to update its stance on 'conversion therapies' in 2013 and once again in 2018. The latter added recommendations regarding gender identity conversion efforts, recommending that 'ethical practitioners respect the identities for those with diverse gender expressions' and 'encourages legislation which would prohibit the practice of "reparative" or conversion therapies that are based on the a priori assumption that diverse sexual orientations and gender identities are mentally ill'.[26]

Other mainstream mental health organisations, both in the US and abroad, have weighed in on conversion practices, including the American Academy of Child and Adolescent Psychiatry,[27] the Royal College of Psychiatrists,[28] and the Pan American Health Organization of the World Health Organization,[29] to name a few. In 2017, a 'Memorandum of Understanding' against conversion therapy was issued in Great Britain that was signed by the National Health Service and over 25 UK medical regulatory bodies.[30]

In June 2019, Lee Jaffe, MD, the President of the American Psychoanalytic Association issued a formal apology to the LGBTQ+ community on the occasion of the 50th anniversary of the Stonewall Riots in New York City. He noted, 'It is long past time to recognize and apologize for our role in the discrimination and trauma caused by our profession'.[31]

Finally, as per OutRight Action International, 'conversion therapies' have been condemned by 'the German Medical Association; the Australian Psychological Society; The Psychological Society of South Africa; the Lebanese Psychiatric Society; the Hong Kong College of Psychiatrists and the Hong Kong Psychological Society; the Chinese Psychological Association; the Indian Psychiatric Society; and the Psychological Association of the Philippines'.[32]

---

[26] D Scasta and P Bialer, 'Position Statement on Conversion Therapy and LGBTQ Patients' (American Psychiatric Association, December 2013); American Psychiatric Association, 'Position Statement on Conversion Therapy and LGBTQ Patients' (2018) www.psychiatry.org/getattachment/4ed6298d-e24c-4b8e-a0dd-3a3035e2e216/Position-2013-Homosexuality.pdf.

[27] SL Adelson et al, 'Practice Parameter on Gay, Lesbian, or Bisexual Sexual Orientation, Gender Nonconformity, and Gender Discordance in Children and Adolescents' (2012) 51(9) *Journal of the American Academy of Child and Adolescent Psychiatry* 957.

[28] Royal College of Psychiatrists, 'Position Statement on Sexual Orientation' (Royal College of Psychiatrists, April 2014).

[29] Pan American Health Organisation. '"Therapies" to Change Sexual Orientation Lack Medical Justification and Threaten Health' (Pan American Health Organisation, 17 May 2012) www3.paho.org/hq/index.php?option=com_content&view=article&id=6803.

[30] British Association for Counselling and Psychotherapy, 'Memorandum of understanding on conversion therapy in the UK' (BACP, 2022).

[31] American Psychoanalytic Society, 'APsaA Issues Overdue Apology to LGBTQ Community' (APSA, 21 June 2019) https://apsa.org/wp-content/uploads/2022/10/StonewallApology.pdf#new_tab.

[32] A Bishop, 'Harmful Treatment: The Global Reach of So-Called Conversion Therapy' (Outright Action International, 2019) 16.

IV. 'Conversion Therapy' Bans

Starting in 2012, the state of California passed legislation making it a matter of professional misconduct for a licensed mental health practitioner to offer conversion practices to minors under the age of 18.[33] Many states followed suit; in the US today, 20 states and the District of Columbia have banned these practices for minors; some states have introduced partial bans.[34] Internationally, conversion therapy bans have been introduced in Brazil (1999), Samoa (2007), Fiji (2010), Argentina (2010), Ecuador (2014), Malta (2016), Uruguay (2017), Taiwan (2018), Germany (2020), Canada (2021), Chile (2021) and New Zealand (2022). On top of this, some countries have provinces and territories with bans.

In 2018, the European Parliament voted by a wide margin for an amendment to the annual EU report on fundamental rights, which, for the first time ever, condemned 'gay cure' therapy and urged Member States to ban the destructive practice.[35]

In 2020, the United Nations issued a 'Report on Conversion Therapy by Independent Expert on Protection against Violence and Discrimination Based on Sexual Orientation and Gender Identity'. The report called for:

> a global ban on practices of 'conversion therapy', a process that must include: clearly defining the prohibited practices; ensuring public funds are not used to support them; banning advertisements; establishing punishments for non-compliance and investigating respective claims; creating mechanisms to provide access to all forms of reparation to victims, including the right to rehabilitation.[36]

V. Concluding Remarks

Legal bans on 'conversion therapies' were never on my mind when I began writing about them more than a quarter of a century ago. In fact, I wrote from the perspective of a gay psychiatrist and psychoanalyst who had experienced homophobia and heterosexism firsthand in almost every step of my professional training.[37]

---

[33] J Drescher et al, 'The Growing Regulation of Conversion Therapy' (2016) 102(2) *Journal of Medical Regulation* 7.

[34] Movement Advancement Project, 'Equality Maps: Conversion "Therapy" Laws' (MAP, 1 January 2023) www.lgbtmap.org/equality-maps/conversion_therapy.

[35] European Parliament's Intergroup on LGBT Rights, 'European Parliament Takes a Stance Against LGBTI Conversion Therapies For The First Time' (European Parliament's Intergroup on LGBT Rights, 1 March 2018) http://lgbti-ep.eu/2018/03/01/european-parliament-takes-a-stance-against-lgbti-conversion-therapies-for-the-first-time/.

[36] UNHRC, 'Practices of So-Called "Conversion Therapy": Report of the Independent Expert on Protection against Violence and Discrimination Based on Sexual Orientation and Gender Identity' (1 May 2020) A/HRC/44/53.

[37] J Drescher, 'Anti-Homosexual Bias in Training' in T Domenici and RC Lesser (eds), *Disorienting Sexuality: Psychoanalytic Reappraisals of Sexual Identities* (New York, Routledge, 1995); J Drescher,

My initial goal in writing (and later presenting) about what we were then calling 'reparative therapy of homosexuality' was to educate my fellow professionals about iatrogenic harm being done to patients. Counter to the common wisdom, there *was* harm in trying. Consequently, I wrote about conversion practices, encouraged others to write and publish about it,[38] and participated in updating the position statements of both APAs.

Yet, it was famously repeated in my youth that the personal is political. In fact, in 2012, when California became the first US state to ban 'conversion therapy' for minors by licensed professionals, I was initially sceptical of the legislation's efficacy. Why? Most people seeking 'conversion therapy' are not minors and most of the practitioners are not licensed. At the time I referred to this as a very big hammer for a very small nail.

However, after its passage, the legislation was challenged in the courts.[39] Both the California Psychiatric Association and the California Psychological Association refused to weigh in on the lawsuits with amicus briefs because at that time they did not support the state's intrusion into the patient-therapist relationship. Consequently, the national organisations, the two APAs, following the lead of their respective state groups, did not weigh in on the lawsuits either.

For that reason, I was approached by the National Center for Lesbian Rights to assist in writing an amicus brief in support of the law.[40] I did so because, despite my doubts, I thought overturning the legislation would be inevitably spun by anti-gay political and religious groups, practitioners and ex-gay groups as legitimising harmful practices. Similarly, when the 2013 law in the state of New Jersey was challenged in court,[41] I was approached by the state's District Attorney office to submit a declaration in support of that legislation as well. None of those challenges succeeded in overturning those bans, and other states followed with similar legislation.

Further complicating matters, another reason for my initial scepticism about the efficacy of state bans derived from my perception that state medical boards tasked with reviewing and adjudicating complaints against licensed practitioners most likely had little or no knowledge about sexual orientation 'conversion

---

'From Pro-Oedipal to Postmodern: Changing Psychoanalytic Attitudes Toward Homosexuality' (1997) 2(2) *Gender and Psychoanalysis* 203; J Drescher (ed), *Homosexuality and the Mental Health Professions: The Impact of Bias* (New York, Routledge, 2000); J Drescher 'Don't Ask, Don't Tell: A Gay Man's Perspective on the Psychoanalytic Training Experience Between 1973 and 1991' (2002) 6(1) *Journal of Gay and Lesbian Psychotherapy* 45; J Drescher, 'Becoming a Psychoanalyst' in L Hillman and T Rosenblatt (eds), *The Analyst's Voice: Narratives on Developing a Psychoanalytic Identity* (New York, Routledge, 2018).

[38] A Shido et al (eds), *Sexual Conversion Therapy: Ethical, Clinical and Research Perspectives* (New York, Haworth Press, 2001); J Drescher and KJ Zucker (eds), *Ex-Gay Research: Analyzing the Spitzer Study and its Relation to Science, Religion, Politics, and Culture* (New York, Routledge, 2006).

[39] *Pickup v Brown*, 728 F.3d 1042 (9th Cir 2012).

[40] Brief of amicus curiae Dr Jack Drescher MD in Support of Defendants-Appellees and Urging Affirmance, *Pickup v Brown*, 728 F3d 1042 (9th Cir 2012).

[41] *King v Christie*, 981 F Supp 3d 296 (3rd Cir 2013).

therapies', let alone those associated with gender identity. I raised this concern about licensing boards' lack of experience or basic knowledge in this area to the LGBTQ+ Committee of the Group for Advancement of Psychiatry, a psychiatric think tank of which I am a member. In an effort to inform and educate state regulators, the Committee produced a report that was published in the *Journal of Medical Regulation*, the official journal of the Federation of State Medical Boards.[42] The statement was awarded the Federation's 2017 Award for Excellence in Editorial Writing. Nevertheless, to date, I am unaware of any case brought in any US State against a licensed mental health professional for having tried to convert the sexual orientation or gender identity of a minor.

Further, I did not know when I began writing about conversion practices that my personal concerns would later echo at an international level. I never imagined I would be asked to participate at a meeting chaired by a UN Independent Expert (2020) to talk about my professional and clinical experiences. Or that I would learn about widespread conversion practices around the world. Adding to the US history of violence – lobotomies, aversion techniques and misuse of electroconvulsive therapy – was the practice of 'corrective rape' to change homosexuality in women.

In closing, what started out as my effort to address a clinical and ethical issue regarding iatrogenic harm to patients has evolved into a symbol of a larger, international culture war issue regarding civil and human rights – and my personal former cannot be disentangled from the political latter. In other words, bans on conversion practices have today come to symbolise the LGBTQ+ movement's struggle for civil and human rights. And at the risk of sounding too binary, nations, states, provinces, cities and municipalities passing these bans do so to declare their support for sexual and gender minority rights. Those resisting usually oppose any cultural normalisation of LGBTQ+ identities. As the quest for full LGBTQ+ rights continues, ongoing awareness of this connection between the personal and the political is something of which everyone involved in today's struggles needs to be aware.

---

[42] Drescher et al, 'The Growing Regulation of Conversion Therapy' (n 33).

Appendix

I'm Your Handyman:
A History of Reparative Therapies[1]

HOMOSEXUALITY IS ASSUREDLY no advantage, but it is nothing to be ashamed of, no vice, no degradation; it cannot be classified as an illness; we consider it to be a variation of the sexual function, produced by a certain arrest of sexual development …[2]

Although psychoanalysts have proffered and claimed homosexual conversions since the time of Freud, a recently coined term, *reparative therapy*,[3] has come to generically define talking cures that claim to change an individual's homosexual orientation to a heterosexual one. Although other treatment modalities such as aversion therapies and psychosurgery have also promised to 'cure' homosexuality, the history of reparative therapies has become inexorably linked with that of psychoanalysis. The strident positions of reparative theorists and practitioners[4] and the tacit acquiescence of their less ideological colleagues, have earned psychoanalytic theory its present mythic status as an implacable foe of lesbian and gay identities. This view persists despite a growing number of authors who criticise the anti-homosexual bias of psychoanalytic theories within a psychoanalytic framework.[5] The perception that psychoanalysis is intrinsically

---

[1] Originally published as J Drescher, 'I'm Your Handyman: A History of Reparative Therapies' (1998) 36(1) *Journal of Homosexuality* 19. Reprinted in A Shidlo et al (eds), *Sexual Conversion Therapy: Ethical Clinical and Research Perspectives* (New York, The Haworth Press, 2001).

[2] S Freud, *The Letters of Sigmund Freud* (New York, Basic Books, 1960) 423.

[3] J Nicolosi, *Reparative Therapy of Male Homosexuality* (Lanham, Rowman and Littlefield, 1991).

[4] R Bayer, *Homosexuality and American Psychiatry: The Politics of Diagnosis* (New York, Basic Books, 1981); C Socarides, 'The Erosion of Heterosexuality' *The Washington Times* (Washington DC, 5 July 1994); C Socarides, B Kaufman, J Nicolosi, J Satinover and R Fitzgibbons 'Don't Forsake Homosexuals who Want Help' *The Wall Street Journal* (New York, 9 January 1997); J Drescher, 'From Preoedipal to Postmodern: Changing Psychoanalytic Attitudes Toward Homosexuality' (1997) 2(2) *Gender and Psychoanalysis* 203; J Drescher, *Psychoanalytic Therapy and the Gay Man* (New York, Routledge, 1998); J Drescher, 'Contemporary Psychoanalytic Psychotherapy with Gay Men: With a Commentary on Reparative Therapy of Homosexuality' (1998) 2(4) *Journal of Gay and Lesbian Psychotherapy* 51.

[5] K Lewes, *The Psychoanalytic Theory of Male Homosexuality* (New York, Simon and Schuster, 1988); R Isay, *Being Homosexual: Gay Men and Their Development* (New York, Farrar, Straus and Giroux, 1989); N O'Connor and J Ryan, *Wild Desires and Mistaken Identities: Lesbianism and Psychoanalysis* (New York, Columbia University, 1993); J Glassgold and S Iasenza (eds), *Lesbians and Psychoanalysis: Revolutions in Theory and Practice* (New York, The Free Press, 1995); T Domenici and R Lesser (eds), *Disorienting Sexuality: Psychoanalytic Reappraisals of Sexual Identities* (New York, Routldge, 1995); A D'Ercole, 'Postmodern Ideas about Gender and Sexuality: The Lesbian Woman Redundancy' (1996) 13(2) *Psychoanalysis and Psychotherapy* 142; S Kiersky, 'Exiled Desire: The Problem of Reality in Psychoanalysis and Lesbian Experience' (1996) 13(2) *Psychoanalysis and Psychotherapy* 130.

hostile to homosexuality led the reviewer of a book affirmatively reformulating psychoanalytic theory and practice with lesbians and gay men[6] to sceptically muse, 'some of the contributors discuss how they are readapting or selectively using psychoanalysis so that its inherent antigay bias is eliminated. If that bias is eliminated, what is left?'[7]

This paper reviews the history and theoretical assumptions of psychoanalytically-oriented practitioners, beginning with Freud's juvenilisation of gay people to the later analysts who pathologized and attempted to change same-sex attractions. The evolution of reparative therapists from medically concerned practitioners into antigay political activists is also discussed.

I. Freud

It is not for psycho-analysis to solve the problem of homosexuality.[8]

Although he never dedicated a major work solely to the subject of homosexuality, Freud's contributions on the subject range across a period of almost twenty years.[9] The contradictions in his voluminous works make Freud's position opaque to the casual, modern reader. Attempts to find 'the real Freud' are too often motivated by those who seek his agreement with their own point of view. When diametrically opposed camps claim Freud as a theoretical ally, it confirms Bayer's assertion that 'the status of homosexuality is a political question, representing a historically rooted, socially determined choice regarding the ends of human sexuality'.[10] Taken out of the historical context in which he wrote, and depending upon the author's selective citations, Freud can be portrayed as either virulently anti-homosexual[11] or as a closeted friend of gays.[12] This section is an attempt to offer a portrait of Freud's complex position in the historical context in which he theorized and lived.

---

[6] T Domenici and R Lesser (eds) ibid.

[7] J Marrow, 'New Wine, Old Bottle' (1996) 2(4) *The Lesbian Review of Books* 13.

[8] S Freud, 'The Psychogenesis of a Case of Female Homosexuality' (1920) 1(2) *International Journal of Psycho-Analysis* 125, 148.

[9] S Freud, 'Three Essays on the Theory of Sexuality' (1905); S Freud, '"Civilised" Sexual Morality and Modern Mental Illness' (1908); S Freud, 'Analysis of a Phobia in a Five-Year-Old Boy' (1909); S Freud, 'Leonardo da Vinci and a Memory of his Childhood' (1910); S Freud, 'Psycho-analytic Notes on an Autobiographical Account of a Case of Paranoia' (1911); S Freud, 'On Narcissism: An Introduction' (1914); S Freud, 'Some Neurotic Mechanisms in Jealousy, Paranoia and Homosexuality' (1923) all in *The Standard Edition of the Complete Psychological Works of Sigmund Freud* (London, Hogarth Press, 1953); S Freud Psychogenesis, ibid.

[10] R Bayer (n 4) p 5.

[11] Nicolosi (n 3).

[12] N McWilliams, 'Therapy Across the Sexual Orientation Boundary: Reflections of a Heterosexual Female Analyst on Working with Lesbian, Gay, and Bisexual Patients' (1996) 1(2) *Gender and Psychoanalysis* 203.

Freud's attitude toward homosexuality was tolerant for its time. He signed a statement calling for decriminalization of homosexual acts in 1930's Germany and Austria.[13] This action was based on his belief that people should not be treated as criminals if their behaviours originated from a 'psychic disposition' beyond their control. Unlike today's reparative therapists, Freud did not believe that criminalization and social opprobrium were acceptable therapeutic tools. He also empathically noted:

> it is one of the obvious social injustices that the standard of civilization should demand from everyone the same conduct of sexual life – conduct which can be followed without any difficulty by some people, thanks to their organization, but which imposes the heaviest psychical sacrifices on others.[14]

In disputing degeneracy theory's[15] pejorative views, Freud observed that homosexuality is 'found in people whose efficiency is unimpaired, and who are indeed distinguished by specially high intellectual development and ethical culture'.[16]

Freud believed a sublimated homosexuality was necessary for normal heterosexual function. Similarly, all homosexuals had some heterosexual feelings. There was no social equivalent of 'coming out' in Freud's era and so he never expressed an opinion on that subject. However, one can surmise he did not believe overt homosexual behaviour was socially acceptable. Freud scolds a patient who asks why people shouldn't express their homosexual feelings as well as their heterosexual ones:

> Normal people have a certain homosexual component and a very strong heterosexual component. The homosexual component should be sublimated as it now is in society; it is one of the most valuable human assets and should be put to social uses. One cannot give one's impulses free rein. Your attitude reminds me of a child who just discovered everybody defecates and who then demands that everybody ought to defecate in public; that cannot be.[17]

A significant difficulty in understanding Freud's work stems from the fact that when discussing homosexuality, he is primarily elaborating other theoretical concepts such as libido and bisexuality (1905), narcissism (1910, 1914), projective mechanisms (1911, 1923), or unsatisfactory Oedipal resolutions (1920, 1923). Because each is addressing a different metapsychological issue, Freud's four theories of homosexuality[18] are often contradictory. Each uses a narrowly constructed 'hypothetical homosexual'[19] to make a different theoretical point.

---

[13] H Abelove, 'Freud, Male Homosexuality, and the Americans' in H Abelove, MA Barale and D Halperin (eds) *The Lesbian and Gay Studies Reader* (New York, Routledge, 1993).
[14] S Freud, Civilised Sexual Morality (n 9) p 192.
[15] R Krafft-Ebing, *Psychopathia Sexualis* (New York, Putnam, 1886).
[16] S Freud, Three Essays (n 9), p 138.
[17] J Wortis, *Fragments of an Analysis with Freud* (New York, Charter Books, 1954) pp 99–100.
[18] K Lewes (n 5).
[19] J Drescher, *Psychoanalytic Therapy* (n 4).

Moreover, Freud's position on homosexuality cannot be understood in the language of the contemporary debate about homosexuality. In fact, his 'original intent' is sometimes obscured when his opinions are brought into the modern controversy. For example, in a posthumously published Letter to an American Mother, Freud reassured a woman that her homosexual son was not ill.[20] In the late 20th century it is argued that lesbians and gay men are not ill and their homosexuality is defined as intrinsic to their nature.[21] It follows, according to this argument, that lesbians and gay men should be accorded minority status and full civil rights.

Although similar arguments were made by Magnus Hirschfeld in Freud's time,[22] they were not germane to his letter. Freud was using the term 'illness' as a synonym for symptom formation, by which he meant the product of intra-psychic conflict.[23] Homosexuality was not defined as an illness because it was thought to represent the unconflicted expression of an infantile sexual wish.[24] However, although an arrested libidinal development was not an illness, neither did Freud believe that it implied health.[25] In Freud's view, one could still justify psychotherapeutic intervention to transform a person's sexual orientation.

Freud theorized that early childhood development was organized into psycho-sexual stages of libido. This hierarchical ordering of pleasure moved from oral to anal to genital stages. It placed genital (heterosexual) intercourse above the former, more infantile forms of gratification. Adult sexuality was defined as genital-genital (penile-vaginal) intercourse and oral and anal sexuality were labelled as foreplay or immature vestiges of childhood sexual expression. Homosexuality could be due to a 'libidinal arrest' or failure to reach the final psychosexual stage of genitality due to a blockage of the energic force. An alternative explanation was that an individual had reached the more mature, genital stage but due to trauma reverted to an earlier stage. This was termed a 'libidinal regression'. For Freud, changing an individual's same-sex orientation to a heterosexual one meant helping them achieve a higher level of psychosexual development. Rather than a cure, effecting a sexual orientation conversion was seen as a metaphor for helping the patient grow up. Thus, in qualifying his reassurances to the 'American Mother', Freud explained that illness was not a necessary criterion for change:

> By asking me if I can help, you mean, I suppose, if I can abolish homosexuality and make normal heterosexuality take its place. The answer is, in a general way, we cannot promise to achieve it. In a certain number of cases we succeed in developing the blighted

---

[20] S Freud, *Letters* (n 2).

[21] S LeVay, *The Sexual Brain* (Cambridge MA, The MIT Press, 1993); D Hamer and P Copeland, *The Science of Desire* (New York, Simon and Schuster, 1994).

[22] V Bullough, *Homosexuality: A History* (New York, Meridian, 1979).

[23] S Freud, 'Inhibitions, Symptoms and Anxiety' (1926) in *The Standard Edition of the Complete Psychological Works of Sigmund Freud* (London, Hogarth Press, 1953).

[24] S Freud, Three Essays (n 9); S Freud, Psychogenesis (n 8).

[25] J Drescher, 'A Discussion Across Sexual Orientation and Gender Boundaries: Reflections of a Gay Male Analyst to a Heterosexual Female Analyst' (1996) 1(2) *Gender and Psychoanalysis* 223.

germs of heterosexual tendencies which are present in every homosexual, in the majority of cases it is no more possible.[26]

In Psychogenesis of a Case of Homosexuality in a Woman, Freud documents a reparative therapy attempt. This is his only reported case in which he is nominally charged with changing someone's sexual orientation. His patient was an eighteen year old girl who had fallen in love with an older woman. Following a stern rebuke from her father, the young woman attempted suicide. She was subsequently brought by her parents for psychoanalytic treatment to change her sexual orientation. In the paper, Freud pointed out the difficulties in achieving the father's goal for his teenage daughter:

> Parents expect one to cure their nervous and unruly child. By a healthy child they mean one who never causes his parents trouble and gives them nothing but pleasure. The physician may succeed in curing the child, but after that it goes its own way all the more decidedly, and the parents are now far more dissatisfied than before. In short, it is not a matter of indifference whether someone comes to analysis of his own accord or because he is brought to it--whether it is he himself who desires to be changed, or only his relatives, who love him (or who might be expected to love him). Further unfavourable features in the present case were the facts that the girl was not in any way ill (she did not suffer from anything in herself, nor did she complain of her condition) and that the task to be carried out did not consist in resolving a neurotic conflict but in converting one variety of the genital organization of sexuality into the other. Such an achievement – the removal of genital inversion or homosexuality – is in my experience never an easy matter ... In general, to undertake to convert a fully developed homosexual into a heterosexual does not offer much prospect of success than the reverse, except that for good practical reasons the latter is never attempted.[27]

Freud hypothesized that the young woman's early oedipal rivalry with her mother was reactivated in puberty when her parents had another child:

> It was just when the girl was experiencing the revival of her infantile Oedipus complex at puberty that she suffered her great disappointment. She became keenly conscious of the wish to have a child, and a male one; that what she desired was her *father's* child and an image of *him*, her consciousness was not allowed to know. And what happened next? It was not *she* who bore the child, but her unconsciously hated rival, her mother. Furiously resentful and embittered, she turned away from her father and from men altogether. After this first great reverse she forswore her womanhood and sought another goal for her libido.[28]

Freud called his lesbian patient a spurned man-hater, labelled her dreams as 'false and hypocritical',[29] and disparaged her as a feminist who suffered from penis envy.[30]

---

[26] S Freud, *Letters* (n 2).
[27] S Freud, Psychogenesis (n 8) p 150.
[28] Ibid p 157.
[29] Ibid p 165.
[30] Ibid p 169.

He claimed *her* transferential animosity toward men was an insurmountable obstacle that forced him to end the treatment and exile her lesbian desire.[31] He advised the family to have the young woman continue with a female analyst. No report of the existence, success or failure of any subsequent treatment is known. However, that report was irrelevant to Freud's purposes, because the aim of this paper was to further expand upon his previous psychoanalytic theories. In fact, the unsatisfactory outcome of the case only confirmed the correctness of Freud's views that homosexuality was not a neurosis, but a difficult-to-treat psychic disposition.

II. Reparative Therapy's Gilded Age

The psychiatrists were always in desperate need to find a biological foundation for homosexuality; in their fight against barbaric, medieval laws, naturally they picked upon inherited homosexuality.[32]

Despite Freud's pessimism about changing homosexual motivations to heterosexual ones, analysts persisted in seeking ways to do so. Psychoanalysts were in the vanguard of redefining socially denigrated behaviours in psychological terms and consequently generated the hope that medical intervention might be able to change them. When psychoanalysis reached its highest influence in psychiatry and academia during the 1940's and through the 1960's, many gay men and women voluntarily sought psychoanalytic treatment for their same-sex feelings.[33]

Although Freud's libidinal model offered little hope for converting homosexuality, psychoanalytic opinion began to change. After Freud's death in 1938,[34] psychoanalytic theories proliferated that differed significantly from his own but that nevertheless remained within the mainstream of the psychoanalytic movement.[35] These new paradigms offered alternative explanations for same-sex attraction that created "therapeutic possibilities." In the post-Freudian psychoanalytic world, the theories of Sandor Rado laid the foundations for what would later come to be called 'reparative therapies'.

---

[31] S Kiersky (n 4).

[32] P Roazen and B Swerdloff, *Heresy: Sandor Rado and the Psychoanalytic Movement* (Northvale, Aronson, 1995).

[33] M Duberman, *Cures: A Gay Man's Odyssey* (New York, Dutton, 1991); R Isay, *Becoming Gay: The Journey to Self-Acceptance* (New York, Simon and Schuster, 1996).

[34] E Jones, *The Life and Work of Sigmund Freud* (New York, Basic Books, 1961).

[35] J Greenberg and S Mitchell, *Object Relations in Psychoanalytic Theory* (Cambridge MA, Harvard University Press, 1983).

2.1. Rado

Rado's 1969[36] theory of homosexuality grew out of the refutation of Freud's belief in psychological bisexuality.[37] Rado believed the theory of libidinal bisexuality was based on a faulty analogy with anatomical bisexuality. That is, underlying Freud's theory was the later disproved 19th century belief in embryonic hermaphroditism, the hypothesis that the potential to become an anatomical man or a woman was present in every embryo.[38] However, after Rado deconstructed Freud's biological metaphors, he succumbed to the same epistemological snare. He too relied upon the physiological and evolutionary models *of his own era* as concrete metaphors for psychological experience:

> In *adaptational psychodynamics* we analyse behaviour in the context of a biological organism interacting with its cultural environment. The human organism, like other living organisms, may be defined as a self-regulating biological system that perpetuates itself and its type by means of its environment, its surrounding system. From this it follows that life is a process of interaction of the organism and its environment ... In the theory of evolution, the crowning achievement of eighteenth and nineteenth-century biologists, *adaptive value is a statistical concept which epitomizes reproductive efficiency* in a certain environment. This is strongly influenced by the type's ability to survive. Hence, 'more adaptive' means more able to survive and reproduce.[39]

Rado declared, with great authority but without any supporting scientific research or evidence, that heterosexuality is the only nonpathological outcome of human sexual development: 'I know of nothing that indicates that there is any such thing as innate orgastic desire for a partner of the same sex'.[40] Starting from that unproven, but firmly-held assumption, he offered the following theory of homosexuality's etiology:

> The male-female sexual pattern is dictated by anatomy ... by means of the institution of marriage, the male-female sexual pattern is culturally ingrained and perpetuated in every individual from earliest childhood ... [homosexual] pairs satisfy their repudiated yet irresistible male-female desire by means of shared illusions and actual approximations; such is the hold on the individual of a cultural institution based on biological foundations ... Why is the so-called homosexual forced to escape from the male-female pair into a homogenous pair? ... The familiar campaign of deterrence that parents wage to prohibit the sexual activity of the child. The campaign causes the female to view the male organ as a destructive weapon. Therefore the female partners are reassured by the absence in both of them of the male organ. The campaign causes the male to see in

---

[36] Although this volume was published toward the end of his life, it is based on ideas and lectures that Rado developed and taught in the 1930's and 40's.

[37] S Rado, *Adaptational Psychodynamics: Motivation and Control* (New York, Science House, 1969).

[38] Ibid, pp 215–216.

[39] Ibid, p 4 (emphasis added).

[40] Ibid p 210.

the mutilated female organ a reminder of inescapable punishment. When ... fear and resentment of the opposite organ becomes insurmountable, the individual may escape into homosexuality. The male patterns are reassured by the presence in both of them of the male organ. Homosexuality is a deficient adaptation evolved by the organism in response to its own emergency overreaction and dyscontrol.[41]

2.2. Bieber

Bieber, Dain, et al (1962) conducted a psychoanalytic study that they claimed confirmed Rado's theory of homosexuality: constitutional factors were insignificant and parental psychopathology was the cause of homosexuality. They examined 106 homosexual men and 100 male heterosexual controls in psychoanalytic treatment to identify family patterns presumed to be responsible for homosexuality. The authors' initial assumptions were consistent with the theory they subsequently claimed to confirm:

> We have selected the patient-mother-father unit for analysis ... We believe that personality for the most part is forged within the triangular system of the nuclear family. It follows then that personality maladaptation must also be primarily rooted here.[42]

> We assume that heterosexuality is the biologic norm and that unless interfered with all individuals are heterosexual.[43]

> We consider homosexuality to be a pathologic biosocial, psychosexual adaptation consequent to pervasive fears surrounding the expression of heterosexual impulses. In our view, every homosexual is, in reality, a 'latent' heterosexual.[44]

They claimed that of their 106 homosexual men:

> 29 patients had become exclusively heterosexual during the course of psychoanalytic treatment. The shift from homosexuality to exclusive heterosexuality for 27 per cent of the H[omosexual]-patients is of outstanding importance since these are the most optimistic and promising results thus far reported.[45]

2.3. Socarides I

Socarides contests Freud's view that homosexuality is a developmental arrest and redefines it as conflictual. His conflict model suggests therapeutic interventions to bring unconscious struggles into awareness in order to reduce homosexual

---

[41] Ibid pp 212–213.
[42] I Bieber et al, *Homosexuality: A Psychoanalytic Study* (New York, Basic Books, 1962) pp 140–141.
[43] Ibid p 319.
[44] Ibid p 220.
[45] Ibid p 276.

symptoms. He reshapes Freud's metapsychological constructs[46] and claims that homosexuality is a neurotic condition in which the libidinal instinct has

> undergone excessive transformation and disguise in order to be gratified in the perverse act. The perverted action, like the neurotic symptom, results from the conflict between the ego and the id and represents a compromise formation which at the same time must be acceptable to the demands of the superego ... the instinctual gratification takes place in disguised form while its real content remains unconscious.[47]

Because homosexuality is now defined as a compromise between intrapsychic forces, it meets the psychoanalytic definition of an illness. His claims, like Freud's, are neither provable or unprovable since the metapsychological constructs of id, ego and superego are not subject to direct observation and can only be understood inferentially.

Socarides holds the parents of gay men and women responsible for causing homosexuality. The recent emergence of his gay son from the closet[48] adds poignancy to his 30-year-old description of the fathers of homosexual men: 'The family of the homosexual is usually a female-dominated environment wherein the father was absent, weak, detached or sadistic'.[49] Socarides also claims a psychoanalytic conversion rate of 35% for his homosexual patients.[50]

2.4. Ovesey

Ovesey's work approaches the post-modern sensibility in his explanation of how categories of masculinity and femininity are socially constructed:

> The social order is so arranged that status accrues to men solely by virtue of the fact that they are men. The polarities of masculinity and femininity are identified respectively with positive and negative value judgments. Masculinity represents strength, dominance, superiority; femininity represents weakness, submissiveness, inferiority. The former is equated with success; the latter with failure. It is true that these values are cultural stereotypes that express primarily the historical prejudices of the men in the culture. However, it would be safe to say that men and women alike make use of them in appraising each other's behaviour.[51]

Men who have dreams or fantasies in which they appear submissive to or dependent upon other men are not necessarily experiencing homosexual feelings, but

---

[46] S Freud, 'Inhibitions, Symptoms and Anxiety' (1926) in *The Standard Edition of the Complete Psychological Works of Sigmund Freud* (London, Hogarth Press, 1953).

[47] C Socarides, *The Overt Homosexual* (New York, Grune and Stratton, 1968) pp 35–36.

[48] A Nagourney, 'Father Doesn't Know Best' *Out Magazine* (February 1995) pp 75–77, 113–115; D Dunlap, 'An Analyst, a Father, Battles Homosexuality' *The New York Times* (New York, 24 December 1995).

[49] C Socarides, *Overt Homosexual* (n 47) p 38.

[50] C Socarides, *Homosexuality: A Freedom too Far* (Phoenix, Adam Margrave Books, 1995) p 102.

[51] L Ovesey, *Homosexuality and Pseudohomosexuality* (New York, Science House, 1969) p 76.

pseudohomosexual ones. These feelings are symbolic of competition and status issues commonly found in heterosexual men. Despite his awareness of how cultural forces value masculine attributes while feminine ones are denigrated, Ovesey treats male homosexuality's low cultural status as a fact of nature that requires no further deconstruction. In fact, he warned that 'those who lack conviction that homosexuality is a treatable illness but believe instead that it is a natural constitutional variant, should not accept homosexuals as patients'.[52]

In Ovesey's approach to treating male homosexuality, we see the standard recommendation of reparative therapists to abandon neutrality or objectivity and function as behavioural therapists:

> There is only one way that the homosexual can overcome this phobia and learn to have heterosexual intercourse, and that way is in bed with a woman … Sooner or later, the homosexual patient must make the necessary attempts to have intercourse, and he must make them again and again, until he is capable of a sustained erection, penetration, and pleasurable intravaginal orgasm.[53]

In order to achieve these goals, the reparative therapist becomes a dating consultant for the patient:

> Most homosexuals do not move readily toward women. More often, the patient protests that he is not ready for sex with a woman. He is, of course, right. The therapist should reassure him that for the present he is only asked to see women socially, to date them; nobody is asking that he jump into bed with them. Later, when he is comfortable with a date, he will begin first to neck, then to pet, and eventually go even further, but certainly not now. If the patient is at all serious about treatment, he will accept this compromise and gradually, with some pressure from the therapist, if necessary, begin to go out … There is a place, just as in the therapy of other phobias, where the patient may be threatened with termination if he unduly procrastinates about entering the phobic situation. In other words, the homosexual patient should be given an ultimatum for insufficient efforts to perform heterosexually.[54]

III. Contemporary Reparative Therapy: Traditional Values for a Postmodern Era

> We refused most emphatically to turn a patient who puts himself into our hands in search of help into our private property, to decide his fate for him, to force our own ideals upon him, and with the pride of a Creator to form him in our own image and see that it is good … we cannot accept (the) proposal either--namely that psycho-analysis should place itself in the service of a particular philosophical outlook on the world and should urge this upon the patient for the purpose of ennobling his mind. In my

---

[52] Ibid p 119.
[53] Ibid pp 106–107.
[54] Ibid pp 120–121.

opinion, this is after all only to use violence, even though it is overlaid with the most honourable motives.[55]

Rado's adaptational model of homosexuality dominated American psychiatry until a year after his death in 1972.[56] In 1973, the American Psychiatric Association deleted homosexuality from its Diagnostic and Statistical Manual.[57] Although Rado's theory is no longer the dominant mental health paradigm, it continues to surface in new forms.

Contemporary reparative therapists must contend with the fact that the terms of scientific and social debate have shifted. They have had to grapple with five significant factors that their predecessors did not: 1) Their patients and potential patients are aware of affirmative identities for lesbians and gay men as that community's public visibility increases; 2) there is a growing, significant scientific and social science literature that defines homosexuality as a normal variant of human sexuality; 3) rigid categories of masculinity and femininity are being increasingly deconstructed by feminist and queer theorists; 4) there is a growing body of research on anti-homosexual attitudes and 5) homosexuality's diagnostic status as an illness has been rejected by conservative psychoanalytic organizations.[58] Despite these cultural changes, the theoretical formulations underlying reparative therapies have changed little since the time of Rado. However, as the following section illustrates, reparative therapists have modified their rhetorical strategies in their adherence to traditional approaches to homosexuality. They have also moved beyond rhetoric to significant political action.

3.1. Siegel: The Neocon

In the reparative therapy literature, Siegel prefaces her work by presenting herself as an accidental tourist, for whom 'a series of coincidences placed me into the position of analysing twelve women who thought they had 'chosen' homosexuality as a lifestyle'.[59] She identifies herself as a reparative therapy neoconservative, a former liberal whose clinical experiences have led her to regard her previous, more tolerant beliefs as part of an idealistic youth that she has disavowed for a new, albeit unpopular, truth:

> My [lesbian] patients had convinced me on an irrational level that there was indeed a choice for them … To be a liberal and liberated woman and yet to review homosexuality as the result of untoward development seemed at times a betrayal of all I then believed.

[55] S Freud, 'Lines of Advance in Psycho-analytic Therapy' (1918) in *The Standard Edition of the Complete Psychological Works of Sigmund Freud* (London, Hogarth Press, 1953).
[56] P Roazen and B Swerdloff (n 32).
[57] R Bayer (n 4).
[58] The American Psychiatric Association issued its first anti-discrimination statement on December 15, 1973. The American Academy of Psychoanalysis issued a non-discrimination statement in 1990. The American Psychoanalytic Association issued one in 1991.
[59] EV Siegel, *Female Homosexuality: Choice with Volition* (New York, Routledge, 1988) p xi.

But viewing my patients through the lens of psychoanalytic thinkers and clinicians soon showed me that allowing myself to be seduced into perceiving female homosexuality as a normal lifestyle would have cemented both my patients and myself into a rigid mode that precluded change of whatever nature.[60]

In her treatment of twelve lesbian patients, Siegel claims more than half became 'fully heterosexual'. She defines homosexuality as preoedipal in origin. In the Radoite tradition, she believes her patients 'tried to heal their defective body images by seeking others like themselves'.[61] She bases her work on the theories of Socarides[62] to whom she dedicates her book. Like Socarides, she uses Mahler's model of separation[63] and individuation as universal metaphors of normal development.

As reparative therapy increasingly moves away from the scientific mainstream, its mystical presuppositions become more apparent. Siegel, for example, defines the psychoanalytic concept of narcissism as 'an energy' which allows individuals to adapt to 'the reality of life, what I have called *Lebensbejahung*, the cathexis of life'.[64] In the tradition of classical psychoanalysis, she interprets from what she believes to be an objective position and has an inflated sense of her own capacity for neutrality. She presents her clinical narratives as historical facts that she has unearthed in the course of analysis. Her approach is somewhat formulaic, marked by a belief that all her patients go through similar 'stages' of transference phenomena. She would have her readers believe she had no preconceived ideas about homosexuality or heterosexuality and came to her eventual conclusion that homosexuality is pathological through a scientific process of observation. It is beyond the scope of this paper to address the influence of the analyst's beliefs on the narratives that emerge in a patient's treatment and the subject has been addressed elsewhere.[65] However, Siege's clinical approach appears to undermine her own attempts to position her work among self-psychology and intersubjective theorists, given their emphasis on co-constructed narratives.

3.2. Nicolosi: The Moral Majority[66]

Psychoanalytic theorists traditionally couched their moral condemnations of homosexuality within scientific and pseudo-scientific metaphors. The Radoite

---

[60] Ibid p xii.

[61] Ibid p 8.

[62] C Socarides, *Overt Homosexual* (n 47); C Socarides, *Homosexuality* (New York, Jason Aaronson, 1978).

[63] M Mahler, F Pine and A Bergman, *The Psychological Birth of the Human Infant: Symbiosis and Individuation* (New York, Basic Books, 1975).

[64] EV Siegel (n 59) p 21.

[65] J Drescher, 'Psychoanalytic Subjectivity and Male Homosexuality' in R Cabaj and T Stein (eds) *Textbook of Homosexuality and Mental Health* (Washington DC, American Psychiatric Press, 1996).

[66] With acknowledgment of the contributions of David Smith, M.D at a presentation comparing the language of reparative therapists and religious fundamentalists at the 1995 meeting of the American Psychiatric Association, Miami, FL.

tradition, in particular, anthropomorphized the concept of evolution, turning it into a force of nature that 'expected' individuals to behave in ways for which they were designed. Consequently, the will of the deity was replaced by the will of evolution in psychoanalytic literature. This approach is embodied in the work of Kardiner:

> Sex morality is not an arbitrary set of rules set down by no one knows who, and for purposes that no one understands, but is what man found expedient in his long evolutionary march, his social evolution … If we find a culture, such as our own, that not only has survived but has to its credit the highest accomplishments ever recorded for man, then the patterns of morality – or the mores by which it governs the relations of the constituents to one another – must have a high degree of effectiveness … at the time sex custom entered recorded history, it already was more or less settled. Monogamy, for example, was an established custom in the Homeric legends … we can assume that 'human nature' has certain constant features and that human interaction, within certain limits, can be predicted on the basis of man's biological make-up … What is more certain is that in man the capacity for love is more extensive owing to the fact that human infants need the proximity of protecting parents for a longer period than do any other mammals. This dependency is the nucleus about which the emotion known as love develops.[67]

One can only wonder what Kardiner understood about the relationship between Achilles and Patroclus in The Iliad. This moralizing tendency within psychoanalysis did not go unobserved and was subsequently embraced by religious institutions that traditionally condemned psychoanalytic thought. Thus, in a document entitled, The Norms of Priestly Formation, homosexuality is ironically described in heretical psychoanalytic terminology:

> The existence of a close link between emotions and sexuality and their interdependence in the wholeness of a personality cannot be denied, even though these two things are diversely understood. In order to talk about a person as mature, his sexual instinct must have overcome two immature tendencies, narcissism and homosexuality, and must have arrived at heterosexuality[68]

Nicolosi's approach marks a significant shift in the reparative therapy literature. This reparative therapist offers a deliberate fusion of spiritual and psychoanalytic thought:

> Each one of us, man and woman alike, is driven by the power of romantic love. These infatuations gain their power from the unconscious drive to become a complete human being. In heterosexuals, it is the drive to bring together the male-female polarity through the longing for the other-than me. But in homosexuals, it is the attempt to fulfill a deficit in wholeness of one's original gender.[69]

---

[67] A Kardiner, *Sex and Morality* (London, Routledge, 1955) pp. 22–31.
[68] National Conference of Catholic Bishops, *Norms for Priestly Formation* (Washington DC, US Catholic Conference, 1982) p 167.
[69] J Nicolosi (n 3) pp 109–110.

In addition to the Radoite theory of homosexuality, Nicolosi draws on literature from the field of pastoral counselling. He offers a religious treatise on homosexuality thinly disguised as a scientific document. In the new religious *cum* scientific paradigm, mental health is defined as conformity to traditional values and norms. Nicolosi's reparative therapy 'acknowledges the significance of gender difference, the worth of family and conventional values, and the importance of the prevention of gender confusion in children'.[70] He criticizes contemporary normal variant theories of homosexuality with the fervour of a religious fundamentalist. In doing so, he argues not as a scientist, but as a preacher:

> The logic of the following assumption has always eluded me: because perhaps 4 percent of all people are homosexual, then homosexuality *must be a normal variation* of human sexuality. The fact that it occurs in other cultures and in subhuman species, under certain conditions, is also seen to prove its normalcy. Such logic would be equivalent to concluding that since a given percentage of people will break a leg skiing each winter, then a broken leg is a natural condition and one should not attempt to avoid it.[71]

Nicolosi's misuse of psychoanalytic concepts to buttress his moralizing approach has been criticized elsewhere.[72] His entire work is characterized by an idealization of heterosexuality, the use of denigrating stereotypes of gay people, and a tendency to treat his own biases as universal truths:

> Gay couples are characteristically brief and very volatile, with much fighting, arguing, making-up again, and continual disappointments. They may take the form of intense romances, where the attraction remains primarily sexual, characterized by infatuation and never evolving into mature love; or else they settle into long-term friendships while maintaining outside affairs. Research, however, reveals that they almost never possess the mature elements of quiet consistency, trust, mutual dependency, and sexual fidelity characteristic of highly functioning heterosexual marriages.[73]

3.3. Socarides II: The Comeback Kid

Socarides, is the perennial reparative therapist who keeps going and going. He was a prominent opponent of the American Psychiatric Association's decision to delete the diagnosis of homosexuality from its Diagnostic and Statistical Manual and a leader in the opposition's clamor for a referendum on the decision. Bayer remarked, 'It [was] rather remarkable that the same psychiatrists who had charged the APA's board with an unscientific and unseemly capitulation to political pressure now invoked the referendum procedure'.[74] After losing that political battle, Socarides and other psychoanalysts continued to maintain

---

[70] ibid p 23.
[71] ibid p 132.
[72] J Drescher, *Psychoanalytic Therapy* (n 4).
[73] Nicolosi (n 3) p 110.
[74] Bayer (n 4) p 142.

that homosexuality was always pathological. As a result, while other psychiatric organizations assimilated their lesbian and gay members, psychoanalytic institutions continued to maintain discriminatory policies in training and promotion of lesbian and gay analysts.[75]

In his public announcements, Socarides has amazingly tried to portray himself as a defender of gay rights. In this Orwellian approach, he is referring to an individual's right to seek treatment to change a homosexual orientation:

> The homosexual must be granted freedom from persecutory laws as well as full civil rights – and this constitutes an integral part of our approach to homosexual individuals … while we ask for civil rights, we also ask for the legitimate psychiatric rights of homosexuals to seek help for what they correctly feel is a disorder.[76]

However, despite Socarides' often-repeated opposition to antigay discrimination, he and other reparative therapists filed affidavits *in support* of Colorado's antigay Amendment Two,[77] which was eventually overturned by the Supreme Court. That law would have prevented any municipality from offering civil rights protections specifically to lesbians and gay men. Furthermore, in the case of *Campbell v. Sundquist*,[78] Socarides submitted an affidavit as part of the state's unsuccessful defence of Tennessee's Sodomy laws. His actions are consistent with the reparative therapy belief that social opprobrium must be reinforced if gay men and women are to be motivated to change their homosexual orientations.

In 1991, the American Psychoanalytic Association issued a non-discriminatory statement regarding the acceptance of lesbian and gay candidates and the promotion of training and supervising analysts in their affiliated institutes.[79] This was a *de facto* repudiation of Socarides and his view that homosexuality was always a sign of psychopathology and serious mental illness. However, the rejection of his life's work by the psychoanalytic mainstream did not deter Socarides from seeking out other forums to continue expounding his views. These have included editorials in politically conservative newspapers,[80] a book written for a nonprofessional audience that recycles his pathologizing theories and demonizes his political enemies,[81] and starting an organization of his own with himself as its first President.

3.4. NARTH

Diminishing professional interest in their approaches has led reparative therapists to form their own organization: The National Association for Research and

---

[75] Drescher 'Anti-homosexual Bias in Training' (n 37).
[76] C Socarides, 'Response to Judd Marmor, M.D.' *Psychiatric News* (May 20 1994).
[77] *Socarides Aff, Romer v Evans* Case No 92 CV 7223, 8 October 1993.
[78] (1996) 926 S.W.2d 255.
[79] R Isay, *Becoming Gay* (n 33).
[80] C Socarides, *Erosion* (n 4); C Socarides et al (n 4).
[81] C Socarides, *A Freedom too Far* (n 50).

Therapy of Homosexuality (NARTH). To avoid any repetition of the embarrassment and defeats they experienced in the clinical, scientific and political debates in other professional organizations, NARTH's officers have taken the position that it is unacceptable for current and potential members to publicly question the group's belief that homosexuality is an illness. To disagree would undermine the organization's raison d'être of providing an environment in which reparative therapists do not have their pathologizing beliefs challenged:

> NARTH is an association founded to study homosexuality. We make the assumption that obligatory homosexuality is a treatable disorder. Our members hold many variations of that essential view.
>
> The NARTH officers may opt to deny or remove membership when an individual's written statements or public speeches show a clear antipathy to this position. We do not always choose to exercise this option, but will do so when, in our judgment, a potential member is likely to be disruptive because he or she is blatantly opposed to our goals.
>
> Our criterion of discrimination is philosophical; we do not ... discriminate on the basis of sexual orientation. In fact, many of our members are ex-gays or homosexual people in a state of transition toward heterosexuality.[82]

Agreement with NARTH'S prevailing dogma appears to be the primary criterion for membership, not an individual's professional background. The heretical belief that homosexuality is a normal variant of human sexuality is unwelcome and those who articulate that view risk excommunication if they voice it publicly. However, neocon converts to NARTH's beliefs, ex-gays and potential ex-gays, are always welcome. These organizational approaches are consistent with the activities of a fundamentalist religious denomination, not a scientific association.

In the current political climate, NARTH's dogmatic views have been marginalized in professional and scientific organizations. It is uncertain if NARTH will have some future impact on clinical practice and thought in those mainstream mental health professions that presently accept homosexuality as a normal variant of human sexuality. For the present, however, reparative therapists have demonstrated their willingness to ally themselves with religious denominations that condemn homosexuality. Because they are unable to find reputable scientific support for their positions, these anti-homosexual religious organizations have turned to reparative therapists to treat their flocks and to provide a veneer of modern respectability. NARTH, in turn, appears to be emulating the tactics of creationists who obscure their increasingly, fundamentalist religious political agendas behind scientific and pseudo-scientific language.[83] Anti-homosexual politics make strange bedfellows and Freud, the devoutest of atheists,[84] would find this wedding of psychoanalysis and fundamentalism astonishing.

[82] Letter from J Nicolosi to R Roughton (10 June 1996).
[83] L Tiffen, *Creationism's Upside-Down Pyramid: How Science Refutes Fundamentalism* (Amherst, Prometheus Books, 1994).
[84] P Gay, *A Godless Jew: Freud, Atheism and the Making of Psychoanalysis* (New Haven, Yale University Press, 1987).

IV. Conclusion

There is no point telling people who have difficulties that they are ill.[85]

This paper reviewed the history of psychoanalytic theories of homosexuality and therapies designed to change a homosexual orientation to a heterosexual one. The evolution of one branch of psychoanalytic theory into an anti-homosexual political movement illustrates the permeability of boundaries between clinical issues and political ones. The deletion of homosexuality from the Diagnostic and Statistical Manual, has led to increased political activism and a rightward swing of reparative therapists. In removing the diagnostic label of illness, anti-homosexual political, religious and mental health forces were deprived of an important tool of repression. The growing political activism of reparative therapists underscores how much actual repression was previously wrought by the diagnostic label itself. In their open support of antigay legislation, reparative therapists have moved from the traditional psychoanalytic centre and have been embraced by conservative religious and political forces opposed to homosexuality. In doing so, they have apparently adopted religious organizational practices themselves, preaching dogma and stifling dissent. The increasing marginalization of reparative therapists from the psychoanalytic mainstream illustrates how psychoanalysis *per se* is neither gay-affirming nor condemning, although psychoanalytic practitioners may fall into either of these categories.

[85] DW Winnicott, *Talking to Parents* (Cambridge MA, Perseus Publishing, 1993).

4

Feeling Pain and Shame

The Emotional Grammar of Banning 'Conversion Therapy'

SENTHORUN RAJ

To think that God and the people around you would suddenly recognize your worth if you were seen as damaged and admitted it. This was LIA's [Love in Action] currency, the trading of literal and proverbial scars, and I hated it. Everyone was trying to one-up everyone else, to render the most painful account. After all, Jesus was most identifiable by his scars, and we were being asked to take up His cross and follow Him. Some deeper cynicism was threatening to take control of my thoughts.[1]

In the closing of his memoir, *Boy Erased*, Garrard Conley recalls an encounter with a counsellor which triggered him to leave the 'conversion therapy' he had solicited about a year earlier. What is particularly striking about the passage quoted above is that it centralises pain, and how pain and injury function as the moral currency by which people are 'valued' in 'conversion therapy'. They are 'scarred' individuals who must recognise, confess, and confront their brokenness if they aspire to live 'normal' (read: heterosexual) lives. Conley's memoir also reveals his own pain at having to endure a series of interventions that were based on 'self-annihilation'.[2] Yet, the exposure of these differing modes of pain also highlights Conley's emerging cynicism about what he has experienced. This is an emotional response to the pain he has endured, as well as the hostility he now feels towards that pain. The cynicism disrupts the assumptions on which the 'conversion therapy' he experienced was built.

The emotional articulations of pain in the closing chapter of *Boy Erased* also speak to the pressing demands to recognise the harms of conversion practices and to ban them. Specifically, in this chapter, I am drawn on one hand, to how those who advocate 'conversion therapy' instrumentalise the pain and shame of LGBTQ+ people as a means of pursuing 'healing' interventions (also referred to as

---

[1] G Conley, *Boy Erased: A Memoir of Identity, Faith and Family* (Glasgow, William Collins, 2016) 318.
[2] ibid 328.

'reparative interventions') to render them 'normal'. Correspondingly, on the other hand, I am mindful of how those who oppose conversion practices use the pain and shame faced by LGBTQ+ people who experience conversion practices as a means of pursuing 'healing' law reforms (which we might also note are reparative interventions) designed to ameliorate the pain and shame LGBTQ+ people have experienced. By exploring these competing articulations of pain and shame, through their different reparative registers, I wish to not only confront the shameful and painful harms of conversion practices, but also to expose how pain and shame become part of an 'emotional grammar' that structure law reform attempts to remedy these harms. In this chapter, I use emotional grammar to refer to emotions that underpin, and are produced by, textual referents (spoken words, written texts) that communicate ideas and make them understandable to others. This grammar frames and shapes modes of communication in law reform.[3] Such analysis is important if we, as lawyers, advocates, legislators, and scholars, are committed to promoting the rights of LGBTQ+ people and to crafting reforms that address the harms of conversion practices.

This chapter begins by examining personal testimonies of conversion practices to foreground how emotions like pain and shame are apparent in people's experiences of those practices. The second section explores how emotions, particularly pain, come to matter in law and the problems that instrumentalising pain generates for law reform. Drawing on the work of Sara Ahmed, Lauren Berlant, and Wendy Brown, I sketch out how we might 'read' pain and shame as an emotional grammar, manifested through a textual register (Hansard), which reflect the movements and attachments between individuals (those who experience 'conversion therapy') and institutions (legislative bodies that seek to proscribe 'conversion therapy'). In the third section, I use the work of these scholars to map the emotional grammar of a recent parliamentary debate in the UK about the need to include trans people in a 'conversion therapy' ban. This involves scanning the text of Hansard for emotions and using these emotions as the conceptual structure for understanding the operation of law.[4] In doing so, legal scholars and practitioners can explore the circulation of pain and shame in legal debates to ban conversion practices. I conclude the chapter by showing how critically navigating the emotional grammar of law reform is useful for a 'reparative reading' of law. This enables us to feel the law's capacity to repair homo/bi/transphobic pain and shame while also allowing us to think more generatively about the law's shame in its failures to secure LGBTQ+ wellbeing, freedom, and dignity. Using Eve Sedgwick's idea of a reparative reading, I challenge both the reparative promise of conversion practices in 'fixing' LGBTQ+ people and the reparative promise of law reform in 'fixing' the homo/bi/transphobic harms associated with those anti-LGBTQ+ practices.

---

[3] I have discussed this concept in much greater depth elsewhere. See S Raj, 'Legally Affective: Mapping the Emotional Grammar of LGBT Rights in Law School' (2023) 31 *Feminist Legal Studies* 191.
[4] For a greater discussion of affective reading in law, see S Raj, *Feeling Queer Jurisprudence: Injury, Intimacy, Identity* (Oxford, Routledge, 2020) 8–12.

I. Pain, Shame, and Anti-LGBTQ+ Conversion Practices

Conversion practices can be traced historically to psychoanalytic theories that pathologised homosexuality as 'arrested psychosexual development' that warranted correction.[5] In writing about 'the queer child', Kathryn Bond Stockton notes how the haunting association between homosexuality and children in psychoanalysis spotlighted those children 'in trouble' who, without corrective intervention, would not approach adult heterosexuality.[6] In terms of 'the transgender child', Jules Gill-Peterson observes how psychoanalytic hostility towards the existence of trans children led to counselling practices that aimed to make trans children identify with the sex assigned to them at birth.[7] Indeed, the discursive power of psychoanalysis from the 1950s onwards led to an increasing number of interventions that aimed to 'cure' homosexuality or trans identification (by characterising gay and trans people as victims of mental deficits or those who experienced childhood trauma) rather than interventions aimed to punish homosexuality or trans life (which typically viewed LGBTQ+ people as evil predators with no morality).[8] Psychoanalytic approaches to address these deficits relied on psychodrama, urging individuals to relive and work through their 'childhood trauma'.[9] When these psychological interventions failed to achieve their goal, some individuals turned to more physically invasive methods like hormone treatment, nausea-inducing drugs to induce 'aversion', electroshock therapies, and even castration.[10]

In a religious context, from the 1970s, pastors and priests also problematised homosexuality as an issue of 'sexual brokenness' that ought to be addressed pastorally with prayer, scripture reading, fasting, support, and counselling.[11] Religious conversion practices, unlike their secular counterparts, did not necessarily seek to 'reorient' individuals towards heterosexuality. Rather, in line with spiritual beliefs, these practices sought to suppress homosexuality or trans identity by cultivating chastity and sublimation of sexual desire into 'socially acceptable and productive activity'.[12]

---

[5] D Haldeman, 'Gay Rights, Patient Rights: The Implications of Sexual Orientation Conversion Therapy' (2002) 33 *Professional Psychology: Research & Practice* 260, 260.

[6] KB Stockton, *The Queer Child: Or Growing Sideways in the Twentieth Century* (Durham, Duke University Press, 2009) 7.

[7] J Gill-Peterson, *Histories of the Transgender Child* (Minneapolis, University of Minnesota Press, 2018) 148–49. For more detailed discussion of trans conversion practices, see F Ashley, *Banning Transgender Conversion Practices: A Legal and Policy Analysis* (Vancouver, University of British Columbia Press, 2022).

[8] G Herek, 'Sexual Orientation Differences as Deficits' (2010) 5 *Perspectives on Psychological Science* 693, 695.

[9] A Jowett et al, 'Conversion Therapy: An Evidence Assessment and Qualitative Study' (GOV.UK, 29 October 2021) section 4, www.gov.uk/government/publications/conversion-therapy-an-evidence-assessment-and-qualitative-study/conversion-therapy-an-evidence-assessment-and-qualitative-study.

[10] Herek (n 8) 695.

[11] T Jones et al, *Preventing Harm, Promoting Justice: Responding to LGBT Conversion Therapy in Australia* (La Trobe University, 2018) 13.

[12] ibid 11.

In both religious and psychological settings, an emphasis on trauma and cure, rather than predation and punishment, reflected an emotional shift in public discourse about homosexuality: gay people could be pitied or sympathised with as victims of their deficits rather than feared or loathed as perpetrators of deviance.[13] This emotional framing of homosexuality in different institutional settings, across an array of conversion practices, is important to note because pain functions as the means by which psychological and religious interventions were delivered to LGBTQ+ people. Conversion practices purportedly relieved the suffering of those with sexual deficits by making them see the promise of living a 'straight' life (even if this notion of 'straightness' simply meant suppressing homosexuality rather than being or acting heterosexual). In other words, alleviating pain was the pressing moral justification for advocating these practices.

Most psychological associations have largely denounced their role in the stigmatising effects caused by conversion practices, along with their dubious efficacy, and embraced a more supportive role for LGBTQ+ people.[14] Yet, conversion practices persist under a religious and pastoral care guise.[15] In examining more contemporary manifestations of conversion practices, we can observe how pain is also both a method and consequence of the practices themselves. One individual has written on the pain of experiencing prayer-based interventions in a church setting, 'part of the trauma of these abusive practices is that you, the victim, are always left with the burden of being told it is your fault, that you are not healed'.[16] In this example, pain functions as the consequence of intervention, as the person is burdened by the shame of their failure to change, and this causes them pain. Writing in the context of receiving 'spiritual guidance' for their homosexuality, another individual has spoken about how 'you'd have to re-live painful experiences from childhood and you're forced to identify things that you'd done wrong in the past. It was traumatic. I nearly always ended up

---

[13] In making this claim, I do not wish to obscure the discursive conditions that enable homophobic and transphobic violence beyond the context of conversion practices, nor do I wish to ignore how LGBTQ+ people remained the subject of criminal sanctions. For more discussion on systematic legal and social violence against LGBT people, see D Meyer, *Violence Against Queer People: Race, Class, Gender, and the Persistence of Anti-LGBT Discrimination* (New Brunswick, Rutgers University Press, 2015) and EA Stanley, *Atmospheres of Violence: Structuring Antagonism and the Trans/Queer Ungovernable* (Durham, Duke University Press, 2021).

[14] Most health and psychological associations in the UK, including the National Health Service, have signed a memorandum of understanding on the harms of 'conversion therapy' and the need to eliminate it. See 'Memorandum of Understanding on Conversion Therapy in the UK' (British Association of Counselling and Psychotherapy, 2 November 2022) www.bacp.co.uk/events-and-resources/ethics-and-standards/mou/. See also EM Maccio, 'Self-Reported Sexual Orientation and Identity Before and After Sexual Reorientation Therapy' (2011) 15 *Journal of Gay & Lesbian Mental Health* 242, 252.

[15] M McMurchie, '"The Dustbin of Quackery?": Senate Bill 1172 and the Legal Implications of Banning Reparative Therapy for Homosexual Minors' (2014) 87 *Southern California Law Review* 1519, 1524.

[16] J Ozanne, 'As a Lesbian Woman, I was Subjected to Conversion Practices. We Must Protect Trans People against This Abuse' (*The Guardian*, 1 April 2022) www.theguardian.com/commentisfree/2022/apr/01/ban-conversion-practices-trans-people-lesbian-gay-people.

in tears'.[17] Here, pain is the method of the practice as the person re-lives memories that cause tears for them in order to recognise their purported brokenness, which is a precondition of their healing.

Conversion practices also cultivate shame, because interventions like sexual violence, electroshock treatments, hormonal interventions, behavioural therapies, individual prayers, and psychological counselling rely on stigmatising LGBTQ+ people by seeking to treat their so-called 'failure' and 'brokenness'.[18] In public testimony for a US parliamentary committee, one survivor noted:

> Because of an innocuous limp wrist or subtle lisp, I was made to feel by licensed doctors that there was something wrong with me ... But in the name of professional mental health and the licensure of the state, I was made to feel shame and engage in a fruitless labor that left me sad and broken.[19]

Shame, in this example, manifests through stigma. In this testimony, a 'limp wrist' and 'subtle lisp' are social markers that 'blemished' the survivor's character by impugning his masculinity.[20] Shame is an intense feeling of the 'subject being against itself'.[21] The survivor spoke about how he came up against himself: self-consciousness towards his bodily comportment, expressed in his 'limp wrist' and 'subtle lisp', made him believe he was 'broken'. Shame was a 'negative' (to the extent it negates the self) emotion that arose from the survivor's perceived failure to approximate a norm of masculinity that was neither 'limp' nor 'subtle'.

However, this survivor recognised the 'fruitlessness' of conversion practices and the shame they felt and, in doing so, their testimony invited the state to feel shame at its failures to 'protect vulnerable populations from harm'.[22] We can see the 'binding' force of shame here – it connects us to others who we think bear witness to our perceived failures and to social norms that we fail to live up to.[23] Shame need not be disclosed; it may be a secret we keep to ourselves, but it materialises within the self through our relation to others. In this example, an individual gay man subjected to a conversion practice felt shame by believing they were 'failing' at

---

[17] F Tomazin, '"I am Profoundly Unsettled": Inside the Hidden World of Gay Conversion Therapy' (*The Age*, 9 March 2018) www.theage.com.au/national/i-am-profoundly-unsettled-inside-the-hidden-world-of-gay-conversion-therapy-20180227-p4z1xn.html.

[18] Jowett et al (n 9) 18–29. It is important to note that there is enormous variability in how 'conversion therapy' is articulated and practised across different sites. See other chapters in this collection for more detailed accounts of conversion practices.

[19] M Levovitz, 'Testimony on Sexual Orientation Change Efforts' (2015) 19 *Journal of Gay & Lesbian Mental Health* 96, 97.

[20] E Goffman, *Stigma: Notes on the Management of a Spoiled Identity* (Hoboken, Prentice-Hall, 1963) 14.

[21] S Ahmed, *The Cultural Politics of Emotion* (Edinburgh, Edinburgh University Press, 2004) 103. Shame also has a relationship with positive affects like desire. Shame exposes that which we find pleasurable (such as same-sex attraction) as it is only objects that can generate desire or enjoyment that can make us blush. See EK Sedgwick, *Touching Feeling: Affect, Pedagogy, Performativity* (Durham, Duke University Press, 2003) 116.

[22] Levovitz (n 19) 98.

[23] Ahmed (n 21) 107.

being masculine enough, both in terms of their individual therapist's expectations and broader social norms they are failing to realise.[24] The intensity of shame, as a mode of self-negation, relied on an individual feeling 'exposed' (by their perceived failure) before another and a desire to turn away from that exposure (of failure).[25] The redirection of shame and pain towards the state, evident in the testimony, urged action to rectify failure. In other words, the exposure of the state's role in sustaining conversion practices negated the state's self-presentation as a guardian of children and the state sought to turn away from such failure through law reform.

The above discussion shows how pain and shame materialise as both individual results of conversion practices and political expressions underpinning action (through law reform) to eliminate conversion practices. This individual-institutional affective relationship invites us to think more carefully about how emotions like pain and shame come to matter in legal interventions designed to cure or repair injury.

II. Manifesting Pain and Repair in Law

Before examining the emotional register of banning 'conversion therapy', I need to define a little more precisely what I mean by the terms 'affect', 'emotion' and 'feeling'. When sharing their personal testimonies about enduring conversion practices, each survivor quoted above named emotions and feelings explicitly as part of their narratives ('painful', 'sad', 'shame'). Emotions and feelings, however, are not self-evident states that are objectively discoverable to either ourselves or others. To undertake an account or analysis of emotion, I need to contextualise how it is conceptualised alongside terms like affect and feeling. Gilles Deleuze, drawing on the work of Baruch Spinoza, talks about affect as an ethology: moments of action, non-conscious experience, or unstructured potentials.[26] Affect is kinetic. It is a relationship between speed and duration. Affects – as the manifestation of these intensities or movements – can be broadly defined as the embodied or intersubjective flows of 'prepersonal feeling'.[27] Affects are movements: the experience of moving and being moved. Affects are not confined to bodies, but rather manifest

---

[24] While my chapter focuses on the relationship between pain and shame in conversion practices, some testimonies also foreground the association between shame and fear. One survivor noted they were 'afraid and confused' about their sexuality and sought out conversion practices in response to fear of being 'kicked out' of (a religious) school if they did not change. See J Beer, 'Testimony on Sexual Orientation Change Efforts' (2015) 19 *Journal of Gay & Lesbian Mental Health* 94, 94.

[25] Ahmed (n 21) 103. In this example, we see how shame is a form of 'internalised social policing': see D Caron, 'Shame on Me: Or The Naked Truth of Me and Marlene Dietrich' in D Halperin and V Traub (eds), *Gay Shame* (Chicago, University of Chicago Press, 2009) 126.

[26] G Deleuze, 'Spinoza and Us' in J Crary and S Kwinter (eds), *Incorporations* (New York, Zone Books, 1992) 626; and G Deleuze and F Guattari, *A Thousand Plateaus: Capitalism and Schizophrenia* (Minneapolis, University of Minnesota Press, 1987) 31–33.

[27] E Shouse, 'Feeling, Emotion, Affect' (2004) 8 *M/C Journal* 1, 1–2.

in the relationship between bodies in any given space.[28] By way of contrast to affect, emotion is framed as a distinctive political and social marker that 'sticks' to a body or community, often produced through subject-object relations.[29] As Patricia Ticineto Clough argues, emotions are considered the narrative subtraction from affect.[30] The former is given social intelligibility while the latter has an excess or remainder that resists representation. Feeling, then, becomes personalised recognition of our affective and emotional histories. As Eric Shouse argues, feelings come to embody a biographical reality because they represent the localised interpretation of our emotional histories and affective sensations.[31] Feeling is political.[32] Feeling is a mode by which we recognise or understand our experiences and communicate about them with others.[33] Emotion and feeling, however, can be taken together as an expression of a more cognitive social and individuating phenomenon, unlike unstructured affects.

In this chapter, I do not press the distinctions between affect, emotion, and feeling. I focus narrowly in this chapter on how emotions and feelings are cultural expressions we give to our bodily states that signify movement and attachment.[34] I look at how emotions have a social or relational quality: they are modes of 'impression' that reflect the experience of coming into contact with objects, spaces, or individuals who 'press' into us.[35] In writing about what emotions do, Sara Ahmed notes that while we are 'moved' by emotion, it also operates as a kind of 'glue' to ground the body to a particular space, sign, or object.[36]

I take this understanding of emotion to think about how pain and shame in particular ground individuals to (legal) institutions in the context of banning conversion practices. In the conversion practices described above, pain and shame function as an organising social principle that foregrounds individual vulnerabilities, attachments to injury, and the promise of repair. For proponents of conversion practices, interventions aimed at suppressing or changing sexual orientation and gender identity manifest through a desire to 'fix' bodies that are deemed to be 'sexually broken' (shame) and are in 'pain' because of their shame. For those who experience these practices, rather than alleviate pain or shame, the stigmatising effects of conversion practices cultivate pain and stigma, and some turn to law for recognition of their pain and shame as a means of triggering reform to eradicate these practices. For those who do not directly encounter conversion practices, the

---

[28] Deleuze (n 26) 628.

[29] Shouse (n 27) 1–2.

[30] PT Clough, 'Introduction' in PT Clough (ed), *The Affective Turn: Theorizing the Social* (Durham, Duke University Press, 2007) 2.

[31] Shouse (n 27) 1.

[32] L Berlant, *The Queen of America Goes to Washington City: Essays on Sex and Citizenship* (Durham, Duke University Press 1997) 5–6.

[33] A Lorde, *Sister Outsider* (Berkeley, Crossing Press, 1984) 59; JW Scott, 'Evidence of Experience' (1991) 17 *Critical Inquiry* 773, 776.

[34] Ahmed (n 21) 11.

[35] ibid 6.

[36] ibid 12.

symbolic degradation that these ongoing practices represent also evoke pain and shame. These practices demean the identities of all LGBTQ+ people by reproducing social images of LGBTQ+ people as disordered, broken and abnormal, which further ground the painful stigma that gets projected onto LGBTQ+ people in other contexts of family, social, and public life.[37] In other words, pain and shame circulate between individuals who are both materially and symbolically degraded by anti-LGBTQ+ stigmas and institutions that seek to harness the pain and shame of LGBTQ+ people being 'sexually broken' through the different modes of 'conversion therapy' they offer LGBTQ+ people. Importantly, too, pain and shame emerge through LGBTQ+ people's rejection of conversion practices and its continued impunity, which triggers banning 'conversion therapy'.

I discussed the logic of how shame works above, but it is important to flesh out the emotional logic of pain. Pain is an embodied experience of alienation or 'againstness', one which we struggle to express through language.[38] Despite linguistic challenges, I argue that pain, when given linguistic expression, reveals our vulnerability to a situation, object, or person. To speak about pain is to make an injury or trauma recognisable to others.[39] This process is co-constitutive. The trauma we recognise brings to the fore the psychic (as well as physical) dimensions of pain.[40] It is important to reiterate that I am not seeking here (as with my discussion of shame above) to provide an authoritative account of what pain means. Instead, I am keen to show how pain organises political and legal investments in banning conversion practices.

Pain is an emotion commonly associated with the shame of conversion practices. Pain in this context might be experienced in 'private' terms (such as the individual who experiences shame from being told they are diseased) while it may also be expressed in 'public' terms (such as the individual who speaks before a parliamentary inquiry about the abuse they have endured). In thinking about the relationship between privatised experiences and public expressions of pain, Lauren Berlant argues that we must distinguish between pain as the shock or surprise that arises from an experience of violence or subordination and 'adversity' as the conditions of that subordination.[41] For Berlant, this public pain must be understood through its relationship to public sentimentality. Public sentimentality works by appropriating the pain of the subordinated subject (LGBTQ+ people who experience the harms of conversion practices either directly or

---

[37] See I Trispiotis and C Purshouse, '"Conversion Therapy" as Degrading Treatment' (2022) 42 *Oxford Journal of Legal Studies* 104, 111–12; M Warner, *The Trouble with Normal: Sex, Politics, and the Ethics of Queer Life* (Cambridge, Harvard University Press, 1999) 1–40.

[38] E Scarry, *The Body in Pain: The Making and Unmaking of the World* (Oxford, Oxford University Press, 1985) 52.

[39] Ahmed (n 21) 21.

[40] A Cvetkovich, *An Archive of Feelings: Trauma, Sexuality, and Lesbian Public Cultures* (Durham, Duke University Press, 2003) 3.

[41] L Berlant, 'The Subject of True Feeling: Pain, Privacy and Politics' in A Sarat and TR Kearns (eds), *Cultural Pluralism, Identity Politics and the Law* (Ann Arbor, University of Michigan Press, 1999) 77.

symbolically) and 'moving' that pain to the consciousness of privileged citizens (non-LGBTQ+ people who feel pain at seeing others' harms). Through such appropriation, we (as non-injured subjects) are 'moved' by the pain of register-ing the pain of others. This movement works to conflate pain with adversity, and in doing so, narrows our ability to respond to the wellbeing of LGBTQ+ people as it foregrounds individual experiences of being pained and shamed through conversion practices. This focus on direct experience, without accounting for the symbolic or structural impacts of stigma facilitated by conversion practices, backgrounds broader discursive conditions that make homo/bi/transphobic stigma and injury possible in the first place.[42] We need to confront the broader context of how social norms and political structures pain or injure LGBTQ+ people if we are to effect an end to these practices.

This kind of public pain, when translated into law reform, generates ethical and political problems. Berlant asserts:

> Feeling politics takes all kinds: it is a politics of protection, reparation, rescue. It claims a hard-wired truth, a core of common sense … It seems to dissolve contradiction and dissent into pods of basic and also higher truth.[43]

Focusing exclusively on individual pain cultivates sites of uncontested truth, where pain exists as a kind of 'obvious thinking' to injustice and pain appeals to 'common sense'.[44] Such appeals are dangerous because they zone feeling beyond contestation or critique. Berlant reminds us that we must not just be critical about how pain is inflicted on minoritised groups, but we must also be critical of how that pain shapes demands for protection and reparation in problematic ways. When an individual's experience of pain is fetishised in law and trans-formed into a legal object, it institutionalises the capacity of law to remedy it. In legislative debates about 'conversion therapy', we ought to pay attention to whose pain is taken seriously (such as survivors of conversion practices) and be mindful of how the debate might reduce the individual to a state of pain while decoupling that suffering from the state's investment in perpetu-ating social stigma, inequality, and violence. Institutionalising responses to this individualised form of violence might obscure two other dimensions of violence that we need to take seriously. First, there is systemic or structural violence: the political and economic conditions that produce identities and bodies through their marginalisation. Second, there is 'symbolic' violence: language which marks and excludes bodies by imposing a particular field of meaning on them.[45]

---

[42] See JL Moghul et al, *Queer Injustice: The Criminalization of LGBT People in the United States* (Boston, Beacon Press, 2011).
[43] Berlant (n 41) 58.
[44] ibid 59.
[45] S Zizek, *Violence: Six Sideways Reflections* (London, Profile Books, 2008) 1–5.

For example, focusing on only those who have experienced 'conversion therapy' directly, obscures its more insidious forms of structural and symbolic violence that affect all LGBTQ+ people. As Ahmed argues, fetishising pain removes injury from its history of production, and commodifies it into a discrete entity with no spatial or temporal character.[46] As Wendy Brown illustrates in her work on political movements, 'wounded attachments' are a poor basis for politics as they rely on 'ressentiment'. Ressentiment is an example of 'slave morality' – one that binds individuals who experience powerlessness to an affective logic of 'returning' (or revenging) that injury against the individuals who caused it by utilising the very power structures that have subordinated them.[47] The ability to 'return' injury to those who have caused it enables the individual to claim a political space, but in doing so, the political foregrounding of injury entrenches the repressive power of state apparatuses.[48]

However, as the debate on banning 'conversion therapy' illustrates, activists have also emphasised the structural logics of homo/bi/transphobia, particularly in relation to stigma, in attempts to seek more carefully tailored legal remedies for its formal banning.[49] Rather than background structural anti-LGBTQ+ violence, the relationships between individual and institutional harm are brought into sharp relief.

The emotional grammar of pain, and its articulation of repair, is central to banning conversion practices – whether it involves 'ressentiment' as paternalist welfare intervention in response to unregulated conversion practices, or, conversely, as anti-statist 'ressentiment' for those who resist legal regulation as a threat to freedom of religion or freedom of speech.[50] In addition to producing an injured (survivors of conversion practices) and injuring subject (conversion practices), such politics generate emotions as well. Specifically, they nurture our 'hurt' feelings by building them with resentment, anger, and righteousness.[51] Brown urges us to rethink the attachments and sentiments these wounds generate. Rather than entrenching identities by painfully relating them to particular forms of injury and repair, we should be open to 'loosening' pain.[52] In order to loosen our attachments to pain and injury, as lawyers and scholars, we need to confront their emotional grammar. By exploring the emotional dynamics of a legislative attempt to ban conversion practices in the UK, the next section uses the affective reading described above to map the emotional grammar of reform.

---

[46] Ahmed (n 21) 32.

[47] W Brown, *States of Injury: Power and Freedom in Late Modernity* (Princeton, Princeton University Press, 1995) 67.

[48] ibid 66.

[49] See, for example, 'SOGICE Survivor Statement' (Sexual Orientation and Gender Identity Change Efforts Survivors, 31 August 2018) www.socesurvivors.com.au/.

[50] Brown (n 47) 67.

[51] ibid 68.

[52] ibid 134.

III. Mapping Emotion in Legislative Debates about Banning 'Conversion Therapy'

A. The Emotional Grammar of 'Conversion Therapy' Bans

State attempts at banning 'conversion therapy' manifest in an array of regulatory forms. These can include professional regulation involving disciplinary sanctions for those who advocate conversion practices, civil sanctions that provide tortious or consumer remedies against those who undertake conversion practices, and penal sanctions like fines and custodial sentences for more serious forms of conversion practices.[53] While existing pro-LGBTQ+ legal scholarship supports some form of legal intervention, there is considerable debate about whether civil or criminal penalties are the most desirable form of intervention.[54]

In order to understand the different impetuses behind each regulatory approach, we ought to think about the emotional claims underpinning them. The justifications for 'conversion therapy' bans are sourced in states' international human rights obligations, which relate to the protection of dignity and prevention of degradation. Legal scholars note that conversion practices function as a form of 'degrading treatment' that undermines a person's moral self-worth.[55] As Ilias Trispiotis and Craig Purshouse note, conversion practices rely on cultivating structural stigmas against, and disempowerment of, LGBTQ+ individuals, by characterising being gay or trans as inferior and deficient identities and characterising being cis or straight as the only desirable identities.[56] States like the UK have an obligation under Article 3 of the European Convention on Human Rights to prohibit such degrading treatment against LGBTQ+ people.[57] The UN Independent Expert with oversight on this issue adds that bans on conversion practices fulfil state duties to guarantee the right to health, protect against discrimination, and ensure the dignity of children.[58] However, some scholars (even those vehemently opposed to conversion practices) evince that rights to freedom of religion and free speech

---

[53] Ashley (n 7) 65–70; R Wagenländer and C Nash, *The Cooper Report: Recommendations on Legislating Effectively for a Ban on Conversion Practices* (Ozanne Foundation, 2021) 2; C Purshouse and I Trispiotis, 'Is "Conversion Therapy" Tortious?' (2022) 42 *Legal Studies* 23.

[54] See J Taglienti, 'Therapists Behind Bars: Criminalizing Gay-to-Straight Conversion Therapy' (2021) 59 *Family Court Review* 185, 189. Taglienti argues for criminal sanctions in contrast to Jones et al (n 11) 65–71 who argue for prioritising civil (tort, consumer, anti-discrimination) remedies instead. In arguing against broad criminal penalties, survivors draw attention to how those who engage in conversion practices are often those who have themselves experienced conversion practices or those who encourage conversion practices are members of their family. See also 'SOGICE Survivor Statement' (n 49).

[55] Trispiotis and Purshouse (n 37); Wagenländer and Nash (n 53).

[56] Trispiotis and Purshouse (n 37) 109–10.

[57] ibid 120.

[58] UNHRC, 'Practices of So-Called "Conversion Therapy": Report of the Independent Expert on Protection Against Violence and Discrimination Based on Sexual Orientation and Gender Identity' (1 May 2020) A/HRC/44/53, 14–17.

need be carefully parsed before pursuing legislative or social interventions against conversion practices given that the primary mode of communicating stigma against LGBTQ+ people is through speech and sermon.[59]

Some scholarship has also addressed the emotional significance of using law to destigmatise minoritised sexual and gender identities through legislative bans on conversion practices. Arcangelo Cella notes that legislation to ban 'conversion therapy' reflects a 'conscientious shift' in law from seeing LGBTQ+ people as group deserving of punishing to a group in need of protection.[60] Other legal scholars note that this shift serves a symbolic function: destigmatising homosexuality by rendering gay people as subjects of protection rather than persecution.[61] The language used in statutes typically reflects a public policy commitment to 'safeguard' young LGBTQ+ people specifically from individual harms but also protect LGBTQ+ communities more generally from social harms and indignities that come from psychopathologising their identities.[62] For example, Malta's law prohibiting conversion practices takes a non-psychologising, capacious approach to defining both concepts like sexual orientation, gender identity, and gender expression and conversion practices which manifest in a variety of stigmatising (pseudo)clinical forms.[63] Even the linguistic shift to referring to this as conversion 'practices', rather than as conversion 'therapy', reflects political desires to challenge the historic sanitisation of the stigmatising consequences of the practice (as referencing it as a form of 'therapy' works linguistically to mask how these practices rely on degrading individual dignity and are the opposite of being therapeutic in character).[64]

The turn to criminal law sanctions to address conversion practices also reflects a redirection of public stigma. If conversion practices aim to stigmatise and shame the deviancy of 'queer lifestyles' by drawing attention to the 'pain' they cause LGBTQ+ people, then bans on 'conversion therapy' seek to stigmatise and shame the perpetrators as homo/bi/transphobic deviants by drawing attention to the pain they cause LGBTQ+ people. As James Taglienti argues, criminal law is the appropriate arena to stigmatise proponents of conversion practices given the affective weight of the harms – high rates of suicidal ideation, anxiety, self-hatred, and depression – associated with these practices.[65]

---

[59] P Newman et al, '"Pray That God Will Change You": The Social Ecology of Bias-Based Bullying Targeting Sexual and Gender Minority Youth-A Qualitative Study of Service Providers and Educators' (2018) 33 *Journal of Adolescent Health* 523.

[60] AS Cella, 'A Voice in the Room: the Function of State Legislative Bans on Sexual Orientation Change Efforts for Minors' (2014) 40 *American Journal of Law & Medicine* 113, 113.

[61] D Friedman, 'The Right to Stay Gay: SB1172 and SOCE' (2014) 25 *Stanford Law & Policy Review* 193, 198; Ashley (n 7) 105.

[62] W Fore, 'A Joyful Heart Is Good Medicine: Sexuality Conversion Bans in the Courts' (2014) 21 *Michigan Journal of Gender & Law* 311, 316; 335.

[63] Ashley (n 7) 61–64.

[64] Wagenländer and Nash (n 53) 2.

[65] Taglienti (n 54) 189.

B. The Westminster Debate on Banning 'Conversion Therapy'

It is in the context of navigating pain and shame – the affective weight of conversion harms – that the British government proposed to ban 'conversion therapy'. Following the results of the National LGBT+ Survey in 2018, the British government developed an action plan which included 'protecting people who are vulnerable to harm' by banning conversion practices.[66] Despite promises of reform, the British government has not yet acted and has announced that any reform would only cover sexual orientation.[67] It is in the context of the exclusion of trans people specifically and delay of reform generally in the UK that I now turn to a recent Westminster legislative debate on banning 'conversion therapy' to unpack the emotional grammar at play.

On 6 May 2022, Samantha Harris created a petition on the UK Government and Parliament website requesting trans people be protected in any future 'conversion therapy' ban, following the British government's refusal to proceed with inclusive legislation. The petitioner's request was framed emotionally with a rationale appealing to shame and pain, 'It's shameful that the UK intends to deliberately exclude trans people from a ban in contrast to the approach taken by many countries, despite trans people being at a greater risk of experiencing the harmful & degrading practices'.[68] The petition received over 100,000 signatures within a month and, under existing parliamentary procedures, was debated on 13 June 2022. Conservative MP Elliot Colburn opened the debate with a broad claim about parliamentary duties, 'we have a duty as parliamentarians to protect the people who we serve from harm, so I urge colleagues to join me in exercising that duty'.[69] The parliamentary debate to ban 'conversion therapy' was not framed in terms of partisan political differences. Rather, the parliamentary debate on the need for including trans people in a 'conversion therapy' ban involved politicians from all parties oscillating between expressions of pain, shame, anxiety, anger, frustration, sadness, fear, optimism, and compassion.[70] It is beyond the scope of this chapter to analyse each emotional expression present in the debate. Instead, I focus on how emotions like pain and shame function as the primary object of concern for legislators and the method by which legislators understand that object. In doing so, I examine how these emotions, alongside more positive affects like hope and compassion, circulate in the legislative debate to problematise the harms of conversion practices while privileging the promise of law reform to remedy those harms.

---

[66] Government Equalities Office, *LGBT Action Plan: Improving the Lives of Lesbian, Gay, Bisexual, and Transgender People* (London, HMSO, 2018) 14.

[67] P Brand, 'Government Pledges Watered down Ban on "Conversion Therapy"' (*ITV News*, 10 May 2022) www.itv.com/news/2022-05-10/government-pledges-watered-down-ban-on-conversion-therapy.

[68] S Harris, 'Ensure Trans People Are Fully Protected under Any Conversion Therapy Ban' (Petitions, UK Government and Parliament, 6 May 2022) https://petition.parliament.uk/petitions/613556.

[69] HC Deb 13 June 2022, vol 716, cols 1WH–40WH, 6WH.

[70] ibid 6WH, 8WH, 19WH, 28 WH, and 36 WH.

Each speech in favour of a trans-inclusive ban on 'conversion therapy' relied on characterising conversion practices in terms of pain and harm. I do not propose to examine each speech in detail. Rather, I select some examples to illustrate how pain and harm come to matter in the debate and the consequences of their articulation. Labour MP Luke Pollard described the practice as 'cruel and abhorrent'.[71] Conservative MP Alicia Kearns said it left 'real and enduring psychological scars'.[72] Liberal Democrat MP Wera Hobhouse noted it was 'harmful and repressive'.[73] While I am not seeking to diagnose the emotional experiences of politicians who made these claims, it is worth noting how individual feelings of pain emerged as political feelings in the debate. To echo my earlier discussion of Berlant, we can observe how politicians like Pollard, Kearns, and Hobhouse were 'moved' by registering the pain of LGBTQ+ people (those stigmatised and abused by conversion practices) and how their registration of that pain involved refracting pain through the debate itself.

The refraction of pain in the legislative debate was a precondition for demanding legal action. SNP MP Alyn Smyth noted, 'we should listen to people's experiences and what they say about the harm done ... there is a clear need for legislation on it'.[74] Kearns emphasised, legislation is about 'holding to account those who cause misery ... and give protections to those who urgently need them'.[75] Labour MP Nia Griffin added, 'at a time when trans people are facing appalling abuse ... we should all be taking a strong stance against transphobia in all its forms'.[76] Each of these painful legislative pleas functioned to frame law reform that sought to ban 'conversion therapy' as urgent and necessary to address the pain and harm of LGBTQ+ people. Pain was both the object of debate (pain of LGBTQ+ people who face conversion practices) and a mode through which the debate took place (pain in hearing and talking about conversion practices).

Shame and humiliation also featured prominently in legislative characterisation of conversion practices. Colburn spoke about the 'degrading and shaming' treatment meted out to those considered sexually deficient.[77] Pollard noted that 'violence and humiliation' follow conversion practices.

Shame functioned in this debate to admonish the state and encourage law reform. Kearns claimed, 'the entire manner of this debate should shame us all'. Noting the way trans people are misrepresented in public discourse, Kearns invited the state to feel shame by exposing how the state had failed LGBTQ+ people through its proliferation of 'misrepresentative' stereotypes.[78] Labour MP Nadia Whittmore commented, 'we will hang our heads in shame at trans people's

---

[71] ibid 8WH.
[72] ibid 9WH.
[73] ibid 19WH.
[74] ibid 11WH.
[75] ibid 10WH.
[76] ibid 28WH.
[77] ibid 4WH.
[78] ibid 8WH.

treatment in decades to come'.[79] Labour MP Kate Osborne said, 'history ... will judge those who fail to protect our trans community now'.[80] Whittmore's and Osborne's comments took a historical route (through discussions of section 28 and the AIDS crisis respectively) to weight the state's failures to protect trans people and, in doing so, shamed the state (of which they are part) for not realising its obligations to protect vulnerable people (as Colburn noted at the start of the debate). This inaction left the UK on the 'wrong' side of history.[81] Colburn emphasised that 'it's shameful that the UK intends to deliberately exclude trans people from a ban in contrast to the approach taken by many countries, despite trans people being at a greater risk of experiencing the harmful and degrading practices'.[82] Colburn's remarks took a geographic turn to weigh the state's failures to protect especially vulnerable trans people and, in doing so, shamed the state for not acting on the harms facing trans people. In the debate, shame was an object of scrutiny for legislators who observed how conversion practices demeaned and stigmatised LGBTQ+ people. Shame, moreover, was a mode for understanding the impetus behind (trans inclusive) law reform as the emotional expressions of politicians shamed the (British) state by drawing attention to its failures to protect trans people.

While pain and shame dominate the legislative debate, fear and anxiety were also notable expressions that drew attention to the precarity of trans people facing conversion practices. Osborne noted the need for legislation to 'close all loopholes to prevent the possibility of abuse continuing'.[83] For Pollard, exclusion of trans people from a legislative ban on conversion practices 'would be a loophole that would allow these practices in through the back door'.[84] Osborne's and Pollard's statement projected legislators into the future through the anticipation of forthcoming injuries if the ban were not inclusive.[85] Fear in this context was expressed through the anticipation of LGBTQ+ people's pain (through the continuation of conversion practices). Reflecting on the delay of waiting to consider the inclusion of trans people, Labour MP Annaliese Dodds warned, 'I genuinely fear for the impact in the interim on trans people, who surely only want to live their lives in dignity and free from abuse, just like everybody else'.[86] Here, the anticipation of injury was rendered through the state's delay in pursuing reform and the projected harmful consequences for trans people.

Legislative fears also cautioned against overbroad and unclear reform in relation to trans people. Conservative MP Jackie Doyle-Price claimed, 'we need to ensure that we are not putting people on to irreversible care pathways that will do

[79] ibid 30WH.
[80] ibid 15WH.
[81] ibid 15WH.
[82] ibid 1WH.
[83] ibid 16WH.
[84] ibid 4WH.
[85] Ahmed (n 21) 65.
[86] HC Deb (n 69) 36WH.

them harm'.[87] Alba MP Neale Hanvey continued, 'encouraging somebody down a path that could lead to irreversible medical decisions without the provision of such information and the opportunity to consider all possibilities is an unforgivable dereliction of professional duty'.[88] Fear emerged in these comments through Doyle-Price's and Hanvey's comments anticipating a hurt to gender 'confused' people who could be coerced into undesired healthcare.[89] Numerous MPs responded to these fearful interventions by noting that any legislative proposal would not interfere with clinical conversations that allow young trans people to explore their gender with therapists.[90]

Positive affect also underlined the push to have a trans inclusive ban on 'conversion therapy'. SNP David Linden asserted, 'I do not believe that we can talk about practising love to other people while pursuing a ban on "conversion therapy" that excludes trans people'.[91] Dodds implored 'we can … ensure that every person in the UK is treated with dignity and respect, including LGBT people, and that they will always have the ability to love and live as they need to'.[92] Through each of these statements, legislators enact hope – an attachment to a fantasy of the future – where LGBTQ+ people can thrive as a result of a prohibition against stigmatising conversion practices.[93] The articulations of hope and compassion in the debate rendered the promise of law reform to ameliorate the negative emotions (pain, shame, anxiety, fear) outlined previously.

Taken together, the speeches highlight how emotions function as a grammar that frames a legislative object of discussion ('conversion therapy') and the legislative mode through which that discussion takes place (debating the best way to ban 'conversion therapy'). Compassion – as a recognition of another's suffering and desire to repair it – manifested in every speech in the debate that recognised the harms LGBTQ+ people face from conversion practices and the pressing need for parliament to remedy these harms.[94] By failing to cultivate compassion in the debate and pursue hopeful legislation that could reach a future where LGBTQ+ people could live free from conversion abuse, legislators expressed pain (at the harms of conversion practices), shame (at failures to address conversion practices), and fear (at ongoing conversion practices). All the legislators who spoke in

---

[87] ibid 18WH.

[88] ibid 25WH.

[89] It is beyond the scope of this chapter to discuss the affectively charged context underpinning the legal regulation of gender affirming healthcare. For discussion on how anxiety features in this context, see S Raj, 'Alleviating Anxiety and Cultivating Care: Young Trans People in the Family Court of Australia' (2019) 45 *Australian Feminist Law Journal* 111. For discussion on the efficacy and protocols involved in gender affirming healthcare, see MA Hildago et al, 'The Gender Affirmative Model: What We Know and What We Aim to Learn' (2013) 56 *Human Development* 285.

[90] See the interventions of Elliot Colburn MP, Alicia Kearns MP, Jacob Young MP, and Wera Hobhouse MP: HC Deb (n 69).

[91] ibid 29WH.

[92] ibid 36WH.

[93] L Berlant, *Cruel Optimism* (Durham, Duke University Press 2011) 2.

[94] Ahmed (n 21) 11.

favour of reform presented legislation as a hopeful vehicle to drive their concerns and anxieties about conversion practices towards a destination or future where those practices were eradicated. Yet, this hopeful promise of law reform relied on drafting legislation that could both contain the pain, shame, fear, and anxiety of conversion practices (which harm LGBTQ+ people) without triggering anxieties, frustrations, and fears about legislation overreaching into 'sensitive' conversations about sexuality or gender (which harm all people).

This emotional tension, however, is not easily resolved and nor can it be. Legislative debates are necessarily emotionally fraught terrains. In saying that, if we understand the emotional grammar of law reform, we can confront those tensions more explicitly and craft law reform that is fit for purpose to end conversion practices. This is particularly important if we are to utilise law, alongside other social or cultural interventions that might be needed. The final section outlines how a reparative reading of law reform can prove useful in our pursuits to ban conversion practices.

IV. Reparative Reading of Law Reform

In this final section, I turn to 'reparative reading' as a way to take seriously the emotional harms of pain and shame that are the result of conversion practices, while recognising how those emotions are refracted in surprising ways in law. Pain and shame offer us an emotional lens via which to think reparatively about how we respond more broadly to homo/bi/transphobic cultures that seek to suppress or 'cure' LGBTQ+ lives. As Eve Sedgwick suggests, a reparative reading is an ethical disposition to a text that seeks surprise and possibility rather than certainty and closure.[95] Sedgwick argues:

> To read from a reparative position is to surrender the knowing, anxious paranoid determination that no horror, however apparently unthinkable, shall ever come to the reader as new; to a reparatively positioned reader, it can seem realistic and necessary to experience surprise … Because the reader has room to realise that the future may be different from the present, it is also possible for her to entertain such profoundly painful, profoundly relieving, ethically crucial possibilities as the past, in turn, could have happened differently to the way it actually did.[96]

Reparative reading relies on loosening our 'paranoid' disposition as legal scholars towards uncovering the true meaning of an object and the structures that generate that object (in law these objects might include legislation, case law, and regulation). Before we can undertake a reparative reading, we first need to understand how a 'paranoid' approach to analysis inhibits our ability to learn new things.

[95] Sedgwick (n 21) 123–51.
[96] ibid 146.

A 'paranoid analysis' of conversion practices, for example, exposes the existence
of an underlying system that causes harm (such as homophobic religious institutions) and prescriptively seeks to find methods to address those harms (such as law
reforms designed to ameliorate conversion practices).[97] In the context of banning
conversion practices, legislative interventions rely on a discursive demand for
'truth' on two fronts. As the legislative debate in the UK on ensuring trans inclusion in a 'conversion therapy' ban illustrates, the discourse on banning conversion
practices relies on characterising sexual orientation or gender identity as immutable (a 'truth' that is objectively discoverable and unchangeable) and characterising
law as a secure system of regulation (a 'truth' that law can prohibit what it purports
to criminalise). Much of the pro-LGBTQ+ legal and psychological scholarship on
conversion practices discussed above also takes a 'paranoid' approach, because it
anticipates, and challenges, structures perceived as subordinating (in this context
we can see these systems as heteronormativity within religious and pastoral
institutions).[98] A paranoid reading is important and necessary work to uncover
the stigmatising harms of conversion practices.[99]

However, in doing so, the reification of this form of analysis refuses openness to
surprise. In contradistinction, Sedgwick suggests we might wish to pursue an 'affect
theory', one that relies on 'selective scanning' and 'amplification' of emotion (by the
mapping the emotional grammar I discussed above) in order to resist the tendency
to aggregate or taxonomise in order to 'prove' an object of thought conclusively.[100]
A reparative approach, then, is willing to make affective or motivational errors
by questioning the wishes, desires, and outcomes that underscore what we seek
to address in the first place. Reparative reading, unlike the paranoid one, brings
us a means of 'healing' existing problems of producing thought through active
reimagining what is possible and affirming the potential of something else. In a
legislative debate about 'conversion therapy', reparative critical strategies enable us
to reflect (rather than simply 'expose') that which is hidden or refused visibility by
politicians and scholars in their pursuits to ban the practice.[101] We do not simply
expose what 'interests' or 'moves' us, but we engage with moments of experience
that are far more banal (such 'banality' can emerge by focusing on the emotional
dynamics of law rather than turning to high level doctrine or human rights principle). It becomes crucial to question our attachments to particular ways of relating
to objects/texts (in this case law reform) and be open to the 'surprises' that such
a process engenders. This is not about succumbing to relativism or abandoning
normative critique. Rather, it is a way of taking the pervasive harms of 'conversion

---

[97] ibid 107–108.
[98] ibid 135–36.
[99] On the importance of combining paranoid and reparative readings, see B Bargetz, 'The Distribution
of Emotions: Affective Politics of Emancipation' (2015) 30 *Hypatia* 580.
[100] Sedgwick (n 21) 135–36.
[101] ibid 140.

therapy' seriously while suspending our normative (legal) certainty about how we might end these harms.[102]

In the legislative debate about banning trans 'conversion therapy', I want to 'amplify' the articulation of pain and what it reveals about both conversion practices and law. In their speeches, Kearns, Pollard, and Colborne take homo/bi/transphobic pain and harm as self-evident consequences of conversion practices. The pain of anti-gay or anti-trans stigma, the pain in feeling that your identity is damaged, the pain associated with identity marginalisation that was evident in each speech speak to pains beyond conversion practices. These homo/bi/transphobic harms are the feature of routine social, familial, and educational practices that diminish LGBTQ+ lives.[103] Yet, the pain articulated in the legislative debate distinguishes itself from the pain that LGBTQ+ people routinely face. In the debate, the then Minister for Equalities, Mike Freer MP, even went so far to say, 'there is nothing wrong with a parent disagreeing with their child's trans status or sexual orientation'.[104] While Freer and other MPs spoke painfully about conversion practices as torturous or abhorrent, their expressions of pain did not register how parental disagreement itself could amount to a conversion practice. Psychological literature already notes how parental pressure, even if framed as concern or disagreement, can create a hostile environment for young LGBTQ+ people who subsequently inhibit themselves.[105] We might think of this 'disciplining environment' as part of a 'conversion culture' (even if it is not a discrete conversion practice).[106]

By reading reparatively, we see how the legislative articulation of pain is a reparative gesture aimed at recognising and remedying the harms of some conversion practices (such as clinical counselling to suppress someone's LGBTQ+ identity or religious exorcisms which might result in physical harms). Yet, the failure to feel pained by other interpersonal encounters which result in homophobic pain and shame (such as familial disagreement or hostile religious views that pressure people to stop identifying as LGBTQ+) reveals the limits of the current legislative discourse of legal reparation. Reading pain reparatively in this context opens us up to affirming the possibilities of law in prohibiting conversion practices while illuminating that law's reparative possibilities are not enough to address

---

[102] Brenda Cossman makes these points ably in her reparative reading of legal and political responses to #MeToo. See B Cossman, *The New Sex Wars: Sexual Harm in the #MeToo Era* (New York, NYU Press, 2021) 141–60.

[103] For a discussion of how routine familial interventions create conditions of social pressure to conform to 'normalcy', see C Ryan et al, 'Parent Initiated Sexual Orientation Change Efforts with LGBT Adolescents: Implications for Young Mental Health and Adjustment' (2020) 67 *Journal of Homosexuality* 159.

[104] HC Deb (n 69) 38WH.

[105] Herek (n 8) 695.

[106] Michel Foucault has written extensively on how spatial architectures police bodies and cultivate forms of self-governance. See M Foucault, *Discipline and Punish: the Birth of the Prison* (New York, Pantheon Books, 1977).

the more insidious homo/bi/transphobic harms within conversion culture. That is, we can accept the imperfections of law in failing to resolve some of the more insidious forms of homo/bi/transphobic harm while also accepting the practical and symbolic benefits of regulating professional psychological bodies or specific conversion practices to prevent some of these homo/bi/transphobic harms from materialising.[107]

Reading shame reparatively also affirms what law needs to do in order to repair what I call 'conversion cultures' (as the social and political conditions that give rise to conversion practices) structured by homo/bi/transphobic stigmas. The legislative debate fixated on shame as the individual emotional results of the stigmatic harm enabled by conversion practices (when LGBTQ+ people are deemed 'broken' or deficient as part of counselling or pastoral care). This experience of shame was recognised and refracted through the legislative debate. Kearns, Whittmore, and Osborne each spoke explicitly about their shame at not only having to debate the need to ban 'conversion therapy' generally but also how the deliberate exclusion of trans people from a 'conversion therapy' ban was shameful. These expressions of shame emerged from a specific articulation of the state (manifested here as parliament seeking inclusive reform) coming up against another articulation of itself (manifested here as the government refusing inclusive reform) as it bore witness to its failure to realise its purported goals of protecting vulnerable people.[108]

By reading shame reparatively, we might question whether law can realise this desire and the answer might surprise us. Homo/bi/transphobic stigmas are inherent to protected forms of religious, familial, and political expression, which any purported ban would not cover.[109] Law has sustained – and continues to sustain – violence against LGBTQ+ people.[110] Opening the law to shame, to read its expressions of shame, points to the ambivalence we should have towards law reform. Could a law stop a parent from using guilt to manipulate their trans child to avoid transition? Could a law prevent a preacher from claiming homosexuality was sinful to a room of students in a religious school? While law's shame might encourage legal action to counter discrete homo/bi/transphobic conversion practices that reach a particular threshold of severity (as evident in the legislative debate discussed above), that reparative action is unlikely to reach diffuse practices that weave into everyday practices like parenting or teaching which are not the subject of current 'conversion therapy' bans. Shame here pulls

---

[107] Brenda Cossman outlines what 'reparative regulation' might look like in the context of sexual harm. See Cossman (n 102) 163–95.

[108] The state manifests through different actors across different scales and registers. See D Cooper, *Feeling Like a State: Desire, Denial, and the Recasting of Authority* (Durham, Duke University Press, 2019) 55.

[109] For a discussion of criminal law's failure to address structural homo/bi/transphobia, see Raj (n 4) 50–72.

[110] Stanley (n 13) 21–40.

in different directions: it pulls the state towards a politics of conformity where we seek to cover over that which makes us blush (law reform as a way to cover state failures to prevent LGBTQ+ stigma) and towards a politics of confrontation (state failure to realise a norm opens the state to question the legitimacy of the norm itself).[111]

We can hold onto pain and shame in our reading of legislative responses to conversion practices and use these affects to illuminate how we might challenge homo/bi/transphobia. In registering the pain and shame faced by LGBTQ+ people who endure attempts to 'correct' their identities, the responses of legislators discussed above challenged homo/bi/transphobic stigma by presuming sexuality and gender were fixed bodily categories that could not (as well as ought not) be changed. However, this emotional characterisation obscures how sexuality and gender are politically and socially organised in fluid and dynamic ways, which are reflected across human existence.[112] To say this is not to imply that an individual's sexuality or gender is mutable like one's hairstyle or clothing. And this does not mean we need to abandon legal repair as means to ameliorate the pain and shame faced by LGBTQ+ people, nor do we need to concede that sexuality or gender are capable of 'reorientation'. Indeed, as my discussion of the legal scholarship on conversion practices made clear, regulatory infrastructure has played an important role in preventing some deceptive consumer practices, ineffective forms of psychotherapy, and abusive religious rituals that target LGBTQ+ life.

However, by refusing to let go of either pain or shame and taking an emotionally critical approach to the reparative promise of law reform, we are brought closer to the everyday manifestations of conversion cultures that take shape as homo/bi/transphobic family environments, school settings, and social life that stigmatise LGBTQ+ people. We do not have to objectify LGBTQ+ people's pain or shame through law's narrow terms of engagement as evidenced in the Westminster legislative debate on banning 'conversion therapy'. We should instead pursue a reparative approach to law. This approach would foreground shame and pain to engage civil remedies (such as tort law, professional governance, and consumer regulation) to ban conversion practices. This approach would also confront the limits of law, particularly criminalisation, for repairing harm while embracing non-legal restorative approaches (such as professional training, conflict mediation, and community oversight) to address the systemic homo/bi/transphobic stigma at the heart of 'conversion therapy'.[113]

---

[111] D Gould, 'The Shame of Gay Pride in Early AIDS Activism' in Halperin and Traub (n 25) 225.

[112] See also JM Victor, 'Regulating Sexual Orientation Change Efforts: The California Approach, Its Limitations, and Potential Alternatives' (2014) 123 *Yale Law Journal* 1532.

[113] For discussion of regulatory alternatives to criminal justice, see Cossman (n 102) 167–84.

V. Conclusion

Debates on 'conversion therapy' and legal attempts to proscribe it are emotionally contested. In thinking about my own emotions in relation to the topic of my critical inquiry when writing this chapter, I cannot ignore the anger I felt towards the UK's inaction to remedy homo/bi/transphobic abuse nor my sadness at reading numerous accounts of those who have been harmed by interventions designed to 'correct' their gender identity or sexual orientation. A memoir like *Boy Erased*, for example, evinces how affecting it is to think and write about conversion practices. It is precisely because these issues feel so emotionally pressing to address that I suggest we turn critically to emotion in order to not only take seriously the emotions of those who experience such abuse but also to understand how emotions structure the socio-legal parameters of what we are talking about when we seek to use law to ban 'conversion therapy'.

In opening the chapter, I examined how conversion practices organise around emotions like pain and shame. Proponents of conversion practices seek to address the pain of sexual or social trauma that they perceive leads to sexual or gender 'confusion'. I noted how these proponents seek to alleviate the shame people feel as a result of their 'confusion' through interventions designed to make them 'normal' by changing or suppressing their sexual orientation or gender identity. I then examined how the consequences of these conversion practices also cultivate pain and shame in LGBTQ+ people. Psychotherapeutic or spiritual interventions that seek to 'heal' LGBTQ+ people stigmatise and shame them through processes that deem them broken, corrupt, or deficient. Meanwhile, LGBTQ+ people feel pain, as well as shame, at being burdened by their purported failure to 'change' and be 'normal' (not to mention the physically damaging consequences of more invasive conversion practices).

By navigating each of these differing registers of pain and shame, I was able to consider how these emotions are recognised and refracted through law. Using the work of Sara Ahmed, Lauren Berlant, and Wendy Brown, I was able to map the emotional grammar of a recent 'conversion therapy' debate in the UK parliament about the inclusion of trans people. Specifically, I drew out how legislative recognition of the pain and shame involved in conversion practices triggered law's reparative gestures to ameliorate harm. Yet, legislative expressions of pain and shame have limited reach when recognising or remedying conversion practices. Mapping the emotional grammar captures the socio-legal tensions between individual and institutional expressions of pain and shame.

To confront the pain and shame of conversion cultures that promote anti-LGBT+ stigma, and associated forms of gendered and sexual policing, require us as scholars, activists, and lawyers to develop more creative forms of dialogue, play, and denunciation to ameliorate the harmful effects of these practices.[114]

---

[114] For creative engagements with law and governance, see D Cooper, 'Towards an Adventurous Institutional Politics: The Prefigurative "As If" and the Repurposing of What's Real' (2020) 68 *The Sociological Review* 893. For work on alternative holistic psychological interventions to promote LGBT wellbeing, see Herek (n 8) 693.

Reading law reparatively is vital if we are to confront the possibilities/limits of law's reparative capacity. Holding space to reflect on pain and shame in conversion practices, and how law reform reacts to them, illuminates the structural conditions that maintain homo/bi/transphobic stigma in society. These cultures sit behind conversion practices and require us to critically feel law to resist them.

PART II

The Scope of a Ban

5

'Conversion Therapy' and Children's Rights

NOAM PELEG

'Conversion therapy' is an umbrella term used to describe a range of practices that have one goal: making LGBTQ+ children straight and/or cis-gendered. When it comes to children, 'conversion therapy' is offered by adults to other adults, primarily parents, with the promise to transform children's sexual orientation, gender identity or gender expressions.[1] As the recipients of these practices, children are usually, but not always, coerced to attend these so-called therapeutic sessions by their parents.

'Conversion therapy' has been subject to extensive debates in law and policy over the last couple of years, with some countries banning all, or some forms, of these practices, while others have stopped short of regulating it.[2] Most, if not all, of the discussions about the legality of these practices centre on adults, their rights and interests, whether it is human or civil rights frameworks, such as discussing parents' or providers' right to religious freedom or to free speech, or their legal positionalities under other bodies of the law such as tort law, to name one example.[3]

But while children are victimised by 'conversion therapy', their rights and interests are often overlooked and forgotten, let alone being front and centre of the discussion about the legality of these practices. This chapter seeks to centre children in the discussions about the legality of 'conversion therapy' by taking a child-centred approach[4] to analyse 'conversion therapy' from a children's rights

---

[1] TC Graham, 'Conversion Therapy: A Brief Reflection on the History of the Practice and Contemporary Regulatory Efforts' (2019) 52 *Creighton Law Review* 419, 420.

[2] For a review see F Ashley, *Banning Transgender Conversion Practices: A Legal and Policy Analysis* (Vancouver, University of British Columbia, 2022).

[3] I Trispiotis and C Purshouse, '"Conversion Therapy" As Degrading Treatment' (2022) 42 *Oxford Journal of Legal Studies* 104; S Boulos and C Gonzáles-Cantón, 'No Such Thing as Acceptable Sexual Orientation Change Efforts: An International Human rights Analysis' (2021) 32 *Women and Criminal Justice* 185; PCW Chan, 'No, It Is not Just a Phase: An Adolescent's Right to Sexual Minority Identity under the United Nations Convention on the Rights of the Child' (2006) 10 *The International Journal of Human Rights* 161; IY Nugraha, 'The Compatibility of Sexual Orientation Change Efforts with International Human Rights Law' (2017) 35 *Netherland Quarterly of Human Rights* 176.

[4] N Peleg, 'Marginalisation by the Court: The Case of Roma Children and the European Court of Human Rights' (2018) 18 *Human Rights Law Review* 111, 112.

perspective, using the 1989 UN Convention on the Rights of the Child (UNCRC) as a normative framework. In doing so, it seeks to answer two questions: First, do these so-called therapeutic treatments constitute a violation of children's rights? Second, running in parallel to the first question, can 'conversion therapy' be considered justified if it is a lawful manifestation of parents' autonomy to raise their children, including to guide or influence their children's sexual orientation and gender identity?

A word about terminology, before we start: when talking about children, I refer to anyone below the age of 18, as per Article 1 of the UNCRC. I also use the term LGBTQ+ children while recognising the diverse experiences of children and the heterogeneity of this cohort of children in terms of identities, including gender identities, gender expressions and sexual orientations, the evolving and changing nature of children's identity and the intersectionality with race, religion, ethnicity, (dis)abilities and socio-economic status. This term should be read in an inclusive way, with the aim to respect the different experiences of children in exploring, questioning, coming to terms with, establishing, debating, and forming their own identities. In a similar vein, the analysis of children's rights in this chapter is done in broad terms too, while recognising that the theoretical meaning of rights should be contextualised in children's everyday living. The term 'conversion therapy' is used for convenience only, but refers to practices that are not a recognised therapeutic practice by any established, or reliable, medical association or regulatory body, and – importantly – convert no one.[5] Unfortunately, the branding campaign to legitimise 'conversion therapy' has been successful, and the supporters of these practices have managed to mainstream this title, thus presenting it as something that it is most certainly not.

Adults' discomfort and disapproval of children being and behaving in ways that do not meet heteronormative imaginations are not new, and attempts to alter children's non heterosexual identities and diverse identity expressions are not new either. For example, in her book, Julian Gill-Peterson charts a gloomy history of trans children, and shows how adults have tried to change children's sexual and gender identities using pseudo medical treatments since, at least, the beginning of the twentieth century.[6] These efforts have historically included the medicalisation of non-gender conforming children, and coercing them to a range of biological and behavioural treatments, including surgical interventions (lobotomies, castrations, clitoridectomies, and cauterisation of the spinal cord), convulsive electric shock treatments and hormonal injections. The behavioural methods included cognitive therapy and aversive conditioning, such as pairing electric shocks or nausea-inducing drugs while presenting homoerotic images, to create a psychological linkage between pain and sexual interaction between

---

[5] J Ozanne, "'Conversion Therapy', Spiritual Abuse and Human Rights' (2021) 3 *European Human Rights Law Review* 241, 242.

[6] J Gill-Peterson, *Histories of the Transgender Child* (Minneapolis, University of Minnesota Press, 2018).

same sex partners. As Gill-Peterson shows, for decades, medical doctors and other health care professionals were at the forefront of these methods, with the psychiatric profession only recently condemning these treatments, classifying aversive therapies as unethical and inhumane.[7]

A more common form of 'conversion therapy' these days is called 'speech therapy', where counsellors, some acting on their religious standing in the community such as priests but without having any professional training in psychology or psychiatry, tell 'patients' that due to their behaviour or identity they are alone, unnatural, and abomination(s) to be rejected.[8] This, like in cases of attempted physical conversion, can result in anxiety, depression, shame, hopelessness, and suicide.[9] The American Academy of Child and Adolescent Psychiatry (AACAP) concluded that there is no evidence to support the application of any 'therapeutic intervention' as non-heterosexual orientation is not pathological. Furthermore, based on the scientific evidence, the AACAP determined that any so-called therapeutic interventions with the intent of promoting a particular sexual orientation and/or gender identity as a preferred outcome lack scientific credibility and clinical utility. The AACAP also stated that there is ample evidence to suggest that such interventions are harmful, and when used on adolescents can be life threatening.[10] Another study shows that survivors of 'conversion therapy' are 'more than twice as likely to report having attempted suicide',[11] and some recipients describe the experience as torture.[12] For these reasons the UN Special Rapporteur on Torture and Other Cruel, Inhuman or Degrading Treatment or Punishment formally classified 'conversion therapy' as a form of torture in 2016.[13] Despite this classification, the question of the compatibility of 'conversion therapy' with human rights has begun to generate scholarly interest only recently, and children and their rights, as mentioned before are, by and large, left at the margin of these discussions.

The UN Committee on the Rights of the Child, which monitors the implementation of the UNCRC, gave scant attention to the rights of LGBTQ+ children and to the question of 'conversion therapy' over the years,[14] even when reviewing state parties where these practices are widespread and legal. It was only

---

[7] ibid.

[8] MD Bracken, 'Torture Is Not Protected Speech: Free Speech Analysis of Bans on Gay Conversion Therapy' (2020) 63 *Washington University Law Journal and Policy* 325.

[9] MA George, 'Expressive Ends: Understanding Conversion Therapy Bans' (2017) 68 *Alabama Law Review* 793, 817.

[10] The American Academy of Child and Adolescent Psychiatry, 'Conversion Therapy' (2018), www.aacap.org/aacap/Policy_Statements/2018/Conversion_Therapy.aspx.

[11] A Green et al, 'Self-Reported Conversion Efforts and Suicidality among US LGBTQ Youths and Young Adults, 2018' (2020) 8 *American Journal of Public Health* 1221.

[12] Bracken (n 8) 325.

[13] UNHRC, 'Report of the Special Rapporteur on Torture and Other Cruel, Inhuman or Degrading Treatment or Punishment' (5 January 2016) UN Doc A/ HRC/31/57, para 5.

[14] P Gerber and A Timoshanko, 'Is the UN Committee on the Rights of the Child Doing Enough to Protect the Rights of LGBT Children and Children with Same-Sex Parents?' (2021) 21 *Human Rights Law Review* 786.

in 2016 that the Committee said that 'all adolescents [should enjoy] freedom of expression and respect for their physical and psychological integrity, gender identity and emerging autonomy. It condemns the imposition of so-called "treatments" to try to change sexual orientation and forced surgeries or treatments on intersex adolescents'.[15] While condemning this practice is important, the Committee fell short in analysing the compatibility of 'conversion therapy' with UNCRC, let alone offering its own viewpoint on its compatibility with children's rights.

The chapter continues with the following structure. The next section reviews and analyses recent legal challenges to bans on 'conversion therapy' that utilised human and civil rights language. Critically engaging with the ways in which Courts, especially in the United States, have dealt with the issue, this section highlights that while children are the main victims of 'conversion therapy', their rights and interests have been overlooked. Against this background, the next section will offer a child's rights analysis to 'conversion therapy'. Utilising the UNCRC, the section will focus on issues of harm and abuse, protection from torture, and the child's rights to identity and development. It will then argue that 'conversion therapy' clearly violates a range of rights of the child not only due to the harm that it causes but also because it undermines the child's right to develop and preserve their own identity, including sexual orientation and gender identity. The final section discusses whether parental autonomy can nonetheless be invoked as a justification for subjugating children to 'conversion therapy' when a child's parents are not happy with their child's sexual orientation, gender identity or gender expression.

I. Current Legal and Regulatory Frameworks

This section focuses on how courts in different countries, mainly the United States, have dealt with human and civil rights based claims against regulatory effort to ban 'conversion therapy'. It shows that while the rights of adults are often invoked and discussed, children and their rights are mentioned rarely, if at all. This is the case even though children's victimhood is often cited as justification for limiting alleged rights of adults, providers or parents alike, when banning 'conversion therapy'. This invocation of victimhood perpetuates the image of children as eternal victims, cements their image as lacking in agency and, paradoxically, as both nonsexual and as heterosexual beings.

Attempts to ban or limit access to 'conversion therapy' usually take one of three forms: ban certain types of providers via administrative law; ban certain types of 'therapy' via criminal law; and offer tortious compensation for those who were

---

[15] UN Committee on the Rights of the Child, 'General Comment No 20: The Implementation of the Rights of the Child During Adolescence' (6 December 2016) UN Doc CRC/C/GC/20, para 10.

subject to this form of abuse. Some laws ban specific types of 'therapy', usually the more overt physical types.[16] However, religious actors are often exempt from such limitations and can continue to offer 'spiritual' therapy in the name of protecting their religious freedom. In practice this exemption means that many, if not most, providers are permitted to continue and operate, as religious and 'spiritual' leaders comprise most of the abusers.[17] A more common, and practical, measure is to prohibit medical professionals, mainly registered psychologists, from offering this service and criminalising those who nonetheless continue to offer this practice. In other words, we either see public law attempting to limit or ban 'conversion therapy' by regulating the conduct of 'service deliveries', or attempting to use criminal law to criminalise some forms of therapies.[18] A third option attempts to utilise private law measures, usually in the form of cases brought by victims, or potential victims, against individual providers, asking for tortious compensation.[19]

In the USA, California was the first state to prohibit licensed mental health professionals from providing 'conversion therapy' to minors, and soon after other states, and some local municipalities, have followed.[20] Legal challenges to these laws were based on three key arguments: freedom of speech and religious freedom, both entrenched in the First Amendment to the US Constitution, and parental autonomy. All these arguments focus on adults: either as treatment providers, who claim to hold the First Amendment rights, or as a child's parents, who claim to hold parental autonomy that gives them the power to subjugate their children to – and to consent on their behalf for – these so-called treatments.

Free speech challenges centre on the argument that therapy is essentially a form of speech, as it is conducted verbally (hence the branding of 'talk therapy').[21] As such, it is a protected act under the First Amendment, and banning it is therefore constitutionally invalid. Courts struggled with the attempt to draw a distinction between therapy as an action and therapy as an act of communication, differences which are relevant to the decision whether the First Amendment applies or not, and the subsequent argument that 'talking therapy' is a form of speech, and therefore constitutionally protected, while 'action therapy' can be restricted. The Ninth Circuit Court of Appeal, for example, when deciding a case challenging the constitutional validity of the California ban on 'conversion therapy', concluded that the ban centres on regulating professional conduct. It held that the professional regulation is not an unconstitutional limitation of free speech.[22] By way of contrast, the Third Circuit Court of Appeal, when reviewing New Jersey's ban on

---

[16] Graham (n 1).

[17] ibid.

[18] Bracken (n 8) 325.

[19] Trispiotis and Purshouse (n 3) 107.

[20] JJ Lapin, 'The Legal Status of Conversion Therapy' (2020) 22 *Georgetown Journal of Gender and the Law* 251.

[21] 'First Amendment – Professional Speech – Eleventh Circuit Invalidates Minor Conversion Therapy Bans – *Otto v. City of Boca Raton*, 981 F.3d 854 (11th Cir. 2020)' (2021) 134 *Harvard Law Review* 2863.

[22] *Pickup v Brown*, 740 F3d 1208 (9th Cir 2014), cert denied, 573 US 945 (2014).

'conversion therapy', ruled that providers of 'conversion therapy' are using speech to provide a specialised service, which is designed to alter the patients' behaviours and thoughts. As such, the providers are exercising professional speech, rather than a conduct.[23] And this form of speech, the Court ruled, as with any other speech, is protected under the Constitution.

While some forms of 'conversion therapy', Mason Bracken claims, involve spoken words, nonetheless it is not 'speech' for the purposes of the First Amendment, but rather a means of torture.[24] The same analysis applies under international human rights law, where so-called medical interventions like this fall under the provisions on torture and cruel, inhuman and degrading treatment.[25] Further, the logic behind this prohibition is to protect the patient from abuse, rather than focusing on the administrator of treatment. This approach, unlike the freedom of expression argument, which centres around the provider, focuses on the victim, and in our case the child.

Lapin takes this argument further, arguing that it would be illogical for therapy effectuated by speech to be given greater protection than the same therapy effectuated by physical treatment. Consider that practitioners used to induce nausea, vomiting, or paralysis; provide electric shocks; or have an individual snap an elastic band around the wrist when aroused by same-sex erotic images or thoughts. Practitioners now reframe desires, redirect thoughts, or use hypnosis, with the goal of changing sexual arousal, behaviour, and orientation. 'Why', he asks, 'should a therapist be more protected when he screams "faggot" or "homo" at a client in a mock locker room than when he directs the client to snap an elastic band on his wrist each time the client is attracted to a man?'[26]

The US case law continued to develop around questions of the meaning of professional speech, what sort of speech should be considered as such, the differentiation between speech and conduct, and the subsequent states' power to regulate one and not the other.[27] This constitutional law issue is not the focus of this chapter, but rather the fact that in all of those cases, the debates centred around the rights of adults, mostly the rights of therapy providers. Only a fraction of the cases were concerned with the rights of adults' 'patients', who argued that a ban on 'conversion therapy' violates their own constitutional rights as it prevents them from benefiting from the providers' protected speech.

The religious freedom argument shifts the focus from the action to the humans. The core of this claim is that individuals have the right to exercise their religion without government interference, and that one possible manifestation of their

---

[23] *King v Governor of NJ*, 767 F3d 216 (3d Cir 2014), cert denied, 135 S Ct 2048 (2015).

[24] Bracken (n 8) 325.

[25] For example, OHCHR 'Convention against Torture and Other Cruel, Inhuman or Degrading Treatment or Punishment' (10 December 1984) 1465 UNTS 85, 113.

[26] Lapin (n 20) 251, 261.

[27] For a comprehensive review see J Hampton, 'The First Amendment and the Future of Conversion Therapy Bans in Light of *National Institute of Family and Life Advocates v. Harris*' (2020) 35 *Berkeley Journal of Gender, Law & Justice* 169.

belief is aiding members of their congregation 'to heal', not to sin, and such like. This argument, again in the context of US constitutional law, but in a similar fashion to international human rights law, potentially carries some weight. However, courts in the US have rejected this line of argument, saying that the laws do not prohibit clergymen from engaging in religious 'conversion therapy', nor do they preclude individuals from providing religious counselling to congregants.[28] Courts also concluded that these bans are neutral and generally applicable, and therefore constitutionally valid.[29] But a big question mark remains over the effectiveness of these bans, given all these exclusions, in stopping treatments from being offered to parents and imposed on children. The issue of religious freedom, or freedom of conscience of children, has not been part of these adjudications in any meaningful way.

A third argument against the legality of 'conversion therapy' bans centres around parental responsibility, parental autonomy, and parental rights. In a nutshell, this argument suggests that parents should be able to raise their children as they choose, without government interference, and if parents are unhappy with their child's sexual orientation or gender identity, they have the prerogative to try to change it. I will come back to this argument later, when discussing parental responsibility from a child's rights perspective.

'Consent' is another form of justification that is sometimes invoked by supporters of 'conversion therapy', in an attempt to salvage the legality of 'conversion therapy', and sometimes introduced as an exception to a ban.[30] According to this line of argument, if a child consents to undergoing this treatment, then it should be legal. Ignoring the question whether consent in this space can ever be free, or whether it is obtained as a result of coercion or pressure by parents, I argue that consent – and the entire discourse that utilises concepts, jargon and case law borrowed from the medical law world – is irrelevant. 'Conversion therapy' is not a therapy, or a medical treatment, and therefore using medical law's conception of consent is just not relevant. Moreover, the pain and harm that it causes means that parents are under a duty to talk their child out of engaging with this practice, rather than offering or encouraging it.

II. Systematic Analysis of the Relevant Rights of Children

This section analyses questions concerning 'conversion therapy' from a child's rights perspective, using the 1989 UNCRC as a normative and positive framework.

This section does not look at the morality of 'conversion therapy' but focuses on the rights of children involved. As Trispiotis and Purshouse have argued before,

---

[28] *Welch v Brown*, 834 F3d 1041, (9th Cir 2016) at 1044–45.
[29] Lapin (n 20) 251, 256.
[30] Ozanne (n 5) 241, 248.

not only is 'conversion therapy' morally wrong, but from human rights perspective, it 'fails to respect the equal moral personhood of LGBTQ+ people',[31] and violates the prohibition of torture and/or degrading treatment under European and international human rights law.[32] Boulos and González-Cantón make a similar claim, and argue that all forms of 'conversion therapy', including 'talk therapy', should be considered as degrading and inhuman treatment, and therefore incompatible with international human rights law norms.[33] When it comes to children, I argue that 'conversion therapy' violates other key rights of children, beyond the prohibitions on torture and on inhuman and degrading treatment.

The UNCRC includes a myriad of relevant provisions on the question of 'conversion therapy', which I suggest dividing into three groups: The first group includes a set of specific rights that are directly relevant to 'conversion therapy', and this includes protection for the right to identity (Articles 7–8), freedom of conscience (Article 14), right to privacy (Article 16), right to freedom from abuse (Article 19), protection from harmful traditional practices (Article 24(3)), and protection from torture and other cruel, inhuman or degrading treatment (Articles 37 and 40). The second group includes two articles that regulate parental roles and duties: Article 18, which positions parents with the 'primary responsibility for the upbringing and development of the child', and setting the child's best interests as parents' basic concern; and Article 5 that asks parents to provide children with appropriate guidance in exercising their own rights, in accordance with the child's evolving capacities. The third group is the UNCRC's four guiding principles,[34] namely the right to non-discrimination (Article 2), the right of the child to have their best interests considered as a primary consideration (Article 3), the rights to life, survival and development (Article 6), and the right to participate in decisions concerning their lives (Article 12). Questions about the compatibility of 'conversion therapy' with the UNCRC, or parental capacity to force children to attend this 'therapy', will be analysed from an assumed child's point of view to consider their rights. In other words, a child, and their rights, will be the focal point of analysis, against a reality where children are subject to these treatments, but their rights are rarely addressed or given adequate weight.

It is worth noting from the outset that the UNCRC does not explicitly identify gender in Article 2, which includes an open-ended list of prohibited grounds for discrimination. It also reflects a narrow conception of childhood where children are seen as victims, specifically victims of sexual violence, who require protection. As mentioned, the UNCRC is silent on children's sexual rights and gender identity. Some even go so far as to argue that the UNCRC denied children's sexual

---

[31] Boulos and González-Cantón (n 3) 3.
[32] Trispiotis and Purshouse (n 3) 107.
[33] Boulos and González-Cantón (n 3).
[34] Committee on the Rights of the Child 'General Comment No 5: General Measures of Implementation of the Convention on the Rights of the Child (Arts 4, 42 and 44, para 6) (27 November 2003) UN Doc CRC/GC/2003/4.

agency altogether.[35] But as Sandberg convincingly argued, despite some of these shortcomings, the UNCRC can be utilised, and interpreted to provide meaningful protection for the rights of LGBTQ+ children.[36]

III. Protection from Abuse and Harm, and the Prohibition on Torture

Protection from harm and abuse, as stipulated in Article 19, is a key issue in the context of 'conversion therapy'. The choice to begin the analysis with Article 19 centres on children's dreadful experiences of 'conversion therapy', especially the harmful and painful impacts that this practice has on them. This departs from other approaches, which takes the best interests principle as a focal point.[37] This is not to say that the best interests principle is not important, or a key feature of children's rights, but there are at least three good reasons to start with Article 19. First, there is ample evidence about the harm that 'conversion therapy' causes. Second, the explicit and unequivocal obligations to ban practices that harm the child physically or mentally are less contentious than the obligations that Article 3 might give rise to. Third, Article 3 is often criticised for being subjective, or constructing a narrow view of children and childhood,[38] and for its potential to be hijacked by parents and other adults who euphemistically argue that attempts to alter children's identity is in the children's best interests. In contrast, Article 19 is not often subject to such criticism. Article 19(1) reads:

> States Parties shall take all appropriate legislative, administrative, social and educational measures to protect the child from all forms of physical or mental violence, injury or abuse, neglect or negligent treatment, maltreatment or exploitation, including sexual abuse, while in the care of parent(s), legal guardian(s) or any other person who has the care of the child.

The article provides a broad protection for children from violence, a term that has been defined in general terms by the UN Committee on the Rights of the Child to include 'physical, psychological, or emotional harm to a child's development and sense of dignity'.[39] Moreover, the Committee emphasises that the term 'violence' should not be interpreted in any way to minimise the impact of non-physical and non-intentional forms of harm', and that all forms of harm 'carry equal weight'.[40]

---

[35] R Linde, 'The Rights of Queer Children' (2019) 27 *International Journal of Children's Rights* 719.
[36] K Sandberg, 'The Rights of LGBTI Children under the Convention on the Rights of the Child' (2015) 33 *Nordic Journal of Human Rights* 337.
[37] Nugraha (n 3).
[38] FR Ammaturo and MF Moscati, 'Children's Rights and Gender Identity: A New Frontier of Children's Protagonism?' (2021) 39 *Nordic Journal of Children's Rights* 146, 155.
[39] Committee on the Rights of the Child 'General Comment 13: The Right of the Child to Freedom from all forms of Violence' (18 April 2011) UN Doc CRC/C/GC13, para 19.
[40] ibid para 19.

In our context, this covers all forms of 'conversion therapy', including 'talk therapy', even if some forms of 'conversion therapy' seem harmless to parents.

The latter point is the logical conclusion when Article 19 is read in conjunction with Article 12 that acknowledges a child's right to participate in decisions concerning their life. This means that the perspective of children must be included when interpreting the meaning of harm. In other words, it is children's experience of harm that counts, and not what adults might think to be harmful or painful, or whether certain level of pain is justified. Further, Article 19 directly addresses inter-familial harm caused to children, and subsequently requires states to protect children against harm inflicted by family members, including parents, and it does not matter whether it was inflicted intentionally, or unintentionally.[41] When it comes to 'conversion therapy', even if parents are acting in good faith and compel their child to attend sessions with the intention of supporting their child, the proven harm that 'conversion therapy' causes means that this parental decision is a violation of Article 19.

Two additional articles should be considered in the context of harm and violence: Article 37 and Article 24(3). Article 37 protects the child from torture and inhuman and degrading treatment.[42] Torture, a *jus cogens* norm in international law, as previously argued about the meaning of harm, is a term that need to be interpreted and contextualised too, and that should be done in a way that takes children's perspective and experience into account. An example for such approach is the interpretation that Tobin and Hobbs suggest:

> ... torture should be considered the intentional infliction of severe pain and suffering, whether physical or mental, on a child by a person who has the control or custody of a child. In contrast, the other forms of ill-treatment prohibited under article 37(a) need not involve intentional infliction of harm but must still reach a certain threshold of pain and suffering. The assessment of this minimum level of harm is relative and depends on the circumstances of the case, including: the duration of the treatment; the effects on the child; and other factors such as the age, gender, and health of the child.[43]

This definition centres around children's experiences rather than the experiences of adults, or adults' assessment as to what can be, for example, an acceptable level of pain. Evidence from children's own testimonies, as mentioned earlier in this chapter, provide vivid descriptions for the pain that 'conversion therapy' has caused them, some referring to it as torture, a definition that was also

---

[41] ibid para 4.

[42] Article 37: States Parties shall ensure that: '(a) No child shall be subjected to torture or other cruel, inhuman or degrading treatment or punishment. Neither capital punishment nor life imprisonment without possibility of release shall be imposed for offences committed by persons below eighteen years of age'.

[43] J Tobin and H Hobbs, 'Article 37: Protection against Torture, Capital Punishment, and Arbitrary Deprivation of Liberty' in J Tobin (ed), *Commentary on the Convention on the Rights of the Child* (Oxford, Oxford University Press, 2019) 1420, 1424.

accepted by the UN Special Rapporteur on Torture.[44] Moreover, even if one casts doubts about the characterisation of 'conversion therapy' as either torture or as inhuman or degrading treatment, it is difficult to argue that it is not a violation of Article 37. This is because it is beyond any doubt that it falls under the broad protection provided for the child's right to protection from abuse, as discussed above.

Another dimension where the UNCRC goes beyond other international human rights law instruments is the scope of the prohibition on torture. As in the case of Article 19, this prohibition is not confined to states and their agents, but includes private actors too,[45] including parents. Article 37 requires states to take active measures, including, but not limited to, legislating a prohibition on torture. This ban should be absolute, and include no exceptions for adults who might claim that by offering 'conversion therapy' they exercise their right to religious freedom or freedom of speech. Article 37, as well as the entire international human rights law corpus on torture, is clear that no exception to this prohibition is allowed.

The second article that requires attention is Article 24(3). This article requires states to abolish 'traditional practices prejudicial to the health of children'. The common interpretation of this article, in the literature and by the UN Committee on the Rights of the Child, refers to a wide range of practices, including, but not limited to, female genital mutilation or cutting, breast ironing, early or forced marriage and forced abortion. When states attempt to defend the legality of these practices, they often invoke arguments grounded in religion or cultural practices. But these arguments have been rejected by UN human rights bodies, including by the Committee on the Rights of the Child and the Committee on the Elimination of Discrimination against Women.[46] As mentioned above, efforts to convert children's sexual orientation or gender identity are not new. Moreover, these practices are often, if not always, rooted in parents' religious beliefs, cultures or traditions. It can therefore be argued that 'conversion therapy' is a form of traditional practice, and therefore falls under Article 24(3). Further, nothing in the text of the UNCRC suggests that the interpretation of this provision is confined to western imaginaries about cultures, traditions, and children's sexuality (although it should be noted that the drafting process of the UNCRC shows a clear bias against non-western practices).[47]

---

[44] UNHRC (n 13).

[45] Tobin and Hobbs (n 43) 1428–29.

[46] Committee on the Rights of the Child (n 39); Committee on the Elimination of Discrimination against Women and Committee on the Rights of the Child 'Joint General Comment No. 31. Committee on the Elimination of Discrimination against Women/ General Comment 18 of the Committee on the Rights of the Child on Harmful Practices' (14 November 2014) UN Doc CEDAW/C/GC/31-CRC/C/GC/18.

[47] S Harris-Short, 'Listening to "The Other"? The Convention of the Rights of the Child' (2001) 2 *Melbourne Journal of International Law* 304; S Harris-Short, 'International Human Rights Law: Imperialism, Inept and Ineffective? Cultural Relativism under the UN Convention on the Rights of the Child' (2003) 25 *Human Rights Quarterly* 130.

IV. The Rights to Identity(ies) and Development

The UNCRC recognises the child's right to establish, develop and practise their identity, or identities, in Articles 7 and 8. Article 7 is less relevant in relation to 'conversion therapy', as it mainly focuses on bureaucratic identity, like having a nationality, registration of birth and having a birth certificate. All these are crucial elements of identity in and of themselves, but also serve as prerequisites to being able to enjoy other rights. Further, birth registration is highly relevant to transgender or intersex children, and its importance goes beyond the logistical importance and to the heart of their sense of self. The focus here, though, is on 'conversion therapy'.

The objective of 'conversion therapy' is to change a child's sexual orientation and gender identities and expressions, usually by associating negative attributes to non-heterosexual sexual preferences, and non-cisgender identities. Article 8 of the UNCRC therefore seems more relevant to the discussion here. This article requires state parties to 'respect the right of the child to preserve his or her identity ... without unlawful interference'. It is an open-ended list. Cahn has argued that, given the high level of harassment, bullying, poor mental health, and stigmatisation that non-heterosexual children experience, Article 8 should be read as seeing gender identity as an identity aspect that requires recognition and protection. According to Phil Chan, this aspect of identity is not less important than nationality, which is explicitly mentioned in the text, and the right of children to form a counter-majoritarian identity should be protected.[48] Reading Article 8 together with Article 6(2), which protects the rights to survival and development, can also suggest that the UNCRC supports the right of the child to develop their own intrinsic identity.

When looking at 'conversion therapy', the focus should not only be on the right to develop sexual and gender identities as a process, but also the right to preserve and practise any identity the child might have, or have already developed.[49] What adults try to do with 'conversion therapy' is presumably to alter expressions of an identity that is non-conforming to cis-gender or heterosexual norms, which presumably the child has intended to express. Whether the child has formulated that expression knowingly or not, they have chosen to perform that expression as a reflection of their selves. Adults assume that an identity has already been formed, meaning that the child has grappled, realised, or come to terms with their sexual orientation and gender identity. It also means that the child's parents know about it (whether because the child told them, or for any other reason), and that the parents are not happy with this identity and want to alter it. 'Conversion therapy' therefore interferes with both the right to develop and the right to preserve the child's identity. Therefore, in this context it is imperative to recognise the child's right to

---

[48] Chan (n 3) 170.
[49] Sandberg (n 36) 344.

preserve their identity. The Committee notes, in General Comment number 20, that adolescents:

> explore and forge their own individual and community identities on the basis of a complex interaction with their own family and cultural history, and experience the creation of an emergent sense of self, often expressed through language, arts and culture, both as individuals and through association with their peers ... The process of construction and expression of identity is particularly complex for adolescents as they create a pathway between minority and mainstream cultures.[50]

This right to an identity establishes corresponding duties for parents and the state. For parents, it falls under the general purview of supporting their child's upbringing and development (Article 18) and to act in accordance with the child's best interests. For the state, Tobin and Todres write, the obligation:

> ... consists of two broad elements: an obligation to enable the child to access information that will enable him or her to understand the historical elements of his or her identity; and an obligation to take reasonable measures to ensure that the child can explore, define, express, and enjoy his or her identity without unlawful interference.[51]

Commenting specifically about a child who identifies as being gay, lesbian, bisexual, or transgender, Tobin and Todres suggest that 'states would be required to take effective measures to ensure that the child is able to express and enjoy their sexual orientation or gender identity without fear of discrimination or violence'.[52] Exposing children to 'conversion therapy' fundamentally contradicts this duty.

An issue related to the right to an identity is self-determination. Although the UNCRC does not explicitly recognise a right to self-determination for children, Sandberg suggests that in the context of analysing the relevance of the UNCRC to LGBTQ+ children this right can be inferred from Articles 12 (right to respect for the views of the child) and 16 (right to privacy).[53] But Sandberg also claims that this interpretation is probably only relevant to certain children: those who are 'capable of understanding the consequences of the existing alternatives'.[54] This approach ignores the role, and weight, that should be given to the right to development in this context and process, and that the realisation of the right to development is not subject to the 'age and maturity' limitations that Article 12 is subject to. If the right to development is considered in the analysis, and considering the explicit obligation on parents to support their child's development that Article 18 stipulates, then the age or 'understanding' limitation that Sandberg mentions should be removed in favour of an argument that supports the right of every child to self-determination. While adults might think that, for example, puberty is the relevant age here, this physical change that the child's body undergoes might come months and years

---

[50] UN Committee on the Rights of the Child (n 15) para 10.
[51] J Tobin and J Todres, 'Art 8 The Right to Preservation of a Child's Identity' in Tobin (n 43) 295.
[52] ibid.
[53] Sandberg (n 36) 344.
[54] ibid.

after the psychological and cognitive processes of developing and realising one's identities.

This section has asked whether 'conversion therapy' is a practice that upholds, or violates, the right of children, as stipulated in the UNCRC. It has focused on some key rights like the right to freedom from abuse, freedom from torture, the right to identity, and the right to development. So far, the conclusion is that 'conversion therapy', in all its forms, is a clear violation of the rights of children. But a question that still requires attention is whether, despite all of this, parents should be able to influence, or try to reverse, their child's sexual orientation or gender identity, so that it will correspond with what they believe is right, moral or in accordance with their religious beliefs.

V. Parental Responsibility

The question of whether 'conversion therapy' can be undertaken so that the child's identity matches one that parents think is moral or aligned with their religious convictions, is one that should be considered from a child's rights perspective. This is in sharp contrast to the hegemonic approach, which is often invoked in litigation or advocacy efforts against banning 'conversion therapy'. The hegemonic approach maintains that parents have a right to raise their children in accordance with their own set of moral or religious values. Such values would include influencing and directing their child's sexual orientation and gender identity, without external interference.

This section asks this question even though it has already concluded that 'conversion therapy' is a clear violation of children's rights. If this conclusion is rejected, or if someone asks to salvage the legitimacy or legality of 'conversion therapy' by using a 'parental rights' argument, then there is a need to address this question. Examining the question of parental discretion from a children's rights perspective mandates, first and foremost, a change in terminology. Instead of talking about parental rights, one should talk about parental duties and obligations.

Article 18 is the main article of the UNCRC that frames the child-parent relationship. It constructs the roles of parents in these terms:

> [B]oth parents have common responsibilities for the upbringing and development of the child. Parents or, as the case may be, legal guardians, have the primary responsibility for the upbringing and development of the child. The best interests of the child will be their basic concern.

Article 5 affirms parents' autonomy in raising their children, and their duty to 'provide, in a manner consistent with the evolving capacities of the child, appropriate direction and guidance in the exercise by the child of the rights recognized in the present Convention'. Reading these two articles together from a child's rights perspective shows that the objective of parenting is to support the child's 'upbringing and development' and that parents should be guided by their child's best interests in their decisions. Parents, under the UNCRC, have rights vis-à-vis the state, and are free to exercise their duties and responsibilities towards their child. Moreover, the UNCRC emphasises several times the importance of the family, traditions, and culture to the child, and respect for the child's rights to know, enjoy and practise their family's identities.[55] Parents can raise their children and tell them, for example, that same-sex relationships are a sin, if this is what the parents believe. But the question here is different. In the case of 'conversion therapy', the issue is not about interfering with or limiting parents' ability to raise and educate their children in accordance with their moral values and religious beliefs, but rather a forward-looking one about the scope of the parental prerogative to respond to an identity of their child of which they disapprove.

Parental decisions should also be guided by the principle of the best interests of the child. The best interest of the child, as defined in Article 3, is also one of the four guiding principles of the UNCRC.[56] The objective of the best interests principle is to ensure the full and effective enjoyment of all the rights recognised in the UNCRC, and its meaning is dynamic, rather than pre-determined. Its meaning depends, first and foremost, on the specific child in question, their characteristics, identities, and own views on the issue at stake. In addition to being an explicit consideration that parents should attend to, the best interests principle is a substantive right of the child. It is also an interpretive principle and a procedural rule of the UNCRC. This means that any decision-making process that can affect a child (or children) should include an evaluation of the possible impacts, positive and negative alike, of the decision on the child.[57]

When it comes to 'conversion therapy', one of the key factors that ought to be considered is how the child understands and identifies itself. The child's sense of self, belonging, and right to development also ought to be considered, together with the harm and pain that 'conversion therapy' causes, including the implications this will have on a child's physical and mental health. It is not that parents who subjugate their child to 'conversion therapy' necessarily have bad intentions and knowingly want to harm their child. Most of them are genuinely unhappy with who their child is or hold prejudicial fears for their child. But this dissatisfaction is not a *carte blanche* to do whatever they think is right, just or morally correct.

In the context of US law, Rachmilovitz goes so far as arguing that the parental autonomy of parents who fail to exercise their duty to protect their child's identity development should be limited by the state.[58] She further claims that parents who pressure children into mainstream sexual identities harm those children, infringe upon their identity interests, and therefore are beyond the scope of parental

---

[55] See Arts 7, 8, 10 and 30.
[56] Committee on the Rights of the Child (n 34).
[57] ibid.
[58] O Rachmilovitz, 'Family Assimilation Demands and Sexual Minority Youth (2014) 98 *Minnesota Law Review* 1374.

autonomy and warrant state intervention.[59] Translating this line of argument into the context of the UNCRC, the second half is more relevant. In a nutshell, under the UNCRC, subjugating children to 'conversion therapy' is beyond parental powers.

VI. Conclusion

Looking at 'conversion therapy' from a children's rights perspective, it is clear that these practices, whether spoken or physical, violate a myriad of rights. They harm and torture children, and violate their right to identity, privacy and development. Subjugating children to them falls outside the remit of parental responsibility.

Under the UNCRC, states have the obligation not only to ban practices that are harmful to children, but also to take measures to protect their rights, and to support parents so they can fulfil their duties towards their children's development and upbringing. Banning 'conversion therapy' in legislation is a necessary step, but it cannot be the only one. Not only is the effectiveness of a legalised ban questionable, but it also does not guarantee that the practice will not be carried out against the law. Nor does it solve the root cause, which is the bias against the non-cisgender and/or non-heterosexual children. States are under a duty to educate the public, including children, about the severe negative effects of these sorts of 'treatments'[60] in order to reduce the likelihood that a child will ask to undergo them.

---

[59] ibid 1380.
[60] UN Committee on the Rights of the Child (n 15) para 34.

6

How do Practices to 'Convert' Childhood Gender Diversity Impact a Child's Right to Develop?

HANNAH HIRST

This chapter examines the extent to which practices to convert gender diversity[1] in childhood impact a child's right to develop. It first explains that some children experience conflict between their sex assigned at birth and gender identity, before discussing the prevalence of childhood gender diversity in the UK. While recent events (such as the Cass Interim Review)[2] and case law (eg *R (Bell and Another) v Tavistock and Portman NHS Foundation Trust*[3]) have led to greater media coverage[4] (and subsequent public awareness) of gender-diverse youth, the chapter describes a lack of focus on gender-diverse children's *rights*.[5] The chapter proposes that a rights-based approach, specifically one that focuses on child development, can offer a lens through which prejudicial and harmful practices (such as 'conversion therapy') can be studied. It describes both violent and non-violent forms of 'conversion therapy' for gender-diverse youth occurring in England as

---

[1] This chapter employs the terms 'gender diverse' and 'gender diversity' to describe a range of identities, including trans, non-binary, agender, bigender, gender fluid, omnigender, and polygender youth.

[2] H Cass, 'The Cass Review: Independent Review of Gender Identity Services for Children and Young People: Interim Report' (NHS, 1 February 2022) https://cass.independent-review.uk/publications/interim-report/.

[3] *R (Bell and Another) v Tavistock and Portman NHS Foundation Trust* [2020] EWHC 3274 (Admin); [2021] EWCA Civ 1363.

[4] See, for instance, KC Pang et al, 'Association of Media Coverage of Transgender and Gender Diverse Issues with Rates of Referral of Transgender Children and Adolescents to Specialist Gender Clinics in the UK and Australia' (2020) 3(7) *JAMA Network Open* 1 and KC Pang et al, 'Negative Media Coverage as a Barrier to Accessing Care for Transgender Children and Adolescents' (2022) 5(2) *JAMA Network Open* 1.

[5] For a more detailed discussion on gender diverse children's rights see FR Ammatruro and MF Moscati, 'Children's Rights and Gender Identity: A New Frontier of Children's Protagonism' (2021) 39(2) *Nordic Journal of Human Rights* 146; AM Bucataru, 'Using the Convention on the Rights of the Child to Project the Rights of Transgender Children and Adolescents: The Context of Education and Transition' (2016) 3 *Queen Mary Human Rights Review* 59.

non-therapeutic and ineffective. The chapter then analyses the possible impact of the practice on a gender-diverse child's right to develop into adulthood – not just physically, but also mentally and socially. It considers the approach of the courts and government in England in relation to issues about childhood gender diversity, before critiquing the exclusion of gender-diverse children in plans to enact legislation ending 'conversion therapy'. The final part of the chapter argues that banning all practices (violent and non-violent) that seek to change children's gender identities would not only reflect changing social norms relating to gender/sex and laws in similar jurisdictions (such as Canada),[6] but also ensure gender-diverse youth obtain a 'maximally' open future.[7]

I. Gender-diverse Children

Gender-diverse youth experience incongruity between their gender identity and sex assigned at birth, which results in some children feeling distressed.[8] It is difficult to quantify the number of gender-diverse children in the UK (and worldwide) because of a lack of empirical and child-centred research with such children. Gendered experiences can be very personal and private, meaning that it is common for children (and, indeed, adults) to feel uncomfortable discussing their gender identity with a researcher, or when completing a survey. This is especially the case when a gender-diverse child's parents are unaware and/or when the child has experienced harassment, abuse, and discrimination related to their gender identity. Reports, such as 'Referrals to the Gender Identity Development Service (GIDS)',[9] however, demonstrate an increase in children identifying as gender diverse and wishing to explore psychological and medical options, including the administration of puberty blockers[10] and cross-sex hormones.[11] The latest published statistics from GIDS reveal that 2,590 children were referred to the service in 2018–2019.[12] This represents a six per cent increase compared to the previous year (which had 2,444 referrals).[13]

---

[6] M Blais et al, 'Sexual Orientation and Gender Identity Expression Conversion Exposure and Their Correlates among LGBTIQI2+ Persons in Quebec, Canada' (2022) 17(4) *PLOS ONE* 1; T Salway and F Ashley, 'Ridding Canadian Medicine of Conversion Therapy' (2022) 194 *Canadian Medical Association Journal* 17.

[7] J Feinberg, 'The Child's Right to an Open Future' in W Aiken and H LaFollette, *Whose Child?* (Washington DC, Rowan and Littlefield, 1980).

[8] S Giordano, *Children with Gender Identity Disorder: A Clinical Ethical, and Legal Analysis* (Oxford, Routledge, 2012) offers a thorough analysis relating to childhood gender diversity. Also see R Kaltiala-Heino et al, 'Gender Dysphoria in Adolescence: Current Perspectives' (2018) 9 *Adolescent Health, Medicine and Theraputics* 31.

[9] The Tavistock and Portman NHS Foundation Trust, 'Referrals to the Gender Identity Development Service (GIDS) Level off in 2018–2019' (NHS England, 28 June 2019) www.tavistockandportman.nhs.uk/about-us/news/stories/referrals-gender-identity-development-service-gids-level-2018-19.

[10] Puberty blockers suspend pubertal development.

[11] Cross-sex hormones enhance a person's secondary sex characteristics.

[12] The Tavistock and Portman NHS Trust (n 9).

[13] ibid.

In the wake of the coronavirus pandemic,[14] the closure of GIDS,[15] and modifications to NHS England's Service Specifications post-*Bell*,[16] it is likely that the number of gender-diverse children referred to and awaiting treatment at regional centres in 2023–2024 will be much greater than the aforementioned figure.

Recent events and cases in England concerning the administration of puberty blockers and cross-sex hormones, such as the Cass Review,[17] *AB v CD and Others*,[18] *Bell v Tavistock*,[19] have brought gender-diverse children's identities more into public focus. The long-awaited publication of Hilary Cass's report,[20] detailing her investigation of GIDS, along with high-profile coverage of *AB* and *Bell*,[21] have led to discussions and debates about gender-diverse children in national newspapers such as *The Sun*, *The Daily Mail*, and *The Spectator*. Notable headlines published in these news outlets include: 'The gender self-identification lobby is harming children, women and trans people themselves';[22] '500K OK FOR TRANS CHILDREN'[23] and 'The latest celebrity must have? A trans child!'.[24] These headlines suggest that gender-diverse children lack the capacity to make informed decisions about their bodies and identities. They also imply that gender-diverse youth are the legal property of their parents and do not possess individual rights.

II. Gender-diverse Children as Individual Rights Holders

Despite increasing public awareness of gender diversity in childhood, gender-diverse children have not been included in significant legislation seeking to uphold

---

[14] D Ehrensaft, 'COVID-19 and Transgender and Gender Expansive Children and Youth' (2021) 50(9) *Paediatric Annals* 336; H Hirst, 'The Impact of COVID-19 on Young Trans People' (University of Liverpool, 1 August 2020).

[15] As well as the opening of new regional gender identity clinics for gender-diverse youth in England. See A Gregory, 'NHS to Close Tavistock Gender Identity Clinic for Children' (*The Guardian*, 28 July 2022) www.theguardian.com/society/2022/jul/28/nhs-closing-down-london-gender-identity-clinic-for-children.

[16] NHS England, 'Interim Service Specifications: Specialist Service for Children and Young People with Gender Dysphoria (Phase 1 Providers)' (NHS England, 20 October 2022) www.engage.england.nhs.uk/specialised-commissioning/gender-dysphoria-services/user_uploads/b1937-ii-specialist-service-for-children-and-young-people-with-gender-dysphoria-1.pdf.

[17] Cass (n 2).

[18] *AB v CD and Others* [2021] EWHC 741.

[19] *Bell* (n 3).

[20] Cass (n 2).

[21] *AB* (n 18) and *Bell* (n 3).

[22] H Joyce, 'Why It's Wrong – and Profoundly Damaging – To Make Us All Agree That Someone is Whatever Gender They Say They Are' (*Daily Mail Online*, 3 July 2021) www.dailymail.co.uk/news/article-9753017/HELEN-JOYCE-argues-gender-self-identification-lobby-harming-children-women-trans-people.html.

[23] J Reilly, 'Grant Go Ahead Charity Helping Transgender Kids and Their Families Will Get £500,000 Lottery Grant' (*The Sun*, 20 February 2019) www.thesun.co.uk/news/8465298/transgender-childrens-charity-500k-grant.

[24] J Burchill, 'The Latest Celebrity Must Have? A Trans Child!' (*The Spectator*, 22 October 2021) www.spectator.co.uk/article/the-latest-celebrity-must-have-a-trans-child.

the rights of gender-diverse people specifically. An example of this is the Gender Recognition Act 2004 (GRA 2004), which was, at the time, hailed as 'a pioneering piece of legislation'.[25] The Act was designed to allow gender-diverse people to legally change their gender, subject to satisfying certain criteria.[26] One significant issue with the GRA 2004, amongst many other problems, is that people under the age of 18 are not included in its remit. This means that while a gender-diverse child can socially (and to some extent medically)[27] transition, they cannot alter their gender in their birth and/or death certificate. Peter Dunne argues that this creates 'significant legal and practical obstacles' for gender-diverse youth; such as access to gender-appropriate identity documents, leading to a continual risk of public outings and transphobic abuse/violence.[28]

Risk, harm, and the rights of others (namely, parents and cisgender children) are common themes in scholarly discussions, public debates, and the case law concerning gender-diverse youth, rather than a gender-diverse child's individual rights. This was notably the case in *Bell v Tavistock*,[29] where counsel for the defendants and claimants, and consequently the Court of Appeal, did not refer to, or grapple with, the 'detailed catalogue'[30] of children's rights existing under the United Nations Convention on the Rights of the Child (1989) (UNCRC). Both the European Court of Human Rights and the English courts have recognised and stressed the importance of signatory states (including England, as part of the UK) realising the UNCRC's standards and aims.[31] In *Sahin v Germany*,[32] for example, the Grand Chamber of the European Court of Human Rights stated that:

> The Convention spells out the basic human rights of children everywhere – without discrimination – have: the right to survival; to develop to the fullest; to protection from harmful influences, abuse and exploitation; and to participate fully in family, cultural and social life. It further protects children's rights by setting standards in health care, education and legal, civil and social services. State parties to the Convention are obliged to develop and undertake all actions and policies in light of the best interests of the child (Article 3).[33]

---

[25] C Fairburn, 'The Gender Recognition Process' (Briefing Paper 08746, House of Commons Library, 5 December 2019).

[26] For a detailed examination of the Act see S Whittle, 'The Opposite of Sex is Politics – The UK Gender Recognition Act and Why It Is Not Perfect, Just Like You and Me' (2006) 15(3) *Journal of Gender* 267.

[27] If they meet certain criteria (such as parental permission and the correct Tanner Stage) outlined in NHS England's Service Specifications.

[28] P Dunne, 'Ten Years of Gender Recognition in the United Kingdom: Still a "Model for Reform"?' (2015) 4(1) *Public Law* 530.

[29] *Bell* (n 3).

[30] H Stalford and S Bryne, 'Human Rights, Children's Rights, and Family Law' in R Lamont, *Family Law* (Oxford, Oxford University Press, 2018).

[31] See, for example, *ZH (Tanzania) v Secretary of State for the Home Department* [2011] UKSC 4, [2011] AC 166.

[32] ECtHR *Sahin v Germany*, Application No 30943/9, 13 July 2000.

[33] ibid 40.

To this end, the courts in England have also noted that the UNCRC should be accepted in 'good faith'[34] and its ratification by the government represents a commitment in international law 'to take action to ensure the realisation of all rights in the Convention for all children in their jurisdiction'.[35] Provisions included in the UNCRC, which are of particular significance to gender-diverse youth, include Articles 3 (best interests), 6 (right to develop and survive), 8 (right to an identity), 12 (right to be heard), and 13 (right to expression). These rights, taken together with the European Convention on Human Rights (ECHR) and the common law,[36] offer a framework for positioning gender-diverse children as individual rights holders, with needs and interests separate from adults and cis youth. Soft law provisions, such as the Yogyakarta Principles, also recognise the distinct need to 'protect children from discrimination, violence, or other harm due to their gender expression'.[37] These principles outline a series of human rights related to sexual orientation and gender identity that were published in 2006. Eleven years later, they were revised and expanded to include new grounds of gender expression and sex characteristics, as well as several new principles.[38]

The UNCRC, ECHR, common law, and Yogyakarta Principles can highlight and begin to address the prejudices and inequalities gender-diverse children face as a minority group. Indeed, reports indicate that gender-diverse children are more predisposed to abuse and harassment compared with cis children.[39] Research published by Youth Chances states that more than four in five (83 per cent) of trans children are verbally abused and that three in five (60 per cent) experience threats and intimidation.[40] Rights, to this end, can be a force for good and change; or as Michael Freeman states: 'for treating children seriously and, in doing so, to stress the importance of respect for autonomy, dignity, decency and concern'.[41] For gender-diverse youth, they also offer a lens through which prejudicial and harmful practices, including 'conversion therapy', can be examined and scrutinised.

---

[34] Vienna Convention on the Law of Treaties 1969, Art 26. See, however, the dissenting judgment of Lord Kerr in *R (SG and Others (previously JS and Others) v Secretary of State for Work and Pensions* [2015] UKSC 16, [2015] 1 WLR 1449, in which he argued that the UNCRC ought to be directly applicable in English law.

[35] Committee on the Rights of the Child, General Comment No 5 (2003), 'General Measures of Implementation of the CRC' (17 November 2013) 1.

[36] Such as the House of Lord's decision in *Gillick v West Norfolk & Wisbeck Area Health Authority* [1986] AC 112.

[37] Principle 24H.

[38] The Yogyakarta Principles Plus 10 2017, 'Additional Principles and State Obligations on the Application of International Human Rights Law in relation to Sexual Orientation, Gender Identity, Gender Expression and Sex Characteristics to Complement the Yogyakarta Principles'.

[39] Metro, 'Youth Chances: Integrated Report' (*Metro Online*, 1 August 2016).

[40] ibid.

[41] M Freeman, 'The Sociology of Childhood and Children's Rights' (1998) 46 *International Journal of Children's Rights* 235.

III. Practices to Convert a Gender-diverse Child's Gender Identity

As noted in the introduction and earlier chapters of this book, 'conversion therapy' is a term used to describe a range of pseudo-medical and/or religious practices, which seek to change or suppress a person's sexual orientation or gender identity. In theory 'conversion therapy' could operate both ways, but the focus of this chapter, as the following pages explain, is historic and contemporary 'conversions' from gender diverse to cisgender. The 'conversion therapy' it aims to capture is the set of practices that arise from the position that some sexualities or gender identities are inferior to others and therefore have to be eliminated or suppressed.

The term 'therapy' suggests that LGBTQ+ identities are a disorder or illness requiring treatment.[42] It is now widely accepted that this is untrue. Gender diversity, as noted by the European Professional Association of Transgender Health,[43] is a natural part of human variation, which has occurred in the young population since *at least* the 1930s.[44] Recent studies suggest that 'conversion therapy' provides no therapeutic benefit to gender-diverse children.[45] Robert Wallace and Hershel Russel, for example, stress that it enhances the risk of children fostering openness to shame and vulnerability to depression.[46]

Speaking at the Human Rights Council, the UN Independent Expert on Sexual Orientation and Gender Identity, Victor Madrigal-Borloz, emphasised that children and young people are particularly vulnerable in the context of 'conversion therapy' because early exposure to such interventions is associated with anxiety, depression, post-traumatic stress disorder, suicidal ideation and suicide attempts. To this end, he noted that:

> Practices of 'conversion therapy' are not only ineffective, but they can also be extremely harmful. They often lead to pain and suffering that will last far beyond their occurrence, leaving indelible scars on a person's body and mind.[47]

---

[42] For a more extensive discussion on this matter see J Talbot and F Finlay, 'Conversion Therapy: Change the Law Not the Person' (2022) 27 *Archives of Disease in Childhood* 324177.

[43] The European Professional Association of Transgender Health, 'Internal Rules December 2019' (*Epath Online*, 1 December 2018) epath.eu/wp-content/uploads/2020/09/EPATH-Internal-rules.pdf.

[44] J Gill-Peterson, *Histories of the Transgender Child* (Minneapolis, University of Minnesota Press, 2018).

[45] JJ Westwater et al, 'What about the Family in Youth Gender Diversity? A Literature Review' (2019) 20(4) *International Journal of Transgenderism* 351; C Brown et al, 'Family Relationships and Health and Well-Being of Transgender and Gender-diverse Youth: A Critical Review' (2020) 7(8) *LGBT Health* 407; EM Pariseau et al, 'The Relationship between Family Acceptance-Fejection and Transgender Youth Psychosocial Functioning' (2019) 7(3) *Clinical Practice in Pediatric Psychology* 267; C Munroe et al, 'The Impact of Peer and Family Functioning on Transgender and Gender-Diverse Children's Mental Health' (2020) 29(7) *Journal of Child and Family Studies* 2080.

[46] R Wallace and H Russell, 'Attachment and Shame in Gender Non-Conforming Children and Their Families: Toward a Theoretical Framework for Evaluating Clinical Interventions' (2013) 14(3) *International Journal of Transgenderism* 113.

[47] United Nations, 'Conversion Therapy Can Amount to Torture and Should be Banned Says UN Expert' (OHCHR, 13 July 2020) www.ohchr.org/en/stories/2020/07/conversion-therapy-can-amount-torture-and-should-be-banned-says-un-expert.

Testimony from gender-diverse adults indicates that childhood 'conversion therapy' is, as Madrigal-Borloz suggests, ineffective, as well as harmful. In a personal account, a boy named Louie, for example, explains that he experienced exorcisms and went on retreats to 'healing' camps with other LGBTQ+ Christians arranged by the church he attended during his childhood.[48] He noted that despite undergoing these interventions and 'regularly begging God to save [him] from [his] queer thoughts and to take away the feelings of gender dysphoria' he was not 'healed' of gender diversity/variance.[49] Louie now identifies as a trans man (he/they), but is mindful of the lasting impact 'conversion therapy' has on children over their life course:

> It has taken me over a decade to heal. Part of that has been recognising that what I went through was 'conversion therapy' and allowing myself to accept that I was a victim.[50]

Since the 1960s clinicians and academics have endorsed a range of practices to 'convert' children's gender identities (from diverse to cis) in texts published in peer-reviewed journals[51] on the basis that non-cis identities should be cured. A frequently cited example is Richard Green and John Money's 'Effeminacy in Prepubertal Boys', which examines 11 cases of children born male and experiencing:

> … excessive and persistent attempts to dress in the clothes of the opposite gender, constant display of gestures and mannerisms of the opposite sex, preference for play and other activities of the opposite sex, or a stated desire to be a member of the opposite sex.[52]

Based on interviews conducted with these children, their parents and, in some instances, their siblings, Green and Money set out 14 recommendations to resolve 'the problem of incongruous gender role in early boyhood'.[53] These include: fathers spending more time with their sons; adults educating boys about the biological and reproductive differences between men and women (as assigned at birth);[54] and parents reinforcing heteronormative values through their sexual and everyday behaviour towards each other.[55] Florence Ashley notes that Green and Money view the children's effeminacy as a problem to be 'fixed' as it may augur future challenges to normative gender roles in the form of adult 'homosexuality and transvestism'.[56]

---

[48] Mermaids, 'Conversion Therapy: Louie's Story' (Mermaids Charity, 26 January 2022) mermaidsuk. org.uk/news/conversion-therapy-louies-story.

[49] ibid.

[50] ibid.

[51] See, for example, GA Rekers and I Lovaas, 'Behavioral Treatment of Deviant Sex-Role Behaviors in a Male Child' (1974) 7(2) *Journal of Applied Behavior Analysis* 173.

[52] R Green and J Money, 'Effeminacy in Prepubertal Boys. Summary of Eleven Cases and Recommendations for Case Management' (1961) 27(1) *Paediatrics* 286.

[53] ibid.

[54] Green and Money state that it is derisible for a boy to know not only about 'the baby egg, the baby nest and baby tunnel', but also about the 'swimming race of 200 million sperms' and that he anticipates with pride and without shame the use of his penis in reproduction.

[55] Green and Money (n 52).

[56] F Ashley, 'Homophobia, Conversion Therapy, and Care Models for Trans Youth: Defending the Gender Affirmative Approach' (2020) 17(4) *Journal of LGBT Youth* 361.

Other, less publicised and known, forms of 'conversion therapy' were carried out on gender-diverse children during (before and, in some case, after) this period, including electroshock, electro-convulsive therapies, abusive behavioural therapy employing physical and psychological punishment.[57] Contemporary approaches (or models) addressing gender diversity/dysphoria in childhood, however, endorse various behavioural, social, and medical responses, rather than violent forms of 'conversion therapy'.

A range of conversion practices are currently recommended under the 'live-in-your-own-skin' approach to addressing gender diversity in childhood.[58] The model's 'treatment' goal, based on the belief that younger children have a more 'malleable gender brain' than older children,[59] is to facilitate a child accepting that their gender identity matches their sex assigned at birth. For Ken Zucker, the approach lowers the possibility that:

> As a kid gets older, he or she will move into adolescence feeling so uncomfortable about their gender identity that they think that it would be better to live as the other gender and require treatment with hormones and sex reassignment surgery.[60]

The live-in–your-own-skin model thus implies that transitioning from one gender to another (or taking up a non-binary identity) is negative and, to some extent, harmful. Practices include taking away cross-gender toys and replacing them with gender appropriate toys; altering a young person's friendship circle to include more same-sex contacts; token-based conditioning techniques; and enrolling a young individual in gender appropriate activities.[61] While violence against a child is not recommended under the approach, some of the aforementioned practices lead to gender-diverse children experiencing physical punishment. Diane Ehrensaft describes this occurring when a parent used physical violence against his child to reinforce token-based confiding techniques:

> When he was five, Kyle entered a behaviour modification program. [...] Kyle received blue tokens for 'desirable' behaviours [...] red ones for 'undesirable' behaviours [...]. Blue tokens were redeemable for treats [...]. Red tokens resulted in a loss of blue tokens, periods of isolation, or spanking by father.[62]

If, however, by the onset of puberty a child continues to exhibit and express gender diverse/dysphoric identification, the live-in-your-own-skin approach suggests that children should be supported in transitioning to the affirmed gender.

---

[57] Ban Conversion Therapy 'Stories' (Ban Conversion Therapy, 1 August 2021) www.banconversiontherapy.com/stories, provides first-hand accounts of violent forms of 'conversion therapy' for gender-diverse youth taking place in England.

[58] D Ehrensaft, 'Gender Nonconforming Youth: Current Perspectives' (2017) 8 *Adolescent Health, Medicine and Theraputics* 57.

[59] ibid. Also see K Zucker and S Bradley, *Gender Identity Disorder and Psychosexual Problems in Children and Adolescents* (New York, The Guilford Press, 1995).

[60] Ehrensaft (n 58).

[61] Zucker and Bradley (n 59).

[62] Ehrensaft (n 58) 60.

This may include the administration of puberty blockers, which delay the onset of a child's pubertal development. Although controversial, and beyond the remit of this chapter, research indicates that blockers offer children an environment free from negative psychosocial experiences[63] to explore and/or affirm their gender identity.[64]

'Live-in-your-own-skin' notably differs from the 'gender affirmative' approach which does not manipulate/convert a child's gender identity and/or expressions. Defined as a method of therapeutic care by its proponents,[65] the approach allows children to speak for themselves and provides support for them to evolve into their authentic gendered selves. The model aims to alleviate stress associated with a child's sex assigned at birth, build gendered resilience and secure social support from their family and peers.[66] Both of the aforementioned approaches to addressing gender diversity in childhood can also be distinguished from 'watchful waiting', which observes children's gender identities and expressions over time.[67] If these persist, a child's gender-diverse identity is affirmed through puberty-blocking and/or cross-sex hormone therapy.

Practices outlined in the 'live-in-your-own-skin' approach are not currently endorsed by the NHS.[68] GIDS recommends a combination of the watchful waiting and gender affirmative approaches to managing gender diversity and treating gender dysphoria in childhood.[69] International health organisations expert in gender affirmative healthcare, including the World Professional Association of Transgender Health and American Psychological Association, also stipulate that health professionals should not engage in practices that attempt to alter the gendered expressions or identity of a young person.[70] Limited data on the prevalence of gender-diverse children 'living in [their] own skin' is available in England. This may be because they are most commonly carried out by parents and faith-based organisations behind closed doors and without the oversight of healthcare professionals.[71] More available data is, however, available for gender-diverse adults. Figures from the National

---

[63] Such as depression, self-harm, anxiety and suicidal ideations.

[64] For example, see C Horton, 'Experiences of Puberty and Puberty Blockers: Insights from Trans Children, Trans Adolescents, and Their Parents' (2022) *Journal of Adolescent Research* 1.

[65] Zucker and Bradley (n 59).

[66] Ehrensaft (n 58).

[67] For a more in-depth discussion of watchful waiting, see F Ashley, 'Watchful Waiting Doesn't Mean No Puberty Blockers, and Moving Beyond Watchful Waiting' (2019) 16(6) *American Journal of Bioethics* 3.

[68] The Tavistock and Portman NHS Foundation Trust, 'A Ban on Conversion Therapy Should Include Protections for Trans People' (NHS Online, 1 April 2022) tavistockandportman.nhs.uk/about-us/news/stories/a-ban-on-conversion-therapy-should-include-protections-for-trans-people.

[69] This is another point I discuss at length in my PhD thesis: H Hirst, 'A Children's Rights Perspective on the Administration of Puberty Blockers and Cross-sex Hormones in England' (PhD Thesis, University of Liverpool, 10 May 2023).

[70] E Coleman et al, 'Standards of Care for the Health of Gender Diverse People, Version 8' (2022) 23(1) *International Journal of Transgender Health* 57.

[71] A Jowett et al, 'Conversion Therapy: An Evidence Assessment and Qualitative Study' (GOV.UK, 29 October 2021) www.gov.uk/government/publications/conversion-therapy-an-evidence-assessment-and-qualitative-study/conversion-therapy-an-evidence-assessment-and-qualitative-study.

LGBT Survey, for instance, found that 13 per cent of trans respondents had been offered or undergone 'conversion therapy'.[72]

Having provided a critical overview of 'conversion therapy' for gender-diverse youth, the following discussion considers the impact the aforementioned practices have on the rights of gender-diverse children, particularly the right to develop in the short, medium, and long-term.

IV. How Does 'Conversion Therapy' for Gender-diverse Youth Impact Their Right to Develop?

Article 6(2) of the UNCRC is a provision specifically committed to protecting and ensuring child development. It states that: 'State Parties shall ensure to the maximum extent possible the survival and development of the child'. Broader protection to a child's right to develop is also given in the ECHR[73] and English common law.[74] While Noam Peleg's research has raised the profile of child development in recent years, it can be argued that it remains an under-theorised and overlooked right in comparison to other general principles included in the UNCRC.[75] These are non-discrimination (Article 2), best interests (Article 3), and a child's right to be heard (Article 12). Later parts of this chapter emphasise the importance of child development and describe how 'conversion therapy' undermines gender-diverse children's physical growth, mental development, and social advancements.

A. Physical Growth

A child's right to develop is often understood in physical terms or as physical growth.[76] It is viewed as a means of protecting children's special status as premature adults or, as Nick Lee puts it, their 'journey towards adulthood'.[77] Children, according to this view, are understood as physically 'unfinished products'[78] and 'humans in the making'.[79] A well-known, and often cited, term underpinning a child's right to develop is the

---

[72] Government Equalities Office, 'National LGBT Survey: Research Report' (GOV.UK, 3 July 2018).

[73] For a more detailed discussion on this, see W Vanderhole et al, 'Article 6: The Right to Life, Survival and Development' in W Vanderhole et al, *Children's Rights A Commentary on the Convention on the Rights of the Child and its Protocols* (Cheltenham, Elgar Publishing, 2019).

[74] Reference is made by the courts to the importance of child development in *Re A (A Child)* [2010] EWCC 33 (Fam), *Re J (A Child)* [1999] EWCA Civ 3022, and *In the matter of D (A Child)* [2017] EWCA Civ 1695.

[75] N Peleg, *The Child's Right to Develop* (Cambridge, Cambridge University Press, 2019).

[76] N Peleg, 'The Child's Right to Develop' (PhD Thesis, University College London, November 2012).

[77] M Lee, *Childhood and Society* (Maidenhead, Open University Press, 2001) 5.

[78] C Smart et al, *The Changing Experience of Childhood: Interdependence, Innovation Systems and Industrial Policy: Families and Divorce* (Malden, Polity, 2001).

[79] Peleg (n 76) 16.

'human becomings' conception of childhood.[80] Peleg argues that the human becomings concept perceives children as weak, vulnerable, lacking agency and in need of adult protection/control.[81] It implies that they are not capable of rational/independent thought,[82] or being active social agents[83] and sole rights holders. This conception of children is identifiable in cases concerning gender-diverse youth. In *Bell v Tavistock*,[84] for example, the Divisional Court stated that:

> There will be enormous difficulties in a child under 16 understanding and weighing up this information and deciding whether to consent to the use of puberty blocking medication. It is highly unlikely that a child aged 13 or under would be competent to give consent to the administration of puberty blockers. It is doubtful that a child aged 14 or 15 could understand and weigh the long-term risks and consequences of the administration of puberty blockers.[85]

Equally, at paragraph 46 of the judgment, Dame Victoria Sharp P, Lord Justice Lewis, and Mrs Justice Lieven referred to Professor Sophie Scott's suggestion that 'all the evidence we have suggests that the complex, emotionally charged decisions required to engage with this treatment are not yet acquired as a skill at this age, both in terms of brain maturation and in terms of behaviour'.[86] In my previous research analysing the judgment, and subsequent appeal, I was critical of the court's focus on children's physical growth and pointed out that its narrow perspective meant that other important developmental considerations, such as the right to an identity (Article 8 of the UNCRC), right to be heard (Article 12 of the UNCRC) and right to health (Article 24 of the UNCRC), were overlooked.[87]

'Conversion therapy' can, nevertheless, undermine a child's physical right to develop because, in some cases, the practice results in gender-diverse children never growing up/reaching adulthood. Powerful, and tragic, stories of children dying of suicide demonstrate this. Leelah Alcorn, for example, wrote in a suicide note posted on the social media website Tumblr that she was taken to Christian therapists by her parents at the age of 16 when she told them of her trans identity.[88] Leelah wrote that conversion practices reinforced the notion that gender diversity was 'wrong' and resigned to living her life 'like a man in drag'.[89] Although this testimony is extreme, it is supported by published studies, such as

---

[80] E Uprichard, 'Children as "Beings and Becomings": Children, Childhood and Temporality' (2008) 22 *Children and Society* 305.

[81] E Burnman, *Child, Image, Nation* (Oxford, Routledge, 2021).

[82] Peleg (n 76).

[83] As suggested in the new sociology of childhood. See A James et al, *Theorising Childhood* (Policy Press, 1998).

[84] *Bell* (n 3).

[85] ibid 151.

[86] ibid 46.

[87] H Hirst, 'The Legal Rights and Wrongs of Puberty Blocking in England' (2021) 33(2) *Child and Family Law Quarterly* 115.

[88] F Fox, 'Leelah Alcorn's Suicide: Conversion Therapy Is Child Abuse' (*Time Magazine*, 8 January 2015) time.com/3655718/leelah-alcorn-suicide-transgender-therapy.

[89] ibid.

Jack Turban et al's,[90] which indicate that exposure to 'conversion therapy' in childhood significantly increases a person's lifetime odds of suicide attempts.[91]

Limiting gender-diverse children's access to treatments related to their gender identity, such as puberty blockers and cross-sex hormones, can also lead to *some* gender-diverse children experiencing more significant suicidal ideations leading to death. As noted earlier in this chapter, the live-in-your-own-skin model recommends restricting a gender-diverse child's access to puberty blockers and cross-sex hormones until puberty.[92] Puberty can occur in the later stages of childhood, even at 16 years, meaning that some children cannot tolerate a delay in treatment and the worsening of their psychosocial distress. This was the case when Jayden Lowe took his own life after being informed that a two-year delay in his treatment at GIDS was likely to be extended by another four years, subsequent to being referred to the Gender Identity Service for Adults on his 18th birthday.[93] Suitability for treatment is, however, a highly individualised choice/process and data related to the impact of puberty blockers and cross-sex hormones on a child's bone density and fertility should be taken into account by a doctor prior to its administration.[94]

B. Mental Development

Child development incorporates more than children's physical growth. It is widely accepted that it is a broad concept involving all aspects of children's growth and development.[95] Elizabeth Levin notes that development involves a child's cognitive and emotional development (as well as their physical growth), and the social occurrences an individual experiences from infancy through to the legal age of majority (18 in England and Wales).[96] This (broader) conception of child development has been acknowledged by the English courts, with Baroness Hale noting in *R (SB) v Governors of Denbigh High School*[97] that

---

[90] J Turban et al, 'Association Between Recalled Exposure to Gender Identity Conversion Efforts and Psychological Distress and Suicide Attempts Among Transgender Adults' (2020) 77(1) *JAMA Psychiatry* 68.

[91] For instance, see A Green et al, 'Self-Reported Conversion Efforts and Suicidality Among US LGBTQ Youths and Young Adults, 2018' (2020) 110(8) *American Journal of Public Health* 1221.

[92] Ehrensaft (n 58).

[93] M Roberts, 'Mother's Agony after Her Transgender Son, 18, Took His Own Life Months after Paying for Hormone Therapy from Illegal Clinic Because He Faced a Six-year Wait on the NHS' (*Daily Mail Online*, 1 July 2019) www.dailymail.co.uk/news/article-7200189/Mothers-agony-transgender-son-18-took-life-months-paying-hormone-therapy.

[94] For a more detailed discussion on these issues see Giordano (n 8) and S Giordano and S Holm, 'Is Puberty Delaying Treatment "Experimental Treatment?"' (2020) 21(2) *International Journal of Transgender Health* 113.

[95] Peleg (n 76).

[96] E Levin, 'Child Development' in J Naglieri and S Goldstein et al, *Encyclopaedia of Child Behavior and Development* (New York, Springer Publishing, 2011).

[97] *R (SB) v Governors of Denbigh High School* [2006] UKHL 15.

'important physical, cognitive, and psychological developments take place during adolescence'.[98] Understanding development in this way means that a child's right to develop entails more than just securing their physical maturation/ growth into adulthood. The Committee on the Rights of the Child discussed this matter in its General Comment No 20,[99] when warning against narrow interpretations of child development:

> [The Committee] regrets the widespread negative characteristics of adolescence leading to narrow problem-focused interventions and services, rather than a commitment to building optimum environments to guarantee the rights of adolescents and support the development of their physical, psychological, spiritual, social, emotional, cognitive, cultural, and economic capacities.[100]

Indeed, the UNCRC requires State Parties (and adults more generally) to implement measures and take action to protect a child's mental, moral, social, cultural, personality, and talent.[101] These developmental domains (in addition to physical development) can be identified in various articles of the UNCRC.[102] Part of embracing a child's broader right to develop, involves adults acknowledging children as human 'beings', and understanding that child development occurs in the short, medium, and long-term.[103]

The aforementioned practices to convert a child's gender identity undercut a child's non-physical right to develop (as conceptualised by the UNCRC and the Committee on the Rights of the Child). Of all the developmental domains, it is arguable that 'conversion therapy' impacts children's mental and social development most frequently. In instances where a gender-diverse child does not take their own life, it is possible to see children exhibiting significant mental distress and/or mental health diagnoses.[104] Erika Muse, a trans woman who underwent 'conversion therapy' as a child, described the live-in-your-own-skin model as 'not therapeutic, but abusive'[105] to the Legislative Assembly of Ontario (Canada). She also told the Assembly that the practice 'destroyed [her] as a person' and that she became 'suicidal and depressed'.[106] Carolyn, another trans woman who identified as gender diverse during childhood, told an organisation

---

[98] ibid 93.

[99] Committee on the Rights of the Child, 'General Comment No. 20 (2016) on the implementation of the rights of the child during adolescence' (6 December 2016) UN DOC CRC/C/GC/20.

[100] ibid 15.

[101] N Peleg, 'Developing the Right to Develop' (2017) 25(2) *International Journal of Children's Rights* 380.

[102] Art 18(1) parental responsibilities and state assistance, Art 23(3) children with a disability, Art 27(2) adequate standard of living, Art 29(1)(a) goals of education, and Art 32(1) child labour.

[103] Levin (n 96).

[104] Giordano (n 8), Hirst (n 87), and Green (n 92).

[105] Legislative Assembly of Ontario, 'Affirming Sexual Orientation and Gender Identity Act 2015' (*Standing Committee on Justice Policy*, 3 June 2015) www.ola.org/en/legislative-business/committees/justice-policy/parliament-41/transcripts/committee-transcript-2015-jun-03.

[106] ibid.

dedicated to abolishing 'conversion therapy' in the UK that she received electric shock therapy as a child.[107] The practice took place at a hospital in Blackburn (UK) during the 1960s and was performed by a psychiatrist. Carolyn had been referred by a local vicar and states that she was strapped to a wooden chair whilst images of women were projected onto the wall in front of her. She recalls psychiatrists claiming that her trans identity would desist if she learnt to associate her gender identity with physical pain. The electrical shock practice had a devastating effect on Carolyn mentally, as she notes: '… you could say that the therapy "worked", in that it affected my body. But, in terms of my mind, and my thoughts, it only made me hate myself more.'[108] The mental impact on Carolyn has endured 40 years, and at the age of 55 she still has flashbacks from the 'therapy' she received. Studies similarly indicate poorer mental health outcomes in children subjected to 'conversion therapy', compared with children who are supported in their gender diverse identity.[109] They describe gender-diverse youth at an increased risk of adverse mental outcomes where there is a lack of support from a parent.[110]

C. Social Advancement

A gender-diverse child's social development is also likely to be affected by practices to convert their gender identity. Contemporary approaches to childhood research indicate that children are 'perpetrators of the present',[111] who are competent in their social relations and culture as a social group. To this end, Alison James and Alan Prout note that, 'Children should be actively seen in the construction and determination of the lives around them, the societies they live in, and their own social lives.'[112]

The courts in England have also taken social development into account when evaluating best interests.[113] In *Re G (Education: Religious Upbringing)*,[114] for example, the Court of Appeal spoke of judges adopting a 'holistic approach'[115] to welfare, which bore in mind:

> … a wide range of ethical, social, moral, religious, cultural, emotional, and welfare considerations, everything that is conductive to a child's welfare and happiness or

---

[107] Ban Conversion Therapy, 'Carloyn's Story' (Ban Conversion Therapy, 1 August 2021) www.banconversiontherapy.com/carolyn-story.

[108] ibid.

[109] Westwater et al (n 45), Brown (n 45), and Pariseau (n 45).

[110] ibid.

[111] C Jenks, *Childhood* (Oxford, Routledge, 2005).

[112] James et al (n 83) 13.

[113] Also see *Re A (A Child)* [2016] EWCA Civ 759; *An NHS Trust v MB & Another* [2006] EWHC 507 (Fam); and *Aintree University Hospitals NHS Foundation Trust v James* [2013] UKSC 67, [2014] AC 591.

[114] *Re G (Education: Religious Upbringing)* [2012] EWCA Civ 1233, [2013] 1 FLR 677.

[115] ibid 24.

relates to the child's development and present and future life as a human being, including the child's familial, educational and social environment.[116]

This has been echoed by the Committee on the Rights of the Child in its General Comment No 14, when it discussed Article 3 (the best interests of the child) as promoting the full and effective enjoyment of all the rights recognised in the holistic development of the child.[117]

Most children have diverse social lives.[118] They may have established relationships with adult members of their own family and professionals. A child may also have long-standing relationships with other children. The latter notably exist separately from a child's parents/guardians, and are built on unique experiences, characteristics, interests, and needs.

The '2020 Conversion Therapy & Gender Identity Survey' carried out by the LGBTQ+ charity Stonewall (with 1,504 gender diverse respondents) indicates that practices to convert gender-diverse peoples' gender identities negatively impacted their family relationships;[119] 38 per cent of respondents stated that 'conversion therapy' had made relationships with family members 'much worse', while 23 per cent revealed that it had made them 'worse';[120] 20 per cent of respondents disclosed 'no impact' on familial relations and 5 per cent revealed conversion practices made them 'better'.[121] These findings notably refer to adults, as there is a paucity of empirical research relating to the impact of conversion practices on gender-diverse children's (and LGBTQ+ youth more widely) wellbeing, development, and rights.

The aforementioned statistics from the Stonewall survey are, however, helpful in demonstrating the personal nature and the dissimilar impact 'conversion therapy' has on children's relationships with family. Familial relations post 'conversion therapy' will be different for every child. In some cases, it may improve a child's relationship with their parents/carers and/or wider family, compared with relations prior to 'conversion therapy'. This may be because their newly 'converted'/'cis' identity conforms to parental expectations relating to sex assigned at birth. Although there may be some improvement in the short term between a gender-diverse child and their parents/carers, it is possible that this will not persist into later childhood and, eventually, adulthood. Some children may feel resentment and anger towards those who facilitated/arranged conversion practices to take place, leading to a breakdown in affected parent/child or

---

[116] ibid.

[117] Para IA. Notably, the 'holistic development of the child' is mentioned five times in this general comment.

[118] Committee on the Rights of the Child, 'General Comment No. 14 on the right of the child to have his or her best interests taken as a primary consideration (art. 3, para. 1)' (29 May 2013) UN Doc CRC/C/GC/14.

[119] Stonewall, '2020 Conversion Therapy and Gender Identity Survey' (Stonewall, 1 March 2021) www.stonewall.org.uk/resources/2020-conversion-therapy-and-gender-identity-survey.

[120] ibid.

[121] ibid.

carer/child relationships. An illustrative example is Eli's experience of undergoing 'conversion therapy':

> My parents don't understand why it ['conversion therapy'] is so damaging. They think all therapy is a good thing. It was them who paid for me to see the therapists I did, and they think I was lucky that I was able to have therapy. It is difficult for me to hear that from my parents – today I struggle with PTSD and an eating disorder which are linked to my 'conversion therapy' experiences.[122]

Parents/carers not only play a vital role in a gender-diverse child's mental development/health (as noted above), but also in their social development.[123] Data from empirical studies carried out with children,[124] underpinned by children's rights research,[125] and guidance provided by the Committee on the Rights of the Child[126] highlights the important function of parental guidance and support in a child's social development. Studies demonstrate that parents/carers are fundamental to a child's developing a social skill-set.[127] Indeed, parents/carers provide children with their very first opportunities to develop a relationship, communicate and interact with others. These ideas are echoed by the Committee on the Rights of the Child (in addition to Articles 5,[128] 9,[129] and 18[130] of the UNCRC), preamble, General Comment No 14: 'the family is the natural environment for the growth and well-being of all its members (especially children)'[131] and No 20: 'factors known to promote the resilience and healthy development of adolescents include: (a) strong relationships with and support from the key adults in their lives'.[132]

'Conversion therapy' can also impact a gender-diverse child's right to socially develop by affecting their non-familial relationships. One example, which could be discussed at length, is a gender-diverse child's connection with other children. As noted above, the live-in-your-own-skin model proposes that a gender-diverse child's friendship group should be altered to include more same-sex contacts. This, as well as the suggestion that parents/carers should take away gender 'appropriate' toys, raises issues in relation to Articles 31 (a child's right to play), 27 (a child's

---

[122] Ban Conversion Therapy, 'Eli's Story' (Ban Conversion Therapy, 1 August 2021) www.banconversiontherapy.com/elis-story.

[123] James et al (n 83), Levin (n 96) and Jenks (n 111). Also see A Baldwin, 'Socialization and the Parent-Child Relationship' (1948) 19(3) *Child Development* 127.

[124] See, for example, J Yousins, *Parents and Peers in Social Development A Sullivan-Piaget Perspective* (Chiacago, The University of Chicago Press, 1980); D Phillips et al, 'Child-care Quality and Children's Social Development' (1987) 23(4) *Developmental Psychology* 537.

[125] O O'Neill, 'Children's Rights and Children's Lives' (1988) 29(3) *Ethics* 445; B Mayall, 'The Sociology of Childhood in Relation to Children's Rights' (2000) 8 *International Journal of Children's Rights* 243.

[126] Such as General Comments Nos 14 and 20.

[127] See, for example, M Neitola, 'Parents as Teachers and Guides of Their Children's Social Skills' (2018) 7(2) *Journal of Early Childhood Education Research* 392.

[128] Parental guidance and a child's evolving capacity.

[129] Separation from parents.

[130] Parental responsibilities and state assistance.

[131] Committee on the Rights of the Child (n 118) c 59.

[132] Committee on the Rights of the Child (n 99) 17.

right to a standard of living, which allows physical, mental, spiritual, and social development) and 15 (a child's right to meet with other children, join groups and organisations) of the UNCRC. Peer interactions through play, leisure, and activities can help socially equip a child in the short, medium, and long-term by teaching and nurturing self-confidence, empathy, problem-solving, creative thinking, and communication.[133] Even disagreements between children can have a positive influence on their social development, as Naomi Lott notes:

> These situations require children to improvise, to learn how to deal with conflict, de-escalate feelings and resolve disagreement, and in-so-doing improves social competency and flexibility.[134]

Reducing play and peer interactions with other children may mean that a gender-diverse child is not taught the aforementioned social skills, which are vital to children's economic, social, and cultural rights.[135] Research also emphasises the important role of play in gendered learning, experiences, and knowledge.[136] A study conducted by Sarah Callahan and Lucy Nicholas, for example, explores children's expression of gender through play.[137] Other research illustrates that play not only teaches children about gender fluidity and different gender identities, it also informs their own perceptions and experiences of gender.[138]

Another, and less obvious, impact of 'conversion therapy' is its social consequences for both cis and gender-diverse children. Social interactions with a gender-diverse child can educate cis children about gendered experiences, identities, bodies, and norms.[139] This knowledge can be helpful and/or informative in navigating employment, further education, and relationships in adulthood, where gender-diverse people make up an ever-growing proportion of society. Robert Bittner et al note that the inclusion of gender-diverse children provides a 'pedagogy of possibility' that disrupts cisnormativity,[140] whilst raising acceptance from cis peers.[141] To this end, it can be argued that the suppression of young gender-diverse

---

[133] N Lott, 'Establishing the Right to Play as an Economic, a Social and a Cultural Right' (2022) 30(3) *International Journal of Children's Rights*, 755. Also see A Pellegrini and P Smith, 'Physical Activity Play: The Nature and Function of a Neglected Aspect of Play' (1998) 69(3) *Child Development* 577.

[134] ibid 769.

[135] Lott (n 133).

[136] S Rameaeni et al, 'Gender, Power and Play in Early Childhood Education' (International Conference on Educational Sciences, Bandung, 2017).

[137] S Callahan and L Nicholas, 'Dragon Wings and Butterfly Wings: Implicit Gender Binarism in Early Childhood' (2019) 31(6) *Gender Education* 705.

[138] See, for instance, B Martin, *Children at Play: Learning Gender in the Early Years* (Stoke-on-Trent, Trentham Books, 2011).

[139] C Horton, 'Thriving or Surviving? Raising Our Ambition for Trans Children in Primary and Secondary Schools' (2020) 11(5) *Frontiers in Sociology* 1.

[140] R Brittner et al, 'Queer and Trans-Themed Books for Young Readers: A Critical Review' (2016) 37(6) *Discourse: Studies in the Cultural Politics of Education* 984.

[141] SD Snapp et al, 'Students' Perspectives on LGBTQ-Inclusive Curriculum' (2015) 48(2) *Equity and Excellence in Education* 249.

identities through 'conversion therapy' has implications for the right of all children to develop and access information (Articles 6 and 13 of the UNCRC).

V. The English Government's Duties and Position on Ending 'Conversion Therapy' for Gender-diverse Children

In light of the implications of 'conversion therapy' on the right of gender-diverse youth to develop physically, mentally, and socially, this chapter addresses the action signatories to the UNCRC should (and are likely to) take to end conversion practices targeting gender diversity in childhood.

A. A Duty to Act

The UNCRC came into force on 15 January 1992, subsequent to its ratification on 16 December 1991.[142] Whilst Wales has incorporated the UNCRC into national law[143] and Scotland has taken steps to involve gender-diverse people in plans to ban 'conversion therapy',[144] there has been little effort made by politicians in England to ensure gender-diverse children's 'open futures'.[145] The most notable example of this was the government's announcement in April 2022 that gender-diverse adults and children would be excluded from a ban on 'conversion therapy'.[146] This lack of support for tackling harmful and ineffective practices, which seek to convert gender-diverse children's gender identities, arguably undercuts the government's duty as a State Party to the UNCRC to:

> Introduce measures to help [children] thrive, explore their emerging identities, beliefs, sexualities and opportunities, balance risk and safety, build capacity for make free, informed, and positive decisions and life choices.[147]

The enactment of legislation to make 'conversion therapy' for gender-diverse youth (and LGBTQ+ people more widely) unlawful in England would characterise such

---

[142] See M Freeman, 'Children's Rights as Human Rights: Reading the UNCRC' in J Qvortrup et al, *The Palgrave Handbook of Childhood Studies* (London, Palgrave Publishing, 2009).

[143] S Lyle, 'Embracing the UNCRC in Wales (UK): Policy, Pedagogy and Prejudices' (2013) 40(2) *Educational Studies* 215.

[144] See, for example, Scotland's Expert Advisory Group on Ending Conversion Practices 'Report and Recommendations' (Gov Scot, 4 October 2022) www.gov.scot/publications/expert-advisory-group-ending-conversion-practices-report-recommendations/pages/2/.

[145] Feinberg (n 7).

[146] S Gallagher and J Parry, 'Conversion Therapy: Ban to Go Ahead but Not to Cover Trans People' (*BBC Online*, 1 April 2022) bbc.co.uk/news/uk-60947028.

[147] Committee on the Rights of the Child (n 99) 16.

a measure. It would mean that a gender-diverse child would, to some extent,[148] be able to explore and live in a gender authentic to them, without the possibility (and fear) of adult interference with their body, identity, and experiences. A ban would also achieve the obligation set out in Article 19(1) of the UNCRC, that:

> State Parties shall take all appropriate legislative, administrative, social, and educational measures to protect the child from all forms of physical or mental violence, injury or abuse, neglect or negligent treatment, maltreatment or exploitation, including sexual abuse, while in the care of parents, legal guardians or any other person who has care of the child.

This provision is particularly significant in the context of 'conversion therapy' for gender-diverse youth because, as noted earlier, it is most often parents/carers (along with religious organisations) who facilitate practices to 'convert' their child's gender identity. It may be the case these parents believe 'conversion therapy' serves their child's best interests. However, as demonstrated in the discussion above, practices to alter gender diversity in childhood can impact not just a child's physical maturation into adulthood, but also their mental and social development.

B. The Best Interests of the Child and Keeping Pace with Ever Changing Social Norms in England and Similar Societies

On the subject of best interests, it is noteworthy that the courts in England have stressed that the word 'welfare' (which is used interchangeably with best interests in English common law) 'must be taken in its widest sense'[149] and its evaluation will change according to developments in society.[150] Reference to changing social norms in cases concerning children's best interests is also made as far back as 1970 by Lord Upjohn in *J v C*:[151]

> The law and practice in relation to infants ... have developed, are developing, and must, and no doubt will, continue to develop by reflecting and adopting the changing views, as the years go by, of reasonable men and women, the parents of children, on the proper treatment and methods of bringing up children; for after all that is the model which the judge must emulate for ... he must act as the judicial reasonable parent.[152]

This statement was described as 'crucial' by Munby LJ, 42 years later in *Re G (Children)*.[153] In this case, he stated that although the concept of welfare remains the same as it was in 1925, understandings of the concept have changed and

---

[148] Depending on the support of adults, most notably parent(s)/carer(s).
[149] *Re G (Children)* [2012] EWCA Civ 1233, 27.
[150] J Dolgin, 'Why Has the Best Interests Standard Survived?: The Historic and Social Context' (1996) 16(2) *Children's Legal Rights Journal* 2.
[151] *J v C* [1970] AC 668.
[152] ibid 722.
[153] *Re G (Children)* (n 149).

continue to change.[154] A noteworthy part of his judgment, which can be applied to changing conceptions of 'conversion therapy' and parenting, reads:

> A child's welfare is to be judged today by the standards of reasonable men and women in 2012, not by the standards of their parents in 1970, and having regard to the ever-changing nature of our world: changes in our understanding of the natural world, technological changes, changes in social standards, and perhaps, most important of all, changes in social attitudes.[155]

Social understandings of 'conversion therapy' in England have shifted hugely in the past 30 years. In recent years (and months), calls have been made by charities,[156] health organisations,[157] activist groups,[158] politicians,[159] and citizens[160] to end 'conversion therapy' for gender-diverse people. In June 2022, a petition letter signed by 149,167 people informed a debate in the House of Commons concerning the exclusion of trans people in a legislative ban on 'conversion therapy'.[161] Importantly, the government's plans to discount gender-diverse people (and youth) from a ban on 'conversion therapy' stood in sharp contrast with other 'similar societies'.[162] In Canada, for example, 'conversion therapy' for gender-diverse youth has been criminalised after the passing of Bill C-6 in the House of Commons.[163] The amendments to the Criminal Code prohibit causing another person to undergo 'conversion therapy'; removing a child from Canada to subject them to 'conversion therapy' abroad; profiting from providing 'conversion therapy'; and advertising or promoting 'conversion therapy'.[164] These changes to the code notably apply to all Canadians regardless of age. In the wake of legislative action on 'conversion therapy' abroad, the English government must be careful

---

[154] President of the Family Division, 'Changing Families: Family Law Yesterday, Today and Tomorrow – A View from South of the Border' (University of Edinburgh, 20 March 2018) www.judiciary.uk/wp-content/uploads/2018/03/speech-pfd-changing-families-edinburgh.pdf.

[155] *Re G (Children)* (n 149) 33.

[156] Such as Mermaids, Stonewall, and Mind.

[157] Including the British Medical Association: L Patel, 'UK's Ban on Conversion Therapy Should Include Transgender People' (British Medical Association Online, 20 June 2022) www.bmj.com/content/bmj/377/bmj.o1453.full.pdf.

[158] See C Clark, 'Thousands Protest Trans People's Exclusion from "Conversion Therapy" Ban outside Downing Street' (Gay Times Online, 1 May 2022) www.gaytimes.co.uk/originals/conversion-therapy-trans-ban-protest-downing-street.

[159] Such as Nadia Whittome, Kate Osborne, Jeremy Corbyn, and Theresa May.

[160] For example, in the form of Parliamentary petitions. See UK Government and Politics, 'Ensure Trans People Are Fully Protected under Any Conversion Therapy Ban' (GOV.UK, 13 June 2022) petition.parliament.uk/petitions/613556.

[161] ibid.

[162] Thorpe LJ's judgment in *Mabon v Mabon* [2005] EWCA Civ 634 discusses England 'falling out of step' in comparison to other similar societies in terms of children's rights and participation.

[163] Blais et al (n 6).

[164] T Salway et al, 'Details of "Conversion Therapy" Practices and Concordance with Legislative Definition: Findings from a Non-probability Community-based Survey in Canada, 2020' (MedRxiv, 16 November 2021) www.medrxiv.org/content/10.1101/2021.11.15.21266353v1.

that they, in the words of Thorpe LJ, do not 'fall out of step with similar societies' in matters related to children's rights and youth participation.[165]

C. The Government's Position and Likely Legislative Action on 'Conversion Therapy' for Gender-diverse Youth

If legislation was enacted under the current government to make it unlawful for a gender-diverse child to undergo 'conversion therapy', it is likely that this would only cover physical acts (such as spanking and electric shock therapy), and not the 'live-in-your-own-skin' model. This is because high-profile members of the Conservative party have called for 'caution' and 'reasonableness' on matters concerning childhood medical transition.[166] In 2019, the then-Prime Minister, Boris Johnson, stated that he did not think 'it was reasonable for kids to be deemed so-called "*Gillick* competent" to take decisions about their gender or irreversible treatments that they may have'[167] and that he believed 'there should be parental involvement at the very least'.[168]

The government's and courts' deference to parental consent in the context of gender affirmative treatments (puberty blockers and cross-sex hormones) indicates that a legislative ban on gender-diverse youth 'living in [their] own skin' would be unlikely. In *AB v CD and Others*,[169] the High Court ruled that a gender-diverse child may gain access to puberty blockers and/or cross-sex hormones without court permission. This position was reaffirmed by the Court of Appeal, when Lady Justice King, Lord Chief Justice Maldon and Sir Geoffrey Vos ruled that children do not always require a specific issue order from the High Court (Family Division) to undergo puberty blocking and/or cross-sex hormone therapy in *Bell*.[170] This reliance/focus on parental consent is emblematic of the wider legal framework concerning children's medical treatment and the state's involvement in parents/carers rearing their child(ren).[171] Lord Donaldson famously stated in *Re W (A Minor) (Medical Treatment: Court's Jurisdiction)*[172] that parental consent can provide 'a flak jacket' ensuring legal protection for doctors when medical treatments/interventions are administered to children.[173] The courts and government

---

[165] *Mabon* (n 162).

[166] A Allegretti and L Brooks, 'Johnson Says Biological Males "Should Not Compete in Female Sporting Events"' (Guardian Online, 6 April 2022) www.theguardian.com/politics/2022/apr/06/johnson-says-trans-athletes-should-not-compete-in-sport-that-does-not-match-biological-sex.

[167] ibid.

[168] ibid.

[169] *AB* (n 18).

[170] *Bell* (n 3).

[171] Also see Art 19 UNCRC.

[172] *Re W (A Minor) (Medical Treatment: Court's Jurisdiction)* [1993] Fam 64.

[173] But equally the consent of a competent child can ensure this. See E Cave, 'Goodbye Gillick? Identifying and Resolving Problems with the Concept of Child Competence' (2014) 34(1) *Legal Studies* 103.

have, over the years, been cautious not to become overly involved in child-rearing and, more specifically, in addressing the status of gender-diverse children's rights in England.[174] This inaction is concerning in the context of 'conversion therapy' for gender-diverse youth, where it can be argued that the developmental harm inflicted upon children outweighs concerns/questions about parental rights/ powers.

For the reasons outlined above, it is questionable whether the English government (as a signatory to the UNCRC) has upheld the duties it owes gender-diverse children. The following analysis builds on this, by suggesting that future legislation, ending 'conversion therapy' (in a similar vein to Canada), should contemplate whether it ensures a 'maximally open future'[175] for gender-diverse youth.

VI. Ensuring a Maximally Open Future for Gender-diverse Youth by Ending 'Conversion Therapy'

Originally coined by Joel Feinberg, a 'child's right to an open future' is a set of autonomy 'rights-in-trust', which cannot be exercised by a child until they acquire the capability to act autonomously.[176] These 'C' rights (child-only rights) ensure that a child has future options when reaching/entering adulthood.[177] Robert Darby notes that they can be 'permanently foreclosed when adults take deliberate steps to restrict children's future options',[178] such as 'conversion therapy' for gender-diverse youth. Feinberg's thesis can be compared to the 'human becomings' depiction of childhood (discussed earlier in this chapter), which distinguishes between children and adults based on physical and cognitive attributes.[179] While, for the reasons discussed above, this is problematic in terms of child development, the right to an open future does nevertheless limit the rights of parents (which, as noted above, currently prevail over gender-diverse children's rights) and impose duties on the state to protect a child's right to develop.[180]

An important and valuable part of Feinberg's right to an open future in the 'conversion therapy' context is his employment of the language of maximisation. According to Feinberg, one 'should send the child into the adult world with as many open opportunities as possible thus maximising his chances of fulfilment'.[181]

---

[174] See, for example, the Supreme Court's judgment in *In the matter of D (A Child)* [2019] UKSC 42.
[175] Feinberg (n 7).
[176] ibid.
[177] ibid.
[178] RJL Darby, 'The Child's Right to an Open Future: Is the Principle Applicable to Non-Therapeutic Circumcision?' (2013) 39(7) *Journal of Medical Ethics* 463.
[179] Uprichard (n 80).
[180] M Lotz, 'Feinberg, Mills, and the Child's Right to an Open Future' (2006) 37(4) *Journal of Social Philosophy* 537.
[181] Feinberg (n 7) 134–35.

This language is notably echoed in Article 6(2) of the UNCRC, which states that 'State Parties shall ensure the *maximum* extent possible the survival and development of the child'. Feinberg offers no context in which a child's maximally open future should be ensured. However, Richard Arnerson and Ian Shapiro suggest that it should apply to children as 'widely as possible to the variety of ways in life'.[182] A maximally open future might, therefore, apply in the context of 'conversion therapy' for gender-diverse youth and offer a lens through which legislation can offer children affected by (or at risk of) practices to convert their gender identity, the greatest possible scope for personal choices and future options as adults.

In October 2021 the government sought to introduce a legislative ban on 'conversion therapy' in England and Wales.[183] This included a prohibition on physical/violent acts, as well as so-called 'talking therapies' (outlined above) for gender-diverse youth. Then, in April 2022, the Conservative government announced that only LGB 'conversion therapy' would be unlawful in its proposed Bill, and that practices seeking to convert children's (and adults) gender-diverse identities would remain legal.[184] More recently, Michelle Donelan published a statement, made in her capacity as Secretary of State for Digital, Culture, Media and Sport, that trans people would be included in 'a draft Bill which will set out a proposed approach to ban conversion practices'.[185] Little detail relating to the Bill's impact on gender-diverse youth in England and Wales was provided by Donelan, other than that:

> The legislation must not, through a lack of clarity, harm the growing number of children and young adults experiencing gender related distress, through inadvertently criminalising or chilling legitimate conversations parents or clinicians may have with their children.[186]

A more thorough description of the Bill is required to assess its impact on a gender-diverse child's open future. At present it is unclear which practices the government is seeking to end and whether a range of gender identities will be included in legislation. If the government is to take its duty as a State Party to the UNCRC seriously, then it should consider ending *all* forms of 'conversion therapy', including so-called 'talking therapies', for *all* gender-diverse children, as this would better guarantee gender-diverse youth a maximally open future. Unlike Erika, Carolyn,

---

[182] R Arneson and I Shapiro, 'Democratic Autonomy and Religious Freedom: A Critique of Wisconsin v. Yoder' in I Shapiro and R Hardin, *Nomos XXXVIII: Political Order* (New York, New York University Press, 1996).

[183] Government Equalities Office, 'Closed Consultation: Banning Conversion Therapy' (GOV. UK, 9 December 2021) www.gov.uk/government/consultations/banning-conversion-therapy/banning-conversion-therapy.

[184] V Clarke, 'UK Conversion Therapy Ban to Include Trans People' (BBC Online, 17 January 2022) www.bbc.co.uk/news/uk-64304142.

[185] HC Deb 17 January 2023, vol 726, cols 3WS–4WS.

[186] ibid.

and Louie (whose testimonies are described above), it would reduce the possibility that a gender-diverse child would enter adulthood with trauma and mental health issues attributed to 'conversion therapy' in childhood.[187] This type of ban on 'conversion therapy' would mean, for the reasons outlined earlier in this chapter, that a child's physical growth, social advancement, and mental development are not compromised by practices seeking to 'convert' their gender identity and that they are sent 'into the world with as many [socially] open opportunities as possible'.[188]

Education and educational resources would be needed to support the implementation of legislation banning all forms of 'conversion therapy' for gender-diverse children. Adults and children (of all gender identities) should be informed about the risks and harms associated with 'conversion therapy' in childhood. This may be conducted through the dissemination of information[189] (in the case of children this should be completed in a child-friendly way)[190] and as part of infant-secondary school education (perhaps in relationships and sex education classes). The private nature of 'conversion therapy' means that children and adults are unable to identify and report practices which seek to convert a child's gender identity to an appropriate person/body. Education, in this sense, can safeguard a child's 'right while he [she or they] are still a child to have future options kept open until he [she or they] are a fully-formed self-determining adult [or *Gillick* competent child] capable of deciding for themselves'.[191] It would also enable the government to uphold its duty under Article 24(2)(e) of the UNCRC: 'To ensure that all segments of society, in particular parents and children, are informed, have access to education and are supported in the use of basic knowledge of child health.'

Professional adults, particularly doctors, nurses, teachers, and social workers, should also be trained to recognise the signs of 'conversion therapy' among gender-diverse youth. At present there is a lack of teaching and awareness among these professionals about the physical, social, and mental impact of 'conversion therapy' on gender-diverse children's development. Legislative efforts will certainly be ineffective (ie those who have facilitated a practice(s) will not be held to account) if children and adults are uneducated about 'conversion therapy', and unsupported when disclosing their experiences.

---

[187] Ban Conversion Therapy (n 107 and n 122).

[188] Feinberg (n 7).

[189] Online and in public places, such as schools, GP surgeries and leisure centres.

[190] Children's rights scholars, such as Bronagh Byrne, emphasise the importance of creating child-friendly information: see B Bryne et al, *Creating Child-Friendly Versions of Written Documents: A Guide* (Luxembourg, European Union, 2021).

[191] Feinberg (n 7).

VII. Conclusion

Data demonstrates that an increasing number of children in England identify as gender diverse.[192] Children's rights, particularly those incorporated in the UNCRC, offer a means of recognising and understanding gender-diverse children as individual rights-holders. They have needs and interests connected to, but also separate from, cis children and adults, and face a range of prejudicial and harmful practices connected to their gender identity, including 'conversion therapy'. These 'therapies' are ineffective and thwart gender-diverse children's physical, mental and social development. Despite this, and the duties owed to gender-diverse youth by the English government as a signatory to the UNCRC, it was announced in April 2022 that a legislative ban on 'conversion therapy' would only apply to LGB people.[193] This raises issues in relation to the best interests principle, which must be judged with regard to the present day's social standards and attitudes,[194] as well as Article 19(1) of the UNCRC. Excluding children (and, indeed, gender-diverse adults) from a Bill making 'conversion therapy' unlawful would stand in sharp contrast to the position of similar societies, such as Canada, where it is a criminal offence to practise, advertise, promote and/or profit from the practice.[195] It remains unclear whether the English government will uphold all gender-diverse children's rights and guarantee them a maximally open future when (and, indeed, if) legislation is enacted ending all forms of 'conversion therapy' for LGBTQ+ people.

---

[192] The Tavistock and Portman NHS Foundation Trust (n 9).
[193] Clarke (n 184).
[194] *Re G (Children)* (n 149).
[195] Blais et al (n 6).

7

Ensuring Trans Protection within a Ban on Conversion Practices

LUI ASQUITH

The existence of gender-related so-called 'conversion therapy'[1] in the UK appears undeniable. The Government Equalities Office LGBT Survey (GEO LGBT Survey) shows that 5 per cent of the LGBTQ+ population have been offered conversion practices and 2 per cent of respondents have undergone it.[2] The risk of exposure to these practices approximately doubles for a transgender (trans) individual, at 8 per cent and 4 per cent respectively.[3] Gender-related conversion practices are rooted in the belief that an individual's gender identity must accord with the sex and legal gender they were assigned at birth. If it does not, practices aim to modify the individual from trans to cisgender[4] to remedy the perceived inferiority via a process of 'cisgender indoctrination'.[5]

Gender-related conversion practices are an unjustifiable form of discrimination against trans people on the basis of their gender identity, against which they are protected under Article 14 of the European Convention on Human Rights (ECHR).[6] There is consensus amongst the medical profession that there are no clinical benefits to conversion practices, and there is no recognised evidence of its effectiveness.[7] It is likely, however, to be traumatic and cause long-lasting harm to

---

[1] From now termed 'conversion practices'.

[2] Government Equalities Office, *National LGBT Survey: Research Report* (HMSO, 2018) 33.

[3] Government Equalities Office, 'The Prevalence of Conversion Therapy in the UK' (Gov.uk, 2021) para 1.1.

[4] Someone who has a gender identity that matches their sex assigned at birth.

[5] A Bishop, 'Harmful Treatment: The Global Reach of So-Called Conversion Therapy' (Outright Action International, 2019).

[6] *P v S and Cornwall County Council* (ECJ) C-13/94 ECR 1-2143 [1996] ICR 795.

[7] British Association of Counselling and Psychotherapy et al, 'Memorandum of Understanding on Conversion Therapy in the UK' (BACP, 4 March 2022) www.bacp.co.uk/events-and-resources/ethics-and-standards/mou. See also, British Medical Association, 'Conversion Therapy: House of Commons, e-petition debate' (BMA, 13 June 2022) www.bma.org.uk/media/5733/bmae-petition-debate-ban-on-conversion-therapy130622.pdf. See also RL Spitzer, 'Spitzer Reassesses His 2003 Study of Reparative Therapy of Homosexuality' (2012) 41(4) *Archives of Sexual Behavior* 757 in which the researcher

the trans individual who undergoes it.[8] Even when there is no bodily injury and no intense physical or mental suffering, it has been argued that conversion practices amount to a 'serious violation of human dignity' with all forms 'amounting *at a minimum* to degrading treatment' (emphasis added).[9] United Nations experts have recognised the capacity for gender-related conversion practices to amount to ill-treatment or torture.[10] Further, the nature of these practices violates an individual's right to physical integrity and self-determination.[11] A trans person having the autonomy to determine their gender identity and how they wish to express that gender identity – without predetermination and an undue policing of bodies – is a prerequisite to a trans person living a life with dignity.[12] Therefore, any prospective ban must protect the trans individual to ensure the full enjoyment of their rights and freedoms. From a rights-based perspective, there is no justification to defend a ban that excludes the trans individual. On the contrary, there is a moral and legal imperative to defend all trans people from this violent and discriminatory practice.

Within this context, this chapter aims to assist any legislative interventions in this area by considering the international context, which shows how trans people can be effectively protected from conversion practices. The chapter will argue that for a ban to be effective: (i) terminology is important; 'gender identity and expression' work well when describing the characteristics in need of protection within the context of the ban; and (ii) exemptions are required to protect the individual's right to explore who they are. Using the ECHR, this chapter will show that well-defined exemptions would allow individuals and professionals to engage in talking therapy or other forms of therapeutic support (so long as it is without predetermination), as well as give continued access to appropriate and good practice healthcare interventions. An exemption that endorses the human rights principle of true 'freedom' could also be helpful to mitigate the risk of any exemption being exploited while protecting an individual's right to autonomy. The chapter will explain that a ban that does not protect free exploration and the right to access good practice healthcare will not protect all trans individuals from conversion practices and would lead to the continuation of human rights violations.

---

responsible for the most cited study issued an apology to the gay community for making 'unproven claims of the efficacy of "reparative therapy"'.

   [8] ibid.

   [9] See Chapter 1 in this edited collection, by I Trispiotis. Also, I Trispiotis and C Purshouse '"Conversion Therapy" as Degrading Treatment' (2022) 42 *Oxford Journal of Legal Studies* 104.

   [10] UNHRC, 'Report of the Special Rapporteur on Torture and Other Cruel, Inhuman or Degrading Treatment or Punishment' (14 February 2017) UN Doc A/HRC/34/54, para 49; UNHRC, 'Practices of So-called "Conversion Therapy": Report of the Independent Expert on Protection against Violence and Discrimination Based on Sexual Orientation and Gender Identity' (1 May 2020) UN Doc A/HRC/44/53.

   [11] Commissioner for Human Rights, 'Human Rights and Gender Identity' (CommDH/IssuePaper (2009)2, Council of Europe, 2009).

   [12] UNGA, 'Protection against Violence and Discrimination Based on Sexual Orientation and Gender Identity' (15 July 2021) UN Doc A/76/152.

I. The Importance of Terminology: The Use of 'Gender Identity' and 'Expression' within a Ban

A small number of people experience incongruence between their sex/legal gender and their deeply felt internal and individual experience of gender. This experience includes (as defined by the Yogyakarta Principles[13]) the personal sense of the body and other expressions of gender (ie 'gender expression') such as dress, speech and mannerisms, commonly referred to as 'gender identity'.[14] Those who experience this incongruence can be described as 'transgender' or 'trans', with existing data indicating that some people's experiences of gender identity does not fall within the male or female binary.[15] Such people, usually identifying as 'non-binary', constituted 7 per cent of the Government Equality Office's LGBT Survey's respondents and among the transgender respondents, 52 per cent identified as non-binary.[16] Government literature defines them as follows:

> They may regard themselves as neither exclusively a man nor a woman, or as both, or take another approach to gender entirely. The word non-binary is used here as an umbrella term. Different people may use different words to describe their individual gender identity, such as genderfluid, agender or genderqueer.[17]

How a trans individual decides to express and present their gender identity can include a 'gender confirmation' process also termed a 'transition', which refers to the 'process (or part of a process) for the purpose of reassigning the person's sex by changing physiological or other attributes of sex'.[18] Transitioning is a self-elected and self-determined process, which can involve social, medical and/or legal changes. For example, this can include a change of pronouns (social); medical interventions, such as hormone treatments for the alleviation of gender dysphoria (medical);[19] and changing one's legal gender by acquiring a Gender Recognition Certificate (legal).[20] Since the experience of gender identity varies, so do transition experiences: some decide not to undergo any transition-related changes, for various reasons, including those who want to but cannot, for example due to financial, social or medical barriers.[21]

---

[13] International Commission of Jurists and International Service for Human Rights, 'The Yogyakarta Principles' (2007) 6, http://yogyakartaprinciples.org/wp-content/uploads/2016/08/principles_en.pdf.

[14] Office for National Statistics, 'Gender identity, England and Wales: Census 2021' (ONS, 6 January 2023).

[15] ibid.

[16] *National LGBT Survey* (n 2) para 3.3.

[17] C Fairbairn et al, 'Non-binary Gender Recognition: Law and Policy' (House of Commons Library, 31 March 2022) s 1.1.

[18] Equality Act 2010, s 7.

[19] NHS Gender Identity Programme Board, 'Service Specification: Gender Identity Services for Adults (Non-Surgical Interventions)' (NHS England, 7 November 2022).

[20] Gender Recognition Act 2004, s 4(1).

[21] M Chen et al, 'Characteristics of Referrals for Gender Dysphoria over a 13-Year Period' (2016) 58(3) *Journal of Adolescent Health* 369.

A ban on conversion practices can only be fully effective if it protects all those at risk. A definition of who is protected therefore needs to cover, as far as possible, all those experiencing gender variation and incongruence with their assigned sex/ legal gender. In order to do so, such definitions should not predetermine what qualifies an individual to be 'trans' with reference to their having to have undergone any particular transition process. Not only is there no moral justification to protect only one cohort of the trans population who have undergone a particular kind of transition, but also the law must maintain the freedom for individuals to determine the confines of their 'transition' and respect their right of bodily autonomy. To protect only those who have undergone specific process (such as medical treatment) would impose invasive requirements on those excluded, which would infringe their rights and freedoms.[22]

To address this risk of exclusion, a ban on conversion practices can focus on protecting not just individuals who have undergone a certain process or meet a certain transition threshold, but rather individuals who share a certain *characteristic* which is at risk of being 'suppressed, cured or changed'.[23] Several states, including Canada (2021),[24] New Zealand (2022),[25] France (2022)[26] and Malta (2016),[27] as well as territories, including those in Australia – Victoria and Queensland (2022)[28] – have done just this. These jurisdictions all use the term 'gender identity' and 'gender expression' to describe the characteristics vulnerable to gender-related conversion practices. Using this description, rather than the status or description of being 'trans', prevents the focus from being on selected processes of transition. This is akin to the use of the characteristic, 'sexual orientation' in order to protect lesbian, gay and bisexual people.

The successful application of the Equality Act 2010 (EqA 2010) should offer reassurance to UK legislators in this approach. Defined characteristics have been used as a tool to protect individuals from discrimination for over a decade and the courts are well-accustomed to applying them. The characteristic we use that protects trans individuals under the EqA 2010 is 'gender reassignment' which is defined at section 7 as follows:

(1)   A person has the protected characteristic of gender reassignment if the person is proposing to undergo, is undergoing or has undergone a process (or part of a process) for the purpose of reassigning the person's sex by changing physiological or other attributes of sex.

---

[22] UNGA (n 12).

[23] Ban Conversion Therapy Legal Forum, 'The Cooper Report: How to Legislate Against Conversion Therapy' (Ozanne Foundation, 2021) 1.

[24] Bill C-4, An Act to amend the Criminal Code (conversion therapy), 1st Sess, 44th Parl, 2021 (assented to 8 December 2021), SC 2021, c2 4.

[25] Conversion Practices Prohibition Legislation Act 2022.

[26] Loi No 4021 du 23 mars 2021, Proposition de loi interdisant les pratiques visant à modifier l'orientation sexuelle ou l'identité de genre d'une personne.

[27] Act No LV of 2016 – Sexual Orientation, Gender Identity and Gender Expression Act.

[28] Change or Suppression (Conversion) Practices Prohibition Act 2021.

(2)   A reference to a transsexual person is a reference to a person who has the protected characteristic of gender reassignment.

(3)   In relation to the protected characteristic of gender reassignment—

(a)   a reference to a person who has a particular protected characteristic is a reference to a transsexual person;

(b)   a reference to persons who share a protected characteristic is a reference to transsexual persons.

When considering how to define the protected group, a consideration of the effectiveness of section 7 is an obvious starting point, which can then be compared to the use of 'gender identity and expression'. We see immediately that the section 7 definition may limit protection from conversion practices in two ways: (i) the use of 'transsexual'; and (ii) the requirement for someone to have at least proposed undergoing some form of transition. Let us consider each in turn.

A. The Use of 'Transsexual'

'Transsexual' was (and can still be) associated with trans people who undergo medical intervention.[29] We have already identified the need to ensure the definition does not include medical intervention as a precondition to protection to ensure a trans individual's bodily autonomy is respected. If the use of 'transsexual' could invite such an interpretation, then it should not be used. However, it was section 7 that, in a landmark move, eradicated the need for medical supervision before protection from discrimination was provided. Instead, there was (and still is) only the need to *propose* to undergo a transition process in order to be protected under section 7, which is in no way dependent on the process being medical. The nature of 'transsexuality' was therefore moved away from its firm association with physical intervention, in line with judicial thinking in the run-up to the introduction of the EqA 2010. For instance, in *Bellinger v Bellinger*[30] Lord Nicholls considered a distinguishing mark of gender to be 'self-perception'.[31]

The use of the term has also not inhibited section 7 from being interpreted as protecting those who experience gender outside of the binary model, in spite

---

[29] Transsexualism no longer is classified as a mental disorder in the International Statistical Classification of Diseases and Related Health Problems (ICD). Now the ICD-11 classifies 'gender incongruence' as a sexual health condition; this classification continues to enable healthcare systems to provide healthcare needs related to gender. The previous version, ICD-10 defined transsexualism as '[a] desire to live and be accepted as a member of the opposite sex, usually accompanied by a sense of discomfort with, or inappropriateness of, one's anatomic sex, and a wish to have surgery and hormonal treatment to make one's body as congruent as possible with one's preferred sex'.

[30] *Bellinger v Bellinger* [2003] UKHL 21, [2003] 2 AC 467.

[31] ibid para 6.

of non-binary genders still not being recognised as a legal gender option in the UK.[32] When it comes to protection from discrimination, judicial decision-making has protected those outside of the gender binary structure. For instance, in the case of *Mx M (gender identity – HJ (Iran) – terminology) El Salvador*[33] the Upper Tribunal confirmed that a non-binary gender identity could form the basis of an asylum claim. And in the case of *Taylor v Jaguar Land Rover Ltd*[34] the Employment Tribunal determined that 'non-binary' and 'gender fluid' identities are protected by section 7 and the claimant was considered as having the protected characteristic '… beyond any doubt'.[35] Such case law comfortably incorporates non-binary and gender-fluid protection and supports the idea that, whilst the word 'transsexual' would likely not be used if the EqA 2010 were to be drafted now, its continued use does not prevent the breadth of legal protection. Such case law therefore indicates that the characteristic of gender reassignment is somewhat kindred to that of 'gender identity',[36] as it is being interpreted as a characteristic that moves beyond the strict notions and application of masculinity and femininity. 'Transsexual' as a term should therefore not be seen as a disabler of protection for all trans experience in itself.

B. 'Proposing to Undergo'

Curiously, the majority of states that have banned conversion practices do not offer a full definition of gender identity within their respective statutes, with the exception of Malta and Victoria, Australia. The former states:

> '[G]ender identity' refers to each person's internal and individual experience of gender, which may or may not correspond with the sex assigned at birth, including the personal sense of the body (which may involve, if freely chosen, modification of bodily appearance and, or functions by medical, surgical or other means) and other expressions of gender, including name, dress, speech and mannerisms …[37]

And the latter holds:

> '[G]ender identity' means the gender expression or gender-related identity, appearance or mannerisms or other gender-related characteristics of a person, with or without regard to the person's designated sex at birth. (Note. Gender identity includes the

---

[32] The Gender Recognition Act 2004 enables a person to change the legal gender recorded on their birth certificate, either from male to female or vice versa. It currently makes no provision for the recognition of any other gender.

[33] *Mx M (gender identity – HJ (Iran) – terminology) El Salvador* [2020] UKUT 313 (IAC).

[34] *Taylor v Jaguar Land Rover Ltd* (Birmingham ET 1304471/2018).

[35] ibid para 178.

[36] See E White and N Newbegin, *A Practical Guide to Transgender Law* (Somerset, Law Brief Publishing, 2021) 13.

[37] Act No LV of 2016 (n 27) s 2(c).

gender identity that the person had or has had in the past, or is thought to have had in the past)[38]

There are distinctions between these two definitions. Victoria does not acknowledge 'change' at all, in contrast to Malta which makes an explicit reference to 'modifications' people may decide to make as being included – and thereby protected – under the characteristic of gender identity, so long as they are freely chosen. This ensures that the ban does not impede access to healthcare provision. One reason why Victoria's definition may not make the same point is because as exempting healthcare provisions to ensure the continuation of access is covered by its exemption at Part 2, section 7(3) of the Act.[39]

C. One-Way or Two-Way

Both Malta and Victoria, Australia approach the definition broadly, in line with the Yogyakarta Principles.[40] So broad, one could argue, that it is not trans-focused enough. Indeed, neither definition would prevent a cisgender person from being protected under the characteristic. This is in contrast to Canada which makes the ban 'one-way':

> … conversion therapy means a practice, treatment or service designed to …
>
> (b) change a person's gender identity to cisgender;
> (c) change a person's gender expression so that it conforms to the sex assigned to the person at birth;[41]

It is anticipated at the time of writing that current UK governmental thinking would make the ban a 'two-way' ban. When the Consultation on *Banning 'Conversion Therapy'* went live, the Ministerial Foreword stated:

> The proposed protections are universal: an attempt to change a person from being attracted to the same-sex to being attracted to the opposite-sex, or from *not being transgender to being transgender,* will be treated in the same way as the reverse scenario …*Our proposed interventions are therefore symmetrical* and universal, protecting everyone.[42] (emphasis added)

As stated at the beginning of this chapter, there is no moral justification for excluding anyone from protection who is in need of protection, and the principle of universal protection – which here includes cisgender people – is one that an international

---

[38] Discrimination Act 1991 (ACT) Dictionary.
[39] Sexuality and Gender Identity Conversion Practices Act 2020 (ACT).
[40] International Commission of Jurists (n 13) p 6.
[41] Bill C-4 (n 24) s 320.101(b) and (c).
[42] Government Equalities Office, 'Closed Consultation: Banning Conversion Therapy' (GOV.UK, 9 December 2021) www.gov.uk/government/consultations/banning-conversion-therapy/banning-conversion-therapy.

human rights-based approach would generally support. But if legislating to restrict any behaviour is understood as an act of paternalism,[43] legislation needs to be justified as necessary, and for our purposes that necessity is to protect from conversion practices. The logic therefore follows that cisgender people need to be subject to risk of such harm to justify and necessitate state intervention.[44] There is currently no evidence that credibly supports the idea that cisgender people are being converted into being trans and it could therefore be argued that a definition that allows for a two-way application is unnecessary. However, it may offer greater flexibility by reducing the need to meet an expectation as to what being trans looks like. It could therefore in turn reduce the likelihood of gender-policing and in turn afford greater protection to the trans individual. When we consider the vast array of gender identity manifestations among the trans community, there is a need to ensure the characteristic does not insist on any form of prerequisite and the approach of Malta and Victoria perhaps provides for that more effectively. There may be fear that such a two-way approach would be abused; for example, it could be used to suggest someone presenting as trans is in fact a cis person who has been coerced into being trans. However, misuse of the law should not preclude a definition being as broad as the trans community need it to be to ensure protection for all experiences.

D. 'Gender Expression' and 'Gender Identity'

In a similar vein, a legal ban on conversion practices must explicitly protect a trans person's freedom to 'express' their gender identity how they wish. This secures a trans person's right to bodily autonomy and, crucially, their freedom to decide whether to undergo medical intervention or not, which some people require in order to experience an 'appearance congruence'.[45] The inclusion of the specific characteristic of 'gender expression' within the ban would also help protect individuals from the notion that there is a gender norm and a legitimate societal objective in adopting particular gender roles, forms of expression, and behaviours according to the sex assigned at birth. Not only would this add a layer of protection for those with perhaps more complex gender identities, but it would have benefits for LGBTQ+ communities more broadly. It would protect every person who does not fit the cis-hetero-norm and their right to express themselves.

Within the context of trans protection, one's 'gender expression' is closely connected with possible transition-related decisions. These can include social

---

[43] C Man-Yiu Tam, 'Conversion Therapy Bans and Legal Paternalism: Justifying State Intervention to Restrict a LGBTQIA+ Individual's Autonomy to Undergo Conversion Therapy' (2021) 7(1) *LSE Law Review* 1.

[44] R Young, 'John Stuart Mill, Ronald Dworkin, and Paternalism' in CL Ten (ed), *Mill's On Liberty: A Critical Guide* (Cambridge, Cambridge University Press, 2009) 211.

[45] Chen et al (n 21).

changes of expression in clothing, hairstyle and name, as well as changes to sexual characteristics. However, any ban must also acknowledge and protect those who are unable to express who they are. These are clearly a particularly vulnerable population who must be protected by the ban, since they already face barriers to expressing themselves. For example, some may be living in hostile and suppressive environments, whilst others may actively resist transitioning as a result of self-loathing. Although the use of 'expression' can therefore protect a trans person regardless of how they present their gender identity, it does not necessarily explicitly protect those whose expressions are suppressed. A legal ban on conversion practices must reach these individuals also. By section 7 requiring one to have, at the very least, proposed to undergo some form of transition, there is an immediate lack of recourse for those individuals living in suppressive environments who cannot be said to meet this threshold because they cannot express themselves for safety reasons, or as a result of self-loathing causing them to reject their trans nature.

This latter category must not be forgotten: many of those who have undergone gender-related conversion practices may be unhappy with being trans and be actively suppressing the idea of transition. A catch-22 must be avoided, whereby an individual falls outside of the definition due to the lack of gender expression and therefore cannot access protection, when in fact their lack of expression is a result of conversion practices to which they have already been subjected. A broad definition of gender identity *and* gender expression is therefore essential to ensure that all forms of trans people are captured. To only include gender expression, or indeed to provide a transition threshold as discussed above, would exclude a population who are already victim to the very practice that the ban is intended be prevent.

II. Protecting Transition-Related Healthcare and Support

The process of a person determining: (i) their gender identity; and (ii) how they want to express their gender identity can be significantly assisted by responsible professional and/or peer support to help them come to a considered, informed and non-judgemental decision. There is therefore a consensus among the medical profession that a ban must not '[...] deny, discourage or exclude those with uncertain feelings around sexuality or gender identity from seeking qualified and appropriate help'.[46] Appropriate help may include: (i) exploring an individual's experience with their gender identity (which may include conflict); (ii) performing clinical assessments of suitability prior to medical intervention; (iii) prescribing hormone treatment in line with clinical guidelines; and

---

[46] BCAP (n 7).

(iv) for individuals who are unhappy with being trans, support to help them live comfortably with it and reduce distress.[47] Access to these forms of care is vital to assist in ensuring bodily autonomy for trans people. Any ban on conversion practices that criminalises or restricts such access would represent an imminent threat to their human rights.[48]

However, with 19 per cent of those LGBTQ+ people who have undergone conversion practices confirming they were conducted by healthcare providers or medical professionals,[49] it is crucial to ensure that healthcare settings fall within the protective scope of a ban. Any ban must ensure those perpetrating conversion practices within a healthcare setting are captured by the ban, whilst also making sure that an individual is not prevented from accessing responsible and required care. We know that many trans people seek medical interventions in order to feel comfortable with themselves, and/or to explore and understand themselves. We also know that many people seek talking therapies. This is especially crucial for those who have not settled on their gender identity, which can be at any age. Ensuring the exception cannot be used to undermine access to support and healthcare is therefore a task of the utmost importance, as is the need to ensure that individuals can offer counsel and discussion to an individual without fear of prosecution.

The particular challenge of protecting access to healthcare can be expected to be subject to significant political pressure, especially in relation to under-18s, which is considered particularly controversial. But the UN Independent Expert on Sexual Orientation and Gender Identity and Expression has emphasised:

> Some claim that gender-affirming care for children and youth is harmful to their mental health, that it is a result of external indoctrination, that it should always be considered as forced intervention or that 'gender dysphoria' resolves itself before adulthood. None of these arguments is supported by scientific evidence.[50]

Responsible gender affirmative care is not about approving and agreeing to anything a young person may say they want. Instead, it is a form of counselling, psycho-therapy or healthcare decision-making process which seeks to help people come to a consensual, comfortable, and self-accepting place with their gender identity.[51] It is founded on the position that no gender identity, expression or experience is any more valid, 'natural' or 'normal' than any other.[52] The ban must ensure that room is provided for exploration and for their self-determined outcome to be respected. Individuals offering counsel and guidance within this context can therefore be reassured that they would not be prosecuted. Further, professionals must still be permitted to allow an individual to make decisions relating to their own healthcare

---

[47] ibid.
[48] UNGA (n 12).
[49] *National LGBT Survey* (n 2) 93, para 5.7.2.
[50] UNGA (n 12).
[51] Ban Conversion Therapy Legal Forum (n 23) p 1.
[52] ibid.

in line with the current legal consent framework in place at any particular time. Again, we return to the principle of bodily autonomy. For instance, the ban must not undermine the doctrine of *Gillick* competence and the ability of a competent young person to make healthcare decisions. *Gillick* holds that young people below the statutory age of consent for medical interventions should be able to affirm treatment of which they have sufficient understanding, having been provided with all the facts and possible consequences of a particular decision they are considering. Those aged 16 and above are presumed to have sufficient capacity to decide on their own medical treatment, unless there is significant evidence to suggest otherwise. [53]

We saw a direct application of *Gillick* to trans healthcare for under-18s in the case of *Bell v Tavistock and Portman NHS Foundation Trust*.[54] On appeal, it was decided that there was nothing about the nature or implications of treatment with puberty blockers that allowed for a real distinction to be made from the consideration of contraception in *Gillick*.[55] In practice, this means that trans young people continue to be subject to their doctor's judgement, who will decide on whether the young person in question: (i) requires clinical intervention; and (ii) has the capacity to consent to said intervention. A ban on conversion practices must ensure this position is respected, notwithstanding pressure to ignore this legal position.[56]

Ensuring an effective and safe healthcare pathway is of course crucial and we can recognise the complexities associated with young people's consent to transition-related interventions. While those who provide gender-related support and healthcare should not be exempt from the scrutiny of a ban, a clinician practising in this area of healthcare must be protected from claims which derive from the prima facie belief that young people should not have access to this type of healthcare. Indeed, it is right that the clinicians, who are the providing the young person with information and assessing their maturity, understanding and capacity to consent, should be appropriately protected in doing so. It would be wrong for Parliament to disturb this key role for clinicians, by not protecting an area of healthcare that has been clinically approved as necessary for some.

A. How to Formulate the Exemption?

We see a commonality in the laws of other states using exemptions, which aim to allow for responsible support services to continue to be available without fear of prosecution. Each state differs slightly in how it carves out its exemptions to protect gender-related support and healthcare. Victoria's Change or Suppression

---

[53] *Gillick v West Norfolk and Wisbech Area Health Authority* [1986] 1 AC 112, 174 (per Lord Fraser), 188–218 (per Lord Scarman); Family Law Reform Act 1969, s 8 and Mental Capacity Act 2005.

[54] *Bell v Tavistock and Portman NHS Foundation Trust* [2021] EWCA Civ 1363.

[55] ibid [76].

[56] See for example, M Forstater and H Joyce, 'Why Gender Identity Should Be Left out of the "Conversion Therapy" Ban' (*The Guardian*, 20 April 2022) www.theguardian.com/society/2022/apr/20/why-gender-identity-should-be-left-out-of-the-conversion-therapy-ban.

(Conversion) Practices Prohibition Act 2021 offers a comprehensive list of practices it aims to preserve, with section 5 stating that conversion practices do not include:

(a)   assisting a person who is undergoing a gender transition; or
(b)   assisting a person who is considering undergoing a gender transition; or
(c)   assisting a person to express their gender identity; or
(d)   providing acceptance, support or understanding of a person; or
(e)   facilitating a person's coping skills, social support or identity exploration and development.

Although its intention is clear, this section potentially exposes itself to a risk of abuse at subsection (d) and (e), as protection is not subject to the condition that support must be 'without a predetermined expectation' as to someone's (for our purposes) gender identity. This omission leads to a significant loophole as *acceptance, support or understanding* could arguably be used to defend an individual who is supporting an individual undergoing self-elected conversion practices. Similarly, there's nothing at (e) that would prevent someone *with* a predetermined purpose, providing 'coping skills, social support or identity exploration' and claim they fall within the exemption.

To help explore this point, we can look to a case study to show how the use of 'without predetermination' within a defined exemption can mitigate the risk of it being exploited.

> Case Study: A, 16, is experiencing gender dysphoria and goes to see B, a psychotherapist for children and young people. B does not believe anyone under the age of 18 can be trans and tries to persuade A that their dysphoria is 'a phase' and that they are actually a lesbian rather than a trans male made to think they need to be a man because of the clothes and mannerisms they want to use. A makes it clear they do not identify as lesbian. B 'accepts' his confusion and commits to supporting A to cope and understand that they are a lesbian and help them develop a comfort with this.

We can see from this case study that, in the absence of the phrasing 'provide acceptance, support or understanding of a person *without predetermination*' (emphasis added), B could argue that they were satisfying their obligation under (2)(d) and (e). However, when 'without predetermination' is included, it reinstates the principle of self-determination and places the burden instead on the alleged perpetrator to show there was no expectation from them. It does not matter if A is trans, a lesbian, both – or indeed neither. What matters is that A has the freedom to explore who they are without expectation as to what the outcome should be. And once the individual has freely settled on their identity (which may in future change again), that this is respected.[57]

---

[57] France, for example, has attempted to close this loophole. See Loi n° 2022-92 du 31 Janvier 2022 interdisant les pratiques visant à modifier l'orientation sexuelle ou l'identité de genre d'une personne.

B. Freedom of Thought, Religion and Belief

Any ban will inevitably have to deal with a conflict of human rights. Specifically, the freedom of thought, conscience and religion (Article 9 of the ECHR) is engaged in this conflict. The argument that a ban should not erode the ability of one to make a choice in line with their religion or belief is a powerful one. Article 9 establishes an absolute and unconditional right to *hold any* thought, conscience and religion and to *change* it:

> Everyone has the right to freedom of thought, conscience and religion; this right includes freedom to change his religion or belief and freedom, either alone or in community with others and in public or private, to manifest his religion or belief, in worship, teaching, practice and observance.

Case law dealing with Article 9 (often closely linked with Article 10, which protects freedom of expression) establishes that maintaining the absolute elements of this freedom plays a role in preserving a broad liberal democracy.[58]

However, the right to *manifest* is different. Article 9 qualifies the freedom to manifest one's religion or belief:

> Freedom to manifest one's religion or beliefs shall be subject only to such limitations as are prescribed by law and are necessary in a democratic society in the interests of public safety, for the protection of public order, health or morals, or for the protection of the rights and freedoms of others.

We can see that the Convention allows for limitation of one's freedom to manifest one's thoughts, conscience and religion to ensure the needs of society, such as the protection from harm. Any ban must therefore protect the absolute elements of Article 9, whilst ensuring that it only encroaches necessarily and proportionately on one's right to *manifest* religion or belief.

The data shows that the vast majority of conversion practices take place within religious settings,[59] so the case for some degree of limitation is impossible to ignore. Indeed, it is difficult to see how the state could justify a blanket exemption to protect religious-based conversion practices from conviction in the name of Article 9. This is especially so when we consider the finding at the beginning of this chapter that conversion practices amount at least to degrading treatment, and under certain circumstances may constitute inhuman treatment or even torture – all of which are *absolutely* prohibited by Article 3 of the ECHR. For Article 3 to be applied in line with its purpose and legal status, the *qualified* freedom to manifest found in Article 9 cannot prevail, as a matter of human rights law: the qualified right must accede to the absolute one. Any argument that a

---

[58] G Moon and R Allen, 'Substantive Rghts and Equal Treatment in Respect of Religion and Belief: Towards a Better Understanding of the Rights, and Their Implications' (2000) 6 *European Human Rights Law Review* 580, 581.
[59] *National LGBT Survey* (n 2) 93, para 5.7.2.

degree of degrading and inhumane treatment, and even torture, must be risked to protect the rights of others to manifest their religious beliefs cannot succeed. Furthermore, the state has a positive obligation 'to take measures designed to ensure that individuals within their jurisdiction are not subjected to torture or inhuman or degrading treatment or punishment, including such ill-treatment administered by private individuals'.[60]

The only way to comply with the obligations under Article 3 and Article 9 is to include all religious settings within the ban, without exemption. This will help ensure that true freedom is enjoyed by the trans individual, whilst only restricting Article 9 necessarily and proportionately in accordance with Article 9(2) of the ECHR.[61] Proportionality would *not* be achieved by only partially exempting religious settings or practices from the ban, as there is no evidence that any particular religious setting, or way of manifesting, is safer than any other when it comes to the risk of harm which could amount to a violation of Article 3. An exemption for any religious conversion practices would therefore undermine the efficacy of the prohibition.[62]

III. Conclusion

This chapter has sought to demonstrate how a government could approach an effective ban on conversion practices relating to all trans people. Specifically, it has focused on the use of gender identity and gender expression as the defined characteristics to include in the ban. It has illustrated that a ban must be based on an adequate definition of both, which must not include a 'transition threshold' and allow for those living in suppressive environments.

It has also illustrated the need to protect an individual's ability to freely explore their gender identity without predetermination, alongside the ability to access responsible healthcare provisions – they are not at odds with one another. An exemption can be used to this effect but should include reference to support and care being 'without a predetermined outcome' to help ensure an individual's true autonomy when exploring their gender identity without fear of prosecution. Further, we have found that, in order to satisfy its obligations under the ECHR and to ensure the risk of an exemption being undermined is mitigated, qualified freedoms found in Article 9(2) of the ECHR must be appropriately restricted where it is necessary and proportionate in order to avoid the degrading treatment of people subject to conversion practices.

---

[60] *A v United Kingdom* (1999) EHRR 611 at [22].
[61] Ban Conversion Therapy Legal Forum (n 23) s VI A(1).
[62] ibid 1, s VI B.

8

Exorcism and Other Spiritual Modes of 'Conversion Therapy'

Balancing Religious Liberty and Individual Rights

JAVIER GARCÍA OLIVA AND HELEN HALL

In the political debate around legislative action to prohibit conversion practices, both the viability and desirability of religious exceptions have been hotly debated.[1] Given the diversity of legal and cultural contexts between jurisdictions, it is unsurprising that law-makers around the world have adopted a variety of approaches when defining the scope of proscribed conduct.[2] The aim of this chapter is to explore: (1) why religious exemptions in relation to spiritual practices, including exorcism, raise particular challenges when it comes to framing prohibitions or exemptions in secular law; and (2) why these challenges do not justify, let alone necessitate, excluding such spiritual methods of purported LGBTQ+ conversion from legislative bans.

In order to do this, we shall begin by setting out the parameters of our study, and explaining both our adopted terminology, and the rationale behind it. We shall then go on to the look at the reasons why introducing secular legal oversight in this arena is complex and is sometimes touted by opponents of reform as not merely unworkable, but as an intolerable threat to religious freedom.[3] First, we shall consider issues which are applicable to all spiritual conversion practices, and are presented as obstacles to legal prohibition, and then we shall address matters which exclusively affect conversion by exorcism. In the process of discussing all

---

[1] See, for example, the discussion in T Jones et al, 'Preventing Harm, Promoting Justice: Responding to LGBT Conversion Therapy in Australia' (La Trobe University, 2018) 31–35; J Walker and K Phillips, 'Legislative Summary of Bill C-6: An Act to Amend the Criminal Code (Conversion Therapy)' (Publication No 43-2-C6-E, Parliament of Canada, 2021).

[2] Government Equalities Office, 'Conversion Therapy: An Evidence Assessment and Qualitative Study' (GOV.UK, 29 October 2021) App 3.

[3] See, for example, R Kiska, 'Is a Conversion Therapy Ban Compatible with Human Right' (Christian Concern, 2022) christianconcern.com/wp-content/uploads/2018/10/CC-Resource-Briefings-Conversion-Therapy-Ban-Opinion-Roger-Kiska-220407.pdf.

these concerns, we shall engage not only with the reasons why they are being raised, but also our basis for ultimately dismissing each one as an insurmountable obstacle to reform. Finally, we shall discuss why it is possible to include spiritual conversion practices in secular prohibitions. We maintain that this approach is required in any society committed to adequately safeguarding the vulnerable people whom such laws are intended to protect.

In order for our discussion to make sense, we must first set out the scope of our analysis, along with the definitions that we propose to use. It is crucial to stress that for present purposes, we are not simply interested in conversion practices which take place within a religious context, although the truth is that in societies where cultural prejudice towards the LGBTQ+ community is diminishing, and the values of equality and diversity are already enshrined in law by democratic consensus, a very high number of conversion practices are connected to faith-based ideology.[4]

For instance, in 2018, the UK Government's National LGBT Survey found that just over half of the reported experiences of conversion practices had been carried out by a religious organisation or group,[5] and even though this is without doubt an extremely significant number, the percentage of conversion practices which could properly be described as taking place 'in a religious context' was far higher than the 51 per cent in this category. The findings also showed that 16 per cent of the individuals subjected to 'conversion therapy' indicated that it had been carried out by a family member, while 9 per cent underwent such practices from a member of a community with which they also identified. In the current analysis, it is not productive to dive into the academic and philosophical rabbit-hole of the interaction between religion and culture, but it is reasonable to hypothesise that religious values played some part in the motivation of at least some relatives and community members carrying out such practices,[6] and the same point could be made about the factors driving individuals to undergo purported therapy from a medical or healthcare professional. Furthermore, it is also significant that 11 per cent of participants in the survey indicated that they preferred not to say who had conducted the conversion practice to which they were subjected, and it is highly likely that there are faith-based activities within this hidden pool.[7] Considering the situation in the round, the total number of experiences with a religious backdrop was far higher than 51 per cent, and any meaningful prohibition will encompass many situations with a faith-based dimension.

Nevertheless, the focus of this chapter is narrower, and we propose to concentrate on conversion practices which are believed to operate through spiritual

---

[4] S Cowan, 'The Best Place on the Planet to be Trans? Transgender Equality and Legal Consciousness in Scotland' in S Raj and P Dunne (eds), *The Queer Outside the Law: Recognising LGBTQI People in the United Kingdom* (Palgrave Macmillan, 2020) 187.

[5] Stonewall, 'Everything You Need to Know about Conversion Therapy' (Stonewall, 2021) www. stonewall.org.uk/everything-you-need-know-about-conversion-therapy.

[6] M Abdulla, 'Culture, Religion and Freedom of Religion or Belief' (2018) 16(4) *The Review of Faith and International Affairs* 102, 102.

[7] Government Equalities Office, 'National LGBT Survey: Summary Report' (GOV.UK, 2018).

means and are grounded in an understanding that change to sexuality or gender identity may come about via some supernatural agency, operating independently of the human participants. These types of practices may take many forms, inter alia: prayer, ritual, pilgrimage, ingesting or inhaling a substance believed to have a purifying effect, and exorcism.[8]

'Exorcism' is an important subcategory of such spiritual conversion practices, and one which merits independent consideration, for the reasons which we shall outline below. The very term exorcism is emotive and evocative, as for many it triggers images of lurid cinematic depictions of black-clad priests engaged in a violent battle for the body and soul of a writhing, screaming demoniac.[9] Nevertheless, despite the scope for sensationalism with the word, and the risk of its associations with horror fiction generating the impression that it is either trivial or removed from reality, we have opted to use it. It is a widely recognised term in popular, as well as academic, discourse,[10] and unlike some possible alternatives (eg deliverance ministry[11] or ruqyah[12]), it is not tied to a particular religious or spiritual context.

We would define exorcism as any rite or practice, aimed at freeing a person, object or place from a negative, external spiritual influence.[13] This conception gathers together an enormous range of beliefs, and an equally diverse spread of physical out-workings of the same. The external influence may be understood as some form of intelligent, non-human entity,[14] the soul of a departed person,[15] or even a living practitioner of magic.[16]

As we shall discuss, the key common thread is that the sufferer is subject to the control, or at least sway, of a will and identity which is not their own. Equally, the methods to free the person from this possession are immensely varied, and may involve simple, quiet spoken prayers, the infliction or physical violence or bodily hardship, chanting, music, ritual drinks, burning of incense and a host

---

[8] BBC News, 'Conversion Therapy: Gay Man Talks of Church Exorcism Trauma' (BBC News, 2 February 2022) www.bbc.co.uk/news/uk-england-south-yorkshire-60208017.

[9] M Cuneo, 'Of Demons and Hollywood: Exorcisms in American Culture' (1998) 27(4) *Studies in Religion* 455, 455.

[10] A De Antoni, 'Possession and Exorcism in Contemporary Society' (2019) 9 *Ritsumeikan University Research Report* www.ritsumei.ac.jp/research/radiant/eng/connect/story7.html.

[11] The term deliverance ministry is most frequently applied in Christian contexts. See further, M Perry, *Deliverance Ministry: Psychological Disturbance and Occult Involvement* (London, SPCK, 1996).

[12] Islamic exorcism; see further, C Suhr, *Descending with Angels: Islamic Exorcism and Psychiatry: A Film Monograph* (Manchester, Manchester University Press, 2019).

[13] JG Oliva and H Hall, 'Exorcism and the Law: Is the Ghost of the Reformation Haunting Contemporary Debates about Safeguarding Versus Autonomy?' (2018) 180 *Law and Justice* 51.

[14] J Walton and H Walton, *Demons and Spirits in Biblical Theology: Reading the Biblical Text in its Cultural and Literary Context* (Eugene, Cascade Books, 2019); A El-Zein, *Islam, Arabs and the Intelligent World of the Jinn* (Syracuse, Syracuse University Press, 2009).

[15] C Moreman, *Beyond the Threshold: Afterlife Beliefs and Experiences in World Religions* (Washington DC, Rowman and Littlefield, 2010) 110.

[16] J Trachtenberg, *Jewish Magic and Superstition* (New Delhi, Prahbhat Prakashan, 2015).

of other techniques. Many of these actions are far removed from the pseudo-scientific approaches to 'conversion therapy' that are widely associated with the term.[17] Nonetheless, they are a highly significant and damaging part of conversion practices, as experienced by individuals around the world in the twenty-first century and, as such, need to be covered by legal instruments in this area.

As previously stated, there are some special considerations which apply to spiritual conversion practices in the form of exorcism. Yet there are also a number of issues claimed in relation to spiritual conversion practices in general, and we shall first address these, before moving on to the specific field of exorcism.

There are a variety of separate but often interrelated issues, in terms of challenges to the legal regulation and prohibition of endeavours to alter an individual's sexuality or gender identity by spiritual means, and we shall explore them in turn: (1) religious freedom and the limits of secular law; (2) the role of faith and the rejection of empirical methods; (3) the absence of a duty of care; and (4) concerns specific to exorcism.

I. Religious Freedom and the Limits of Secular Law

It is uncontroversial that freedom of religion and conscience must be protected within any constitutional framework committed to maintaining a democratic and pluralistic society.[18] At the same time, it is an equally uncontested principle, for both national and international human rights frameworks situated within the liberal democratic tradition, that freedom of belief does not provide individuals or communities with a carte blanche with regard to the practical expression of their ideology and doctrines.[19] Article 9(1) of the European Convention on Human Rights (ECHR) acknowledges an absolute right to hold beliefs on questions of profound importance, expressly including religious matters. In contrast, the liberty to sustain inner convictions in outward terms only receives qualified protection. The manifestation of belief may be limited when other pressing interests are in jeopardy, and sometimes public authorities have a positive duty to restrict it.[20]

In a nutshell, there is broad consensus that freedom of religion is essential, but not absolute; the difficulty comes in deciding when and where it is permissible, or even required, for state authorities to step in and restrain its exercise. The

---

[17] D Haldeman (ed), *The Case Against Conversion 'Therapy': Evidence, Ethics and Alternatives* (American Psychological Association, 2022) 1–44.

[18] See, for example, the deliberations of the European Court of Human Rights in *Eweida v UK* [2013] ECHR 37.

[19] See, for instance, the European Court of Human Rights in *Osmanoğlu and Kocabaş v Switzerland* Application No 29086/12, 10 January 2017; the UK House of Lords in *R (Williamson) v Secretary of State for Education and Employment* [2005] 2 AC 246; and the Supreme Court of Canada in *R v Jones* [1986] 2 SCR 284.

[20] *R (Dolan) v Secretary of State for Health and Social Care* [2020] EWCA Civ 1605.

jurisprudence of the European Court of Human Rights, and also domestic judges within the United Kingdom, have long sought to walk a tight-rope between holding states to appropriately rigorous standards in safeguarding what is an essential right in liberal democratic paradigms, on the one hand,[21] and ensuring that religious freedom does not trample other rights, on the other.[22] Restrictions on the freedom to manifest religious beliefs will only be justified if they are prescribed by law and necessary in a democratic society, as well as 'in the interests of public safety, for the protection of public order, health or morals, or for the protection of the rights and freedoms of others'.[23] It is not permissible to overegg the pudding, and impose more sweeping or stringent restrictions than required to address whatever conflicting interest demands curtailing religious liberty.[24] So, for example, in *Manoussakis v Greece*, imposing criminal liability on a faith group for using an apartment as a place of worship without having obtained governmental permission was disproportionate, especially since the state authorities had been dilatory in relation to the application.[25]

The European Court of Human Rights recognises that states enjoy a margin of appreciation in determining the balancing between competing rights, although this is not infinitely plastic.[26] Pointing to opposing human rights or considerations in the public interest will not be sufficient to justify limiting Article 9 rights, as it must be possible to show that due weight has been given to the religious interests at stake, and that any restrictions do not exceed what is necessary.

The *Williamson* case provides an instructive example of such a balancing act in practice. Parents and teachers sought to argue that a ban on corporal punishment violated their Article 9 freedom to manifest their faith-based convictions, as their interpretation of Christian scripture mandated physical chastisement as an essential dimension of raising and educating children.[27] The House of Lords was prepared to accept that a religious requirement to beat disobedient minors could come within the ambit of the article.[28] Nevertheless, the state was able to justify prohibiting schools from putting this doctrine into practice, because the limitation was a necessary and proportionate means of protecting the competing Convention rights vested in children. In a similar vein, hospital authorities may forbid nurses from wearing religious jewellery in a way which poses a hygiene risk,[29] organisations offering relationship counselling can expect employees to treat clients equally regardless of their sexuality,[30] and state registrars can be

---

[21] *Metropolitan Church of Bessarabia and Others v Moldova* [2001] App 45701/ 99.
[22] *R (Williamson) v Secretary of State for Education and Employment* (n 19).
[23] ECHR, Art 9(2).
[24] *Manoussakis v Greece* Application No 18748/91, 26 September 1996.
[25] ibid.
[26] *Kokkinakis v Greece* [1993] ECHR 20.
[27] *R (Williamson) v Secretary of State for Education and Employment* (n 19).
[28] ibid [78] per Lady Hale.
[29] *Chaplin v United Kingdom* Application No 59842/10; *Eweida v UK* (n 18).
[30] *McFarlane v United Kingdom* Application No 36516/10, joined with *Eweida v UK* (n 18).

compelled to perform ceremonies for same-sex couples, even if this conflicts with their spiritually-based moral code.[31] In summary, limiting religious freedom will not offend human rights law, where this is a necessary and proportionate measure.[32] Yet courts will be particularly vigilant about any restraints placed upon the purely internal conduct of religious groups and, furthermore, will not regard arbitrating on matters of doctrine as either justifiable or possible. The challenge for spiritual conversion practices is that they, by their very nature, are concerned with the doctrine and worship of faith communities, generally considered by courts as sacred territory into which secular law should not trespass.[33]

It is telling that even in *Shergill v Khaira*, a comparatively recent case in which the UK Supreme Court signalled that courts had become too willing to find matters non-justiciable on religious grounds, the judgment was crystal clear that questions about the correctness of theology or ritual remained off limits: 'the courts do not adjudicate on the truth of religious beliefs or on the validity of particular rites'.[34]

Following this decision, the current position in England and Wales, and indeed Scotland, is that: 'where a claimant asks the court to enforce private rights and obligations which depend on religious issues, the judge may have to determine such religious issues as are capable of objective ascertainment'.[35]

In other words, where there are contractual, tortious or property questions which have a religious context, secular courts will not turn away simply because of this spiritual backdrop. In *Khaira*, the dispute centred on whether one of the litigants could exercise a power to remove and appoint trustees, based on his claim to a particular status within his faith community. The Supreme Court ultimately concluded that secular judges could adjudicate on religious matters (as long as these were amenable to objective determination) in order to decide which parties were trustees with powers and duties to administer trusts of the property in question.[36]

The court was influenced by the Canadian authority of *Bruker v Marcovitz*,[37] which had dealt with a wife suing her husband for damages flowing from his refusal to give her a Jewish religious divorce (a *ghet*).[38] The parties had agreed that once their civil divorce had been obtained, they would attend a rabbinical court and seek a *ghet*, but unfortunately, the husband had failed to honour his promise, leaving his wife unable to enter into another religious marriage. The Supreme Court of Canada ruled that although, following *Syndicat Northcrest v Amselem*,[39]

---

[31] *Eweida v UK* (n 18).

[32] *Ladele v United Kingdom* (51671/10) joined with *Eweida v UK* (n 18).

[33] *R v Chief Rabbi, ex p Wachmann* [1992] 1 WLR 1036.

[34] *Shergill v Khaira* [2014] UKSC 33, [47] per Lord Neuberger, Lord Sumption and Lord Hodge (with whom Lord Mance and Lord Clark agreed).

[35] ibid.

[36] *Shergill v Khaira* (n 34) [59].

[37] *Bruker v Marcovitz* [2007] 3 SCR 607.

[38] *Shergill v Khaira* (n 34) [44].

[39] *Syndicat Northcrest v Amselem* [2004] 2 SCR 551, 2004 SCC 47, [50].

secular judges could not explicitly or implicitly determine subjective questions of religious doctrine or practice, they were nonetheless empowered to give effect to the civil consequences of religious acts.

The upshot of these cases is that, at least in the United Kingdom and Canada, judicial bodies will not shy away from adjudicating on questions rooted in civil law, merely because they arise in a religious or spiritual setting. In commenting on *Shergill v Khaira*, Cranmer expressed the view that while the ruling might embolden future judges to intervene in contexts previously assumed to be out of bounds for secular courts, it would not lead to them 'adjudicating on the truth or falsity of religious doctrines per se, in a vacuum'.[40]

Almost a decade has now passed since this pronouncement, and time has so far proven it to be well-founded, as reported case law does not demonstrate any trend towards judges aiming to expand their jurisdiction and involve themselves in subjective theological debates, or the inner lives of faith communities. They have quite properly adjudicated on civil law questions in religious contexts but have refrained from addressing the merits or veracity of theological assertions.[41]

It should also be stressed that this is not a radical departure, and that the court in *Shergill v Khaira* saw itself as reasserting a long-standing orthodoxy, rather than breaking new ground.[42] Even in the period of caution following *Wachmann*, when judicial bodies in England and Wales, and indeed Scotland, were somewhat leery of cases involving religious subject matters, such rulings were nonetheless still made on a routine basis.[43] Often in practical terms, there was no viable option. For instance, in a family context, a situation may arise where estranged parents cannot agree on the religious upbringing of children, and the children themselves lack capacity to make their own decision. If the same compromise cannot be found within the family, and one or both parties appeal to the courts, then in England and Wales, it will fall to the courts to make a best interests decision pursuant to the Children Act 1989.[44]

It speaks volumes that even in the United States, where the legal and social framework holds the notion of a wall of separation between Church and state especially dear,[45] litigation in a religious context is not per se problematic.[46]

---

[40] F Cranmer, 'Is Religious Doctrine Justiciable? Up to a Point, Yes: *Shergill v Khaira*' (*Law and Religion UK*, 11 June 2014) https://lawandreligionuk.com/2014/06/11/is-religious-doctrine-justiciable-up-to-a-point-yes-khaira-v-shergill/.

[41] See, for example, *Rev Keith Walters v The Active Learning Trust Ltd & Another* [2022] UKET 3324619/2019.

[42] *Shergill v Khaira* (n 34) [47] per Lord Neuberger, Lord Sumption and Lord Hodge (with whom Lord Mance and Lord Clark agreed).

[43] See, for instance, *Percy v Church of Scotland Board of National Mission* [2005] UKHL 73; *Re S (Specific Issue Order: Religion Circumcision)* [2005] 1 FLR 236.

[44] Children Act 1989, ss 1 and 8.

[45] *Reynolds v United States*, 98 US 145 (1879); *Everson v Board of Education*, 330 UK 1 (1947).

[46] For a colourful example, see J Turley, 'Spiritual Slip and Fall: Knoxville Man Sues for Evangelical Injury After Being Touched by God' (Jonathan Turley, 11 July 2008) jonathanturley.org/2008/07/11/spiritual-slip-and-fall-knoxville-man-sues-for-evangelical-injury-after-being-touched-by-god.

Certainly, the degree of permissible intervention in the religious affairs of citizens varies to some extent in the liberal democratic world, according to the specific constitutional culture[47] of the relevant jurisdiction, but a faith-related factual backdrop will never, in and of itself, make a matter non-justiciable. However, it is also universally accepted that secular judges ruling on purely theological claims will always give rise to an unacceptable violation of constitutional boundaries, and arguably the rule of law.[48] If courts were to attempt to adjudicate on matters that could not be objectively determined, it would be impossible to ensure that legal rules were certain, non-retroactive and transparent.

In light of this, it is easy to see why opponents of including spiritual conversion practices within secular prohibitions of conversion activities often vociferously assert that any such provision would constitute an intolerable threat to religious freedom,[49] and those accepted boundaries between Church and state.[50] Campaigners highlight that any proposals for bans encompassing spiritual modes of 'conversion therapy' would, by their very nature, inter alia, prohibit certain forms of prayer.[51] This is because: (1) including spiritual modes of 'conversion therapy' within the proscribed behaviour would cover some activities carried out within prayer and worship; and (2) these types of practices do not, at present, always and necessarily infringe provisions of criminal or civil law. When these two considerations are taken together, it is understandable how it could be argued that the new regulation would redraw the boundaries of judicial authority, as the change would mean that secular judges would at times be adjudicating on the content of prayer, in circumstances not previously giving rise to any claim in civil law.

There are two limbs to this concern: first, the lack of any prior secular law matter in which to root judicial involvement; and second, an objection to the very regulation of prayer, worship or other modes of spiritual engagement.

With regard to the first issue, there most certainly are prior interests in play from a secular law paradigm. For instance, in English and Welsh law, situated as

---

[47] The term 'constitutional culture' is used here to signify the collective norms and expectations which regulate collective life and the operation of the legal framework. See further, J Garcia Oliva and H Hall, 'Peoples and Sovereignty: Constitutional Law Lessons from Greenland and Denmark' [2020] *Public Law* 331.

[48] If courts are making determinations on matters not based on objectively ascertainable criteria, the principles that the law should be known and predictable, and equally applied, are inevitably violated. See T Bingham, *The Law of Law* (London, Penguin, 2011), in particular Chs 3 and 4. See also the deliberations of the Strasbourg court in *Eweida v UK* (n 18); and *Dogan v Turkey* Application No 62649/10, 26 April 2016.

[49] Christian Concern, 'What's Wrong with Banning Conversion Therapy?' (Christian Concern, 9 July 2021) https://christianconcern.com/resource/whats-wrong-with-banning-conversion-therapy/.

[50] In using the terminology 'Church and state' we do not imply that Christianity is in any sense normative or prioritised. We are simply reflecting the widely used terminology within Anglophone contexts, for historical reasons, eg R Thomas, *Church-State Relations: Tensions and Transitions* (Oxford, Routledge, 2017).

[51] D Webster, 'The Challenges around Conversion Therapy' (Evangelical Alliance, 16 March 2021) www.eauk.org/news-and-views/the-challenges-around-conversion-therapy.

it is within the framework of the ECHR,[52] there are the Article 8 (right to private and family life) and Article 3 (right to freedom from torture and inhuman or degrading treatment) interests of recipients of conversion practices,[53] as well as the real possibility of infringement of interests protected by the tort of negligence, in particular personal injury in the form of diagnosable psychiatric harm.[54]

As Purshouse and Trispiotis convincingly demonstrate,[55] there is certainly scope for successful claims arising from psychiatric injury, following experiences of conversion practices. Nonetheless, the challenge for claimants in meeting the required evidential burden, particularly in respect of causation, and the obvious risk of the litigation process itself becoming a retraumatising experience, should not be underestimated. The serious drawback to negligence as a legal device in respect of conversion practices is that, *at best*, it holds some promise of redress for damage already suffered, but it can only hope to have an indirect impact in terms of preventing harm, should a number of successful claims incentivise faith groups and their insurers to change their policies with regard to conversion activities.

Therefore, the aim of protecting the health of individuals, and thereby safeguarding interests within the umbrella of Article 8, can far more realistically be met by targeted legislation to outlaw conversion practices. Another material consideration is that new secular law to ban conversion practices would, by definition, earth judicial deliberation within an identifiable, discoverable state law framework with objectively applicable criteria, meeting both the objection to judges assessing spiritual questions divorced from civil law interests, and legitimate concerns about the rule of law.

It goes without saying that introducing a prohibition on 'conversion therapies' in jurisdictions currently without such provision would change the legal landscape, but this is precisely why campaigners are advocating for such reform.[56] Moreover, all constitutional frameworks are constantly evolving, and respecting religious freedom does not mean requiring them to remain static. In some instances, religious tribunals rule on bodies of doctrine which they understand to be divinely appointed and unchanging, but judges in courts of the state necessarily deal with an evolving legal landscape.

To put it simply, in pragmatic terms, religious organisations operate in the temporal sphere and have to conform to the same laws as non-religious groups, unless they are afforded special exemptions.[57] For instance, if the secular legal framework determines that rules about storing and using personal data[58] or fire

---

[52] Human Rights Act 1998.

[53] ECHR, Arts 3 and 8.

[54] *Page v Smith* [1995] UKHL 7; *Brayshaw v The Partners of Aspley Surgery and O'Brien* [2018] EWHC 3286 (QB).

[55] C Purshouse and I Trispiotis, 'Is "Conversion Therapy" Tortious?' (2022) 42(1) *Legal Studies* 23.

[56] See, for example, Ban Conversion Therapy Legal Forum, 'The Cooper Report: How to Legislate against Conversion Therapy' (Ozanne Foundation, 2021).

[57] See, for example, Equality Act 2010, Sch 11.

[58] Data Protection Act 2018.

safety[59] are going to be modified, then faith communities have to adapt, along with the rest of the voluntary sector, and exactly the same logic applies to generally applicable rules around attempting to change a person's sexuality or gender identity. The absence of exceptional treatment in respect of a universal ban cannot alone be sufficient to justify an assertion of infringing religious freedom, and it should be remembered that criminal sanctions, in particular, are the most coercive form of state power, and should be used sparingly in the interests of civil liberties.[60] If the social evils of conversion practices are great enough to demand that the freedoms of citizens in general are curtailed, for example, in respect of freedom of expression,[61] then there are likely to be compelling reasons not to grant an enclave of legal protection for faith groups.

This consideration closely relates to the second aspect of objections to regulating spiritual conversion practices, viz the thought of state oversight of prayer, worship or other modes of spiritual engagement. Once again, it must be highlighted that religious practices are not the target of prohibition, it is merely that they will not raise a shield against sanction for universally unlawful behaviour. In other words, there is no mainstream current or historical proposal within England and Wales, or any other liberal democratic regime, to prohibit prayer, worship or other forms of spiritual practice and ritual, but the point is, that as an overarching principle, criminal conduct is not magically transmuted into licit behaviour on the basis that it happens within a religious setting.

In the view of many advocates for reform, this default position should apply to conversion practices.[62] Consider, for instance, the analogous case of criminal law in relation to hate speech. If, for example, a religious minister were to make comments during a sermon or extemporary prayers which stirred up racial hatred, and the minister in question had the required mens rea, then this expression would be as much a criminal offence as if an atheist, far-right extremist made similar declarations.[63] As Edge argues, the courts do indeed have a complicated task in balancing the competing interests at stake when statements alleged to be hate speech are made in religious contexts,[64] but it is important to stress that Edge is not suggesting that the solution to this would be to give faith groups *carte blanche*, in the form of an all-encompassing shield against liability.

Furthermore, the recognition that some religious speech may be hate speech worthy of prosecution is in harmony with the ECHR, in particular Article 17.[65]

---

[59] The Regulatory Reform (Fire Safety) Order 2005, SI 2005/1541 (England and Wales).

[60] M Matravers, 'Political Theory and Criminal Law' in A Duff and S Green (eds), *The Philosophical Foundation of Criminal Law* (Oxford, Oxford University Press, 2013) 67–82.

[61] Protected in the United Kingdom by ECHR, Art 10.

[62] P Maheshwari-Aplin, 'Conversion Therapy: Why We Need a Ban with No Exemptions and Excuses' (*Stonewall*, 20 October 2021) www.stonewall.org.uk/about-us/news/ban-conversion-therapy-why-we-need-ban-no-exemptions-and-no-excuses.

[63] Public Order Act 1986, s 18.

[64] P Edge, 'Oppositional Religious Speech: Understanding Hate Preaching' (2018) 20(3) *Ecclesiastical Law Journal* 278, 285–87.

[65] ECHR, Art 17: 'Nothing in this Convention may be interpreted as implying for any State, group or person any right to engage in any activity or perform any act aimed at the destruction of any of the

As decisions like *Glimmerveen and Hagenbeek v Netherlands*[66] and *Kuhnen v Germany*[67] claim, the Convention framework will not allow individuals or groups to weaponise their rights as a vehicle for stripping third parties of theirs.

Thus, considered in the round, there can be no doubt that legislative schemes which catch spiritual conversion practices within a net of proscribed activity are not inimical to human rights, nor an unprecedented encroachment on religious liberty. In such a scenario it would not be that prayer, worship or ritual were being criminalised, but rather that they would not raise a defence to criminal behaviour.

In order to ascertain whether such criminal behaviour had in reality taken place, courts would have to scrutinise factual paradigms with a religious setting, but this is an exercise common to *any* situation in which civil law interests or criminal provisions arise, and state courts undertake such exercises on a regular basis.

In light of this, it is necessary to move on to our next consideration: the role of faith and the rejection of empirical method. Even if we have challenged the argument that criminal law *in principle* should not extend its reach to conversion practices which are spiritual in nature, is it possible to claim that it cannot logically be caught *in practice*?

II. The Role of Faith and the Rejection of Empirical Method

Are purely spiritual conversion practices qualitatively different, and as such in need of separate categorisation from purported 'therapies' with a pseudo-scientific basis, as well as practices aimed to influence individuals, using persuasion, argument and social pressure? If the hope for transformation is not being attributed exclusively to human agency, either on the part of the person delivering or the person undergoing the conversion practice, is it in fact an attempt on their part to *change* the recipient's sexuality or gender identity? Advocates of this position would suggest that conversion through prayer or ritual is all about opening up the possibility for a spiritual agent to change the person, and not intending to directly cause that transformation.

This approach, for instance, is expressed by the conservative Christian commentator MacNutt:

> [This is] the best solution: simply, homosexuality can be healed. That is, a homosexual can become a heterosexual; the homosexual orientation can be changed through prayer for inner healing and the power of the Holy Spirit.[68]

---

rights and freedoms set forth herein or at their limitation to a greater extent than is provided for in the Convention.'

[66] *Glimmerveen and Hagenbeek v Netherlands* 18 DR (1987).

[67] *Kuhnen v Germany* 56 DR (1988).

[68] F MacNutt, 'Homosexuality: A Cure?' (2000) 13(3) *Healing Line* 1.

Despite being premised on the understanding that a supernatural entity (in this instance, the Christian God) is the agent of transformation, we would argue that it remains appropriate, and indeed necessary, to classify appeals to such forces as conversion practices, and there are a variety of reasons for this.

First, and significantly, offers of such interventions are cast in terms of guaranteed success, provided that the participants are willing to persist with the process. For instance, MacNutt goes on to state:

> Prayer for healing of homosexuality takes time. Although I know of several healings that were nearly instantaneous, most took much longer – for example, receiving prayer once a week for six months or more.[69]

As we can see in this statement, there is no suggestion that the endeavour might ultimately be unsuccessful, and this is not an isolated case: many other religious perspectives either promise a complete success rate, or caveat this with a warning that the individual must genuinely desire to be cured.[70] Such activities are no less damaging than any other form of conversion practice, and potentially heighten the trauma by blaming the recipient should the process ultimately not bring about the intended result.[71]

It would be disingenuous to claim that these sorts of conversion practices are being offered with anything other than the explicit aim of altering a person's sexuality or gender identity and, this being the case, there is no reason for them not to come within the fold of any well-drafted legislative prohibition, regardless of the mechanism to which the participants attribute the change sought. There is no evidence that conversion by means of religious ritual, supplication or meditation is any less dangerous than talking 'therapies' in relation to long-term psychological damage, and peer-reviewed empirical studies attest to the harm caused by all types of conversion practices.[72]

Moreover, not only do these spiritual forms of conversion practice pose the same risk as far as adverse effects are concerned when no permanent change in sexuality or gender identity is forthcoming, but the worldview of those also offering and receiving such interventions ordinarily excludes any assessment of empirical evidence of potential benefit and detriment. Support for efficacy of

---

[69] ibid.

[70] L O'Neill, 'Gay Nurse's Challenge to Derry Pastor Who Cures Homosexuality' (*The Belfast Telegraph*, 23 August 2017) www.belfasttelegraph.co.uk/news/northern-ireland/gay-nurses-challenge-to-derry-pastor-who-cures-homosexuality-36058526.html.

[71] G Nunn, 'I Felt This Crushing Guilt: How Faith-based LGBTQ Conversion Practices Harm Young Australians' (*The Guardian*, 6 April 2021) www.theguardian.com/world/2021/apr/07/i-felt-this-crushing-guilt-how-faith-based-lgbtq-conversion-practices-harm-young-australians.

[72] A Forsythe, 'Humanistic and Economic Burden of Conversion Therapy among LGBTQ Youths in the United States' (2022) 176(5) *JAMA Pediatrics* 493; What We Know Project, 'What Does the Scholarly Research Say About Whether Conversion Therapy Can Alter Sexual Orientation Without Causing Harm?' (Cornell University, 2016) whatweknow.inequality.cornell.edu/topics/lgbt-equality/what-does-the-scholarly-research-say-about-whether-conversion-therapy-can-alter-sexual-orientation-without-causing-harm/.

practices is likely to be found in unverifiable, anecdotal evidence,[73] and even if presented with the consensus of the clinical and academic opinion that 'conversion therapy' is ineffective and harmful to health and wellbeing, this would not be deemed a relevant factor because a miracle is by definition not dependent upon rational, scientific principles.[74]

Individuals who understand supernatural forces as being capable of transcending the ordinary laws of biology and chemistry will not be interested in research data. Moreover, in many faith contexts, a questioning stance will be seen as a sign of doubt or negativity, which in itself may put the requested divine favour in jeopardy.[75] In addition, there will often be immense social pressure on an individual offered the possibility of undergoing a conversion practice to embrace it. Already marginalised by their position as an LGBTQ+ person within a social setting which explicitly condemns this, they are being provided with an opportunity to demonstrate their loyalty to shared values, publicly reidentify with the majority within their community, as well as trading rejection, condemnation and stigmatisation for acceptance, and potentially even enhanced status and approval.[76] Some faith traditions, for example, Christianity, explicitly glorify the virtues of those who have been deemed morally problematic, but have opted to return to the community's values.[77]

In light of all of these extrinsic forces on individuals to comply with spiritual conversion practices when offered, it can be seen that the need for protection is as great as – if not greater than – in other contexts. The importance of safeguards is further heightened by the effective absence of any duty of care for individuals offering spiritual services, and the implications of this for recipients.

III. The Absence of a Duty of Care

Spiritual conversion practices are not anchored to any objectively agreed principles when it comes to the imposition of a duty of care, and of liability in tort. There have been no reported cases in England and Wales of attempts to establish a professional or quasi-professional duty on the part of religious ministers, but we should bear in mind the well-known Californian decision in *Nally v Grace*

---

[73] D Verhaagen, *How White Evangelicals Think* (Eugene, Cascade Books, 2022) Ch 8.

[74] A Tarango, 'Jesus as the Great Physician: Pentecostal Native North Americans within the Assemblies of God and New Understandings of Pentecostal Healing' in CG Brown (ed), *Global Pentecostal and Charismatic Healing* (Oxford, Oxford University Press, 2011) 107, 112.

[75] R Scott, *Miracle Cures: Saints, Pilgrimage and the Healing Power of Belief* (Berkeley, UC Press, 2010) 149–66.

[76] R Crapo, *Cultural Anthropology: Understanding Ourselves and Others* (Madison, Brown and Benchmark, 1996) 72.

[77] See, for instance, the Parable of the Prodigal Son (Luke 15:11–32) or the Parable of the Lost Sheep and Coin (Luke 15:1–10).

Community Church.[78] This tragic case referred to a young student who died from suicide, and whose parents pursued to sue his church for negligence in pastoral care (even though his pastors had tried extremely hard to help him in accessing treatment for his mental health, and the family had actively resisted this, as they regarded psychiatric treatment as somehow shameful).

The court robustly rejected the decision. Part of the reasoning related to concerns about separation between Church and state, but there was also lengthy consideration of the impractical and undesirable nature of any development of tortious liability for clerical malpractice. It was found that it would be impossible to assess whether a minister had met the standard required of a reasonable and competent spiritual adviser, as this depended on a subjective consideration of faith-based matters.

This reasoning is clear and rational, which may explain the dearth of subsequent journeys to develop a tort of clergy malpractice, either in the US or other common law contexts. Certainly, the analysis of the court in respect of the impossibility of establishing an objective duty of care would transfer to the context of England and Wales. One material consideration is that religious ministers ordinarily have no special expertise in mental health, so would be in no better position than anyone else to diagnose, or even recognise, warning signs about the onset of illness or the deterioration in someone's condition. Moreover, they obviously lack the statutory powers vested in police officers[79] or medical doctors[80] to impose enforced intervention in appropriate circumstances.

In addition to this, religious ministers are in the role of offering spiritual advice and, therefore, are not holding themselves out as being able to facilitate any standard of care for other matters, such as mental health, physical wellbeing or financial management. It is also a material aspect that some faith groups adhere to practices which will result in demonstrable harm as far as many outsider observers are concerned, eg refusal of blood transfusions.[81] Clearly, if spiritual advisers were treated by civil law as taking on responsibility for protecting the interests within the purview of the tort of negligence, this would mean satisfying two sets of competing demands: the teaching of a faith which maintains that spiritual benefits demand earthly sacrifice, versus the legal obligation to give reasonable advice to avoid personal injury (including psychiatric harm), property damage and in some circumstances, economic loss.[82]

All things considered, it is readily apparent why a tort of clergy malpractice is unlikely to gather much momentum, or prove workable in the improbable event that it does.[83] At first sight, it might seem that this finding lends support to the

---

[78] *Nally v Grace Community Church*, 47 Cal 3d 279 (1988).

[79] Mental Health Act 1986, s 136.

[80] ibid ss 2, 3 and 5.

[81] Jehovah's Witnesses, 'Why Don't Jehovah's Witnesses Accept Blood Transfusions?' (JW.ORG, 2014) www.jw.org/en/jehovahs-witnesses/faq/jehovahs-witnesses-why-no-blood-transfusions.

[82] *Hedley Byrne & Co Ltd v Heller & Partners Ltd* [1964] AC 465.

[83] See *Nally v Grace Community Church* (n 78).

view that spiritual conversion practices should be excluded from legal prohibition of conversion activities more widely, but our contention is that a much closer examination in fact leads to the opposite conclusion.

As discussed above, we by no means discount the possibility that some conversion practices resulting in harm could plausibly give rise to successful claims in negligence. Nevertheless, such an action would be based not upon a general duty of care imposed on religious ministers or spiritual advisers to safeguard the welfare of those for whom they had a pastoral role, but in the reckless exposure of recipients of conversion practices to the foreseeable risk of psychiatric harm.

We would argue that such claims would be entirely proper, given the well-recognised peril associated with conversion practices, and the vulnerability of recipients, who are frequently under immense social and psychological pressure to participate.[84] This would promote the interests of justice and a fair distribution of loss, fundamental issues of the law of tort,[85] but an exemption for spiritual modes of conversion would erode the chances of such claims being successful.

The very existence of a provision allowing for spiritual conversion practices to take place would convey the message to courts that such activities were within the scope of acceptable behaviour for faith communities. If they were invariably an unjustifiable risk, why would Parliament have specifically allowed for their continuance? Conversely, although a free-standing action in tort would operate independently of any criminal law framework which was constructed, the existence of such sanction would assist claimants seeking to show that a religious adviser performing or instigating a conversion practice had acted recklessly. Taking this into consideration, we would assert that the absence and unworkability of an overarching duty of care for spiritual advisers makes the need for a clear prohibition of spiritual conversion practices all the more pressing.

In summary, our investigation so far has consistently demonstrated the imperative to ensure that spiritual conversion practices, in general, are within the ambit of any prohibition on such activities, and we now turn to the paradigm of exorcism, a subcategory of spiritual conversion activities. All of the foregoing reflections apply to exorcism, but there are additional reasons specific to this context that render protection in this arena especially critical.

IV. Considerations Specific to Exorcism

We have already examined the social pressure on individuals to assent to spiritual conversion practices, broadly defined. Nonetheless, understandings of sexuality

---

[84] For instance the British Medical Association advocate for a complete and effective ban: see British Medical Association, 'Parliamentary Brief – Conversion Therapy' (13 June 2022) https://www.bma.org.uk/media/5733/bmae-petition-debate-ban-on-conversion-therapy130622.pdf.

[85] M Geistfeld, 'Compensation as a Tort Norm' in J Oberdiek, *Philosophical Foundation of the Law of Torts* (Oxford, Oxford University Press, 2014) 65–85.

or gender identity linked to possession may generate situations of even greater contextual duress, whether or not this is intentional or conscious as far as family members or representatives of the faith community are concerned.

At one level, possession provides an explanation for the individual's situation, whether the negative force is a demon, jinn, deceased spirit or malevolent human magician, and what might otherwise be characterised as deviant behaviour is comprehensible to members of a social group.[86] In addition, not only is a person's sexuality or gender identity rendered comprehensible if it is attributed to an external, negative influence, the stigma and ascribed culpability may be reduced, or even replaced, with sympathy or enhanced status.[87] Instead of regarding what is construed as a problem or deficiency as having an internal source, it is possible to point to an external cause. The narrative of possession may be much more palatable than viewing sexuality or gender identity as an intrinsic part of a person, both for the individual concerned, and family members and associates. This interpretation has the potential to temporarily lift a weight of guilt or shame, and also offer hope, because there are steps which may be taken to cure the problem.

However, alongside what may be experienced initially as positive aspects of the possession narrative, it is important to stress that there is also a darker side, present from the beginning. Some understandings of possession attribute it to the negative or careless behaviour of the victim or their close relatives, the latter being especially likely to be blamed in the case of a child or teenager.[88]

A plethora of different dangers are identified as potential causes, and many of these are connected with areas which young people may explore and experiment, eg sexual relationships, occult rituals or paranormal investigation.[89] Given that these activities frequently attract the disapproval of parents and community leaders, there is a high chance of vulnerable individuals ascribing their turmoil over sexuality or gender identity to transgression of community norms.

There is also the core point that believing your body and soul to be undertaken by a malicious and invisible enemy is bound to be a terrifying experience for many people, and the incentive to cooperate with anyone who claims to be able to free you is immense. When all of these considerations are taken together, it is undeniable that those presenting or being presented for exorcism are acutely vulnerable.

However, the special dangers associated with this practice go far beyond the inherent vulnerability of those accepting it, under varying degrees of duress, and

---

[86] P Almond, *Demonic Possession and Exorcism in Early Modern England* (Cambridge, Cambridge University Press, 2004) 38.

[87] T Pires, 'A Brazilian Exorcist at the Beginning of the Twentieth Century: The Supernatural as an Empowerment Strategy' in G Giordan and A Possamai (eds), *The Social Scientific Study of Exorcism in Christianity* (New York, Springer, 2020) 53.

[88] G Dow, 'Healing and Deliverance Addresses' (Bishop Graham Dow's Personal Website, 2020) www.bishopgrahamdow.com/healing-and-deliverance.

[89] N Squires and R Ray, 'Emergency Need for Exorcists after Surge in People Dabbling in Satanism and Black Magic' (*The Telegraph*, 26 August 2016) www.telegraph.co.uk/news/2016/09/26/urgent-need-for-more-exorcists-as-increasing-number-of-people-da/.

there are two principal considerations to explore: (1) the methods employed; and 2) the difficulties around withdrawal of consent.

In relation to the first, as we noted above, there are a wide variety of beliefs and rites within the umbrella of exorcism, and it should be pointed out that not all of them involve any physical discomfort or danger. Nevertheless, it is important to appreciate that some of the modes of exorcism involve subjecting the possessed body to physical ordeals, either with the aim of bringing about spiritual cleansing for the besieged soul, or with rendering the invaded body an extremely unpleasant place for the parasitic entity to inhabit. Such practices carry an obvious and inherent danger, and there have been numerous cases of individuals from diverse cultural backgrounds being killed in the course of exorcism rituals.[90]

Furthermore, there is some doubt as to whether exorcism rituals could come within the 'religious mortification' exemption to the criminal prohibition on giving operative consent to actual bodily harm or more serious injury, as recognised in *R v Brown*.[91] In our view,[92] the better conclusion is that it does not, and this was apparently the approach taken by an English court in *Rabiya Patel*.[93] In a harrowing incident, family members were persuaded by a spiritual adviser to beat to death a young woman suffering from mental illness, having been assured that this was the only means to cure her and free her from a jinn. The victim had apparently cooperated with the initial stages of the process, but there was no suggestion that any defence of consent might be raised. It should, however, be noted that the family were utterly distraught by the outcome, and everyone except the spiritual adviser accepted responsibility for their part in the events.

An appellate court in New Zealand in the case of *R v Lee*[94] was critical of the English approach and opted for a different analysis. A detailed treatment of *R v Lee* is beyond the scope of our current discussion, but the court considered that rejecting the possibility of consent to actual bodily harm in relation to exorcism represented an unwarranted degree of paternalism.[95]

We would respectfully disagree and suggest that the stance of English authorities is to be preferred in the realm of exorcism. The victim in *Lee* was a relatively new arrival to New Zealand, spoke almost no English, suffered from mental health problems and lived in the house of the pastor who brutally beat her to

---

[90] O Lambert, 'The Real Story Behind the Exorcism of Janet Moses' (News Australia, 3 August 2016) www.news.com.au/lifestyle/real-life/true-stories/the-real-story-behind-the-exorcism-of-janet-moses/news-story/02b55149f2c5573cf0b111680c68af07; The London Free Press, 'LFP Archives: The Seven Day Exorcism that Killed London Teen' (The London Free Press, 13 August 2022) https://lfpress.com/news/local-news/lfp-archives-the-seven-day-exorcism-that-killed-a-london-teen; D Trujillo, 'Mother of Girl Killed in Apparent Exorcism Faces Judges in San Jose' (NBC Bay Area, 9 August 2022) www.nbcbayarea.com/news/local/mother-girl-killed-apparent-exorcism-court-appearance/2973108.

[91] *R v Brown* [1994] 1 AC 212.

[92] H Hall, 'Exorcism, Religious Freedom and Consent: The Devil in the Detail' (2016) 80(4) *The Journal of Criminal Law* 241.

[93] *Rabiya Patel* [1995] 16 Cr App R (5) 827.

[94] *R v Lee* [2006] 5 LRC 716 (New Zealand).

[95] ibid 289–318.

death. It is difficult to conceive of someone more vulnerable and less able to ask for help in what was a situation of domestic abuse, and allowing consent to be operative in such circumstances would be a step backwards, rather than forwards, for human rights protection.

It is true that Lee's situation (the victim had the same surname as the defendant) was extreme, but it illustrates all too graphically the potential for catastrophic accidents within exorcisms. Those undergoing such rites may be highly motivated to comply, for all of the reasons set out above, and the very idea of beating, starving or freezing out an evil spirit places individuals at acute risk.

In relation to exorcism as a type of conversion practice, press reports in the UK detail incidents of participants in rituals being required to fast (from water, as well as food) for a three-day ordeal, with no prior questions about their health.[96] That said, even forms of conversion exorcisms which do not involve the infliction of bodily harm or physical pain may be extremely traumatic, as victims may be faced with shouting for a prolonged period, sometimes from a crowd of people, and often accompanied by the use of frightening language or images. Inevitably, the impact of this kind of environment can be most disturbing, with victims reporting physiological symptoms like struggling for breath, and ongoing anxiety.[97]

Whilst we have been at pains to stress that by no means all modes of exorcism pose a risk of immediate and ongoing harm (beyond those associated with any spiritual conversion practice), it cannot be denied that a significant number of those rites are, by their very nature, unsafe.

Once we have carried out this analysis of the methods employed, we must now turn to our second consideration: the difficulty of withdrawing consent. Whilst there is huge pressure on individuals to agree to undergo conversion by exorcism, the unpleasant nature of the actual experience may be such that the recipient wishes to end it, but unfortunately, the beliefs underpinning the rite may make this extremely difficult. If it is the understanding of those involved that the physical body in front them has been hijacked, in whole or in part, by a hostile entity, they may interpret requests to stop, and even desperate pleas for mercy as coming from that being, rather than the human person. If the objective is to make the body an unpleasant place to dwell, they might even consider the begging of the victim as proof that the battle is being won and intensify their efforts.

For those without any experience of this sort of contexts, this may seem farfetched, but a twenty-first century Texas appellate court refused to allow a church member to claim in battery or false imprisonment when pinned down for an exorcism ritual, on the basis that permitting such an action would present too great a risk to religious freedom.[98] The judicial view was that only terminating

---

[96] J Parry, 'This Is the Reality of Gay "Cure" Conversion Therapy Taking Place in Liverpool' (*Liverpool Echo*, 3 July 2018) www.liverpoolecho.co.uk/news/liverpool-news/echo-goes-undercover-gay-cure-13468107.

[97] BBC News (n 8).

[98] *Pleasant Glade Assembly of God v Schubert* (2005) No 02-02-264-CV.

membership of a church known to practise exorcism would be sufficient to indicate a revocation of consent.

The truth is that it is almost inconceivable that an English court would come to a similar conclusion, and that the decision must be understood in light of a conservative, US approach to Church-state relations,[99] combined with a cultural setting in which casting out demons was a common practice for faith groups. Yet, although the possibility of a claim in tort is much stronger in England and Wales, the fundamental point is that communities practising exorcism may well not regard a request to stop as something which they should heed.

Alongside the obvious implications of interpreting the voice of the victim as that of the demon, there is the real possibility for a group of people engaged in an exorcism to simply lose control and perspective. There are well documented cases of apparently devoted families slowly killing their loved ones in the course of exorcism rituals and failing to recognise the danger of their actions. In addition to the facts of *Rabiya Patel*, there is the now infamous story of Janet Moses, which has entered the popular culture via a Netlfix documentary. Janet drowned after her relatives forced a large quantity of water into her, even after she had begun to lose consciousness.[100] The improvised ritual which her family carried out could have stopped at any point, but those involved chose to refuse intervention from neighbours, elders or spiritual advisers.

The circumstances of the young woman's death are undoubtedly complex, and a detailed consideration of them is beyond the remit of this analysis, but for present purposes, they are a salutary reminder of the potential for group actions in an exorcism situation to rapidly escalate. They also illustrate, strikingly, the added potential for danger when they take place in a domestic setting, and the possibility of wider safeguards and oversight is greatly reduced. The protective policies of a faith community will not avail recipients of exorcism conversions, which happen behind closed doors in a private home.

It should not be underestimated that the stigma and discrimination associated with LGBTQ+ people in some communities increase the likelihood of families trying to carry out such rites in secret.[101] For example, in 2015, a former Muslim gave interviews about experiences of home-based exorcisms that had been forced upon him as a teenager and had left him suicidal.[102]

In many respects, exorcism as a conversion practice raises particularly acute risks for those on the receiving end of such rituals. From the outset, there is intense pressure to accept the narrative of possession, in preference to understandings of

---

[99] *Nally v Grace Community Church* (n 78).

[100] NZPA, 'No Jail Terms for Makutu Manslaughter Culprits' (*The Dominion Post*, 19 August 2009) www.stuff.co.nz/dominion-post/news-old/2752940/No-jail-terms-for-makutu-manslaughter-culprits.

[101] Stonewall (n 5).

[102] E Mclleand, 'My Father Tried to Cure My Homosexuality by Performing an Exorcism on Me Says Former Muslim Extremist' (*The Mail Online*, 3 November 2015) www.dailymail.co.uk/news/article-3301339.

the situation which would ascribe sexuality or gender identity to internal rather than external factors. To begin with, there may be the carrot of positive regard or treatment as the victim of spiritual attack, but this is frequently accompanied by the stick of repercussions if the person does not wish to cooperate in addressing this via the expected means, as well as a genuine fear of the possession, often underscored by guilt at perceived wrongdoing which brought it about. When this is overlaid with the perilous nature of some exorcism practices, and the very real difficulty of withdrawing consent and escaping once the process has begun, there is alarming potential for individuals to suffer a wide variety of negative outcomes. Taking all of the foregoing into account, it is hard to comprehend how any legal framework which failed to encompass conversion by exorcism could be construed as adequate or appropriate.

V. Conclusion

Our exploration of this topic has shown that any prohibition of conversion activity must be broadly drafted to proscribe spiritual conversion practices. It is a demonstrable reality that these represent a significant proportion of attempts made to alter sexuality or gender, both in England and Wales, and internationally.

We have shown that as a matter of overarching principle, including spiritual conversion within a wider legal ban does not pose any threat to freedom of conscience or belief, as courts can and do regularly adjudicate on matters of criminal or civil law which happen to arise in a religious context, and this field would pose no greater threat to religious freedom than these existing provisions. There are no proposals for any prohibitions aimed specifically at worship or ritual, but there is equally no reason to carve out an exception for religiously motivated conduct when constructing a prohibition. If there are pressing reasons to outlaw conversion practices, and we are persuaded that this is the case, then there is no rational basis for permitting such dangerous and abusive behaviour merely because it is carried out under the guise of faith. We do not permit hate speech simply because it is expressed in a religious setting, and conversion practices are no different. For example, if a preacher makes statements stirring up hatred against a group of people on the basis of their sexuality or race, the fact that this is done in the context of a sermon will not provide a defence.[103]

We have also proved why omitting spiritual conversion from any new law would erode its effectiveness, and allowing exorcism in particular would continue to expose extremely vulnerable people to acute risk of serious harm, up to and including death.

---

[103] P Edge, 'Oppositional Religious Speech: Understanding Hate Preaching' (2018) 20(3) *Ecclesiastical Law Journal* 278.

In light of all of this, the ultimate question is not whether legislative bodies operating in liberal democratic contexts *can* prohibit spiritual conversion practices. As we have stated, bearing in mind their human rights obligations and the necessity of maintaining a coherent framework, this point has been answered in the affirmative. The real unknown is whether and when they will demonstrate a proper desire to take this bold but necessary step, bearing in mind that it is a *sine qua non* for making any ban on conversion practices meaningful in the real world.

PART III

Beyond a Ban

9

The Religious Dimension – Confronting Spiritual Abuse

JAYNE OZANNE

Religious practices that inflict harm on individuals, however well-intentioned and commonplace, constitute spiritual abuse. It is well past time that this harmful form of abuse, wrapped carefully in the respectable cloak of religion, was acknowledged, challenged and outlawed. Abuse is abuse, no matter where it occurs or who conducts it. There must be no exceptions regarding whom the law protects and holds to account, for people's very lives are at stake.

As many will testify, religious belief is the impetus behind most forms of modern day 'conversion therapy' in both the Western world and in developing countries, where religious or cultural norms form an integral part of the national identity.[1] Indeed, even in former Warsaw Pact countries such as Hungary and Poland, where atheism was for many years the norm, the use of conversion practices has been promoted and legitimised by conservative religious leaders who associate the acceptance of LGBTQ+ people with Western liberalism, and which therefore must be rejected.[2] What is more, even in countries that are committed to equality legislation and which are progressive in their values and outlook, we find pockets of resistance amongst certain religious and cultural leaders who seek exemptions from the law so that they can continue with their barbaric practices on the grounds that their right to religious freedom trumps all others' rights.[3]

Sadly, spiritual abuse is one of the most pernicious forms of abuse as it is inflicted by people in positions of power who exercise significant moral authority within their communities, leaving their victims defenceless and in a vacuum

---

[1] UNHRC, 'Practices of So-Called "Conversion Therapy": Report of the Independent Expert on Protection Against Violence and Discrimination Based on Sexual Orientation and Gender Identity' (1 May 2020) A/HRC/44/53; A Bishop, 'Harmful Treatment: The Global Reach of So-Called Conversion Therapy' (Outright Action International, 2019).

[2] Ban Conversion Therapy Legal Forum, '2022 Hungarian "Conversion Therapy" Research' (Ozanne Foundation, 2022).

[3] H Dixon, 'Church Leaders Willing to be "Criminalised" if Conversion Therapy Ban is Introduced' (*The Telegraph*, 7 December 2021).

of despair. Given the collective norms and beliefs of those around them, there are sadly few to whom they can turn – their family, friends, teachers, doctors and mental health practitioners are typically all part of the problem rather than the solution. That is why we need legislation that clearly states what is and is not acceptable within these communities and addresses the concept of spiritual abuse head on, without exception or excuse.

However, the law can only draw a clear line in the sand and provide a means to punish those who choose to step over it. It cannot itself change the hearts and minds of those determined to continue with these damaging practices due their religious beliefs, no matter how well intentioned. To do this we need a programme of work that will challenge the harmful theology underpinning these spiritually abusive beliefs and highlight the harm that is being done in God's name.

This chapter therefore seeks to look at why these beliefs continue to be held so fiercely, despite the mounting evidence of the harm that they cause,[4] and what is being done by religious leaders to challenge their own colleagues. It also sets out what more needs to be done, and what additional steps governments and institutional organisations can take to address matters that purport to be supported by a right to religious freedom.

But first we must understand what religious conversion practices are and why so many adults willingly 'consent' to them, as I myself once did. Of course, there are many who tragically have no choice in the matter – especially children – who are forced to undergo them. But unless we understand those who 'consent' we will not be able to understand the level of coercion at work.

I. Religious Conversion Practices

> Religious conversion practices are any practices aimed at an individual or group of individuals with the 'predetermined purpose' aimed at changing, 'curing' or suppressing a person's sexual orientation and/or gender identity.[5]

The above definition is that proposed in the 2021 Cooper Report by the Ban Conversion Therapy Legal Forum in the UK, a group of highly respected international human rights lawyers, campaigners, survivors, academics, service providers and parliamentarians from across all the political parties, chaired by Baroness Helena Kennedy KC. The report sought to recommend to the UK Government how best to legislate effectively for a complete ban on conversion practices.

Central to the definition is the concept of 'predetermined purpose', where the outcome of the practice is already fixed – that is, that an individual must conform to an accepted 'norm' within their religious or cultural community.

---

[4] UNHRC (n 1).
[5] Ban Conversion Therapy Legal Forum, 'The Cooper Report: How to Legislate Against Conversion Therapy' (Ozanne Foundation, 2021).

Typically, this means suppressing or changing a LGBTQ+ person's true identity and in certain circumstances also involves 'curing' the individual from what is perceived to be either a mental, emotional or spiritual illness – or indeed a mix of all three.

These practices can take numerous forms and are practised by a wide range of individuals – few of whom will have had any formal training but most of whom will have some form of standing within their community, thus creating a power imbalance. According to research, most religious practices involve some element of prayer.[6] However, other religious practices used include fasting, flagellation, exorcisms and even corrective rape.[7] These can be conducted during acts of worship, in front of the whole religious community, or in a one-on-one setting. When conducted in a psychotherapeutic setting, they will typically involve intensive questioning into early sexual experiences and relationships in order to identify causes of trauma that explain the 'unwanted' or 'deviant' feelings, which are then purportedly 'cured' through healing prayer techniques.[8]

A. Prevalence of Religious Conversion Practices

In July 2017 the UK government launched a nationwide survey open to anyone living in the UK over the age of 16 and who identified as 'LGBT' (an umbrella term to include anyone from any minority sexual orientation, gender identity or with a variation in sex characteristics).[9] The aim of the survey was to develop a better understanding of the experiences of LGBTQ+ people and intersex people. Over 108,000 valid responses were received, making it the largest national survey to date of LGBTQ+ people anywhere in the world. Importantly, the findings showed that 2 per cent of the 108,000 respondents had undergone conversion practices and an additional 5 per cent had been offered them.[10] The survey also highlighted that transgender respondents were twice as likely to undergo and be offered conversion practices (13 per cent versus 7 per cent).[11] Furthermore, the official summary noted that:

> Faith organisations were by far the most likely group to have conducted conversion therapy (51% of those who received it had it conducted by faith groups), followed by healthcare professionals (19% of those who received it had it conducted by healthcare professionals).[12]

---

[6] UNHRC (n 1).

[7] Ozanne Foundation, 'Faith & Sexuality Survey 2018: Executive Report' (Ozanne Foundation, 2019).

[8] Ban Conversion Therapy Legal Forum (n 2).

[9] Government Equalities Office, 'National LGBT Survey: Summary Report' (2018) 6.

[10] ibid 14.

[11] ibid 91.

[12] ibid 14.

To investigate this further, the UK government commissioned Dr Adam Jowett from the University of Coventry to lead a review of evidence into the efficacy of conversion practices as well as a qualitative research study to examine the first-hand experience of conversion practices in the UK. The results, after much delay, were finally made public in October 2021 and concluded that:

> A previous systematic review of evidence on sexual orientation change efforts concluded that they appear to be aimed mainly at people with conservative religious beliefs. This may vary according to religious denomination, how questioning someone is of their religion, and the extent to which they internalise negative messages from their religion about their sexual orientation or gender identity.

> Studies have found that religious fundamentalism or strong religious beliefs significantly predict participation in conversion therapy. However, most of the evidence comes from North America and there is a general lack of representation of people from non-Judeo-Christian religions.[13]

My own Foundation has conducted research studies under the scrutiny of eminent advisory boards into conversion practices in the UK, Hungary and the Caribbean, as well as a study amongst transgender and non-binary respondents in the UK. Each survey highlights the significant role that religion plays in terms of those advocating conversion practices and those conducting them, and shows that religious belief is the primary source of motivation for the vast majority of those seeking out and undergoing these harmful practices. Notably, the 2018 Faith & Sexuality Survey concluded:

> Few said they had sought advice from the medical profession but nearly half said they had sought it from religious leaders and a fifth from 'specialised religious ministry/ faith healer'. The influence of religious leaders is profound. They were the most likely to be identified as the person who had advised or forced attempts at sexual orientation change, far more so than parents, and yet were the least likely person respondents said they were open with.

> The primary motivations for attempting to change were due either to their religious beliefs or internalised homophobia. This was evidenced by the fact that nearly two-thirds of those who admitted attempting to change their sexual orientation said they had done so because they were 'ashamed of my desires' and a quarter 'did not want to be associated with LGBT people or their lifestyle'. Nearly three quarters said they had done so 'because I believed that my desires were "sinful"' and over half said it was 'because my religious leader disapproved'.[14]

The impact of this on a victim's psyche is profound – and now well documented.[15] To grow up believing that one is intrinsically disordered and 'sinful' is a weight that is just too heavy to bear for many. This is made significantly worse by the knowledge

---

[13] A Jowett, 'Conversion Therapy: An Evidence Assessment and Qualitative Study' (Government Equalities Office, 2021) s 5.3 (citations omitted).
[14] Ozanne Foundation (n 7) 5.
[15] UNHRC (n 1); Ozanne Foundation (n 7) 16.

that all those in authority within a victim's religious or cultural community often believe that they have brought this 'problem' upon themselves. That is, that something must have happened in their past to make them have these unwanted feelings or a 'false' sense of identity. Sadly, many will also interpret a failing to get healed as due either to a lack of faith or because of some other 'hidden sin' that is not being disclosed. To children who are naturally keen to be loved and accepted by their family and friends this is a living hell that few will survive without significant long-term psychological damage. They are keenly aware of the shame that they have brought on their families which, coupled with their own high levels of self-loathing, is crushing. For many, suicide is the only way out of the impossible situation they are in.[16] The fact that this happens to many at the most formative stages of their lives – when they should be revelling in the joys of first love and experiencing unconditional love by those around them – makes this even more distressing.

B. Understanding Religious Conversion Practices

Given the weight of evidence that now exists across the international community regarding the mental health trauma caused by these barbaric practices, one has to ask why religious leaders have not relented, called a halt to these practices and apologised for the harm they have caused.

Whilst some religious leaders notably have (see below), there is a significant number who continue to lobby governments for the right to continue their abuse with impunity, claiming that they have a legitimate right to do so under the right to freedom of religion or belief, protected among others under Article 9 of the European Convention on Human Rights (ECHR). Even if a country does decide to make conducting conversion practices a criminal offence, there are still many religious leaders who are prepared to continue to conduct these practices – believing their allegiance to God takes precedence over their duty to comply with the law of the land.[17]

To understand why this is and what must be done to finally end religious conversion practices, we must first understand the various stages an individual typically goes through, including their motivations and beliefs that are held by them and those around them. That said, it is important to note that there are many who have no choice and are forced by their families and religious leaders to undergo these practices. Urgent and immediate steps must therefore be taken by governments to punish these abusers and support their victims, using both criminal and civil law. This must include sentence uplifting for criminal offences that are motivated by the pre-determined purpose of seeking to change, 'cure' or suppress a person's sexual orientation or gender identity.

---

[16] Jowett (n 13).
[17] Dixon (n 3).

Independent of whether someone chooses to willingly 'consent' or is forced to undergo religious conversion practices, most tend to go through the following three-stage process.

i. Stage One – The 'Silent Hell' Phase

People come to the self-realisation that they are 'different' to the accepted sexuality or gender identity norms of their religious or cultural community at very different times. For some, they will know from the very first moment that they start to interact with other children, others when they hit puberty and for some not until they have left home and been able to break free from the expectations placed on them by their immediate friends and family. I have spoken to many who have told me that they knew right from their first innocent interactions at playschool, and yet others who have taken a lifetime to understand who they truly are.

The one thing nearly all have in common is the dread of those close to them finding out. They know that they bear a secret that is likely to bring both division and shame on them and their family. Whilst some are secure in the knowledge that the unconditional love they experience from one or both parents will mean they will have some support, others are not so sure and most fear the reaction of those close to them when they find out. The 'coming out' process is always perceived as a 'one-way' process – for the genie can never be put back into the proverbial bottle, and this genie has such potentially dire consequences it is best left securely locked away.

For those who have their own personal faith, the problem is exacerbated by a growing dread that they are also unacceptable to God and, in some cases, fear they are destined to eternal damnation. This is an incredibly heavy burden for a young child to bear, especially when they are unable to share it with anyone around them for fear of being 'found out'. Knowing how disappointed – and, more often than not, angry – those close to them will be by the news that their child will not conform to their community's norms, many start to 'plea bargain' with God. They will make deals and promises, they will fast and pray, they will become overly zealous in their faith – all with the hope that it will change who they are. But to no avail. Their desperation leads quickly to depression or worse – to self-harm, suicidal ideation or in many cases attempts to take their own lives.

It is a living hell for so many at such a young tender age, when they should be rejoicing in who they are and experiencing the joy of first loves – knowing they are loved and that they are loveable. Instead, many begin to despise their bodies, and find themselves becoming increasingly isolated.

Something then typically happens to bring the individual into Stage Two: there is either a mental health incident, when the internal conflict and anguish they are suppressing becomes too much for them to deal with on their own, or the individual is outed by someone in their community. Too often this is by a jealous sibling or an angry classmate, rupturing what can often be one of their few trusted relationships and so causing even more pain and shame to the individual concerned.

Whatever the cause, the genie is now out of the bottle, and those in positions of authority around the individual – typically religious or cultural leaders, not to mention their parents – will believe that something must be done.

ii. Stage Two – The 'Healing Prayer' Phase

Whilst different religious communities hold a variety of beliefs and approaches to the idea of 'healing prayer', I have purposefully chosen to name this stage 'healing' because it is usually based on a desire to 'make whole' something that is perceived as sick or 'disordered'. The latter word is one that both the Catholic Church and Anglican Church have used in relation to LGBTQ+ people and is consistent with views held by many religious leaders from across the world's major religions.[18]

Despite the large amount of scientific and medical evidence, there are still many around the world who believe homosexuality and gender dysphoria to be illnesses that have been brought on by some form of childhood trauma or unhealthy relationship, notably with one or both parents.[19] This has led to countless parents blaming themselves for the fact that their children do not conform to the traditional norms expected by their community, leading many to feel shame about both their parenting skills as well as their child's 'unnatural condition'. This in turn leads to many fractured relationships between children and their parents, with both sides blaming the other for the rejection that they are experiencing by those close to them. This would be upsetting when all the parties involved are adults but is far more so when one party is still only a child.

Once the knowledge of the 'illness' is made public, the individual's religious or cultural leaders are typically informed and approached to seek their views. The logic that many are then subjected to is that 'if God requires people to live a certain way, then God's healing power will transform those people ("sinners") to live in accordance with those rules'. As such they will subject themselves, or be forced to be subjected, to hours of 'healing prayer' by those who often care deeply for them – wanting them to be 'healed' so that they can go on to live 'normal', healthy and fulfilling lives.

In my own case, I opened myself up to being questioned by those I hardly knew about the most intimate parts of my past, so that they could then try and identify the 'keys' as to why I had such 'unnatural' feelings. The prayer sessions were intense – often lasting hours and sometimes even whole days (this is not just a 'quick cup of tea and a chat'). The expectation that God would act was real, with

---

[18] Catholic Church, *Catechism of the Catholic Church* (Huntington, Our Sunday Visitor, 2000) para 2357; F Seper, *Persona Humana* (Vatican City, Sacred Congregation for Doctrine of the Faith, 1975) s 8; Anglican Communion, 'Resolutions of the Thirteenth Lambeth Conference' Res I.10.

[19] L Payne, *The Broken Image* (Wheaton, Crossway Books, 1981); SL Jones and MA Yarhouse, *Homosexuality* (Westmont, Inter-Varsity Press, 2000); G Harrison, 'The Science Behind Same-sex Attraction' (2008) 1 *Nucleus* www.cmf.org.uk/resources/publications/content/?context=article &id=2078.

doubt seen as a weakness and failure to get healed a sign that I was not strong enough in my faith. This creates a perfect storm – an individual desperate for love and acceptance is prayed for by people they love, who want them to be healed by a God of love. If the prayer does not work – then it must be the individual's fault, causing them to feel even more wretched and unloved. It is a vicious cycle that adds ever-increasing levels of anguish and pain.

This phase can last from weeks to years. However, there will normally come a time when either the individual or their family decides to seek more special-ised interventions from so-called 'professionals' who claim to have some form of expertise in this area. These are typically people with specific spiritual (eg deliver-ance) or counselling gifts – or a mix of the two. Notably, there is nearly always a charge for this stage – or rather an expectation that the person seeking healing will be prepared to give generously to show how much they desire and have faith in their healing.

iii. Stage Three – The 'Professional' Intervention Phase

It is a basic consumer marketing truth that wherever there is a need, there will always be people offering a means to meet that need. There are few exceptions to this rule, not even in religious contexts where people require solutions to 'unnat-ural' or 'spiritual' problems. Indeed, it is also a basic truth that the greater the desperation behind the need, the more a person is willing to pay.

Whilst spiritual remedies to spiritual problems have existed for years, the growth in deliverance or exorcism ministries has been spurred on by the relatively recent growth in the charismatic renewal movement within the evangelical wing of the Christian church. This has encouraged people with little or no training to offer spiritual deliverance (aka exorcisms[20]) to people suffering from a range of problems that have befallen them: from physical illness to financial problems to mental health issues. Those offering these services do so primarily 'out of love' for their fellow Christians and rarely charge an actual transaction fee. However, they will nearly always ask for a donation or gift towards their ministry, often asking the person they are 'helping' to give an amount that they think is commensurate with the healing that they seek. This can be coupled with a teaching that one must always show thanks for the healing one is about to receive – if for no other reason because it shows one has faith that it is going to work. This is rarely a business transaction and so cannot be traced through tax returns or business accounts.

Perhaps the more common form of 'professional services' with regards to reli-gious conversion practices are religious psychotherapists or counsellors, many of whom may have received some counselling training earlier in their careers, but who now use a mix of spiritual guidance, prayer and counselling in order to try and 'heal' their patient. I have been through hundreds of hours of sessions like this

---

[20] See Ch 8 of this edited collection, by JG Olivia and H Hall.

myself – both at international conferences, in group sessions and in one-to-one sessions – paying literally thousands of pounds for the privilege of their time.

What is perhaps most distressing about this stage is the earnestness that exists both with the 'professional' who is offering to help and the individual who is so desperate for any 'cure' that will enable them to live a 'normal, healthy and happy' life. The yearning to be healed can become all-consuming and leads many to a very dark place mentally as the more that they try to get healed, the bigger the disappointment they experience when they realise they are not. Similarly, when parents are paying for their children to participate in these sessions, the child will often be made aware of the acute financial burden their parents are undertaking on their behalf and will become even more distressed when they know deep down that the sessions are not working.

The harm this stage can cause is well documented.[21] Sadly, not all survive it – as the high level of attempted suicide rates have tragically shown (there is unfortunately no official data on suicide statistics).[22] Others do fortunately survive, often by coming to a point of realisation that the only way out is to accept themselves for who they are and walk away. However, this comes at a significant cost, as it means near certain rejection by their religious and/or cultural communities and, more upsettingly, often by their families too. Unfortunately, this option is rarely available to those children who are dependent on their parents for both financial and emotional support, putting many at grave risk of harm until they are old enough to leave home and fend for themselves.

That said, it is important to note that there is now mounting evidence that shows that some do escape, particularly given the higher-than-average levels of teenage homelessness amongst LGBTQ+ children from certain religious or ethnic backgrounds.[23] Interviews show that many had been told they would be sent abroad for 'conversion therapy' courses or threatened with either physical or sexual harm. Their stories are heartbreaking, and lead us to ask the simple question: 'If the evidence of harm is so great then why do religious leaders continue with these barbaric practices?'

II. Hermetically Sealed Hermeneutics

The inability to engage with the pain and abuse that religion can cause LGBTQ+ people is a question that the Anglican Bishop of Oxford, Right Reverend Dr Steven Croft, poses in his essay on same-sex relationships, published in October 2022. Entitled *Together in Love and Faith: Personal Reflections and Next Steps for*

---

[21] UNHRC (n 1); Jowett (n 13); Ozanne Foundation (n 7) 16.

[22] The Trevor Project, '2022 National Survey on LGBTQ Youth Mental Health' (The Trevor Project, 2022); Ozanne Foundation (n 7) 16.

[23] Albert Kennedy Trust, 'Impakt: Safe Homes and Better Futures for LGBTQ+ Young People' (Albert Kennedy Trust, 2021).

the Church,[24] it sets out his journey as a senior evangelical bishop in the Church of England in relation to lesbian, gay and bisexual people. In the essay, he movingly acknowledges and apologises for the pain and hurt that the Church has caused so many LGBTQ+ people, asking: 'Why was it so hard to hear the extent of the pain and distress of my fellow Christians?'[25] He goes on to admit:

> It is very difficult as a Church leader to acknowledge pain, and discomfort within your own community – especially if you are the cause of that pain or see it as a challenge to deeply held beliefs. It is much too easy to dismiss the experiences of a small number of individuals as particular to them.[26]

In other words, the heart (or, indeed, the head) will not hear what it does not want to hear. It is far easier to dismiss the testimony of one or two individuals as 'exceptions', rather than engage with the truth of their lived experience. The irony of this approach is that most of the major world religions recruit new members by encouraging individuals to testify to their lived experience of the impact their faith has had on their lives. Indeed, it is very common, particularly in evangelical settings, for Christians to be invited to 'share their testimony'. So why are the lived experiences of LGBTQ+ individuals not heard? Why are the numerous testimonies offered in TV documentaries, research studies, health journals and government reports not heeded and taken on board?

The answer lies far deeper than an inability to accept uncomfortable truths. For many it lies in their theological understanding of the nature of God, of sin and of judgement. In short, many hold that their religion teaches that these individuals have brought their suffering upon themselves because of their 'perverted' or 'ungodly' desires. It is an 'hermetically sealed hermeneutic' that leaves LGBTQ+ people with no way out. They are hurting because they are 'ungodly' and because they are not healed – it is a circular airtight argument that is not open to reason or challenge. No wonder so many are keen to claim that conversion practices work.

A good example of how impenetrable this belief is to proof of harm is in the prologue of *God, Gays and the Church: Human Sexuality and Experience in Christian Teaching* by Dr Lisa Nolland, Chris Sugden and Sarah Finch. Here they address the question raised by Reverend Hugh Lee about 'those gay and lesbian people who have tried to change their sexuality because the Church has told them that they should do, and who have been really hurt and have found that that was not God's will for them'.[27]

They respond by saying there are two problems with Reverend Lee's statement. First, that they do not believe that God's will is person- and context-specific, which

---

[24] S Croft, *Together in Love and Faith: Personal Reflections and Next Steps for the Church* (Oxford, Diocese of Oxford, 2022).
[25] ibid 12.
[26] ibid 13.
[27] L Nolland et al, *God, Gays and the Church* (London, The Latimer Trust, 2008).

many will take issue with. The second problem, they say, relates to the 'walking wounded'. They answer this by stating:

> It may well be the case that, in some people's lives, issues were not addressed at the right time, or in the right way, or with the necessary expertise. However, simply citing failed cases of 'cure' is no proof that the diagnosis is wrong![28]

In other words, people must try harder. They go on to explain that what is needed is resolve to:

> Improve the operation of the programmes, so that they can help more people reach greater levels of wholeness and well-being, and we also encourage those who struggle to have another 'go' to get a different mode of help, perhaps – but not to abandon the quest.[29]

A more recent response to the acknowledgement of the pain and suffering that these teachings cause is to say that the suffering people are enduring, particularly by suppressing who they are, is a good and holy thing. Ed Shaw, a same-sex-attracted Christian who believes that as such he must remain celibate and single for life, sets out the argument in his book *The Plausibility Problem*:

> So why on earth would anyone sign up for a life of suffering as a celibate same-sex attracted Christian? And how can I encourage others to do the same? In a word: Jesus.[30]

> For he teaches us that suffering for a good purpose is not to be avoided but embraced .... Oddly, the self-sacrifice that Jesus calls us to ends up not really being self-sacrifice at all. It is actually in our own best interests – in the long term.[31]

It is fair to say that different religions approach their teachings on this subject in a variety of ways, each using their own scriptures as a basis for their beliefs. The central issue for all religions, though, is how these scriptures are then interpreted. Typically, those with a conservative mindset will refuse to accept that there is any question about the traditional interpretations of their core texts. For them there is only one 'true' interpretation – that is, the one that they have always held. Indeed, to consider otherwise is viewed as deeply heretical, which if pursued or promoted must lead to the individual being rejected by their community.[32] This is another example of an 'hermetically sealed hermeneutic', where there is no room for questioning or disagreement of traditional interpretations and where people are ostracised for daring to do so. A good example of this is in the UK Evangelical

---

[28] ibid 20.

[29] ibid 21.

[30] E Shaw, *The Plausibility Problem: The Church and Same Sex Attraction* (Nottingham, Inter-Varsity Publishers, 2015) 116–17.

[31] ibid 120.

[32] A/HRC/53/37: Freedom of religion or belief, and freedom from violence and discrimination based on sexual orientation and gender identity – Report of the Independent Expert on protection against violence and discrimination based on sexual orientation and gender identity (Advance unedited version) pars 51–52.

Alliance's 'Affirmations' of how they recommend their member churches and church leaders respond pastorally to questions regarding homosexuality:

> We believe both habitual homoerotic sexual activity without repentance and public promotion of such activity are inconsistent with faithful church membership. While processes of membership and discipline differ from one church context to another, we believe that either of these behaviours warrants consideration for church discipline.[33]

It is deeply concerning to see such a rigidity of thinking that does not allow for reason, science or human suffering to shape and refine religious teaching – a practice that has been embraced by most religions for thousands of years (indeed ever since we thought that the world was flat).

III. Recognising 'Spiritual Abuse'

This strict adherence to a certain religious teaching, despite all the evidence of the harm that the teaching is known to inflict, is the root cause of 'spiritual abuse'. It is *this* that governments, with the support of religious leaders, must look to identify and legislate against in order to safeguard and protect people. There is much precedent for this, with actions already taken by many governments to outlaw female genital mutilation, forced marriage and corporal punishment. As a former UN Special Rapporteur on Freedom of Religion or Belief, Dr Ahmed Shaheed, has said:

> Countries already restrict manifestations of religion to protect those within their jurisdiction from harm. Religious or cultural practices such as female genital mutilation, early and forced marriage and 'honour' killings are rightly condemned as human rights abuses, with many countries criminalising their commission. However, some pay less attention when it comes to ending harmful gendered practices that are less easily characterised as 'contrary to western values'. The fact that conversion practices are conducted within almost all major faith communities in the UK cannot be an excuse for the state to treat it differently from other gendered practices that both constitute and cause serious harm.[34]

So how and why does spiritual abuse occur? Typically, it is when someone in a position of power or authority in a spiritual context invokes a 'divine right' or religious teaching to treat someone in their care in an abusive way. This concept of 'spiritual abuse' has been researched in some depth by Dr Lisa Oakley from Manchester Metropolitan University, who in 2013 defined it as follows:

> Spiritual abuse is coercion and control of one individual by another in a spiritual context. The target experiences spiritual abuse as a deeply emotional personal attack. This abuse may include: manipulation and exploitation, enforced accountability, censorship of

---

[33] A Goddard and D Horrocks, 'Biblical and Pastoral Responses to Homosexuality' (Evangelical Alliance, 2012) www.eauk.org/resources/what-we-offer/reports/biblical-and-pastoral-responses-to-homosexuality.

[34] A Shaheed, 'There is No Legal Defence of LGBT+ Conversions' (*The Guardian*, 23 April 2021).

decision making, requirements for secrecy and silence, pressure to conform, misuse of scripture or the pulpit to control behaviour, requirement of obedience to the abuser, the suggestion that the abuser has a 'divine' position, isolation from others, especially those external to the abusive context.[35]

This definition has since been key in helping generate public discussions about the existence and differing forms of spiritual abuse.[36] As such it focuses on the abuse perpetrated by an individual (normally a person in authority) over another individual (normally a congregant).

In this context, religious conversion practices are a clear example of spiritual abuse, as they involve an individual being subjected to practices by people in religious authority over them. However, few governments are prepared to recognise religious conversion practices as abusive, as they appear loath to upset the conservative Christians in their midst. It is noticeable that whilst it is acceptable to talk about spiritual abuse when it relates to the practices of certain faith or ethnic groups, such as with female genital mutilation, there is a reluctance to do so when it relates to practices that are viewed as more 'mainstream', such as 'healing prayer' or religious counselling.

This raises the question as to whether governments, and indeed religious organisations, truly accept the harm that these forms of religious conversion practices inflict on individuals, often children, and whether instead they perceive them as a 'benign' set of practices that are relatively harmless and should therefore be allowed to continue. An example of the willingness to side with religious organisations rather than victims is the response of the UK Equality and Human Rights Commission to the UK government's 2021 consultation on 'conversion therapy', which stated:

> Encouraging people to comply with religious doctrine that requires refraining from certain types of sexual activity should not fall within the definition of conversion therapy.[37]

> Conversion therapy will need to be carefully defined in any legislation in order to ensure that harmful practices are caught whilst mainstream religious practices such as preaching, teaching and praying about sexual ethics or gender roles, including in relation to children and young people under 18, are not criminalised.[38]

The issue of spiritual abuse is made considerably worse by the fact that most religious organisations have been left to 'mark their own homework' with regard to safeguarding against 'spiritual abuse'. As a result, few have taken this form of abuse as seriously as they should. For instance, it has only been in the last decade that

---

[35] L Oakley, *Breaking the Silence on Spiritual Abuse* (London, Palgrave Macmillan, 2013).

[36] H Williams, 'Spiritual Abuse: This Way to the Exit' (*Church Times*, 16 August 2019).

[37] Equality and Human Rights Commission, 'Response Submitted to UK Government Consultation: Banning Conversion Therapy' (EHRC, 2022) para 6.

[38] ibid para 10.

the Church of England has started to recognise their major safeguarding failures. This has been brought into sharp focus with the Independent Inquiry into Child Sex Abuse (IICSA) and other high-profile sexual abuse cases, particularly within conservative evangelicalism.[39] This has left victims extremely exposed, given that few religious leaders were initially willing to listen or act on their concerns. Indeed, it is only in the last few years that some religions have started to understand the full nature of the safeguarding challenges that they face and the need to ensure adequate training and protections.

In April 2021 the former Archbishop of Canterbury, Lord Williams of Oystermouth, highlighted the need for independent assessment of religious practices that are deemed abusive. Drawing on the findings of the IICSA, he raised the following question, recognising that there must be necessary limits to certain religious practices:

> Is the Church of England, or indeed any other religious body, capable of monitoring its own practice without independent assessment? In other words, you need some external input into the workings of a religious community in order to create and to settle what are acceptable limits of behaviour, to rule out the abuse and manipulation and whatever else that there may be.[40]

It is therefore clear that spiritual abuse needs to be recognised by governments and religious organisations alike, and that the religious organisations require governments to help determine the acceptable limits of these practices. This should and must be focused on the wellbeing of individuals so that they are protected from harm, rather than protecting the religious organisations. This is particularly true when it relates to safeguarding people with protected characteristics. To do this effectively, governments cannot be seen to give preference to any one religion over another, nor indeed any religious practice over another. As the highly respected human rights lawyer, Jonathan Cooper, said in a legal paper on banning conversion practices:

> In matters of faith, the state must also remain neutral. It is not the role of government to prefer one religious doctrine over another, or one faction of a faith group over another. It is the role of the state to ensure that human rights are protected and that includes guaranteeing that when the right to religion and belief is manifested, harm is not caused.[41]

The most effective way for governments to ensure complete clarity as to what is and is not a harmful practice is to define this in law, especially in a society committed

---

[39] Independent Inquiry Child Sexual Abuse, *Child Protection in Religious Organisations and Settings: Investigation Report* (London, HMSO, 2021) s C.4.

[40] R Williams, 'UK Parliamentary Briefing Organised by MOU Coalition against Conversion Therapy' (28 April 2021).

[41] J Cooper, 'Why Conversion Therapy Needs to Be Banned' (The Labour Campaign for Human Rights, 2021).

to upholding and protecting the human rights of all. That is why specific legislation to ban religious conversion practices is required, setting out the consequences for those who continue with their abuse.

IV. Safeguarding from Spiritual Abuse

There is much that religious leaders and religious organisations can themselves do – and indeed are doing – to set out what are and are not acceptable religious practices in relation to LGBTQ+ people within their own religious institutions. This section looks at what has been achieved to date and provides some good practice for other religious organisations to consider.

The first official statement agreed by a religious organisation in relation to condemning conversion practices was a motion agreed in 2017 by the Church of England's General Synod.[42] This is a debate I led, where I sought to unite the Church of England – despite its differing views on the nature of same-sex relationships – in its condemnation of these harmful practices. Much to the surprise of many there was some resistance to the motion from conservatives, who wanted to be able to continue with various spiritual practices as they did not believe them to be harmful. Fortunately, the majority of Synod thought otherwise, notably amongst the House of Bishops, where all but one voted to condemn the practices and call on the government to ban them.

My approach had been to ask the Synod to endorse a statement that a group of eminent health care professionals had made – the Memorandum of Understanding on Conversion Therapy (MOU).[43] The slightly amended motion chose to endorse the 2015 MOU, which had the backing of the Royal College of Psychiatrists, the British Association for Counselling and Psychotherapy, the Royal College of General Practitioners and many other groups. The agreed motion read as follows:

> That this Synod: (a) endorse the Memorandum of Understanding on Conversion Therapy in the UK of November 2015, signed by The Royal College of Psychiatrists and others, that the practice of gay conversion therapy has no place in the modern world, is unethical, potentially harmful and not supported by evidence; and 3 (b) call upon the Church to be sensitive to, and to listen to, contemporary expressions of gender identity; (c) and call on the government to ban the practice of Conversion Therapy.[44]

---

[42] Church of England, 'General Synod Backs Ban on Conversion Therapy' (Church of England, 8 July 2017) www.churchofengland.org/news-and-media/news-and-statements/general-synod-backs-ban-conversion-therapy.

[43] British Association for Counselling and Psychotherapy, 'Memorandum of Understanding on Conversion Therapy in the UK' (BACP, 2022).

[44] Church of England (n 42).

Since then, the MOU has been updated to include condemnation of gender identity as well as sexual orientation conversion practices, and has the support of over 25 health, counselling and psychotherapy organisations.[45]

Importantly, other religious organisations have also followed suit by agreeing similar public condemnations of conversion practices. For instance, in July 2021 the Methodist Conference of the Methodist Church of Great Britain agreed the following statement:

> The Conference agrees:
>
> (1)   to support and adopt the 'Memorandum of Understanding on Conversion Therapy in the UK' definition of conversion therapy as quoted above,
> (2)   to call on all Methodists to refuse to offer or participate in offering conversion therapy in any form.
> (3)   that no conversion therapy can take place in the name of the Methodist Church.
>
> The Conference directs the Methodist Council to consider, draft and publish a policy on 'Conversion Therapy' in light of points (1) to (3) of this response. The Conference calls on the UK Government to ban 'Conversion Therapy' without further delay and therefore also directs the Methodist Council to consider further the most appropriate way in which to engage with HM Government on this issue.[46]

Then in December 2021 the Quakers in Britain and the Quaker Gender and Sexual Diversity Community added their voice to the growing calls to ban 'conversion therapy'. In responding to the UK government's consultation on conversion practices they set out their religious reasons for opposing conversion practices and highlighted evidence as to why a ban is needed, stating: 'Quakers believe that conversion therapy is a form of inhuman and degrading treatment, and that freedom of religion or belief cannot be used legally to justify it.'[47]

Pope Francis has said a variety of things that have led to some confusion about where he stands on conversion practices. In September 2018 he made some remarks, later clarified by the Vatican, suggesting children should seek psychiatric help.[48] In contrast, in March 2021 he gave a speech to moral theologians where he urged them to 'enter into a relationship with the members of God's people and to look at life from their perspective in order to understand the real difficulties that they encounter'.[49] Many interpreted this as him condemning conversion practices because of his insistence that moral theology could not just be about principles and formulations, but must respond to the reality of the person in need, urging

[45] British Association for Counselling and Psychotherapy (n 43).

[46] The Methodist Church, 'Methodist Conference Votes on Banning Conversion Therapy' (1 July 2021) www.methodist.org.uk/about-us/news/latest-news/all-news/methodist-conference-votes-on-banning-of-conversion-therapy.

[47] Quakers in Britain, 'Quakers Back Ban on Conversion Therapy' (Quakers in Britain, 8 December 2021) www.quaker.org.uk/news-and-events/news/quakers-back-ban-on-conversion-therapy.

[48] F DeBernardo, 'Vatican Clarifies Pope Francis' Remark about Psychiatry' (New Ways Ministry, 1 September 2018) www.newwaysministry.org/2018/09/01/vatican-clarifies-pope-francis-remark-about-psychiatry.

[49] G O'Connell, 'Pope Francis: Moral Theology Must Concern Reality and People, Not Just Principles' (America Jesuit Review, 23 March 2021) www.americamagazine.org/faith/2021/03/23/pope-francis-speech-moral-theology-cdf-statement-240303.

all those present to remember, 'knowledge of theoretical principles alone ... is not enough to accompany and sustain consciences in discerning the good to be done'.[50]

In November 2019, in-between these two events, I had the privilege of meeting the Pope at the Vatican and was able to present him with copies of both my autobiography, *Just Love*, and the results of our 2018 Ozanne Foundation Faith & Sexuality survey. On hearing the trauma that I and others had gone through he grabbed my hands and asked me to pray for him on this matter.

These public condemnations of conversion practices have not been confined to Christian denominations. In June 2021 both the Hindu Council UK and the Buddhist Dharma Centre in England wrote open letters to the trustees of my Foundation stating that 'conversion therapy' had 'no place in the modern world', with both organisations going on to call for a full ban by the UK government.[51] And that was just the start: as I write, dozens of orthodox rabbis are coming together around the world to make a public statement to condemn conversion practices too.

Perhaps the most significant condemnation by religious leaders, however, is that made by those who signed the Global Interfaith Commission on LGBT+ Lives 2020 Declaration.[52] This brought together hundreds of senior religious leaders from around the world to agree to a statement that sought to 'declare the sanctity of life and the dignity of all'. Sponsored by the UK Foreign, Commonwealth and Development Office, the initiative was launched by my Foundation to amplify the voices of senior religious leaders who wished to celebrate and affirm all LGBTQ+ people. The declaration opened by apologising for the harm that religious teaching has caused and continues to cause around the world and asked for 'forgiveness for those whose lives have been damaged and destroyed on the pretext of religious teaching'. It then went on to call for an end to the criminalisation and violence against LGBTQ+ people, before ending with this important statement:

> We call for all attempts to change, suppress or erase a person's sexual orientation, gender identity or gender expression – commonly known as 'conversion therapy' – to end, and for these harmful practices to be banned.[53]

The first signature was that of the late Archbishop Desmond Tutu and by the time of our launch we had over 400 senior religious leaders from 35 countries, including 10 archbishops, 63 bishops and 66 rabbis. A special Act of Celebration was held in Westminster Abbey, London to mark its launch, which was hosted by the Dean of Westminster with the Dean of St Paul's giving the address.[54] Since then, over 1500 people have added their names to the Declaration.[55]

---

[50] ibid.

[51] L Wakefield, 'Hindu and Buddhist Communities Call for "Immediate" UK Ban on "Unethical" Conversion Therapy' (PinkNews, 18 June 2021) www.pinknews.co.uk/2021/06/18/uk-conversion-therapy-ban-hindu-council-buddhist-dhamma-center-jayne-ozanne.

[52] Global Interfaith Commission on LGBT+ Lives, '2020 Declaration' (Global Interfaith Commission on LGBT+ Lives, 20 December 2020) www.globalinterfaith.lgbt/declaration-2.

[53] ibid.

[54] Global Interfaith Commission on LGBT+ Lives, 'Westminster Abbey' (Global Interfaith Commission on LGBT+ Lives, 16 December 2020) www.globalinterfaith.lgbt/westminsterabbey.

[55] Global Interfaith Commission on LGBT+ Lives, 2020 Declaration (n 52).

Figure 1 2020 Declaration on the Sanctity of Life and Dignity of All

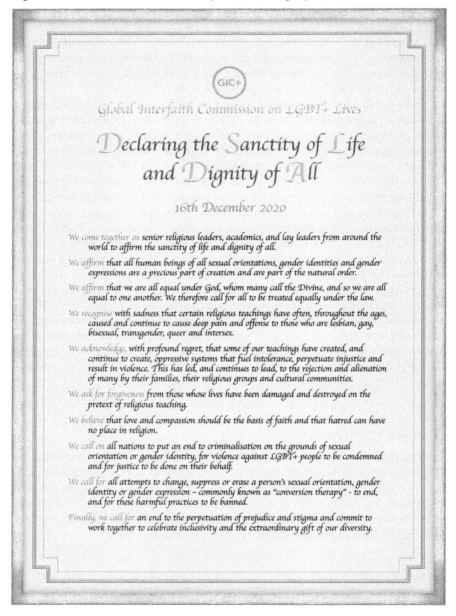

Two years later the Global Interfaith Commission on LGBT+ Lives (GIC+) convened again, thanks to the ongoing support of the UK Foreign, Commonwealth

and Development Office. This time we brought together over 150 senior religious leaders from 30 countries from around the world to agree and publicly endorse a set of six safeguarding principles to protect LGBT+ lives.[56]

To inform our discussions, we commissioned research in Hungary and the Caribbean on the nature and impact of conversion practices, particularly religious conversion practices, on LGBTQ+ people living there. The results were harrowing and showed the true extent of the abuse. The Chair of our Research Advisory Board, Professor Zoe Playdon, surmised the impact of this in her Foreword:

> The majority of respondents were children when they were recruited into these degrading attempts to change their sexuality or gender identity. Defenseless and at a critical stage of their adolescent development, they turned for help to those they trusted in what should have been places of safety – their church, their doctor's surgery, their home – and found there only prejudice and harm.
>
> Their abusers are emboldened by a toxic culture whose constant negative message is that it is not acceptable – to God, to medicine, to society or to their family– for LGBT+ people to be who they intrinsically are. The implicit requirement is that they must conform in order to belong, to be accepted, and to be loved. Unsurprisingly, many tried to do so. Out of despair, some sought death.
>
> That is why we need the international community to intervene. It is also why we need those with recognised spiritual and moral authority to champion their cause and lead the debate in their own religious communities, which are so often the source of such prejudice. We cannot support these abhorrent practices, and the damage they wreak on society's most vulnerable members, any longer.[57]

The religious leaders attending the conference were united in their resolve to act. Led by our GIC+ Patron, the former President of Ireland Dr Mary McAleese – herself a devout Catholic – we unanimously agreed a set of Safeguarding Principles that were based on the six safeguarding principles from the UK Care Act 2014: empowerment, prevention, proportionality, protection, partnership and accountability.[58] These specifically addressed the issue of eradicating 'any harmful practice that inhibits the flourishing of all', such as conversion practices. It opened:

> All individuals are made in the image of God, whom many call the Divine, and should be free to live a life of dignity consistent with their sexuality and gender identity within their faith communities without fear or judgement.[59]

As before, these Safeguarding Principles to Protect LGBT+ Lives were celebrated in an Act of Dedication amongst the wide group of religious leaders from across all the

---

[56] Global Interfaith Commission on LGBT+ Lives, 'Senior Religious Leaders Agree Principles to Safeguard LGBT+ Lives' (Global Interfaith Commission on LGBT+ Lives, 22 March 2022) www.globalinterfaith.lgbt/safeguarding.

[57] Ban Conversion Therapy Legal Forum (n 2) ii.

[58] Department of Health and Social Care, 'Statement of Government Policy on Adult Safeguarding' (2011).

[59] Global Interfaith Commission on LGBT+ Lives, 'Principles to Safeguard LGBT+ Lives' (n 56).

major faiths, which this time was held in the Chapel of Church House, the institutional home of the Church of England. Since then, the Safeguarding Principles have been taken and used by religious leaders around the world to advocate for change in the way religions treat and safeguard LGBTQ+ people in their care.

Figure 2 2022 Principles to Safeguard LGBT+ Lives

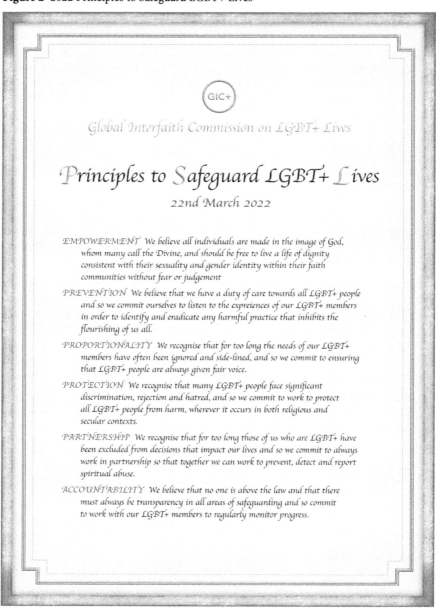

V. Ending Religious Conversion Practices

Whilst there has been much progress in recent years in encouraging religious leaders to recognise the significant harm caused by certain members of their faith traditions, there is still much more that needs to be done. This must start with more religious leaders speaking out about the need for a legislative ban on conversion practices in order to hold ongoing perpetrators to account. As the former Chair and Vice Chair of my Foundation, the former Bishop of Liverpool and Dean of St Paul's, along with members of our Inter-Religious Advisory Board, said in an open letter to the Secretary of State, the Rt Hon Liz Truss (the then Minister for Women and Equalities) in July 2020:

> We urge you to make it clear that the UK will not tolerate those who practise conversion therapy in any form, whether consensual or not, and that those who practise it will be prosecuted. This will have the impact of causing religious leaders to think twice, as they will be loath to risk having a criminal record that would stop them from following their vocation. It will also, importantly, enable victims to know that they will be understood and protected if they find the courage to speak out.[60]

However, still more can and must be done. Returning to the three-stage process that so many experience when undergoing conversion practices, all governments and religious organisations that are committed to eradicating these abusive practices must also consider the following steps.

A. Ending Stage One – The 'Silent Hell' Phase

The most critical thing to end in this phase is the damaging isolation that so many individuals too often experience, and signpost them to safe and appropriate forms of trained support.

This is not as easy as it would appear. Despite the advent of the internet and the plethora of LGBTQ+ groups and even LGBTQ+ faith groups that can now be easily identified and accessed, the greatest need of those trapped in this 'Silent Hell' phase is being sure that whatever they do say will be treated in the strictest confidence. They cannot risk their internal turmoil being shared with anyone they have not approved, and this will typically always stop them reaching out for help.

Trust takes an age to build and a moment to lose. This adage is even more pertinent in a world where the individual knows that those who are purportedly charged with their care – their parents, teachers, doctors, religious leaders – are the ones they fear the most finding out.

A secure dedicated helpline, which they can access anonymously, is critical. As is freely accessible educational materials alongside stories of other LGBTQ+

---

[60] Letter from Paul Bayes et al to Liz Truss (7 July 2020).

people of faith who have survived similar difficulties. I have lost count of the number of people who have reached out to me, as someone who they trust will understand, for help and support. I cannot deal pastorally with these cases, and have sought to refer them on to trained colleagues who I urge them to trust and confide in.

A recent initiative is the advent of LGBTQ+ chaplains, such as those pioneered by my own Diocese of Oxford in the Church of England.[61] However, this may well be too risky for some to reach out to as many will be concerned that their secret will be shared amongst the religious leaders in their diocese.

Independent helplines where the counsellors are trained in faith and LGBTQ+ matters are the key. These should be championed by well-known LGBTQ+ people of faith to help give them legitimacy.

B. Ending Stage Two – The 'Healing Prayer' Phase

Stopping both this and the next stage is the primary aim of a legislative ban on conversion practices, which denounces these abhorrent practices and makes clear to perpetrators that their actions are criminal and will not be tolerated. The Cooper Report,[62] which I published with the support of a highly respected group of international lawyers, parliamentarians, academics and civil society leaders, recommends that any ban should utilise both criminal and civil law. The report explains that criminalisation is warranted because:

> Conversion practices deny human dignity and demean victims in such a way as to amount to degrading or inhuman treatment and may in some circumstances constitute torture. They also destroy an individual's right to a private life, protected by Article 8 ECHR. Human rights law requires that conduct that falls within the scope of prohibited ill-treatment be regulated by the criminal law.[63]

It then goes on to say that in addition to criminalising conversion practices, a ban must be:

> Coupled with ancillary civil protection orders that ensure a victim's safety. This is to protect victims immediately so that they avoid any harm, given they cannot afford to wait for lengthy investigation and prosecution.[64]

However, for civil protection orders to work effectively, there must be significant investment in multi-agency guidelines and training for all other relevant organisations, such as police and social services. This is essential to ensure appropriate

---

[61] Diocese of Oxford, 'LGBTQIA+ Chaplaincy Service' (Diocese of Oxford, 2022) www.oxford.anglican.lgbt.
[62] Ban Conversion Therapy Legal Forum (n 5).
[63] ibid s I (2).
[64] ibid s I (3).

recognition and risk-assessment of conversion practice victims, particularly in religious and cultural settings. As the Cooper Report recognises:

> Without this information, abusive conversion practices may be misinterpreted as a generational, cultural or religious ideological disagreement and the pattern of escalating behaviour that often occurs in the lead-up to conversion practices would be missed.[65]

At the same time, religious leaders must themselves speak out and denounce the harmful theology that fuels the beliefs underpinning these spiritually abusive practices. The silence must be broken and the 'hermetically sealed hermeneutics' exposed. It is incumbent on all leaders to teach how religions have evolved in the light of science, reason and understanding of harm.

The most important step that religious organisations can make is to embrace the GIC+ Safeguarding Principles (set out above) and ensure adequate safeguarding training for all those involved in pastoral care, particularly those involved with prayer ministry. This must include teaching that any religious practice aimed at an individual or group of individuals with the 'predetermined purpose' of changing their sexual orientation and gender identity is illegal.

At the same time a National Reporting Hotline is needed to enable victims to report those religious leaders or religious communities who habitually offer or practise any form of activity that falls within the definition of conversion practices. This will enable patterns of behaviour to be identified and will help the authorities engage with repeat offenders, warning them about their criminal behaviour before instigating, if they are determined to continue, criminal proceedings.

C. Ending Stage Three – The 'Professional Intervention' Phase

Central to this stage is the offering of 'specialist services' by individuals with the predetermined purpose of seeking to change, suppress or 'cure' a person's sexual orientation or gender identity. Often there is an expectation that money will be given for this service, although there is rarely a formal contractual arrangement. People typically find out about the services via word of mouth within their religious or cultural communities, although sometimes they will be advertised publicly. These are the most dangerous forms of religious conversion practices and must be stopped.

Whilst all the steps in Stage Two still apply, there are additional actions that must also be taken, including banning the advertising and promotion of these services as well as criminalising those who force people to travel overseas to undergo conversion practices. This should extend to banning teaching materials that encourage people to try these disreputable practices themselves.

---

[65] ibid s VIII (2(e)).

Once again it is incumbent on religious leaders to speak out, particularly about the arbitrary use of deliverance ministries. They must stress that only those with specific training have the authority to conduct these procedures and never when it relates to any form of conversion practice.

Medical healthcare professionals should be duty bound to pay attention to colleagues who claim to offer specialist services in this area and report any offenders to the relevant regulatory body. It is also highly recommended that countries consider agreeing a 'Memorandum of Understanding on Conversion Practices' amongst their healthcare professionals, like that agreed in England.[66]

Given that money is often exchanged, banks may wish to make a collective decision as to where they stand in relation to hosting the bank accounts of known perpetrators. Ultimately, however, it is the use of criminal legislation that is most likely to stop this stage.

VI. Conclusion

Religious conversion practices are the most common form of conversion practices and whilst legislation can provide some protections for victims, a far broader set of actions by governments and religious organisations is needed to ensure these harmful practices finally come to an end.

This requires senior religious leaders to recognise the harm that is being done within their religious organisations, both by certain toxic theologies and by those who are determined to continue these barbaric practices because they adhere to 'hermetically sealed hermeneutics'.

Safeguarding against spiritual abuse is foundational to protecting LGBTQ+ people within their religious communities. As such, agreement to and promotion of the six Global Interfaith Commission on LGBT+ Lives' Safeguarding Principles will provide some clear guidelines about how to treat LGBTQ+ people. However, these will only be embraced once senior religious leaders start to break the silence and speak out about the harm that religious practices are known to have caused.

Governments must work with religious organisations to raise awareness of the harm that is being caused, and to oversee safeguarding training amongst all those involved in the relevant agencies. Helplines and reporting lines must also be set up alongside specialised support for survivors.

However, all this is contingent on the collective will of both governments and religious leaders to root out and end these abhorrent practices. Key to this is the urgent need to ensure a full and meaningful ban on conversion practices, including all religious practices, that will protect victims and bring those who are determined to continue harming LGBTQ+ people to face justice.

---

[66] British Association for Counselling and Psychotherapy (n 43).

10

Nothing about Us without Us

Listening to and Engaging with Survivors of Conversion Practices

JORDAN SULLIVAN AND NICHOLAS SCHIAVO

This chapter will address the reasons why the lived experience of survivors is fundamental to the work of advocating for legislative bans of conversion practices. It will also address the critical importance of funding, creating, and providing accessible supports for victims of conversion practices; work that must be done alongside legislation. In presenting the Canadian experience, the chapter hopes to inform similar survivor-led movements in other jurisdictions and provide a potential template for global advocacy.

Conversion practices refer to a broad set of behavioural, clinical, cultural, and/or faith-based practices, messages, or pressures, which aim to change, deny, or suppress a person's same-sex attraction, gender expressions, or gender identities discordant with sex assigned at birth. It includes, but is not limited to, 'conversion therapy'. Even when informal and infrequent, conversion practices can do significant damage to LGBTQ+ people.

It goes without saying that many survivors experience a lifelong scarring effect from the trauma they endure. Conversion practices are not just abhorrent while they occur: they continue to have devastating effects on their LGBTQ+ victims long after. This trauma impacts mental and physical health, confidence, intimacy, social relations and career development. That is because conversion practices, at their core, are designed to invalidate an individual's humanity and pathologise the human condition. These practices are committed with a clear goal in mind: to break LGBTQ+ people down by creating a self-sustaining cycle of hate within their victims.

This gruesome reality has been confirmed by countless international reports and peer-reviewed research. Conversion practices are at the very least a confirmed form of degrading treatment, and could at times even amount to torture, in violation of well-established provisions of domestic and international human rights law.[1] In addition to the report by the United Nations Independent Expert on Protection against Violence and Discrimination Based on Sexual Orientation and Gender Identity, other comprehensive and complementary reports on the state of global conversion practices have been developed by the International Rehabilitation Council for Torture Victims,[2] the Global Project against Hate and Extremism,[3] and OutRight Action International[4] among others. Likewise, leading Canadian scholars like Florence Ashley and Dr Travis Salway,[5] and Australian scholars like Tiffany Jones and Nathan Despott have informed the extensive body of research on conversion practices.[6]

I. Biography

Jordan, the first-named author of this chapter, is a trans man and a survivor of religious trauma and conversion practices. Raised in the Seventh-day Adventist church, he was aware of conversion practices since the late 1970s and through gay friends who survived the Quest Learning Centre in the United States during the 1980s.[7] However, most of the advocacy efforts he was involved with – drafting statements, letters and action plans to support bans on conversion practices – were done safely at a distance at places like the national office of the United Church of Canada (which affirmed LGBTQ+ people in 1988, condemned 'conversion therapy' in 2018, and supported the federal criminal ban in 2019). He had not publicly shared his story of experiencing conversion practices.

When Jordan was invited to coordinate the SOGIE CE/CT Survivor Support Project (a community-based research project led by survivors, with survivors, for survivors) he was hesitant to accept the position as he struggled with knowing whether his experience could be classified as SOGIE CE (Sexual Orientation and Gender Identity or Expression Change Efforts) or 'conversion therapy'. He never

---

[1] See Chapter 1 of this edited collection, by Ilias Trispiotis. See also I Trispiotis and C Purshouse, '"Conversion Therapy" as Degrading Treatment' (2022) 42(1) *Oxford Journal of Legal Studies* 104; UNHRC, 'Practices of So-Called "Conversion Therapy": Report of the Independent Expert on Protection Against Violence and Discrimination Based on Sexual Orientation and Gender Identity' (1 May 2020) A/HRC/44/53.

[2] J Bothe, 'It's Torture Not Therapy' (International Rehabilitation Council for Torture Victims, 2020).

[3] W Via and H Beirich, 'Conversion Therapy Online: The Players' (Global Project Against Hate and Extremism, 2022).

[4] A Bishop, 'Harmful Treatment: The Global Reach of So-Called Conversion Therapy' (Outright Action International, 2019).

[5] T Salway and F Ashley, 'Ridding Canadian Medicine of Conversion Therapy' (2022) 194(1) *Canadian Medical Association Journal* E17.

[6] T. Jones et al, 'Supporting LGBTQA+ Peoples' Recovery from Sexual Orientation and Gender Identity and Expression Change Efforts' (2022) 57(6) *Australian Psychologist* 359.

[7] R Lawson, 'The Troubled Career of an "Ex-Gay" Healer: Colin Cook, Seventh-day Adventists, and the Christian Right' (Meeting of the American Sociological Association, San Francisco, 22 August 1998) www.ronaldlawson.net/2018/06/11/the-troubled-career-of-an-ex-gay-healer-colin-cook-seventh-day-adventists-and-the-christian-right.

attended a formalised 'conversion therapy' programme or camp run by a religious organisation. He never experienced healthcare practitioners misdiagnosing him or refusing him access to care. He felt like his experience of conversion practices was not as bad as that experienced by others.

In reality, Jordan spent 33 years internalising conversion practices through prayer, the study of religious texts, disassociation from his body, and suppression/denial of his sexual orientation, gender expression, and gender identity. He spent six years in Christian counselling where conversion practices were used, accessing resources recommended by Exodus International (an ex-gay Christian umbrella organisation active between 1975 and 2012) and Love in Action (an ex-gay Christian ministry founded in 1973). He came out as a lesbian at age 33, and as a trans man at age 51. At the time of writing, he is 62 (and queerly heterosexual), but he spent decades of his life hiding in shame and fear and struggled with suicidal ideation until his mid-30s. He too had experienced SOGIE CE and survived conversion practices.

Jordan's experience is common among many LGBTQ+ people who, for a variety of reasons, do not think of themselves as having experienced conversion practices, nor do they fully understand how the harm they experienced continues to affect them in their lives today. This is a problem that can only be addressed by providing accessible support and education, as we will discuss below.

Today, in his work with the Community-Based Research Centre (CBRC), Jordan works with colleagues, survivors, and key stakeholders across Canada to support the creation of survivor initiatives; develop resources to educate a wide variety of audiences about what 'conversion therapy' is; improve understanding of the federal ban and acknowledge its limitations; and collaborate across sectors to prevent these practices from continuing to harm people.

Nick Schiavo, the second author of this chapter, is Executive Director of No Conversion Canada, a registered non-profit, non-partisan organisation dedicated to ending 'conversion therapy', which he founded in 2018. He is a gay man, public policy professional and human rights advocate but does not have lived experience as a survivor of conversion practices.

II. Listening to Survivors

A. Importance of Testimony

'Nothing about us without us' is a critical element of all advocacy work to ban conversion practices and develop support for survivors. People with lived experience of conversion practices have repeatedly stressed that when legislative bans are being developed, or when survivor resources are created, they must be done in equal partnership with survivors. They should empower survivors and ensure that laws, policies, activities and services reflect the needs of the people they purport to serve. Simply put, working with survivors is important because they have the most at stake.

When pushing for political action, one cannot lose sight of the emotional and human element of this particular issue.[8] In the lead up to the federal ban in Canada, as well as to provincial and municipal bans, our movement utilised lived experience and storytelling as a tool for policy change. Looking back at this period, we believe it was effective. In particular, the voices of survivors coming to the forefront proved pivotal in galvanising support.[9] While peer-reviewed research and statistics will always be required to change public policy, Canada would not have the protections it does today without survivors coming forward and sharing their stories.

One of the other unique challenges in banning conversion practices was combatting the myth of Canadian progressive exceptionalism. There is no doubt that Canada is lucky to have secured several rights for LGBTQ+ communities. Unfortunately, this has created a false belief that the state is now a post-phobia utopia. This view often means that lesser-understood issues within the queer community go unseen and fail to receive the political attention they deserve. With equal marriage and federal human rights protections for gender-diverse people now established, there is a sense of disbelief that conversion practices could and do take place in Canada.

By 2020, a snowball effect within the media was starting to occur as more survivors came forward. As more stories were shared, other survivors found strength in learning that others had similar experiences. While many media stories offered hope, like the territory-wide ban in the Yukon,[10] others fuelled opposition.[11]

B. Sources of Testimony

The recommendations and findings below are based in large part on two crucial surveys. A decisive, game-changing moment occurred with the June 2021 release of the findings from the Community-Based Research Centre's Sex Now Survey, Canada's largest and longest running survey of the health of LGBTQ+ people.

---

[8] See eg Chapters 4 and 9 of this edited collection, by Senthorun Raj and Jayne Ozanne respectively.

[9] D Kinitz, 'How I Ended Up in Conversion Therapy and Why Canada's Proposed Ban is Only a First Step for LGBTQ+ Youth' (The Conversation, 10 March 2020) www.theconversation.com/ how-i-ended-up-in-conversion-therapy-and-why-canadas-proposed-ban-is-only-a-first-step-for-lgbtq-youth-131647.

[10] D d'Entremont, 'How Teens Made Yukon One of the Few Places in Canada to Ban Conversion Therapy' (CBC News, 15 November 2020) www.cbc.ca/news/canada/north/teens-yukon-conversion-therapy-ban-1.5802585.

[11] C Cullen, 'Conservative MP Raising Funds off His Opposition to Conversion Therapy Bill' (CBC News, 12 November 2020) www.cbc.ca/news/politics/derek-sloan-conversion-therapy-1.5799986.

The 2019 edition surveyed approximately 9,214 participants across the country, and found that one in ten, or roughly 47,000, have experienced 'conversion therapy' practices.[12] Experiences were higher (over 10 per cent) among non-binary and trans respondents (20 per cent), those aged 15–19 (13 per cent), immigrants (15 per cent), and racial/ethnic minorities (11–22 per cent). [13] This data played an important role in the passage of Canada's criminal ban, including describing the prevalence and impact of conversion practices in Canada.

In 2019, the Centre for Gender and Sexual Health Equity released a report outlining the nature and scope of conversion practices. The report, 'Ending Conversion Therapy in Canada',[14] was developed following a dialogue in which participants affirmed the need for a multipronged strategy to stem exposure to conversion practices and the associated harms, as well as providing support for survivors.

Inspired by this dialogue, and the Sex Now survey data, a community-based research project was launched: the SOGIE CE/CT Survivor Support Project. The project's primary purpose was to assess what support was needed by survivors and work with Canadian partners to deliver the supports needed to recover. Research activities took place from April to September 2021 and included a survey, focus groups, and interviews.

Participation was open to anyone who identified as an LGBTQ+ person who experienced subtle or blatant pressure to change their sexual orientation or gender identity or expression. Participants included people who experienced conversion practices in secular settings or in religious-based settings; were 15 years of age or older; and who resided in Canada (including Canadian citizens, immigrants, residents, or those with no status). Those who experienced harm outside of Canada were also eligible to complete the survey.

Responses focused around three main research questions:

- What have you found helpful in recovering from your experience of harm?

- What barriers or challenges have you experienced in seeking to recover from the harm?

- If resources were unlimited, what kinds of support would you most wish you could access?

---

[12] Community Based Research Centre, 'New Data Reveals So-Called "Conversion Therapy" Practices Continue to be Common Across Diverse Groups of Sexual and Gender Minorities in Canada' (CBRC, 2 June 2021) www.cbrc.net/new_data_reveals_so_called_conversion_therapy_practices_continue_to_be_common_across_diverse_groups_of_sexual_and_gender_minorities_in_canada.

[13] T Salway et al, 'Experiences with Sexual Orientation and Gender Identity Conversion Therapy Practices among Sexual Minority Men in Canada 2019–2020' (2021) 16(6) *PLOS ONE* doi.org/10.1371/journal.pone.0252539.

[14] T Salway et al, 'Ending Conversion Therapy in Canada: Survivors, Community Leaders, Researchers, and Allies Address the Current and Future States of Sexual Orientation and Gender Identity and Expression Change Efforts' (The Centre for Gender and Sexual Health Equity, 2020).

We will share throughout this chapter what we have learned from the 270 survivors who took part in the SOGIE CE/CT Survivor Support Project research activities and who trusted us enough to share their experience, knowledge, and insights. The project's 2022 findings report, executive summary, and webinar, are available online.[15]

Findings from this project speak predominantly to the experiences of those who identify as white, queer, and gay. Further research that focuses on other groups specifically, given their unique conversion practice experiences at the intersections of other systems of oppression, is critical.

CBRC's work at time of publication, includes: 'Understanding the Experiences of Conversion Therapy Practices among BIPOC, Immigrant, Newcomer and Refugee 2SLGBTQ+ People: A Qualitative Project' and a 'Conversion Practices Public Legal Education and Information (PLEI) Project' about the federal criminal ban. In addition, a centre, that serves as an online exchange of information on conversion practices in Canada, will be launched in 2023.

III. Findings and Recommendations

A. Numbers and Contexts (Scope of the Problem)

While breaking down the data, the myth of Canadian progressive exceptionalism on LGBTQ+ equality begins to fade. As mentioned above, the Sex Now Survey found that 1 in 10 (10 per cent) gay, bi, trans, and queer men and Two-Spirit and non-binary people (GBT2Q) reported experiencing 'conversion therapy' practices.[16] It should be noted, however, that the survey did not account for lesbians, trans women and queer women, so the true number is likely much greater. Other notable findings from the data indicate that 67 per cent experienced conversion practices in religious/faith-based settings and that 72 per cent started conversion practices before the age of 20.[17] These facts proved invaluable in our advocacy efforts.

The data was striking for several reasons. With numbers in hand, there was finally an opportunity to engage policymakers in a difficult conversation about the pervasiveness of this abuse in Canada. An estimated 50,000 Canadians had experienced conversion practices.[18] There was no longer an opportunity to deflect the severity of the issue, the extent to which it was targeted at youth and the extent to which it was being driven by radical, religious actors.

---

[15] J Sullivan et al, 'SOGIE CE/CT Survivor Support Project: Findings from a National Survey, Focus Groups, and Interviews with Hundreds of Survivors, 2021–22' (Community Based Research Centre, 2022).
[16] Salway et al (n 13).
[17] ibid.
[18] ibid.

CBRC's SOGIE CE/CT Survivor Support Project revealed that conversion practices are experienced by survivors in religious contexts, healthcare contexts, and/or in a person's social life (family, friends, and society). Pressures to repress, discourage, or change were experienced in three main ways: over two-thirds experienced pressure to change their sexual orientation, half were pressured to change their gender expression, and roughly a third experienced pressure to change their gender identity.[19]

In religious-based contexts, survivors experienced conversion practices through formal counselling, programs or camps, or were silently internalised in religious settings. Survivors shared:

> I was hung up on a demonic understanding of homosexuality … seeing myself as an agent of evil.

> In the world I knew I didn't trust anyone outside my faith community. [I] was surrounded by people who normalised how dysfunctional things were.[20]

> My church was my only known and trusted community – in which I was hiding. I felt all alone in the universe.[21]

Conversion practices were also experienced by survivors in healthcare contexts, from practitioners who discriminated, did not recognise conversion practices as trauma, did not believe in or understand religious trauma, refused service, misdiagnosed, misgendered, and withheld transitional services. Participants shared:

> Health services discouraged me to continue taking steps towards my transition and qualified my efforts to affirm my gender identity as 'histrionic' or 'borderline' traits.

> I have been diagnosed as 'delusion[al]' that I experienced SOGIECE. Medical staff refuse to see my gender identity, and medical records misgender me.[22]

Survivors also experienced conversion practices in their social lives, from family, friends, peers, and others, as subtle or blatant messages or pressures. This includes verbal and physical harassment, denied access to services, and persistent 'nudges' where they were encouraged to try something cis-heteronormative (eg dating someone of the opposite gender). Survivors shared:

> *Those small subtle statements nearly killed me* and I haven't been able to say it to anyone quite like this.[23]

> I did not actually see myself in this light, but I was subjected to it in a subtle way. The trauma was real … and I have under-appreciated what an impact that has had.[24]

---

[19] Sullivan et al, SOGIE CE/CT Survivor Support Project (n 15) 11.

[20] J Sullivan et al, 'Executive Summary: Findings from the Conversion Therapy/SOGIE CE Survivor Support Project, 2021–2022' (Community Based Research Centre, 2022) 1.

[21] Sullivan et al, SOGIE CE/CT Survivor Support Project (n 15) 14.

[22] Sullivan et al, Executive Summary (n 20) 1.

[23] Sullivan et al, SOGIE CE/CT Survivor Support Project (n 15) 23.

[24] Sullivan et al, Executive Summary (n 20) 1.

It is important to recognise that survivors may experience conversion practices in more than one context. 60 per cent of focus group and interview participants experienced it in religious contexts, 12 per cent in healthcare contexts, and 28 per cent in both religious and healthcare contexts. This was reflected in many of the survey responses as well.

Being ashamed of who you are – your core identity – could amount to degrading treatment in violation of international human rights law, as the United Nations SOGI expert and others have concluded.[25] Overcoming shame is not a quick or simple process. Many survivors, decades after having come out, continue to struggle with the trauma of shame as it impacts their self-worth, their closest relationships, and creates ongoing struggles with being intimate.

Overcoming internalised homophobia/biphobia/transphobia was one of the most significant barriers to healing. Participants spoke of the challenge of deconstructing and replacing non-affirming messages with life-affirming messages, of learning to acknowledge and address their emotions as they moved to a place of acceptance, loving and trusting themselves, and restoring personal agency.[26]

B. Legislative Responses in Canada

First introduced in November 2021, Bill C-4, 'An Act to amend the Criminal Code (conversion therapy)', received Royal Assent on 8 December that year and came into force on 7 January 2022, officially criminalising conversion practices in Canada.[27] The criminal ban applies to all ages and enacts new offences to prohibit:

(a)   causing another person to undergo conversion therapy;
(b)   … removing a child from Canada with the intention that the child undergo conversion therapy outside Canada;
(c)   promoting or advertising conversion therapy; and
(d)   receiving a financial or other material benefit from the provision of 'conversion therapy'.[28]

It followed in the footsteps of earlier, unsuccessful attempts including Bill S-260, Bill C-8 and Bill C-6.[29] Beyond the strength of the law, the Bill is historic for being one of few Bills throughout Canadian history to pass with unanimous consent in both the House of Commons and the Senate. There is no doubt that the passing of

---

[25] UNHRC, 'Practices of So-Called "Conversion Therapy": Report of the Independent Expert on Protection Against Violence and Discrimination Based on Sexual Orientation and Gender Identity' (1 May 2020) A/HRC/44/53. See also I Trispiotis and C Purshouse, '"Conversion Therapy" As Degrading Treatment' (2022) 42(1) *Oxford Journal of Legal Studies* 104.

[26] Sullivan et al, Executive Summary (n 20) 15.

[27] Bill C-4, An Act to amend the Criminal Code (conversion therapy), 1st Sess, 44th Parl, 2021 (assented to 8 December 2021), SC 2021, c 24.

[28] ibid.

[29] R Treisman, 'After Two Failed Attempts, Canada Bans Conversion Therapy' (NPR, 9 December 2021) www.npr.org/2021/12/09/1062720266/canada-bans-conversion-therapy.

the federal criminal ban was a monumental moment for survivors and LGBTQ+ history in Canada.

Due to its political structure, Canada has a variety of bans at different levels of government. We have always held the position that it is integral to have protections at all levels of government. At the federal level, Bill C-4 amended the Criminal Code to create four new, criminal offences to prohibit conversion practices.[30]

Prior to this, provincial bans like Ontario's 2015 Act to amend the Health Insurance Act and the Regulated Health Professions Act 1991 implemented civil prohibitions against conversion practices. To date, Canada has five provinces and territories with a legislative ban or policy against conversion practices including Ontario, Nova Scotia, Quebec, the Yukon and Manitoba.[31] These bans typically operate only within the healthcare system to prevent healthcare professionals from performing conversion practices.[32] They vary widely in their scope, applicability and enforcement.

While there are varying degrees of effectiveness, many argue that Quebec's 2020 'Act to Protect Persons from Conversion Therapy Provided to Change Their Sexual Orientation, Gender Identity or Gender Expression' is the strongest, albeit imperfect, form of a provincial ban in Canada. Quebec's legislation prohibits conversion practices on individuals of all ages and covers both medical-led and faith-led conversion practices, doing so with stringent penalties.[33] This is a welcome departure from weaker and more symbolic gestures such as Manitoba Health's position statement against 'conversion therapy'.[34] These types of declarations signal the intent of a provincial government, but often lack enforcement or regulatory capacity.

Finally, as of 2023, there are 20 municipalities in Canada that have adopted a formal ban, policy, or declaration against conversion practices, or are in the process of doing so. Local level bans are critical as they serve as the first form of protection and are typically the most direct path towards accessing life-saving resources. Passed in 2020, Calgary's 'Prohibited Businesses Bylaw' which banned the practice and promotion of 'conversion therapy', is considered the gold standard model for other Canadian cities to follow, both for its scope and strength.[35] Other municipalities, like Kingston, Ontario, have taken a more proactive approach by

---

[30] Bill C-4 (n 19).

[31] K Wells, 'Conversion Therapy Laws in Canada' (No Conversion Canada, 2020) www.noconversioncanada.com/legislation-map.

[32] Bill 77, An Act to amend the Health Insurance Act and the Regulated Health Professions Act 1991 regarding efforts to change sexual orientation or gender identity, 1st Sess, 41st Leg, Ontario, 2015 (assented to 4 June 2015), SO 2015, c 18.

[33] Bill 70, An Act to protect persons from conversion therapy provided to change their sexual orientation, gender identity or gender expression, 1st Sess, 42nd Leg, Quebec, 2020 (assented to 11 December 2020), SQ 2020, c 28.

[34] Manitoba Health, 'Position on Conversion Therapy' (2015) www.gov.mb.ca/health/conversion_therapy.html.

[35] City of Calgary, by-law 20M2020, Prohibited Businesses By-Law (25 May 2020).

implementing funding for survivor groups.[36] This approach is credited to local survivor Ben Rodgers, who established Canada's first formal organisation dedicated to supporting survivors of conversion practices.[37]

Canadian scholar Florence Ashley offers a variety of frameworks and recommendations for other jurisdictions to consider when developing bans on conversion practices, with an emphasis on trans realities.[38] In their book *Banning Transgender Conversion Practices*, Ashley insists that bans should define conversion practices in greater detail to ensure that everyone knows what practices are prohibited and which are not, which would contribute to preventing conversion practices before they occur and help minimise lengthy legal proceedings.[39]

This is not to say that there are not challenges with relying on the criminal justice system to combat conversion practices. We found that survivors and stakeholders have unique perspectives about the blunt tool of the criminal justice system, with some questioning whether it is the most appropriate path forward.

C. Beyond a Legislative Ban

When it comes to criminalisation, there is a real issue for survivors about the value in coming forward. This issue speaks to the state of the Canadian judicial system and the ways in which it often abandons survivors. Many survivors rightly feel that if they come forward, they will be dismissed. This can create a culture of doubt. For survivors looking to heal, this culture of doubt and disbelief is not one that many are willing to endure.

This potential reticence to come forward is made all the worse by a critical piece of the puzzle missing in Canada: a clear, universal reporting mechanism for those who are being subjected to conversion practices. For those being subjected to this abuse, it is not always clear where they should go or how they can initiate a legal process. We must remain vigilant in monitoring bad actors, institutions and individuals that are committing this abuse and ensure information is shared with authorities where it is safe to do so.

To this end, jurisdictions that implement policies to combat conversion practices should commit to periodic reviews to ensure they are fit for purpose. As the legal frameworks to end this abuse evolve, so do the means and the language with which it occurs. To avoid backlash, many of those who commit conversion practices shield it in alternative language such as 'reducing same-sex attraction'. As a

---

[36] D Chenier, 'Kingston City Council Awards Contract for Conversion Therapy Survivors Program' (Kingstonist, 10 August 2022) www.kingstonist.com/news/kingston-city-council-awards-contract-for-conversion-therapy-survivors-program.

[37] E Ferguson, 'Kingston to Fund Conversion Therapy Support Services' (*The Kingston Whig Standard*, 19 January 2022).

[38] F Ashley, *Banning Transgender Conversion Practices: A Legal and Policy Analysis* (Vancouver, UBC Press, 2022).

[39] ibid.

result it is rare to see people offering 'conversion therapy' because of the social and legal consequences that arise. Rather many groups, particularly those on the religious right, claim to help LGBTQ+ people 'deal with unwanted same-sex behaviour' or fulfil 'God's divine design for human beings' to cast doubt about their intentions. These examples of alternative terminology, and others, still fall under conversion practices.[40]

Canadian scholar, Dr Robert Bittner, articulated this well in his submission to the Senate Standing Committee on Legal and Constitutional Affairs on the former Bill C-6 stating:

> the desire to work around the changing landscape of terms and labels surrounding gender and sexuality has been a mainstay of those practising forms of 'conversion therapy' for decades, and it is because of this that legislation attempting to criminalise these practices be malleable and adaptable to future attempts and circumventing the law.[41]

The inconvenient truth is that these practices still happen in Canada, even with the protections we have for queer and trans people. While it is unlikely you will find advertisements for electroshock 'therapy' in Canada today, many queer people find themselves in situations where they face what can amount to psychological torture because of their sexual orientation, gender identity or gender expression.

D. Support Systems

> At the very beginning, I knew the fewest people, I had the least resources, but I was vulnerable because I had the biggest need.[42]

While legislative bans have been identified by participants as an important form of action, they have also stated that legal bans need to be paired with financial commitments for survivor initiatives and support to pursue judicial proceedings against 'conversion therapy' practitioners. Survivors have made it clear that when they leave spaces where they are being harmed, they face a significant lack of support, often when they are most vulnerable and in need of support.[43]

The vast majority of survivors found that affirming communities and relationships, where their sexual and gender identities are seen, heard, believed, understood, and supported were most helpful in recovery. Meeting similar people within LGBTQ+ communities and queer friendly spaces was pivotal in survivors

---

[40] D Kinitz et al 'The Scope and Nature of Sexual Orientation and Gender Identity and Expression Change Efforts: A Systematic Review Protocol' (2021) 10 *Systematic Reviews* 14 doi.org/10.1186/s13643-020-01563-8.

[41] R Bittner, 'Why a Broad Definition of "Conversion Therapy" is Necessary' (Brief Submitted to Senate Standing Committee on Legal and Constitutional Affairs, 4 July 2021).

[42] Sullivan et al, Executive Summary (n 20) 5.

[43] ibid 5, 28–29.

overcoming internalised homophobia, biphobia, or transphobia, and dispelling the myths told by others about sexual and gender minorities:

> The more involved I get in the LGBTQ community, the more comfortable I become with who I am ... I'm not broken. This is normal and there are lots of people like me in the world.[44]

Finding LGBTQ+ affirming therapeutic support was crucial for many, especially a therapist who was experienced with conversion therapy practices and qualified to address the intersections of trauma, sexuality, and gender. As a young survivor shared:

> I needed therapy for many, many years. Not just related to 'conversion therapy' because I think that experience has a way of sort of cracking us to our foundation, so it was just sort of building myself up as a human again.[45]

Among those who experienced conversion practices in religious settings, many reported that leaving their faith community was the most important step towards healing, while others shared that finding an affirming religious community was important for healing. A survivor shared:

> My big fear was that you can't be gay and Christian, and so having that larger community that was both and held both of those identities, was super helpful.[46]

Survivors talked about the challenge of finding people who shared similar experiences and identities and requested that a survivors' online network be created in Canada. The creation of CT Survivors Connect by Ben Rodgers in 2021, was serendipitous as it offers a way for survivors to find each other. Opportunities to connect with LGBTQ+ people from similar cultures, ethnicities, or practices were also identified. One survivor shared:

> For a long time, I would not even consider myself a 'survivor' because I thought my experiences are just normal and expected for someone who was bi and gender non-confirming in a society that is misogynistic, homophobic and patriarchal. In Canada where I was able to connect with LGBTQ2+ community, I started gaining a different understanding of my past experiences. But I am not coming out within my diaspora community because I still encounter the same sentiment of LGBTQ2 phobia. What would help is the opportunity to connect with other LGBTQ2 people from my ethnic community.[47]

In order to create an accessible support system that addresses the harm and complex trauma experienced, it is essential that support systems consider how racism, ableism, classism, sexism, and misogyny intersect with being a survivor of conversion practices.

---

[44] ibid 18–19.
[45] ibid 20.
[46] ibid 21.
[47] ibid 22.

E. Education

Obviously, support can only come from people who are informed and well-versed in the experiences survivors have dealt with. A number of survivors shared their frustrations at having to defend themselves for engaging in religious-based conversion practices. They were often ridiculed or made to feel stupid while facing an almost total lack of understanding of what 'conversion therapy' is and what it is like to be raised in a fundamentalist or evangelical religious home and faith community.[48] As one survivor shared:

> [People] make you feel like a total fucking idiot for having spent more than two minutes in 'conversion therapy'. Because obviously it doesn't work, and who would do that? Who would go into it? Who could stand it? You must be stupid! They don't say it like that, but like, why would you do that? Did somebody force you into doing that? Zero comprehension, zero understanding. So now I don't say anything. Now I don't say anything.[49]

On top of this, in order to best enable people to come forward with their experiences, they must first have the language to describe what has happened and the knowledge that they were harmed. Survivors spoke of the importance of recognising their experience as trauma and understanding the ways in which their psyche had been harmed. Survivors shared that until they recognised the harm done, they were not ready to reach out for help to heal and recover.[50]

Given the importance of education, No Conversion Canada has been working alongside other national, non-profit organisations to conduct this work. The goal is to develop survivor-led educational materials and legal resources that can provide clear guidance to those being subjected to these harms. This process began by developing survivor advisory boards that are guiding all resource and education materials that can then be developed into regionalised campaigns to share more broadly. This follows other successful models from around the world such as the Australian SOGICE Survivor Statement released in July 2020.[51]

The vast majority of participants in the SOGIE CE/CT Survivor Support Project asked for advocacy support to help people understand that small, subtle statements to change are just as harmful as blatant statements and pressures to change. They identified the need for education and increased awareness about conversion practices, regarding what it is, how it is experienced, the trauma it inflicts on survivors, and how widespread it is. As one survivor shared:

> When I've heard the term SOGIECE, I've always assumed this to be formal change efforts in psychotherapy or religious counselling settings. What I've learned, however,

---

[48] See also Ch 9 of this edited collection, by Jayne Ozanne.
[49] Sullivan et al, Executive Summary (n 20) 17.
[50] ibid 20.
[51] SOGICE Survivors, 'SOGICE Survivor Statement' (SOGICE Survivors, 2020).

is that SOGIECE can also be subtle and insidious and just as intentional and targeted as formalised methods.[52]

The findings demonstrate that the barriers created by ignorance, lack of awareness, and misinformation must be dismantled. Educational campaigns tailored for a wide variety of audiences that aim to address systemic inequities and intersectional identities in the context of conversion therapy are urgently needed.

F. Healthcare

As discussed above, overcoming shame is one of the hardest parts of the recovery process, weaving its way from how survivors are made to feel about themselves. Some survivors believe that the healthcare system shames them again, experiencing discrimination from some healthcare practitioners. As one trans survivor powerfully stated:

> You can walk away from religion and still have your physical and mental needs met, but you cannot walk away from the medical or mental health system and have your physical and mental needs met.[53]

Finding and accessing a counsellor or therapist who has the required training and awareness was mentioned as being a critical support, yet only 12 per cent of participants were able to find one.[54] A fulsome and accessible support system that prioritises safety and personal agency is needed to address complex trauma experienced. These findings are similar to findings from La Trobe University in Australia.[55]

IV. Conclusion

The SOGIE CE/CT Survivor Support Project's findings and recommendations were released a few months after Canada's federal ban on conversion practices came into effect and thus did not have an impact on the current Canadian legislation. They do, however, speak to the need for additional legislation and policy development by all levels of government to enable the funding and policy mechanisms essential to strengthen prevention of 'conversion therapy' and to support survivors. While criminalising 'conversion therapy' is a critically important step in

---

[52] Sullivan et al, Executive Summary (n 20) 23.
[53] ibid 14.
[54] ibid 15.
[55] T Jones et al, 'Preventing Harm, Promoting Justice: Responding to LGBT conversion therapy in Australia' (La Trobe University and Human Rights Law Centre, 2018); Jones et al (n 6).

curbing its most visible forms, the law alone will not be sufficient in dismantling the systemic homophobia and transphobia that conversion practices emerge from.

As we continue our work beyond the ban, we are aware that there is not a 'best practices' manual out there for us all to follow. The way forward lies in creating resources that address critical knowledge gaps, meeting the needs of community-based services for LGBTQ+ people, and ensuring affirming trauma-informed care for survivors. While we celebrate the historic importance of Canada's conversion practices ban, we must not get complacent and instead must stand on guard to keep our community safe as we look towards a true end to these abusive practices once and for all.

11

'Conversion Therapy' and Transformative Reparations

NATASA MAVRONICOLA AND LEE DAVIES

We base our analysis in this chapter on the understanding that 'conversion therapy' amounts to a serious violation of human rights, notably of the absolute right not to be subjected to torture or to inhuman or degrading treatment, as convincingly argued in a recent article by Ilias Trispiotis and Craig Purshouse,[1] and elaborated further by Trispiotis in Chapter 1 of this collection. Our focus in this chapter is on unpacking the full scope of the wrong of 'conversion therapy', including the socio-political factors that surround and give shape to it, and looking 'beyond the ban' to explore how the wrong may be made right through the lens of transformative reparations. We examine 'conversion therapy' as a historical wrong and an ongoing set of practices that was and is embedded in, and shaped by, problematic systemic and structural conditions. We then consider how the harms of 'conversion therapy', as well as the conditions enabling and perpetuating it, may be addressed through transformative reparations: we define this concept, locate it in scholarship and practice, and contemplate how transformative reparations could be concretised in relation to 'conversion therapy' in a country such as the UK.

I. The Wrong of 'Conversion Therapy'

A. A Violation of Human Dignity

We understand practices conventionally known as 'conversion therapy' as including any practice(s) 'intended to alter a person's sexual orientation, gender expression, gender identity, or any combination thereof'.[2] As the contributions to

---

[1] I Trispiotis and C Purshouse, '"Conversion Therapy" as Degrading Treatment' (2022) 42 *Oxford Journal of Legal Studies* 104.
[2] DE Conine et al, 'LGBTQ+ Conversion Therapy and Applied Behavior Analysis: A Call to Action' (2022) 55 *Journal of Applied Behavior Analysis* 6, 6.

this book indicate, such practices take a range of forms. Documented practices of 'conversion therapy' range from 'talk therapy' to electroshocks, enforced isolation or confinement, beatings, and 'corrective' rape.[3] While a vast range of 'techniques' and modes of intervention can be identified as 'conversion therapy',[4] what all of them hold at their centre is the goal of altering sexual and gendered desire, behaviour, and identity so as to be congruent with the supposed 'norm' through targeted treatment.[5]

The term 'therapy' is loaded with connotations of scientific and medical legitimacy. Indeed, some practices which (purportedly) attempt to change someone's sexuality or gender identity may display superficial resemblance to routinely performed therapeutic practices such as talking therapies.[6] This is not the case, of course, with all practices falling within the ambit of 'conversion therapy', notably so-called 'corrective' rape. More fundamentally, by identifying such practices as therapeutic, the term 'conversion therapy' casts the sexualities or gender identities being 'converted' as problematic and in need of 'cure'. This is discriminatory against LGBTQ+ persons. The International Lesbian, Gay, Bisexual, Trans and Intersex Association (ILGA) accordingly recommends that inverted commas are used where 'conversion therapy' is referred to.[7]

We share the view of other authors in this collection that 'conversion therapy' runs counter to human rights, that it amounts at least to inhuman and/or degrading treatment,[8] and that where it involves the infliction of severe pain or suffering, on the basis of discriminatory attitudes towards certain sexual orientations or gender identities, the practice can amount to torture.[9] More broadly, given its fundamentally discriminatory character, we consider that 'conversion therapy' is contrary to the egalitarian underpinning of human rights: to the elevated and equal status ascribed to the human person within the human rights edifice, which we tend to refer to as human dignity.[10] 'Conversion therapy' treats LGBTQ+ people 'as if they are not of equal moral worth to others' (specifically to those who conform to cisheteronormative expectations), as Trispiotis and Purshouse put it.[11] Given the clear incompatibility of 'conversion therapy' practices with human rights norms,

---

[3] D Alempijevic et al, 'Statement on Conversion Therapy' (2020) 72 *Journal of Forensic and Legal Medicine* 101930. See also J Bothe, 'It's Torture Not Therapy' (International Rehabilitation Council for Torture Victims, 2020).

[4] LR Mendos, 'Curbing Deception: A World Survey on Legal Regulation of So-called "Conversion Therapies"' (ILGA World, 2020) 17.

[5] D de Groot, 'Bans on Conversion "Therapies" – The Situation in Selected EU Member States' (2022) *European Parliamentary Research Service* PE 733.521, 1–4.

[6] See Alempijevic et al (n 3).

[7] Mendos (n 4) 13–20.

[8] See Trispiotis and Purshouse (n 1).

[9] S Boulos and C González-Cantón, 'No Such Thing as Acceptable Sexual Orientation Change Efforts: An International Human Rights Analysis' (2022) 32(1–2) *Women and Criminal Justice* 185, 193–94. See also Mendos (n 4) 59.

[10] See the analysis in N Mavronicola, *Torture, Inhumanity and Degradation under Article 3 of the ECHR: Absolute Rights and Absolute Wrongs* (Oxford, Hart Publishing, 2021) Ch 3.

[11] Trispiotis and Purshouse (n 1) 127.

taking practical and effective measures to end such practices and offer appropriate relief to (potential) victims is both imperative and overdue across all too many countries, including the UK.

For the purposes of this chapter, we wish to consider the wrong of 'conversion therapy' as both a historical phenomenon and ongoing set of practices embedded in, and facilitated by, a range of institutional, systemic and structural factors. Understanding the wrong in its full scope, we argue, necessitates looking beyond the ban to more transformative approaches to redress and protection.

B. The Wrong's Full Scope: Structural Discrimination, Pathologisation and Othering

Examining the full scope and scale of the phenomenon of 'conversion therapy' is beset with challenges, particularly because such practices are often shrouded in secrecy. Barriers include the use of non-disclosure agreements, the re-labelling of such practices to avoid detection, the trauma which such practices inflict leading to a reluctance by victims to discuss their experiences,[12] and indeed the broader structures of oppression and stigma in which such practices are embedded. Both current and historical data on such practices are therefore likely to underrepresent its prevalence. It is estimated by the European Parliament that 5 per cent of the LGBTQ+ community in Europe have been offered such 'therapies', though, as expected, other sources have indicated a much higher number.[13] As to geographical range, the United Nations Independent Expert on sexual orientation and gender identity reports such practices as being documented in at least 68 countries, though likely to take place in some form or another throughout the world.[14]

A recent UK Government-sponsored study suggests that current 'conversion therapy' practices in the US and UK predominantly take the form of: spiritual techniques, including prayer, exorcism, and pastoral counselling; psychological techniques, including talking or behavioural therapies; and 'pseudo-scientific forms of religious counselling that combine spiritual and psychological techniques'.[15] It identifies religious forms of 'conversion therapy' as chiefly being driven by perceptions that same-sex attractions and trans identities are caused by evil spiritual forces or that they amount to a test from God, and shaped by convictions that same-sex sexual behaviour and expression of one's trans identity are sinful or

---

[12] Government Equalities Office, 'Conversion Therapy: An Evidence Assessment and Qualitative Study' (GOV.UK, 29 October 2021) www.gov.uk/government/publications/conversion-therapy-an-evidence-assessment-and-qualitative-study/conversion-therapy-an-evidence-assessment-and-qualitative-study.

[13] de Groot (n 5) 2.

[14] UNHRC, 'Practices of So-Called "Conversion Therapy": Report of the Independent Expert on Protection Against Violence and Discrimination Based on Sexual Orientation and Gender Identity' (1 May 2020) A/HRC/44/53 paras 24, 27.

[15] Jowett et al (n 12).

immoral. The study finds that, in the psychoanalytic and cognitive-behavioural context, 'conversion therapy' is often animated by views that sexualities and forms of gender identity or expression that do not conform to the cisheteronormative standard amount to disorders or addictions which can be cured.[16] In agreement with multiple other studies on the subject,[17] the UK study finds that 'conversion therapy' practices tend to inflict significant harm and have no discernible 'therapeutic' benefits.[18] Importantly, the UK study underlines the enduring lack of evidence on the full scale of the phenomenon of 'conversion therapy' and of the form that 'conversion therapy' practices take, and the still nascent character of legislative interventions around the world to end 'conversion therapy' practices and offer reparation to victims.[19]

'Conversion therapy' is rooted in pervasive institutional, systemic and structural discrimination, pathologisation and othering. Structural discrimination, as distinct from isolated instances of individual discrimination, may be understood as the interlocking of social or socio-political forces, systems, institutions and their policies and practices, to assert, produce or perpetuate discriminatory policies, practices and beliefs, and generate inequities between groups of people.[20] Often, prejudicial or stereotypical beliefs and attitudes towards particular groups combine with structural forces, creating an 'us and them' narrative that feeds into policies and practices of institutional actors whose actions mould or are moulded by those forces.[21] Building on pathbreaking scholarship on racism, Shreya Atrey refers to 'structural racism' as 'embedded not in the minds of individuals, but in the social, economic, cultural and political forces which define ... relationships between people.'[22] We would argue that a similar approach must be taken to appreciate the full extent of discrimination, pathologisation and othering that underpins 'conversion therapy' practices.

The ideological underpinnings and conditions that shape 'conversion therapy' practices and their prevalence, legitimisation and/or sanitisation, must be viewed in their historical light. Efforts to alter same-sex sexual attraction have historically been grounded in dominant views that cast homosexuality as deviant and harmful to a range of societal and individual interests. These attitudes have been expressed in various ways, from profound social stigma, marginalisation and (all too frequently state-sanctioned) violence, to criminalisation and punishment. When Alan Turing was subjected in 1952 to what is often referred to as 'chemical castration', the context of his treatment was the criminalisation of same-sex sexual

---

[16] ibid.
[17] See, for example n 3 and n 14 above.
[18] Jowett et al (n 12).
[19] ibid.
[20] LT Dean and RJ Thorpe, 'What Structural Racism Is (or Is Not) and How to Measure It' (2022) 191(9) *American Journal of Epidemiology* 1521.
[21] MC Angermeyer et al, 'Public Attitudes Regarding Individual and Structural Discrimination: Two Sides of the Same Coin?' (2014) 103(1) *Social Science and Medicine* 60.
[22] S Atrey, 'Structural Racism and Race Discrimination' (2021) 74 *Current Legal Problems* 1, 5.

activity (deemed an act of 'gross indecency' under section 11 of the Criminal Law Amendment Act 1885), which meant that he was offered the 'choice' between being put in prison and taking oestrogen pills that were aimed at suppressing his sex drive. As the Human Dignity Trust highlights, LGBTQ+ persons have faced forms of legal proscription for centuries, initially under religious laws, and later under secular laws which often drew on the theological traditions that preceded them.[23] Moreover, colonial powers, such as Great Britain, imposed laws criminalising LGBTQ+ people 'over diverse indigenous traditions where same-sex activity and gender diversity did not always carry the same social or religious taboo'.[24] Today, the Human Dignity Trust points out that 66 states criminalise homosexuality, and 12 of these states can or do impose capital punishment for same-sex intimacy, while 14 states criminalise the gender identity or expression of trans persons.[25]

The idea that LGBTQ+ persons are deviant and dangerous, and that they even pose a threat to the 'nation', has also motivated other forms of law and policy initiatives around the world. One prevalent type of law and policy initiative besides the criminalisation of some forms of sexual activity or gender expression is legislation aimed at suppressing the 'promotion' of homosexuality.[26] The latter type of legislation deepens the marginalisation of LGBTQ+ persons by suppressing their access to information and support, and further fostering abuse. In the UK, section 28 of the Local Government Act 1988 added an amendment to the Local Government Act 1986 which prohibited the 'promotion of homosexuality' by local authorities, providing that a local authority 'shall not intentionally promote homosexuality or publish material with the intention of promoting homosexuality' or 'promote the teaching in any maintained school of the acceptability of homosexuality as a pretended family relationship'. It remained in place until its repeal in Scotland in 2000 and in England and Wales in 2003.[27]

Drescher observes that for a great deal of Western history, discourse on homosexuality has been conducted under the almost exclusive aegis of religious morality, which paints homosexual conduct as sinful, deviant and thus as a site of legitimate punishment/intervention.[28] An additional layer to this narrative was the

---

[23] Human Dignity Trust, 'A History of LGBT Criminalisation' (Human Dignity Trust, 2023) www.humandignitytrust.org/lgbt-the-law/a-history-of-criminalisation.

[24] ibid. See also A Gupta, 'This Alien Legacy: The Origins of "Sodomy" Laws in British Colonialism' (Human Rights Watch, 17 December 2008) www.hrw.org/report/2008/12/17/alien-legacy/origins-sodomy-laws-british-colonialism.

[25] Human Dignity Trust, 'Map of Criminalisation' (Human Dignity Trust, 2023) www.humandignitytrust.org/lgbt-the-law/map-of-criminalisation.

[26] See the discussion of the situation prevailing in Russia in R Buyantueva, 'LGBT Rights Activism and Homophobia in Russia' (2018) 65(4) Journal of Homosexuality 456, 458.

[27] See S King-Hill, 'LGBTQ+ History Month 2022: The Legacy of Section 28' (University of Birmingham, 8 February 2022) blog.bham.ac.uk/socialsciencesbirmingham/2022/02/08/lgbtq-history-month-2022-the-legacy-of-section-28.

[28] J Drescher, 'Out of DSM: Depathologising Homosexuality (2015) 5(1) Behavioral Sciences 565, 568. See further R Clucas, 'Sexual Orientation Change Efforts, Conservative Christianity and Resistance to

idea that 'indulgence' in such deviant activity was harmful or even destructive to 'civilisation'.[29]

Relevant evidence from the US and the UK, while incomplete, suggests that religious organisations or individuals motivated by religious beliefs are at the forefront of 'conversion therapy' practices.[30] These often involve prayer, study of religious texts, and appeals to divine punishment and reward.[31] They are driven by perceptions of sexualities and forms of gender identity or expression which do not conform to cisheterosexual norms as evil and sinful. Such 'spiritual' methods may often combine with (pseudo-)scientific techniques that employ psychological methods such as 'talking therapy'. Indeed, a UK Government-sponsored study from 2018 establishes that medical professionals are the second largest providers of 'conversion therapy', after religious institutions.[32] At the same time, it is to be noted that the NHS and a number of health, counselling and psychotherapy organisations have signed a Memorandum of Understanding (initiated in 2015 and updated in 2017 and 2022) seeking to end 'conversion therapy' practices in or associated to healthcare provision of healthcare settings (broadly conceived) in the UK.[33]

Somewhat distinct from moral or 'divine' judgement, pathologisation takes centre stage in (nominally) therapeutic environments and institutions that offer or have offered 'conversion therapy'. This pathologisation of non-cisheteronormative identities has both historical roots and present-day relevance. In a study published in 2015, Stonewall found that one in ten healthcare and social work professionals had witnessed colleagues express the view that homosexuality can be cured.[34] Such perspectives view LGBTQ+ persons not necessarily as engaging in deviant moral choices but rather as acting in ways that result from an underlying pathology which is curable or which can be medically treated or managed.[35] This is captured in the words of psychoanalyst Edmund Bergler, writing in 1956: 'I have no bias against homosexuals; for me they are sick people requiring medical help'.[36] Of course,

---

Sexual Justice' (2017) 6(2) *Social Sciences* 54; A Moreno et al, 'Cross-cultural Perspectives of LGBTQ Psychology from Five Different Countries: Current State and Recommendations' (2020) 11(1–2) *Psychology & Sexuality* 5.

[29] R Alter, 'Sodom as Nexus: The Web of Design in Biblical Narrative' in RM Schwartz (ed), *The Book and the Text: The Bible and Literary Theory* (Oxford, Blackwell, 1990) 151.

[30] Jowett (n 12).

[31] A Przeworski et al, 'A Systematic Review of the Efficacy, Harmful Effects, and Ethical Issues Related to Sexual Orientation Change Efforts' (2021) 28(1) *Clinical Psychology: Science and Practice* 81, 82.

[32] Government Equalities Office, *National LGBT Survey: Research Report* (HMSO, 2018) 93.

[33] British Association of Counselling and Psychotherapy et al, 'Memorandum of Understanding on Conversion Therapy in the UK' (BACP, 4 March 2022) www.bacp.co.uk/events-and-resources/ethics-and-standards/mou/.

[34] C Somerville, 'Unhealthy Attitudes: The Treatment of LGBT People within Health and Social Care Services' (Stonewall, 2015) 17.

[35] See the pathologisation prevalent in medical approaches discussed in J Drescher, 'Queer Diagnoses: Parallels and Contrasts in the History of Homosexuality, Gender Variance, and the Diagnostic and Statistical Manual' (2010) 39 *Archives of Sexual Behavior* 427.

[36] E Bergler, *Homosexuality: Disease or Way of Life?* (New York, Hill and Wang, 1956) 28–29.

this framing of LGBTQ+ identities upheld and indeed reified the basic binaries and stratification of sexuality and gender identity and expression.[37] Moreover, as Toscano and Maynard observe, moral theories of good and evil remain at least implicit in pathologisation discourse,[38] and purportedly benevolent interventions grounded in the supposed normative inferiority of the fundamental identity or interests of LGBTQ+ persons remain antithetical to human dignity.[39] Importantly, the identification of homosexuality as a form of pathology or 'disease' is indisputably connected to the ultimate attempt at its 'eradication'. As Giles points out, discussing the Nazis' persecution of persons identified as gay or lesbian: 'The literature of the period is full of disease metaphors ... In the late 1930s and beyond, the efforts to halt the spread of this "disease" resulted in the arrest of thousands', and ultimately to internment and mass killings.[40]

Today, 'conversion therapy' practices and the pathologisation of LGBTQ+ persons that has often underpinned them have been denounced by a range of prominent professional bodies.[41] Yet legacies of pathologisation and attempts to 'cure' non-cisheteronormative identity and expression remain. Notably, appeals to scientific integrity and supposed patient 'autonomy' remain prevalent in the offer of, and/or support for, 'conversion therapy' practices by organisations such as the Alliance for Therapeutic Choice and Scientific Integrity (ACTSI, formerly NARTH, the National Association for Research and Therapy of Homosexuality) in the US and Core Issues Trust in the UK.[42]

In reference to the UK context, we must not neglect the role of the state vis-à-vis 'conversion therapy' practices. UK state authorities have been involved in the active and even systematic perpetration of 'conversion therapy' practices, as evidenced in the chemical castration of Alan Turing, through to facilitation, condonement, and ultimately still-inadequate opposition to such practices. The large-scale campaign of pathologisation and stigma that prevailed during the peak of the AIDS epidemic, in particular, saw gay men especially painted not only as socially deviant and dangerous, but also as disease carriers who posed risks to the rest of the population.[43] Section 28 prolonged the stigmatisation and ostracisation and led many to experience not just prejudice and persecution, but self-loathing.[44]

---

[37] L Downing, 'Heteronormativity and Repronormativity in Sexological "Perversion Theory" and the DSM-5's "Paraphilic Disorder" Diagnoses' (2015) 44 *Archives of Sexual Behavior* 1139–40.

[38] ME Toscano and E Maynard, 'Understanding the Link: Homosexuality, Gender Identity, and the DSM' (2014) 8(3) *Journal of LGBT Issues in Counselling* 248, 249–50.

[39] Trispiotis and Purshouse (n 1) 113.

[40] GJ Giles, 'The Persecution of Gay Men and Lesbians during the Third Reich' in JC Friedman, *The Routledge History of the Holocaust* (London, Routledge, 2011) 389.

[41] Noted in Clucas (n 28). See the NHS Memorandum (n 33 above).

[42] See the analysis in Clucas (n 28).

[43] TC Correll, '"You Know about Needle Boy, Right?": Variation in Rumors and Legends about Attacks with HIV-Infected Needles' (2008) 67(1) *Western Folklore* 59, 62–63; C Clews, *Gay in the 80s: From Fighting our Rights to Fighting for our Lives* (Leicester, Troubador Publishing, 2017).

[44] P Griffin, 'From Hiding Out to Coming Out: Empowering Lesbian and Gay Educators' (1992) 22(3–4) *Journal of Homosexuality* 167; C Sullivan, 'Oppression: The Experiences of a Lesbian Teacher in an Inner-City Comprehensive School in the United Kingdom' (1993) 5(1) *Gender and Education* 93; C Lee, 'Fifteen Years On: The Legacy of Section 28 for LGBT+ Teachers in English Schools' (2019) 19(6) *Sex Education* 675.

These were circumstances in which efforts to 'convert' stigmatised identities undoubtedly flourished.

In facing 'conversion therapy' practices, LGBTQ+ persons are often trapped in a cycle of abuse, whereby they may (perhaps on the surface, voluntarily) resort to such 'therapy' because of the discrimination, pathologisation and othering they experience in society or within their communities, only to experience further harm and stigmatisation through such 'therapy', and to be thrust back into their societies or communities 'uncured' and potentially face further abuse. This vicious cycle is not fully captured by the identification of individualised instances of ill-treatment by individual perpetrators. Moreover, any notion that the uptake of such 'conversion therapy' practices may be freely consensual and, accordingly, not wrongful, is problematic. As Trispiotis and Purshouse convincingly demonstrate, 'a choice has elevated moral force only when the conditions under which it is made are right', and it is evident that in circumstances of widespread prejudice, histori-cal and enduring disadvantage, and violence, pressure or danger faced by persons because of their LGBTQ+ status, their 'choice' to pursue 'conversion therapy' is neither clearly *free* nor such as to vitiate the fundamentally wrongful character of such practices.[45]

There are several aspects of 'conversion therapy' that we would distil from our analysis above, which lead us to believe that a proper response to the practice must be transformative. First, 'conversion therapy' represents both a contemporary phenomenon and a historical set of practices whose full scale is not wholly known, but which we know to have gravely harmed and to be gravely harming a vast number of LGBTQ+ people in the UK and around the world. Second, 'conversion therapy' tends to take place in institutional settings or other contexts characterised by asymmetrical power relationships, notably where practised by religious organi-sations or medical professionals, or indeed with the active involvement or tacit support of state authorities. Third, 'conversion therapy' is shaped by and in turn shapes cisheteronormative, discriminatory structures of oppression, which cast particular sexualities and forms of gender identity or expression as sinful, deviant and/or pathological, and are harmful both to the immediate victims of 'conversion therapy' and others. Understood in its full scope, therefore, 'conversion therapy' is a widespread and serious violation of human rights, which is often practised by powerful institutional actors enabled by the acts and omissions of state authorities, and which not only harms the individuals subjected to it but also produces and sustains broader 'communities of harm'[46] within a vicious cycle of discrimination, pathologisation and othering.

---

[45] See Trispiotis and Purshouse (n 1) 112, citing TM Scanlon, *What We Owe to Each Other* (Cambridge, Harvard University Press, 2000) 260.

[46] We take this term from F Ní Aoláin, 'Sex-based Violence during the Holocaust – A Reevaluation of Harms and Rights in International Law' (2000) 12 *Yale Journal of Law and Feminism* 43; and F Ní Aoláin, 'Rethinking the Concept of Harm and Legal Categorizations of Sexual Violence during War' (2000) 1(2) *Theoretical Inquiries in Law* 307. We understand 'communities of harm' in this context

II. Transformative Reparations and their Relevance to 'Conversion Therapy'

As other chapters in this collection have convincingly demonstrated, given that 'conversion therapy' constitutes a human rights violation, the state bears obligations to take appropriate measures to prevent and redress it. In this section, we consider reparations for 'conversion therapy' practices, focusing on transformative reparations as measures that both redress the wrong in its full scope and seek to ensure its non-repetition.

Reparations for human rights violations relate to a state's duty, following its commission of a breach of human rights, 'to make full reparation, by restitution if possible and by compensation and/or satisfaction if restitution is not possible.'[47] The concept of *transformative* reparations denotes measures that seek to transform the (unjust) circumstances in which serious wrong-doing was (and is) embedded. Writing in 2009 with particular focus on transitional justice,[48] Rodrigo Uprimny Yepes observed that, given the marginalisation and disadvantage faced by victims of serious human rights violations prior to, and indeed contributing to, the abuse to which they were subjected, reparations that sought to achieve restitution – that is, to restore their situation to the status quo ante – would be both unjust and contrary to the aim of seeking the non-repetition of such abuses.[49] Accordingly, for Uprimny Yepes, the idea of transformative reparations is premised on the conviction that

> the purpose of reparations of massive human rights violations in unequal societies should not be to restore poor victims to their previous situation of poverty and discrimination, but to change or 'transform' these circumstances in which they lived, and that could have been one of the roots of conflict and that anyway are in themselves unjust.[50]

One of the prominent areas in which the idea of transformative reparations has taken hold is in relation to violence against women (VAW). Driven by scholarship and activism seeking an expansive approach to reparations to address the

---

to encompass both individuals to whom the victim-survivors are connected and the wider LGBTQ+ community. See further, R Rubio-Marín et al, 'Repairing Family Members: Gross Human Rights Violations and Communities of Harm' in R Rubio-Marín (ed), *The Gender of Reparations: Unsettling Sexual Hierarchies while Redressing Human Rights Violations* (Cambridge, Cambridge University Press, 2009).

[47] D Shelton, 'Reparations for Human Rights Violations: How Far Back?' (2002) 44 *Amicus Curiae* 3, 3.

[48] R Uprimny Yepes, 'Transformative Reparations of Massive Gross Human Rights Violations: Between Corrective and Distributive Justice' (2009) 27 *Netherlands Quarterly of Human Rights* 625.

[49] On guarantees of non-repetition as a component of reparations for gross human right violations, see UNGA, 'Basic Principles and Guidelines on the Right to a Remedy and Reparation for Victims of Gross Violations of International Human Rights Law and Serious Violations of International Humanitarian Law' (16 December 2005) UN Doc A/RES/60/147 Arts 18 and 23.

[50] Uprimny Yepes (n 48) 637–38.

contributing factors to and consequences of VAW,[51] and informed by burgeoning case law on the subject,[52] the then United Nations Special Rapporteur on Violence Against Women, Rashida Manjoo, wrote a landmark report in 2010 on 'Reparations for women subjected to violence'.[53] In it, she underlined that '[since] violence perpetrated against individual women generally feeds into patterns of pre-existing and often cross-cutting structural subordination and systemic marginalisation, measures of redress need to link individual reparation and structural transformation'.[54] She advanced the argument that

> reparations for women cannot be just about returning them to the situation in which they were found before the individual instance of violence, but instead should strive to have a transformative potential. This implies that reparations should aspire, to the extent possible, to subvert instead of reinforce pre-existing patterns of crosscutting structural subordination, gender hierarchies, systemic marginalisation and structural inequalities that may be at the root cause of the violence that women experience before, during and after ... conflict.[55]

These are vital insights and a call to transformative action that places gender, and attention to cisheteropatriarchal norms, at the heart of reparations for serious human rights violations. We would suggest that these insights, and the call for transforming the unjust circumstances underpinning serious and widespread human rights violations, are transposable to 'conversion therapy', as historically and currently practised, and its context.

The idea of 'transformative reparations' has largely taken shape in mobilisation around transitional justice, understood by the United Nations as the 'range of processes and mechanisms associated with a society's attempt to come to terms with a legacy of large-scale past abuses, in order to ensure accountability, serve justice and achieve reconciliation'.[56] While this is not specified in the quoted definition, there is a tendency to associate transitional justice with transitions

---

[51] See, for example, R Rubio-Marín (ed), *What Happened to the Women? Gender and Reparations for Human Rights Violations* (New York, Social Science Research Council, 2006); Rubio-Marín (ed), *The Gender of Reparations* (n 46); C Duggan and AM Abusharaf, 'Reparation of Sexual Violence in Democratic Transitions: The Search for Gender Justice' in P de Greiff (ed), *The Handbook of Reparations* (Oxford, Oxford University Press, 2006). See too, Coalition for Women's Human Rights in Conflict Situations et al, 'Nairobi Declaration on Women's and Girls' Right to a Remedy and Reparation' (International Meeting on Women's and Girls' Right to a Remedy and Reparation, Nairobi, 19–21 March 2007).

[52] See, for example, *González et al ('Cotton Field') v Mexico* Preliminary Objection, Merits, Reparations, and Costs, Inter-American Court of Human Rights Series C No 205 (16 November 2009); *Opuz v Turkey*, Application No 33401/02, 9 June 2009.

[53] UNHRC, 'Report of the Special Rapporteur on violence against women, its cases and consequences, Rashida Manjoo' (23 April 2010) UN Doc A/HRC/14/22, para 23.

[54] ibid para 24.

[55] ibid para 85.

[56] United Nations Secretary General, 'The Rule of Law and Transitional Justice in Conflict and Postconflict Societies' (23 August 2004) UN Doc S/2004/616, para 8.

from conflict, including civil war, and (particular forms of) authoritarian rule.[57] Irrespective of one's understanding of transitional justice, however, whether that be expansive or restrictive, we consider that there is ample scope and good reason for treating transformative reparations as being relevant and applicable to any serious human rights violations that are embedded in, and shaped by, systemic and structural discrimination, marginalisation, and injustice. Indeed, the phenomenon of 'conversion therapy', which is part of legacies and enduring patterns of violence, discrimination and injustice against persons who do not conform to cisheteronormative expectations across society, invites rethinking of rigid line-drawing about the contexts in which we may speak of a need for societal transition or transformation.[58] In this regard, transformative reparations may be viewed as part of a broader idea: that of transformative *justice*, which may be understood to have at its heart the 'challenging of unequal and intersecting power relationships and structures of exclusion at both local and global levels'.[59] Such transition or transformation is an imperative that need not be confined to post-conflict or otherwise rigidly bounded contexts; yet it demands close attention to the systemic and structural dynamics that shape serious wrong-doing.

What measures would fall within the category of transformative reparations? This is the subject of ongoing debate, research, law and policy interventions, and activist input. Rashida Manjoo[60] has tied the pursuit of transformative reparations to a pillar of the 2005 UN Basic Principles on the right to a remedy and reparation for gross human rights violations: that of guarantees of non-repetition. According to the UN Basic Principles, guarantees of non-repetition

> … should include, where applicable, measures such as: […] (d) Protecting persons in the legal, medical and health-care professions, the media and other related professions, and human rights defenders, […] (f) Promoting the observance of codes of conduct and ethical norms, in particular international standards, by public servants, including law enforcement, correctional, media, medical, psychological, social service and military personnel, as well as by economic enterprises, […] and (h) Reviewing and reforming laws contributing to or allowing gross violations of international human rights law and serious violations of international humanitarian law.[61]

However, those working on transformative reparations have gone substantially further than this provision, placing greater emphasis on the *transformative* character

---

[57] The UN report mentioned above referred to 'conflict and post-conflict societies'. But consider Y Joshi, 'Affirmative Action as Transitional Justice' (2020) 1 *Wisconsin Law Review* 1.

[58] Colleen Murphy unpacks the imperative of societal transformation in her landmark monograph: C Murphy, *The Conceptual Foundations of Transitional Justice* (Cambridge, Cambridge University Press, 2017).

[59] P Gready and S Robins, 'From Transitional to Transformative Justice: A New Agenda for Practice' in P Gready and S Robins (eds), *From Transitional to Transformative Justice* (Cambridge, Cambridge University Press, 2019) 32.

[60] R Manjoo, 'Introduction: Reflections on the Concept and Implementation of Transformative Reparations' (2017) 21(9) *The International Journal of Human Rights* 1193, 1194–95.

[61] UNGA, Basic Principles (n 49) Art 23.

of the necessary interventions to repair and prevent abuses. Manjoo underlines that one key dimension of transformative reparative measures must be the development and implementation of a process – not necessarily judicial – whereby the true nature and full scale and scope of the problem can be identified and acknowledged.[62] This is a critical first step towards further reparative measures, oriented at enabling the identification of the problem in its entirety, rather than purely as it manifests in individual behaviour that is juridically recognised as attracting civil and/or criminal liability. Acknowledgement of the full scope of the violation(s) at issue is, however, also a form of reparation in itself. Victim-survivors and broader 'communities of harm' have repeatedly asserted a right 'to know the truth about the circumstances in which human rights violations took place'.[63]

To realise their transformative potential, reparative measures must involve the participation of the persons (who stand to be) harmed and broader 'communities of harm' in the design, implementation and oversight of the relevant reparations, and must thereby be accessible, inclusive and shaped by the lived experiences of victims-survivors.[64] Substantively, transformative reparations may necessitate a variety of significant initiatives including institutional overhauls, educational measures, and equality-driven public services, and require redistributive interventions that materially improve the lives of victimised persons and communities and redress power asymmetries that expose people to abuse. It is neither possible nor advisable to claim to offer an exhaustive 'list' of concrete forms of transformative reparations. Transformative reparations are ultimately defined by their 'long-term, victim-centred and context-specific' orientation.[65] It is crucial, therefore, that transformative reparations are responsive to the particular characteristics and contextual dimensions of the problem(s) being addressed, and to the needs and demands of the people who have been harmed or stand to be harmed by it.

III. What Might Transformative Reparations Demand in Respect of 'Conversion Therapy'? The Example of the UK

The concretisation of the idea of transformative reparations requires sensitivity to historical and contemporary context. Accordingly, the implementation of transformative reparations in respect of 'conversion therapy' practices in any particular

---

[62] Manjoo (n 60) 1199.

[63] See notably, UN ECOSOC, 'Report of the Independent Expert to update the Set of principles to combat impunity, Diane Orentlicher' (8 February 2005) UN Doc E/CN.4/2005/102/Add.1 principle 4. On the value of truth-knowing, see B Quinney et al, 'Truth is its Own Reward: Completeness of Information, the Feeling of Truth Knowing, and Victims' Closure' (2022) 61 *British Journal of Social Psychology* 389.

[64] See L Laplante, 'Just Repair' (2015) 48 *Cornell International Law Journal* 513.

[65] S Gready, 'The Case for Transformative Reparations: In Pursuit of Structural Socio-Economic Reform in Post-Conflict Societies' (2022) 16(2) *Journal of Intervention and Statebuilding* 182, 183.

country must respond to the phenomenon of 'conversion therapy' in its varied manifestations in the past and present, and the multi-layered conditions that have enabled and sustained it. To be fully effective, they must also provide tools for anticipating and addressing future developments.

The measures currently being proposed to address 'conversion therapy' in the UK[66] include amendments to the criminal law and new criminal law provisions: in particular, rendering the motivation of 'conversion therapy' an aggravating factor in respect of already recognised violent offences (including, notably, sexual violence offences), and rendering criminal the provision of 'talking conversion therapy' to persons under 18, and the provision of 'talking conversion therapy' to persons 18 or over where, the Government says, they 'have not consented or due to their vulnerability are unable to do so'.[67] In addition, the UK Government is considering Conversion Therapy Protection Orders, as well as other tools to stop the promotion and facilitation of 'conversion therapy' practices through the media, charities, and other organisations. As mechanisms to support victims, the Government is proposing 'a helpline and/or instant messaging service with suitably trained call handlers, and an online education resource that details the law on conversion therapy, and forms of support available to victims'.[68] Finally, the UK Government anticipates the development of policy guidance for statutory services to recognise 'conversion therapy' as a problem, identify the challenges faced by victims coming forward, and to provide training for how to protect people from being harmed by 'conversion therapy' practices. In its proposals, the Government suggests that the criminal sanction, which it places at the forefront of its proposed package of measures, will 'interrupt and deter' (profiting from) practices of 'conversion therapy'.[69] It also labels its measures 'universal', in that 'an attempt to change a person from being attracted to the same-sex to being attracted to the opposite-sex, or from not being transgender to being transgender, will be treated in the same way as the reverse scenario'.[70] We note the ongoing debate surrounding the UK Government's approach to 'conversion therapy' in relation to gender identity or expression,[71] and share the view expressed by others in this volume that efforts to end 'conversion therapy' must encompass such practices.

Foregrounding criminalisation and the criminal sanction, and treating it – as the UK Government does – as automatically entailing the deterrence and interruption of such practices, warrants reconsideration. It is well established that the general deterrence achieved through criminalisation and criminal sanction depends on a

---

[66] See Secretary of State for Foreign, Commonwealth and Development Affairs and Minister for Women and Equalities, *Banning Conversion Therapy: Government Consultation*, (Cm 535, 2021).

[67] ibid 9.

[68] ibid 25–26.

[69] ibid 24.

[70] ibid 3 (Ministerial Foreword).

[71] A Adu, 'Conversion Practices Ban Will Include Transgender People, Donelan Confirms' (*The Guardian*, 17 January 2023) www.theguardian.com/society/2023/jan/17/conversion-practices-ban-will-include-transgender-people-donelan-confirms.

range of factors and is not a given.[72] Indeed, as Yvette Russell points out, in the UK the under-resourcing of the police, prosecution services and courts has contributed to prosecution and conviction rates that can lead one to describe many serious offences, notably sexual offences, as having been de facto 'decriminalised'.[73] Moreover, particularly in contexts of significant power imbalance and dynamics of secrecy, shame and stigma, a penal approach may be far from the most effective way of preventing undesirable behaviour or protecting vulnerable people.[74] Besides these fundamental issues plaguing the criminal process, there is a body of research demonstrating that sentence *severity* has no significant deterrent impact on perpetrators,[75] thereby undermining a flagship element of the UK Government's proposals.

There are additional limitations to the criminal approach. One example of such a limitation is that the criminal law is a blunt instrument for dealing with 'complex' or 'guilty' victims: for example, in the context of 'conversion therapy', persons who have themselves been victimised but who may go on to become perpetrators of such abuse.[76] More broadly, the construction of 'victims' and 'perpetrators' in the criminal process remains beset with dominant perceptions of 'ideal victims' as innocent, very young/old and/or otherwise vulnerable, and upstanding citizens, who suffer harm at the hands of a villainous stranger.[77] These dynamics can distort how people view abusive practices, and even result both in denial of victimhood and in further stigma and discrimination. Crucially, as Catherine Donovan and Rebecca Barnes highlight, 'being LGB and/or T can provide opportunities, for those who so wish, to ascribe both culpability and agency to any misfortunes that they might experience', pointing to discourse 'in which the lives of LGB and/or T people – and gay men particularly – are socially constructed to point to hidden deficiencies, of morality typically, but also of more essentialised personality flaws, which explain not only their outsider status in society, but also their liability in any circumstances of their being victimised'.[78] These critical insights disclose some of the profound pitfalls arising in penal pathways to protection and redress.

---

[72] European Committee on Crime Problems, *Report on Decriminalisation* (Strasbourg, Council of Europe, 1980) 75–78. See also LW Sherman, 'Defiance, Deterrence, and Irrelevance: A Theory of the Criminal Sanction' (1993) 30(4) *Journal of Research in Crime and Delinquency* 445; Y Russell, 'Criminal Injustice' in I Rua Wall et al (eds), *The Critical Legal Pocketbook* (Oxford, Counterpress, 2021).

[73] Russell (n 72) 175. See, in respect of sexual offences, Centre for Women's Justice et al, 'The Decriminalisation of Rape: Why the Justice System is Failing Rape Survivors and What Needs to Change' (2020).

[74] See the thorough analysis and further bibliography in S Tapia, *Feminism, Violence against Women, and Law Reform: Decolonial Lessons from Ecuador* (London, Routledge, 2022).

[75] See, among other studies, A von Hirsch et al, *Criminal Deterrence and Sentence Severity: An Analysis of Recent Research* (Oxford, Hart Publishing, 1999).

[76] See L Moffett, 'Reparations for "Guilty Victims": Navigating Complex Identities of Victim–Perpetrators in Reparation Mechanisms' (2016) 10(1) *International Journal of Transitional Justice* 146.

[77] See N Christie, 'The Ideal Victim' in EA Fattah (ed), *From Crime Policy to Victim Policy: Reorienting the Justice System* (Basingstoke, Palgrave Macmillan, 1986).

[78] C Donovan and R Barnes, 'Being "Ideal" or Falling Short? The Legitimacy of Lesbian, Gay, Bisexual and/or Transgender Victims of Domestic Violence and Hate Crime' in M Duggan (ed),

It is also important to attend to the more all-encompassing queer critique of enlisting the police and the carceral state more broadly in emancipatory LGBTQ+ agendas.[79] In a thorough critique of 'queer investments in punitiveness', Sarah Lamble argues that 'pro-criminalization policies can only be sustained on the myth that the criminal justice system punishes those who deserve it, and that imprisonment is about safety, justice and protection for all, and not about warehousing, caging and punishing particular targeted populations'.[80] On this account, reliance on these mechanisms is not only inadequate, but also deeply dangerous, particularly for LGBTQ+ people of colour, LGBTQ+ people with 'irregular' migration status, LGBTQ+ people within 'suspect communities',[81] and others who face particular vulnerability or precarity in their encounters with the carceral state.

Additionally, and crucially, an emphasis on identifying, sanctioning and disin-centivising the individual perpetrator – the 'respondent', as they are referred to in the UK Government's proposals – has ramifications for how the wrong of 'conversion therapy' is understood, and how its prevention, and the protection and redress offered to the victims, is shaped. Rosemary Gartner and Ross MacMillan write that 'the criminal law … fashions individualised solutions to systemic prob-lems, and reinforces prevailing inequalities'.[82] A set of measures that chiefly aims at identifying and punishing the individuals responsible for the violation at issue (the so-called 'bad apple(s)'[83]) can obscure and in this way effectively absolve the 'rotten orchard' (collective or institutional malpractice or discrimination, for example), as well as the wider ecosystem of abuse: the structures and systems that empower abusers and expose or subject people to human rights violations.[84] A focus on punishing those who perpetrate the practice of 'conversion therapy' or its promotion, can serve to atomise and decontextualise the wrong-doing at issue, thereby obscuring the systemic and structural circumstances in which 'conver-sion therapy' (whether nominally consensual or not) occurs and even proliferates.

Revisiting the 'Ideal Victim' Developments in Critical Victimology (Bristol, Bristol University Press, 2018) 84.

[79] See, for example, R Girardi, "'It's Easy to Mistrust Police When They Keep on Killing Us'": A Queer Exploration of Police Violence and LGBTQ+ Victimization' (2022) 31(7) *Journal of Gender Studies* 852; TS Winter, 'Queer Law and Order: Sex, Criminality, and Policing in the Late Twentieth-Century United States' (2015) 102(1) *Journal of American History* 61.

[80] S Lamble, 'Queer Investments in Punitiveness: Sexual Citizenship, Social Movements and the Expanding Carceral State' in J Haritaworn et al (eds), *Queer Necropolitics* (London, Routledge, 2014) 155. See also S Lamble, 'Queer Necropolitics and the Expanding Carceral State: Interrogating Sexual Investments in Punishment' (2013) 24 *Law and Critique* 229.

[81] On the concept of 'suspect community', see P Hillyard, *Suspect Community: People's Experience of the Prevention of Terrorism Acts in Britain* (London, Pluto Press, 1993); C Pantazis and S Pemberton, 'From the "Old" to the "New" Suspect Community: Examining the Impacts of Recent UK Counter-Terrorist Legislation' (2009) 49 *British Journal of Criminology* 646.

[82] R Gartner and R Macmillan, 'The Effect of Victim-offender Relationship on Reporting Crimes of Violence against Women' (1995) 37(3) *Canadian Journal of Criminology* 393, 423.

[83] M Punch, 'Rotten Orchards: "Pestilence", Police Misconduct and System Failure' (2003) 13 *Policing and Society* 171.

[84] On the ecological dimensions of torture (prevention), for example, see D Celermajer, *The Prevention of Torture: An Ecological Approach* (Cambridge, Cambridge University Press, 2018).

A substantial part of these conditions is shaped by acts and omissions of state authorities and other powerful actors. A focus on a criminal ban, and measures that fall within the 'orbit' of said ban,[85] can sideline these conditions. By doing so, such focus can therefore have the implication of absolving these powerful actors, who claim to be acting to counter – or even, in the UK's case, to be leading the fight against[86] – a set of practices that they might in effect continue, through their acts and omissions, to sustain.

Approaching 'conversion therapy' practices through the lens of transformative reparations can go some way to dealing with the problems identified above. Although we maintain some reservations about the primacy accorded to criminal 'solutions' to the issue, we would suggest that transformative reparations are chiefly to be viewed as adding to, rather than necessarily replacing, the pursuit of criminal redress and civil remedies through the relevant legal processes.

We would argue that a key step in putting into effect transformative reparations for 'conversion therapy' would be for the Government to establish a large-scale, independent inquiry into the true nature and full scope and scale of 'conversion therapy' practices in recent (twentieth century) history through to the present. This is an essential step towards understanding 'conversion therapy' practices in contemporary and historical context, and illuminating the multi-layered dynamics of discrimination, pathologisation and othering that have underpinned them. Such a large-scale venture could take the shape of a statutory public inquiry established under the Inquiries Act 2005. Nonetheless, we recognise that this route is not without potentially significant flaws and limitations, notably in the context of Ministerial discretion over the remit of the inquiry and the publication of its final report. We are also acutely aware of the issues that plagued the Independent Inquiry into Child Sexual Abuse (whose findings were recently published), in the course of which there were several resignations and withdrawals from some victims organisations, citing concerns about the scope and independence of the inquiry and the extent to which victims were able to access and participate effectively in it.[87] In our view, if the Government is serious about its commitment to ending 'conversion therapy', it should do what is necessary to secure and safeguard the independence, thoroughness and rigour of any inquiry, and to maximise participation by those concerned in its findings. Alternatively, taking the transformative orientation of such an initiative seriously, the Government could establish a truth commission,

---

[85] We borrow this term from M Pinto, 'Sowing a "Culture of Conviction": What Shall Domestic Criminal Justice Systems Reap from Coercive Human Rights?' in L Lavrysen and N Mavronicola (eds), *Coercive Human Rights: Positive Duties to Mobilise the Criminal Law under the ECHR* (Oxford, Hart Publishing, 2021) 170.

[86] See *Banning Conversion Therapy: Government Consultation* (n 66) at 26–27.

[87] See H Siddique, 'What is the Child Sexual Abuse Inquiry and Why Did it Take Seven Years?' (*The Guardian*, 20 October 2022) www.theguardian.com/uk-news/2022/oct/20/what-is-the-child-sexual-abuse-inquiry-and-why-did-it-take-seven-years.

inspired by equivalent undertakings in transitional contexts.[88] A truth commission would be aimed at establishing the truth about 'conversion therapy' in its historical and present-day institutional, societal, systemic and structural context, repairing the harms it has inflicted, and identifying the transformative interventions necessary to ensure its eradication.

Such large-scale undertakings take time, and we are conscious that they can often stretch to several years. The duration of any truth-seeking initiative should by no means entail a delay in the taking of more immediate measures of protection and redress for those (who stand to be) harmed by 'conversion therapy' practices. Moreover, we would envisage a large-scale truth and reparations initiative triggering an immediate and ongoing cascade of institutional-level initiatives that delve in depth into particular actors' engagement in or contribution to 'conversion therapy' practices. An example of such institutional initiative would be a recent report by the University of Birmingham, which examined 'sexual reorientation work' carried out at the University between (circa) 1966 and 1983, and produced an institutional acknowledgement and apology for the University's role in these practices and the harm that they caused.[89] The report was commissioned after testimony from a survivor of the practice,[90] and was produced by a Steering Group led by academic researchers and composed of both students and staff at the University of Birmingham. It established that psychologist Dr Maurice Philip Feldman (who was employed by the University of Birmingham between 1966 and 1983) and psychiatrist Dr Malcolm J MacCulloch (who was employed by the University of Birmingham between 1967 and 1970/early 1971) had practised 'aversion therapy' (branded 'anticipatory avoidance therapy'), including in the form of electric shock 'treatment', with a view to changing people's sexual orientation.[91] The report made a series of recommendations, including towards the facilitation of further inquiries into this practice, and in favour of the University supporting efforts and campaigns to ban 'conversion therapy' practices. In response to the report, the University's Vice-Chancellor issued an acknowledgement and apology, and indicated that the institution is now 'unequivocal that conversion therapy is unethical, degrading, and harmful'.[92]

We hope that a large-scale investigation into 'conversion therapy' would, by illuminating the practice of 'conversion therapy' from its (recent) history through

---

[88] See, in this regard, J Sarkin, *The Global Impact and Legacy of Truth Commissions* (Cambridge, Intersentia, 2019). On the transposability of truth commissions to systemic human rights violations beyond the paradigmatic transitional justice contexts, see A Cahill-Ripley and LD Graham, 'Using Community-Based Truth Commissions to Address Poverty and Related Economic, Social and Cultural Rights Violations: The UK Poverty Truth Commissions as Transformative Justice' (2021) 13(2) *Journal of Human Rights Practice* 225.

[89] M Moulton et al, '"Conversion Therapy" and the University of Birmingham, c.1966–1983' (University of Birmingham, 2022).

[90] B Hunte, 'Gay "Conversion Therapy": Man Given Electric Shocks Demands Apology' (BBC News, 16 December 2020).

[91] 'Conversion Therapy' and the University of Birmingham (n 89) 10 ff.

[92] ibid 3.

to the present day, help sharpen, broaden and deepen the legislative and practical measures taken to protect people from 'conversion therapy' practices. We would, however, argue that it is important to urgently attend to the limitations of the criminal process and to place enhanced focus on other mechanisms to counter 'conversion therapy' practices, to secure accountability for such practices, and to protect (potential) victims. For example, existing mechanisms could be engaged, or new mechanisms established, to conduct independent oversight of settings in which there are reasonable grounds to believe 'conversion therapy' to be practised, including on the basis of anonymous reporting or whistle-blowing, with a view to identifying and preventing such practices. This would align with the growing emphasis on prevention in relation to torture and other forms of cruel, inhuman or degrading treatment or punishment.[93] An independent expert or body of experts could be assigned and provided with the resources to receive complaints, conduct visits and issue relevant recommendations.

Moreover, the pursuit of transformative reparations demands confrontation of cisheteropatriarchal norms across the institutions and social structures in which 'conversion therapy' practices are embedded. For this reason, an approach that is 'neutral' and formally equal on paper must be considerably more nuanced in practice, in view of the reality of 'conversion therapy' practices and those routinely targeted by such practices. In particular, the bodies tasked with giving effect to protective measures against 'conversion therapy' should be trained and sensitised to the particular dynamics underpinning efforts to bring people's sexuality and gender expression or identity into conformity with the dominant cisheterosexual norm.

More broadly, it is vital to tackle the structural conditions in which 'conversion therapy' operates.[94] This requires multi-layered interventions across education, healthcare, welfare and other public services to meaningfully counter the dynamics of discrimination, marginalisation, pathologisation and othering before they culminate in criminal acts, to recalibrate the cisheteronormativity that pushes people (perpetrators, victims, and others) into viewing 'conversion therapy' practices as 'curing' forms of sexuality or gender identity or expression, and to offer people who (stand to) face such 'practices' or the discrimination, pathologisation and othering that underpins them the resources and capacity to resist, to survive and to thrive as their true selves. To give an example, one of the most vital safeguards for an adolescent who is being forced into 'conversion therapy' by family members would arguably be information on and ready access to safe accommodation and support outside the family home. A recent survey by the Albert

---

[93] See MD Evans, 'The Prevention of Torture' in MD Evans and J Modvig (eds), *Research Handbook on Torture: Legal and Medical Perspectives on Prohibition and Prevention* (Cheltenham, Edward Elgar, 2020).

[94] See DJ Kinitz and T Salway, 'Cisheteronormativity, Conversion Therapy, and Identity among Sexual and Gender Minority People: A Narrative Inquiry and Creative Non-fiction' (2022) 32 *Qualitative Health Research* 1965, 1973.

Kennedy Trust (AKT), a LGBTQ+ youth homelessness charity, found that almost two-thirds of LGBTQ+ young people felt 'frightened or threatened by their family members before they became homeless', and that at the same time less than half of LGBTQ+ young people had been aware of housing support services, with almost a quarter unaware of any support services available to them.[95] A previous report by AKT suggests that LGBTQ+ youth comprise as much as 24 per cent of young homeless people.[96]

We would, moreover, underline that the provision of helplines to (potential) victims of 'conversion therapy' should not be confined to the reporting of criminal or civil offences or to informing them about the law banning 'conversion therapy'. Meaningful and targeted mental health support is needed. Concluding on a study examining the experiences of people subjected to 'conversion therapy', David Kinitz and Travis Salway emphasise the importance of 'trauma-informed mental health care related to grief and loss, supporting religious desires alongside sexual and gender diversity, and reducing shame and stigma while strengthening social supports'.[97] Implementing such a programme of support requires the UK Government to turn its commitment to ending 'conversion therapy' and supporting victims into a substantial investment into appropriate and timely mental health care for LGBTQ+ persons.

IV. Conclusion

Our chapter seeks to offer an additional and, to an extent, alternative perspective on pathways to ending 'conversion therapy' practices and protecting those who have been victimised or who stand to be victimised by such practices, focusing on transforming the conditions in which this occurs. We consider that a fundamental element of a transformative response to 'conversion therapy' practices is a reckoning with the historical dimensions of these practices and the institutional, systemic and structural continuum(s) observable in these practices' various manifestations, coupled with a readiness to foster systemic change and redistribute material resources. While our contribution to this vital discussion is by no means claiming to be exhaustive of the conceptual or concrete issues raised in addressing 'conversion therapy' practices through transformative reparations, we hope it is at least an invitation to reimagine how the law can be mobilised to end, and not simply ban, such practices.

---

[95] J Bhandal and M Horwood, 'The LGBTQ+ Youth Homelessness Report' (Albert Kennedy Trust, 2021) 9.

[96] W Bateman, 'LGBT Youth Homelessness: A UK National Scoping of Cause, Prevalence, Response and Outcome' (Albert Kennedy Trust, 2015).

[97] Kinitz and Salway (n 94) 1973.

INDEX